I WAS AN

UNSOLVED MYSTERY:

AN AMERICAN FUGITIVE STORY

BY THOMAS LION

LEOBRAND BOOKS

MILILANI HAWAII

Pages from Paradise

Leobrand Books

Published by Leobrand Books

Cover concept and design by Leobrand Books.

For information contact:

Leobrand Books
P.O. Box 893548
Mililani, HI 96789

Printing History
First Printing 1998

ISBN: 0-98658515-2-4

Printed in the United States of America

10 9 8 7 6 5 4 3 2 1

To Mom, Dad,
my brothers, my sisters,
my true friends, and others
who during the journey gave energy, kept
hope alive, and encouraged the real
me to bloom again.

Table of Contents

1

Fugitives' Rendezvous

Thursday January 10, 1991, Sunriver Resort, Oregon: I heard tense, angry men shouting, then the whirling of approaching helicopter blades. Sirens wailed. Car doors slammed. A gruff voice bellowed commands over an amplified bullhorn: "You, inside! This is the FBI! We have warrants for your arrests. The house is surrounded. Come out with your hands up!"

That familiar dread took hold of my gut. *Who turned us in?* Was it the realtor I paid in cash, or one of Moon's mysterious friends like Mad Max, Lady Wrestler, or the reckless Hell's Angel? I struggled to throw off the grip of a vodka hangover. Again came the voices.

"I repeat, come out with your hands up!"

The chopper swung into the clearing above our hideout. Half a dozen ninja-clad SWAT team members jumped down into loose, chest-deep snow, creating instant foxholes where they shouldered sniper rifles and waited for orders.

"Come out!"

I broke into a sweat, blinked heavily, and tried to focus my eyes. The room was dark and quiet. I dove off the bed, head spinning, heart pounding, and threw back the drapes.

Steam rose from the hot tub enclosure beneath our balcony. Unbroken snow ran all the way to the cul-de-sac where the first carload of powder hounds challenged the unplowed road. On the horizon, Mount Bachelor's rugged peak ruled over clear blue skies and snow cats labored between trees like mechanized ants grooming downhill ski trails. A helicopter circled the summit, dropping dynamite charges for avalanche control. Not a boogie man in sight.

I shook my head. No one was out there watching us. Just another sleepless night, and another cold crisp morning in Central Oregon. The dream had come again.

Certainly my occasional bouts with paranoia were not unfounded, but after five years of pursuit and threats from every conceivable government agency, I wondered if the authorities really had a clue. Before choosing this path, I read underground publications that claimed the feds were an inept bunch who waited for America's estimated 100,000 fugitives to make fundamental traffic errors, be driven to the surface by emotional or financial hardships, or come in contact with their growing legions of snitches. In the beginning I was skeptical about such teachings, but time has a way of making a man on the run lower his guard.

I emitted a short snort of breath that steamed the window glass, then nodded with self-assurance. I never wanted to be a fugitive, but for what it was worth, I had become quite good at the fugitive game. In my case, money was not a factor, and I was too damn meticulous to get caught.

There once were nine fugitives from the conspiracy. Now there were seven—a direct result of Smiley and Lizzy's unfortunate accident in 1989. Remarkably, one of our people had recovered a revealing government document following the Camelback Raid, but I was never fully convinced that no damning evidence on me was discovered by the Bureau on that fateful day in Phoenix. It was entirely possible that one of the captives had spilled their guts, and I was facing more charges after Arizona. Accordingly—ever since our comrades' demise—my survival instincts had been instructing me to cut the tattered umbilical cord to family, friendship and marriage, give up my futile attempt at living the American dream in the Wild West, and get the hell out of Dodge.

The James Bond part of my brain clicked into high gear, second-guessing my waffling fugitive strategy again. Why did I stay in America? Although my criminal career was over, negotiating with the law was no longer an option. I had three United States passports with real Social Security numbers, and had created employment histories for two identities. All of my groundwork for expatriatism had been quite properly laid. I had over one million dollars invested offshore with my European money manager, Blake, who had befriended me in 1983 before my flight from prosecution began. And now, thanks to the crafty Greek gold dealer, I had a guaranteed escape route with political protection in Athens.

So why did I stay within reach of Big Brother? Why didn't I have my

So why did I stay within reach of Big Brother? Why didn't I have my face altered and my fingerprints removed by Moon's Los Angeles doctor friend? This last Christmas had clearly reminded me why. Try as I might to erase my entire past—including family, friends, and childhood dreams—I simply could not. Over the years my James Bond spy personality had become powerful and cunning, but it was still outweighed by my crazy desire to be normal and an apparent weakness for placing both feet firmly into the Twilight Zone of aliases and invented selves and disappearing correctly...*forever.*

Feeling a chill, I pulled away from the window, slipped on my robe and sized up the master bedroom of yet another fine vacation rental—mainstay of fugitive life. Inside three covered cages on the dresser, our four pet birds began to stir. Beneath our queen bed's covers lay the only woman I had ever totally confided in—my lovely wife. I studied her with mixed emotions, recalling the day I learned Kim was a cop's daughter. Ah, but it was far too late; for by then we were both consumed by the illogical power of overwhelming passion.

As I watched her toss and turn, and heard the faint grinding of her pearly white teeth against that repulsive bite guard, instinct told me I could not remain free with her. If I was the dangerous outlaw they had painted me to be, why didn't I just murder her? There was only one way out for both us. But then there was love, and my hopelessly romantic side.

Suddenly the gush of forced-air gas heat surging through the floor vent at my feet ceased, and I heard angry voices like those in my nightmare again. It was Moon and the lady jeweler with the silicone jugs arguing in the bedroom below ours.

"Why do we have to drive my new car all the way to Vancouver?" the whiney little woman with the New Jersey accent asked. "We've put over 5,000 miles on her in less than a month! Why can't we just fly into Canada from Portland?"

"Because," Moon answered tersely, "that's the way I want it, and you know why. I'm not going through Customs at that airport on this passport, and that's that!"

Something heavy hit their floor. Her suitcase, I guessed.

"Pack all that designer crap in the bottom and leave some scented lingerie on top for the border crossing tomorrow night."

another weekend? I phoned Sunriver Lodge. They have a vacancy. And this new powder is fabulous. Please? I'm tired of moving, and I like your friends. They seem so normal."

"Shhhhhh!" Moon hissed, suddenly aware of how quiet the house had become. "I can't be late for this rendezvous."

"Why does everything have to be so secretive? I thought these people were cool. I thought you said—"

There was the ugly sound of a slap, and I cringed, knowing Moon's hand had crashed across her cheek.

"Bitch! That's your problem. You think too much, ask too many questions, and—"

Whoosh! The heat kicked on again, drowning out their shouting match, and I was flooded with thoughts. Moon's meteoric rise had occurred during the fugitive era. Five years ago he didn't have a pot to piss in; then suddenly his high-tech skills were back in demand and paying handsome dividends. Within days he was wiring millions out of Montreal to Pakistan, proceeds from the Afghanis' last freighter to Vancouver. I did not envy him. Once I had been in his place—a hungry surfer treading water, waiting on a wave which, when it finally came, turned out to be a tsunami of such magnitude and force that there was no option but to ride it for a long, long time. Like me before my attempted retirement, he was yo-yoing between criminal elation and rational fear.

Before our comrades' elimination from the game, they had reintroduced me to Moon, whom I'd met on a mission years ago. All his life he'd been called Sonny. And though I was bored by cutesy nicknames like Star, Spider and Country which were used to excess in the '60s and '70s, one intoxicated night when we all vowed to get serious about our fugitive status and change our names forever, I was the one who tagged Sonny with *Moon.* As he became a trusted friend, I watched him develop into a nightmare for the women he embraced.

In the beginning of our run I always thought Moon would be the first to get caught by the government. His passion for fine Los Angeles restaurants and front row seating at concerts, and his lack of attention to detail in creating new identities disturbed me. His abusive verbal tirades were also appalling, but over the years his strategy of constant movement and coldness in relationships served him well. God knows we had all tried our methods at this game. Sometimes I even thought his idea of buying passports from greedy officials might be the way to go.

I wondered why Moon had insisted on bringing this Lisa, or what ever her name was, to our annual holiday outlaw gathering. Was he getting soft? Did he want to show her he had real friends? Was he trying to recruit her into going underground with him, because Missy had refused? I couldn't understand what he saw in this latest one. They'd been dating for just over a year now—since he bought a diamond bracelet from her jewelry counter for his main squeeze, L.A. Missy—and they were already fighting like cats and dogs. Lisa was just a younger, more compact version of Missy, only colder. Definitely not my style. But who was I to talk? I married a cop's daughter. The sole reason I'd agreed to Lisa coming was because Kim craved feminine companionship, but the two women were incompatible.

At any rate, Moon's love life was not my business. Security was. Survival was. Keeping our Bainbridge Island refuge safe and secret was job one with me, which was why I told Moon's playmate we lived in Portland (as the license plate on my truck proclaimed) and spent most of our time overseas—just in case.

A knot formed in my suddenly queasier stomach. Lisa had phoned Sunriver Lodge? This was a violation of my rules. Who else did she call? I had reserved this rental months in advance with my sacred credit card that led to my secret offshore account, which is why I'd insisted no one use the phone. Another thought crossed my mind. If I could listen to them through the vents, then what had this stranger (and non-fugitive) overheard during our little ski vacation? And how much had moon-struck Moon revealed about us beyond my standard cover story? I hadn't heard anyone call him Sonny in ages. There was always something to consider.

I stared at Kim's long, exposed leg and thigh on the bed, recalled our argument last night, and frowned. I had been peacefully grilling Cornish hens on the deck. She was watching. We were both drunk. She began instructing me on how and when to turn the birds, then kept telling me I was ruining them. I'm all for equal rights, but have always harbored a strong aversion to attempted dominance—be it by beautiful women, greedy business associates, heartless con men, or hypocritical government officials. Anyway, we started arguing. She even went so far as to wrongfully accuse me of ogling Moon's young jeweler one too many times. When the argument spilled into the living room, along with my perfectly cooked hens, I got pissed. Kim had a lightning-quick temper, but it took a lot to get me mad.

That was hours ago and long gone. But it still reminded me of our last trip out of the country to Greece's Isle of Rhodes, when she finally lost her nerve and our fairy tale romance briefly resembled the *War of the Roses.*

Presently, I watched her twitch beneath the covers and envisioned us entwined at the end of the evening with my face buried in her amazing breasts. "At least mine are real," she cooed as I caressed them, "and they didn't cost you a goddamn dime!" Not exactly true, I thought at the time.

I smiled, suddenly entertaining the notion of slipping off my robe and diving under the covers for a romp before venturing to the downstairs of our vacation rental. How many couples in the over-glorified real world still screwed like rabbits, then cuddled through the night following a fight, especially after they'd spent twenty-four hours a day together for nearly seven years? Sure, we were sexual warriors before we met, but such sustained desire certainly said something about our compatibility as well, considering our stress-torn circumstances.

Boozer the parakeet squawked impatiently in her dark cage. Her mate, Pepper, joined in this chorus. Sophia the Latino cockatiel shrieked beside them. Harry Canary came to life.

I walked to the dresser and uncovered them all. "Morning, kids," I whispered. As I opened the parakeets' cage, then Sophia's, Harry Canary serenaded me with a warm-up number. Boozer flew to my finger and began the morning ritual of grooming my moustache. "Boozer-girl. Boooo-Czar! Who loves ya baby?" I asked with a cartoon accent.

My baby blue parakeet squawked out the answer.

A single ray of sunshine streamed into the dark room.

I carried the shy lemon-colored cockatiel to Kim, who was just coming around, and kissed her cheek. "Morning honey," I said cheerfully, thankful for all the birds in my life, regardless of their cost.

"What time is it, honey?" she asked in her sweet, innocent morning voice, while Sophia rubbed soft feathers on her chin.

"Eight-thirty," I replied. "Ready to move out today?"

She nodded, half-awake. Of course she was ready. With our lifestyle, she'd become a professional mover, same as me.

"I told the realtor we'd be out by ten," I said. "I'm going downstairs to brew some coffee."

She scratched Sophia's fragile yellow neck with her fire red fingernail and yawned. "Could you…"

"Yeah, sure," I responded instinctively as I headed for the door. "I'll bring you back a cup."

In the kitchen my best friend Todd was squeezing oranges for the long drive ahead and listening to National Public Radio News. He handed me a glass filled with some carrot-lettuce concoction he'd created with his juicer. "Go on. Drink it," he said softly, his rosy cheeks glowing. "It's good for a hangover."

Typical Todd, always mothering. He was thirty-seven, six-foot-two, solid build, receding hairline. A natural athlete. A health nut pacifist, hippie-era holdover. Hard not to like. Born and raised in the Midwest and addicted to tennis, golf, National Public Radio and Notre Dame football—same as me. Todd was an articulate speaker. He was loyal, patient, and well read. He played college ball and could have been a pro golfer. He was, in fact, the finest fugitive golfer I ever knew. Which is why I nicknamed him Arnie, like legend Arnold Palmer.

I studied the collection of compact discs, classic old movie tapes, and ski stuff spread out on the living room floor. "Almost finished packing?" I asked.

Arnie nodded, simultaneously crunching on a rice cake.

"How about Moon?" I asked.

He pointed to the garage door.

"Did we nuke Iraq yet?"

My friend frowned, then proceeded to give me the *Readers Digest* condensed version of the morning news.

By the time I took Kim her cup of coffee, she already had our big beige Samsonite and one suit bag packed. I slipped into my long underwear, switched to my business mode, and went with luggage in hand to join Moon in the garage.

He was cramming his shiny new Lexus, purchased under the jeweler's name, full of high-tech ski gear, cellular phones and gobs of electronic junk. Moon had tucked himself inside a two-grand ski uniform to keep warm while packing.

"Hand me the football," he said.

I gave him the briefcase that contained all of his ID, books, and other sensitive materials, and watched him stash it. He grabbed his bad knee, reminding me of his mounting problems with failing health. Besides the football, he carried a case of medicine for various emerging ailments. His right knee was shot after years of hotdog skiing, and the only thing keeping him from orthopedic surgery was a fugitive's fear of filling out admittance forms at a major hospital, then finding a way to pay thousands in cash.

Moon was Jewish and proud of it, a mobile, high profile, gadget man who had to have the nicest and newest of everything. He was *Consumer Reports* most loyal reader, an olive-skinned, lanky guy with dark curly hair who viewed our warped world through coke bottle lenses and reminded me of some whiz kid from a '70s era Walt Disney flick. Our man Moon: pilot and former Aspen Ski Patrol member who enjoyed dropping down into twenty feet of powder from the belly of a helicopter, more hyper than me on coffee, definitely Type-A, no phone, no apartment, no pets, a girl in every port, and still playful at forty—when stress wasn't gnawing at his ulcer.

"Hey, Chief!" Moon exclaimed. "Bet you're ready to head home, huh?"

I nodded. Bet your ass. We were the only ones in our group who maintained any facsimile of a home, and we were always eager to go there.

He dug into the trunk of the Lexus and feverishly tossed stuff aside until he reached the spare tire. "Give me a hand with this," he said. I lifted the tire. Moon retrieved a plump manila envelope and gave it to me. "Forty grand in twenties," he said. "Final payment. Want to count it?"

"Did you?" I asked.

He nodded.

"No need then," I said. "You've never been off a dime." I dropped the tailgate on my pickup truck, jumped into its customized bed, opened the lid to a side storage compartment, slid back a false bottom panel, and stashed the manila packet by the wheel well with my other set of identification.

"Is the Gulf War a go yet?" Moon asked anxiously.

I paused to consider the undercurrent of tension that a pending war had added to my plans. "No. Any minute though."

"Far out," my Jewish friend snickered. "Those A-rabs need another good ass whippin'. And like you said, gold prices will soar. My employers will be pleased with this latest purchase," he sighed.

For a moment, I had second thoughts about selling off all of my precious metals prematurely.

"So, what do you think of her?" Moon blurted.

"Who?"

"Lisa!"

"She's pretty. I like her," I lied, hoping my facial expression didn't give away the truth.

Moon cleared his throat. "Bill finally got those Canadian birth certificates from the law students he hired to research the birth and death records. What do you say about coming up to British Columbia in a couple of weeks? If I get the passport, it might be a while before we get together again. We could ski Blackcomb/Whistler with Bill and Leigh."

I shoved gloves and hats in the compartment above my stash and slammed the lid shut. "Why even ask? You know what I'll say."

Moon nodded thoughtfully.

"Thanks, but no thanks," I barked.

Bill, Leigh, and their daughter, Shannon, comprised the northern contingent of our fugitive clan. Leigh had been my high school sweetheart, with whom I cohabited for several satisfying years. Bill and I were former business partners with long-standing, deep-seated differences. At our wives' urgings, I had tried to make peace with him, but my aversion to his domineering and manipulative nature made this impossible. Worse yet, I feared his brash carelessness and did not trust him with so much as my home phone number. Two years earlier I had arranged a new life for Kim and me in Australia with an old friend. But Bill and Leigh's narrow escape from Interpol after fleeing Sidney to Hong Kong—and the messy trail they left behind—rendered the Land Down Under as radioactive as Russia's Chernobyl for the rest of us.

Bitterness engulfed me. I turned to Moon. "Listen, you know how I feel about him. Whatever you two got cooking is cool with me, but if

I were you I'd watch how much I—"

The garage door swung open. It was Lisa. Moon gave her a nasty look.

"I'm sorry, Babe. Did I interrupt something?" she asked, swallowing hard before silently disappearing.

Moon took the floral Fabergé bag which the tiny jeweler had brought and returned to packing the Lexus. I drove my truck into the driveway, cranked up the heat, and left it running so our pets would have a tropical travel environment.

While the women vacuumed, I gave the vacation rental one final going over, searching for any carelessly left items which could be used to trace us in the event Moon encountered trouble at the Canadian border. I scanned every room, got on my hands and knees and looked under each bed, even probed beneath the sofa cushions. In the beginning, the others thought I was crazy and paranoid, but that was before the Phoenix affair.

We said our good-byes. Moon and his jeweler babe climbed into their silver 1991 Lexus. Todd crammed his big body inside the cab of his little Nissan truck, and Kim and I boarded our warm Ford full of squawking birds. The three-vehicle fugitive convoy motored north on Oregon's scenic Highway 97 until Arnie took the fork in the road toward The Dalles and his Hood River hideaway. Moon and Lisa waved as we passed them at the entrance to a Madras, Oregon gas station.

I have not seen any of them since that day.

2

Dream's End

The black 1985 Ford F-150 rolled north across the last stretch of Central Oregon's high desert on Highway 26. I gazed into the rearview mirror at the disappearing peak of Three Sisters, recalling our first peaceful fugitive year spent in a secluded house along the banks of the Deschutes River. My Irish setter Benjamin was still alive, love was new, and life was so much simpler then, before all the madness and the moving resumed.

Meeting with the others always left me confused and melancholy. At least Moon was invariably running from or to something—a woman, an event, a business deal. Lately, it seemed like I was just running in place. But somehow, when it was only Kim and I and the natural beauty I respected above any government's arbitrary laws or political doublespeak, I still managed to feel positive about life. And sometimes, for an hour or so, I'd forget being a wanted man and could view the world though the writer's eye I once possessed. In those rare moments, my life was a dream, and I wanted to drive forever.

I shifted gears and wound downgrade through treeless canyons to reach the shimmering waters of the lower Deschutes. Big city fishermen in expensive outfits waded and cast their lures for elusive winter steelheads. Poorly dressed native Americans from the Warm Springs Reservation staggered alongside the rusting skeletons of abandoned cars as if feeling false warmth after the day's first drink. I lowered the window, listened to the familiar voice of the river, heard happy children's laughter echoing on the wind from the reservation school's playground nearby, and smiled. Kim napped with her head on a pillow propped against my thigh. Carly Simon sang softly on the stereo. I gingerly switched gears and stepped on the gas. The Ford ascended the gray asphalt which parted a forest green sea, en route to Mount Hood—yet another friendly part of Oregon where we had once resided.

Two hours later I pulled into a strip mall across from Portland's Multnomah County Sheriff's building, and returned to my fugitive mindset. I parked in front of the pet store, donned a nerd hat with wide-framed reading glasses, and walked toward *The Letter Box* with two keys in hand.

In recent years the growth of independent postal companies in America has been nothing short of phenomenal. They are listed in the Yellow Pages under headings like Mail Receiving and Forwarding Services, but in the underground they're called *mail drops*. Technically, customers are only renting a box to receive their mail at an *apartment* or *suite* number that corresponds to the company's street address. This creates the illusion that they are actually residing at the location which appears on their mail, business cards, or official documents, and affords them the convenience of having a "home away from home." The best mail drops guarantee confidentiality and twenty-four hour access for odd-hour collections.

These places began as the disgruntled citizen's answer to an inefficient US postal system, but savvy customers quickly found other uses for them. Small business owners unable to afford office space discovered that a wisely chosen mail drop's prestigious street address and professional answering service was extremely useful. Naughty husbands—and wives—could communicate with their adulterous partners. Mail fraud experts conducted nationwide cons without ever exposing their true locations or identities. Terrorists renting U-Haul trucks, escort services courting clients, politicians picking up soft money or hard cash from generous lobbyists—the possibilities were endless.

But to the astute fugitive, the mail drop was essential, for in keeping with the time-tested adage "never shit where you sleep," a wanted person's mail drop had to be where he or she lived *on paper*. Driver's licenses, Social Security numbers, passports—all roads led to your box, far away from home, thus providing a buffer between predators and prey. Each of my mail drops had a different purpose, and at each I maintained a distinct image. Here, at Tim Barnes' Northeast Glisan Street backup box, I was known as the nerd.

My box contained the January '91 issue of *Fly Fisherman*. Apartment number 110 was crammed full of fashion magazines and junk mail for Kim's alter ego, Diane K. Moore. At the bottom of her pile I discovered a disturbing note: "Please see the manager." The bad memory of another fugitive's close encounter during a similar situation put me on alert.

After scanning the parking lot for suspicious vehicles, I cautiously presented the pink piece of paper to the pretty clerk behind the desk. She was a New Delhi immigrant who'd been working days for the past seven months.

"Miss Moore hasn't been in for a while, has she?" the clerk asked.

I shook my head. "She's visiting family back east. Guess I've been so busy watering her plants and watching her pets that I plumb forgot about checking her mail. Huh?" I added, like a nerd.

The bronze skinned girl quickly disappeared into a side room.

I decided to leave if she was not back in two minutes.

A minute and thirty seconds later she handed me another stack of fashion magazines—*Elle*, *Vogue*, *Victoria's Secret*. "There wasn't enough room in her box," she explained, smiling and passing me a plastic bag to carry them in.

"Thanks. Have a n-nice day," I stammered, heading for the door.

In over four years as her client, the owner of *The Home Office*, my other Portland mail drop, had come to know me as a quiet, clean-cut, mobile yuppie businessman with a European-based corporation. Consequently, whenever young Mr. Barnes made an appearance, he wore a suit and tie and wire-rimmed glasses, and carried a worn leather briefcase. If I were dressed for the part, I would have driven across town to 9875 S.W. Barbur Boulevard, Apartment 11, where Timothy Alan Barnes *lived*. Instead, I hit the payphone outside the restaurant next door and dropped a quarter. While the number rang, I watched law-enforcement officials come and go across the street and questioned my "right under their noses" line of thought in choosing Diane K. Moore's only mail drop and Tim Barnes' disposable backup.

"Home Office," the lady owner answered cheerfully. "May I help you?"

"Good afternoon," I replied in a purely professional manner. "Are there any messages for number eleven?"

"No messages, Mr. Barnes."

"Mail?" I quizzed, hoping Blake had sent my new Visa Gold card from London.

"Just a letter from Allstate Insurance. That's it."

"Could you tell me when my account is due, please?" I already knew.

"Not until February."

"All right. Thank you so much. I'll stop in when I return from L.A. next week."

"Have a safe trip, Mr. Barnes."

Great, I thought. No news was better than bad news, but I wished the Gold Card had come.

Back at the truck I found my wife talking to our birds. She studied my face and bit her lip. "Do we have to drive all the way to Barbur Boulevard again?" she asked.

I gave her the magazine bag and she dug into it like an excited trick or treater. "Naaa, let's go home." She shoved a James Taylor tape into the stereo—my reward—and I steered the Ford to Interstate 205.

Within minutes, we were crossing the mighty Columbia River and entering the Evergreen State—our latest adopted home. I briefly admired an easterly horizon dominated by Mount Saint Helens before training my green eyes on the road. Kim's brown eyes devoured fashion magazines. She loved those things. They were her escape, reminding her of carefree teenage modeling days, and she read them all the way to Seattle.

Traffic was light. Soon the Emerald City loomed before us with its King Dome off to the left and Space Needle beyond. In Elliott Bay, the Bainbridge ferryboat made its way to Pier 52 from the island—our island. It was perfect timing, and a tired Seattle commuter's dream. We slipped into the car boarding lot and secured our place in line.

In retrospect, I should have taken a cab uphill to 1206 Pike Street where my alter ego resided, Paul James Kelly, Washington State resident and British real estate consultant. But with a serious case of road fatigue and only fifteen minutes until the ferry's departure, I settled for another trip to the phone booth—forgetting that fugitives cannot afford the price of laziness.

"Hi, Paul!" the gay owner of Mr. Kelly's mail drop greeted me. "What can I do for you?"

I often wondered if he recognized the voice of every client, or if mine simply stood out. His excessive friendliness and tendency to engage in lengthy political conversations would have worried me if he weren't so blatantly liberal, anti-government, and big on privacy. "Just checking in," I said, listening as he flipped through his notepad.

"No messages, Paul. Let's see, you have a brochure from a realtor in Chelan, Washington, a bank statement from First Interstate, and something from Gold Key Mini Storage in Tigard, Oregon."

I slapped my cheek. The big storage unit was due again in two weeks. I hated the exposure those notices gave my stash places, but it was late in the day. We were locked into the ferry line-up. I had no desire to acquire a money order. Paul Kelly's mail would have to sit tight until my next excursion into the city.

"Thanks," I said. "See you next week."

I bought some flowers and an afternoon paper from a parking lot vendor. Horns started honking. Vehicles began boarding. I high-tailed it for the truck.

The thirty-minute voyage was quiet. I read the financial section, occasionally peering out the window past Puget Sound's wintry white-caps to the approaching island. And, as always, I fought a secret sense of foreboding and felt the opposing emotions of joy and fear, which any sane fugitive feels when returning to an empty house after a lengthy vacation.

I fell in love with Bainbridge during our great emergency house hunt of 1989. After the Phoenix raid, we spent several months in isolation. My wife's desire for a social life soon led me to the Seattle area and its nearby islands. Whidbey was too far from the city. Vashon was too rural.

Bainbridge appeared to have been colonized by the ever-evolving citizens of the Woodstock nation: businessmen wearing Nike sneakers with sports coats rode bicycles to the ferry dock, and neighbors shared garden plots and formed food cooperatives. There was a growing artist community with local galleries that displayed promising nouveau works. Island writers were getting published. They had an indoor tennis club. Long-neglected intellectual stimulus was all around. Geographically, Bainbridge was part of a group of islands near an international border with an abundance of natural resources and a relatively mild climate. It was appealing to the old me, and reminiscent of my beloved Lake Tahoe. "Tahoe by the sea," is how I described Bainbridge to my wife. Close to the Emerald City's culture, yet far from its crime, Bainbridge was surrounded by the towering pine trees and water I craved, and one of those rare islands with an optional overland escape route to the wild Olympic Peninsula, via Agate Pass Bridge. Irresistibly perfect. I always needed to be sure there was another way out.

When we disembarked, we were only five minutes from home, but I wasn't done yet. It was time to retrieve items routinely stored when we went away, so nosy landlords or random burglars didn't get lucky during our absence. I turned onto New Brooklyn Road, scanned the tidy mini storage grounds, then motored in past the huge iron gate.

Totem Storage, like most of this nation's 25,000-plus mom and pop-owned-and-operated self-storage facilities, pledged security and privacy to its cash paying customers. (And their lease agreement never asked if I was a fugitive.) Totem met all of my requirements—conveniently located only minutes from the house, casual with no security cameras, and mellow owners who lived on the grounds. As a matter-of-fact, our little 5 x 7, #E-237, was located directly beneath their apartment—the perfect place to stash sensitive documents and valuables.

I parked beside the orange door with the big black 'E' painted on it and jumped into the back of the truck. I took the manila envelope and my Paul Kelly wallet out of the Ford's stash, placed them in a briefcase and toted it and our skis into the storage unit. Inside, I opened the heavy, fireproof, steel safe and grabbed some spending cash and Kim's jewelry box. I slipped Paul Kelly's wallet into my pocket, slid Tim Barnes's into the safe along with the forty grand from Moon, locked up, and left. On the way out, I noticed the owner looking out the window, and waved.

Minutes later, we were back on good old Northeast Tolo Road, coasting down the last hill before the split-rail fence and stopping at the familiar line-up of *real* rural mailboxes, like the type I grew up with back in Indiana. Kim nervously checked ours, #5875, and found nothing but an electric bill.

The black Ford crawled down the long dirt lane past a carpenter's rustic corner house, eternally under construction, past the pleasant realtor couple's cozy cedar chalet, past the pre-yuppie era mobile home at the swampy curve where the lovable Grateful Dead Grandmother lived. Farther and farther into the woods went the Ford, until we came to the worn, red horse barn at the end of our driveway. I looked around, drew a deep breath, and pulled in.

The Brewers' dog Scooter charged the truck, wagging his tail and barking at the top of his canine lungs. Our two cats, Smokey and Punkin, sat like furry bookends on the deck acting cool and nonchalant. As soon as I turned off the engine, our neighbor, Ginny Brewer, called through the pines, "Hi, Paul! Hi, Diane! How was the skiing?"

So much for a quiet, inconspicuous return home.

My wife, who'd had enough socializing for a while, headed straight for the door—birdcage number one in hand. It was nearly dark. I was tired, but Ginny was a good neighbor and a nice person. I trudged across our muddy, idle garden plot to greet her.

It had been a rough winter for the Brewers and many people on Bainbridge Island. A terrible snowstorm blew through just before Christmas. Pipes froze and there was no electricity for days. My experience in home building and renovation, as well as my four-wheel-drive truck, came in handy during the emergency. I dug up and defrosted frozen well lines and repaired burst copper tubing. We hauled people to the tennis club, where an emergency generator provided warm showers. After the storm, Tom Brewer's father passed away, and he, Ginny, and their two boys, Ben and Matt, journeyed back to Michigan for the funeral. We watched their house, dog, and cat for a week. And now they had returned the favor.

"Hi, Ginny," I said, leaning down to pet Scooter by the fallen section of fencing, which we'd decided long ago not to fix. "Skiing was great. How's Tom doing?" I always felt strange saying my own real first name when referring to her husband.

"He's all right," she whispered, tugging at her Washington Huskies sweatshirt. "Your finches are fine. I think there's two new eggs in one of the aviary's nest boxes. The fish were fed this morning." She furrowed her brow. "One of them died. And the cats were..."

Suddenly Scooter shot between Ginny's legs and scrambled back to his own yard.

My tough-guy Manx cat, Smokey, rubbed his massive gray head against my ankle and meowed proudly. I picked him up by his scruff and rough-housed him in mid-air. He purred so loudly I could feel it, then he licked my arm.

"That's some animal you've got there," Ginny remarked. "The boys just love him."

"Me too," I replied. "Thanks for watching our menagerie. By the way, how's your plumbing?"

Ginny smiled warmly. "Everything's back to normal for now." She removed her glasses and patted her short dark hair. "You know, Paul. There's something I've been meaning to tell you."

"Yes," I said, dropping the cat and nearly swallowing my tongue. "What's that?" I asked, fearing whatever revelation I might hear.

"You and Diane are the best neighbors we've ever had."

Paranoia left my mind. Emotion swelled in my heart. After five years of nomadic living, we had finally stayed in one place long enough to get close to some decent, normal people; the way it used to be, the way it was meant to be—but not for a wanted man. I attempted to make a joke of her sincerity. "Us? The best ever? Come on, Ginny. Did I miss island cocktail hour at the Brewer Piano Bar, or what?"

She placed a hand on my shoulder. "No, really. I can't tell you how much we enjoyed that bottle of wine and your fireplace during the storm." She shook her head. "We'd have never gotten out of the driveway if you hadn't chopped that fallen tree in half."

"Forget it. Glad to help. It was great exercise. And, as you know, I am a wild and crazy exercise kinda guy!" I grinned a la comedian Steve Martin, and started to skip off through the mud towards my house.

With a sigh Ginny thrust her chilled hands into her sweatpants pockets. "Yes, Paul, but we appreciated it."

"That's all that matters," I muttered, suddenly feeling too much like my old self—extremely vulnerable and very emotional.

A short time later I attended a toilet bowl funeral for one of my wife's fish. After the flushing, I yanked a Finlandia Vodka bottle out of the freezer, mixed Kim her customary double with soda water, and poured myself one with tonic. I slipped on the furry bear-claw slippers my mom had given me for our last Christmas together, then drummed my fingers on the library table. The momentous time had come to listen to the messages on our telephone answering machine. According to the digital counter there were plenty of calls, undoubtedly all from our fellow members of the Bainbridge Tennis Club, center of our social universe. I depressed the button and we both listened intently as the magical device delivered the treasure of friendship to our diminished isolation.

"Hi, Di! We miss ya, baby," said Donna, an aging but bubbly blond jazz singer. "Hope you enjoyed your trip. The girls are playin' doubles Monday afternoon, and we're savin' you a spot. Gimme a call when you get in. Hi, Paul! Bye-bye."

Click.

"Diane? Doris Van Fleet here," said the smooth and sexy fifty-something wife of a retired Weyerhaeuser timber executive. "Donna said she'd call you about Monday, but sometimes she forgets. Call me, hon. Or better yet, stop by for a drink! And say hello for me to that darling husband of yours."

Click.

"Paul? Pick up the bloody phone if you're there!" demanded Patricia Corlett, a feisty British woman and wife of an island author. "I do hope you're back by now. For God's sake, give me a ring. I need to work up a good sweat with a younger man," she chuckled. "Bye-bye, love."

Fred Schafer, retired dentist and local greeting card artist, was next. "Oh, Paul," he drawled in an Ivy League vernacular befitting his stature, and reminiscent of the millionaire character portrayed on television's *Gilligan's Island*, "if you're still interested in playing weekday doubles with the geriatric league, do give me a call."

Click.

Flora Bloedell, outspoken island heiress who kept a pet donkey, left a message, as did several others in the diverse and curious clique we had become a part of through the club. Flora and I had finished second in the last mixed doubles tournament.

I turned off the machine and switched on the Christmas tree lights, which hung from the Japanese magnolia tree at the edge of our deck. Those little things had sparked the great holiday marital debate of 1990, when I grudgingly gave in to my wife's wishes.

Kim caught me staring at the magnolia tree and shaking my head. She pinched my ass and said, "Don't worry, honey. Next Christmas, you can hang your stupid colored strobe lights on it."

We laughed and took our respective places on the sofa in front of the big bay window. Warmth from the fire in our Ben Franklin's hearth enveloped us, and entertainment was provided by two cats playing with a catnip-filled tennis sock at our feet. Contrary to the picture my pursuers' painted of me, this was how I spent the majority of my life on the lam. And against all logic and instinct, our last year and a half had been spent blending in and falling in love with this island community in Washington State's Puget Sound.

"May I propose a toast, *Meekla*?" I asked, using one of my many mindless pet names for Kim.

She put her hand in mine and nodded.

"Here's to coming home."

We clicked glasses. Kim made a funny face, then asked the standard question with her mouth full of vodka and those vivacious lips pursed provocatively. "Yes, but do you love me?" she mumbled like an amateur ventriloquist.

I looked deep into her big brown eyes and answered without hesitation, "Heart and soul, Meekla. Heart and soul."

She swallowed her drink and echoed solemnly: "To coming home, then."

Friday, January 11, 1991: The clock radio went off at precisely 7:00 A.M. I slapped it, slid out of bed, and began my routine: brew the coffee. Uncover the birds. Feed the cats. Fill the blender with my protein concoction. Flick on the television. Put on my long underwear. Position three sets of free weights and my rowing machine on the living room floor and work up a good sweat while studying London stocks and currencies on the Financial News Network's early report.

Forty-five minutes later, I was that familiar figure in grubby gray sweatpants with a Sony Walkman headset clamped over the earflaps of my funky blue wool hat, jogging down our lane, nodding to neighbors on their way to Winslow's ferry dock while listening to NPR News. Reaching the pavement of Tolo Road, I cursed my laziness, picked up the pace, and scaled the first hill. There, surrounded by dark woods, struggling to ascend the second incline, I tuned in some classical music and cranked up the volume. Violins cried. A piano pounded. Golden shafts of sunlight penetrated gray sea borne mist, lifting my unfulfilled spirit to a higher plane. The snowcapped Olympic Mountains appeared. My heart raced. Man. Nature. Solitude. In my restless and surrealistic world, this was my religion.

"Work! Sweat! Run, boy," I commanded myself.

And I did, only briefly pausing at the pond in Battle Point Park where several wood ducks were still frozen in place—their lifeless webbed feet shackled by thin ice. These ducks, too, were victims of the great storm, taken by surprise one wintry night, didn't see it coming, too slow to survive. I shuddered. After seeing them prior to our Oregon ski trip, I was driven to pen a morbid poem about omens and change.

Work! Sweat! Run, boy.

Six miles later, I was in our driveway again with two playful cats zigzagging one step ahead of me. I stood on the deck dripping sweat and panting steam clouds into frosty air.

"Back to the rowing machine, you wimp!" I said. "No room for weakness. Only the strong survive out here."

Even on the days when every aspect of my life seemed totally, obviously, illogically contradictory, keeping physically fit was unquestionably sane. Exercise kept depression at bay, and I had to be strong. If I became weak, the entire illusion would die.

We had a typical day. I inspected my emergency plumbing work in the basement, dusted the antiques, and chopped some wood. Kim spent the morning with her plants and the aviary we'd built together. At lunchtime, I placed a bird playground constructed out of dowel rods and tinker toys affixed to a TV dinner tray on the living room floor. Kim stocked it with lettuce and millet sprigs, and we turned the parakeets and the Latino Cockatiel loose. They squawked and pecked. We laughed and made love.

When I started rinsing the dishes, the blue parakeet Boozer—instinctively drawn by the sound of running water—flew to the kitchen and began her dance on my shoulders. I stiffened my arms, adjusted the water temperature and volume, and cupped my hands beneath the faucet. Boozer's act ensued. She sidestepped up and down my arms, bobbing and weaving and showering repeatedly in the palm of my hands.

"The neighbor kids were right honey," Kim said, tipping back a beer. "If I filmed you and that crazy bird together and sent the tape to *America's Funniest Home Videos*, you'd win that ten grand first prize for sure."

"Uh huh," I said, "but we don't need the money, and I damn sure don't need the exposure."

"No shit, Sherlock. I'm not one of those dumb blonds you used to date. I'm a cop's daughter. Remember? Anyway, I thought you always wanted to be a TV star?"

"Smartass," I replied while tweaking my blue bird's beak. "I wanted to be a lot of things once upon a time. Hey, how about playing some tennis tomorrow?"

Kim panned the house with a contented smile. "Oh, let's wait until Sunday," she said.

That night we returned from San Carlos Mexican Restaurant in a great mood. En route to the bedroom, the answering machine's little red light caught my eye. I pressed a button, and Moon's voice blasted unexpectedly from the tiny speaker.

"Paul? Diane? You there?"

He sounded tense.

"Pick up the phone if you're there!"

Something was wrong.

"Beep me the minute you get in. It's important." He paused. "A friend of mine was watching one of those cop/snitch television shows Wednesday night..." He sucked air, apparently considering how much he wanted to say on an unsecured line. "Maybe it's nothing," Moon exhaled. "Just beep me when you get in."

Click.

First Kim's jaw dropped, then her purse.

I rewound the tape and listened to the message again and again, staring at that damn answering machine and assessing every word. "One of those cop/snitch television shows Wednesday night. It's important. Maybe it's nothing. Beep me." I thought about the warning Kim's mother had given us so very long ago. My logical mind whirled. My emotional stomach churned. On the outside, I *showed* cool, but inside I felt sick. The look on my wife's face frightened me more than Moon's call.

I went out alone. A cold rain fell. I stood inside a phone booth in front of the Bainbridge Public Library waiting for Moon to return my call. Fifteen minutes passed—twenty. I chewed through several layers of cheek skin. A suspicious-looking car parked beside my truck. Its driver sat staring at me with the motor running. Suddenly, our comfy island refuge didn't feel so comfy. I had to move on.

I stopped at Jiffy Mart and phoned Arnie's Hood River hideaway.

No answer. I desperately needed to talk to Moon, and wanted to do it on a payphone. An island police car cruised past me slowly. I dialed Moon's pager number again, punched in #44, my code for home, and headed there.

He called an hour later from some posh restaurant in Vancouver. By that time, we were nursing the vodka bottle. I'd wanted to hear all the details at a payphone, but never drove drunk. I decided to waive my own rule against having sensitive conversations at home. "Tell me," I said.

"Wednesday night, while we were having dinner in Bend..." He drew a deep breath. "A mutual friend was watching *Unsolved Mysteries*."

"Great! Just great," I said, slapping the tabletop.

Kim wrapped both hands tightly around her drink.

"Go on," I said, straining to stay calm.

"They showed some pictures, talked about the Midwest. Said the people they were after were armed and dangerous. Listen, she didn't catch all of it, just the tail end of the show. She wasn't even sure it was you."

I hung on to every word he said—hell, every syllable.

"The Wrestler is getting a copy of the tape and sending it up here. I should have it by Monday afternoon."

I swallowed hard, speechless. I pictured the buffed professional female wrestler who was part of Moon's crew, and wondered if she could even identify me on TV after having met me only once.

"You there?" Moon asked.

"Yeah," I whispered. "I'm here."

"What do you think?"

"Don't know," I muttered, struggling for something positive to say. "Armed and dangerous?"

"Yeah, I think so," Moon said.

"Have you contacted Bill and Leigh, or Arnie?"

"Tried to. No answer, but I'll try again after dinner. What's your plan?"

I cleared my throat. "It's already been two days and no one's knocking at the door. My neighbors didn't act strange." Kim slumped. She started pulling her hair into little bunches. I thought about running, then made my decision. "I'm going to sit tight until you hear from the

Wrestler. *Sonny*?"

"Yeah, man?"

"If it happens? If I go down? Don't worry about me. I won't take anyone with me. In the meantime, I'll punch in my home code at night so you'll know we're okay. All right?"

"Yeah, sure," he mumbled.

"Talk to you Monday?"

"Sure, Monday."

"Thanks, Moon man."

Click.

Part of me wanted to punch the wall and scream at my wife: "Great! Fucking great. Your deranged daddy finally found a way to rescue himself from the guilt of desertion, and his lost daughter from the clutches of the dangerous fugitive! If that bastard gave a damn about anything but his macho ego he could have said, 'Kimberly? You say Tom's a good man, and I know that you love him. Get him to come in, honey. I'll help settle this. I'll pull in some favors and get him a light sentence. I'll help you while you wait for him, then you can have your life together.'"

In that moment of fear and anger, I could have said a lot of things. But one of the many differences between me and Detective-Daddy-in-Law was that I could control my temper.

"*Unsolved Mysteries*?" Kim asked, rubbing the rash on her neck.

I nodded, massaging my temples.

Her hands shook as she reached for more vodka. She started hyperventilating.

Thud! Crash! Thud-thud-thud.

We heard noises like heavy bodies dropping on wood. Kim whirled around, spilling her cocktail.

Next came the sound of fingernails scraping on window glass.

"Relax," I said, as the last of our pet raccoons jumped from an overhanging pine branch onto our back deck. "Its just Stubby and his gang of masked bandits." Instinctively, I walked to the refrigerator to fetch the beggars some food scraps.

Kim grabbed my shoulder. "Run, Tom," she cried. "I couldn't stand to see you caged."

I gazed into those brown eyes and slowly shook my head. "What about our dream? I thought you were ready to assume the lead role of gourmet chef at our own bed and breakfast place on Lake Chelan."

"Jesus Christ! Quit dreaming, Tom," she screamed, fighting back tears. "I'm tired of playing roles. We will never have a normal life. You will never be a writer, and this nightmare will never end. Just take your money and run. I'll stay here with the pets. If the feds come, at least you'll be safe and free."

For a microsecond, I envisioned myself on some tropical island surrounded by young bare breasted beauties, with no shortage of cash and bottomless tropical drinks. No thanks. Been there, done that. No gardening partner, fishing buddy, playmate, or soul mate. I was committed to my marriage. My response was heartfelt. Kim had certainly heard all that before, but maybe she needed to hear it again. "No, Lady Di. How do we know this is real? Anyway, I would miss you desperately," I added in Shakespearean style.

"God, how I hate your theatrical side," she said, shaking her head. "Is it really worth the risk?"

I wrapped my arms around her, wondering if she was also asking herself that question. Unlike the others, I had never involved my wife in my business. Yet, because of me, she had altered her identity by illegally obtaining a passport, Social Security number, and driver's license. For the first time, I was genuinely concerned about her criminal exposure. "You know me. If the feds were holding you and threatening you with jail time? I'd have to turn myself in."

She went limp in my embrace. Then, showing the spunk that initially attracted me to her, she mustered one last attempt to change my mind. "Can you say LONELY?" She pushed me away. "Because that's all you'll be if you wind up in prison! Those places weren't made for people like you, Tom," she sobbed.

I was proud of her. She was strong, protective, that rare brand of woman capable of wielding a broken beer bottle beside her man during a crucial bar fight, then making a silk teddy scream that same night. I pecked her cheek and led her to the sofa. We sat staring at our reflections in the big bay window, talking in muted and soft tones, taking turns on the vodka bottle, and watching it rain.

It takes a certain breed to live a lie, not just big balls, money, or intellect. As we sat there that night, I realized I was not born to do it. Between the good times, my illusion was draining us both, making us something else, like the settlers in Ray Bradbury's tale *The Martian Chronicles* who slowly spoke, looked, and became Martian.

Beyond our bay window, was someone watching us from those wet woods? Was this the real thing?

Time would tell.

And if they were there, then *they* could have me in my sleep, good and drunk.

Saturday, January 12, 1991: A loud ringing awoke me from an uneasy sleep. I peered through the window blinds, then answered the phone. Arnie was calling from the Safeway grocery parking lot down in Hood River, Oregon. We never telephoned house to house in order to avoid the paper trail.

"I heard from Moon last night," Arnie began nervously.

My best friend understood my decision to stay. He had been around for the other quick moves, and knew what a toll they took. There had been no confirmation about the show. In any case, none of us had unusual features that would stand out in a crowd.

"You know how cool my neighbors are," Arnie said. "If they saw something on TV, they would have warned me."

I hoped my island friends would do the same, or at least have the courage to confront me and ask for my side of the story (as opposed to the media hype version) before turning me in for a cheap thrill or a fist full of dollars. Like us, Arnie belonged to a tennis club. We agreed that's where our biggest exposure was. We vowed to stay close to home and phone each other daily.

"Take care, Bud," Arnie said.

I immediately called the Bainbridge Racquet Club. "Morning, Jene. I'd like to..." I broke into a forced cough. "Please excuse me. I'd like to cancel our court time for Sunday."

"What's a matter, Paul?" asked the receptionist in her thick Scottish brogue. "Are ya catchin' a cold?"

"No, just getting over one." I strained to catch any negative vibes in her voice, but detected none. "Tell Fred and the gang I'll be there on Monday for Men's Doubles."

"Aye, Paul. Monday, noon. Bye, Paul."

Around four, we got up the nerve to leave our nest for pet food and groceries. Over the years we'd become very relaxed with the illusion, but that afternoon my survival mode clicked on, and with it came an ominous regression into fugitive psychology. We both wore hats and dark sunglasses and completed our shopping in record time. I kept my eyes glued to the rear-view mirror of my wife's Volvo as well. No one tailed us though, and on the way out of town, my Leo curiosity led me back to the parking lot of the Bainbridge Public Library.

This time, we bypassed the phone and went inside. Two years earlier, at a clandestine rendezvous with her mother in Toronto, Kim was told that her father was embarrassed by her actions, hell-bent on revenge, and pushing an FBI buddy hard to have me featured on *Unsolved Mysteries.* Promptly warned, we laid low and watched the show religiously for over a year. When nothing materialized, we decided the warning was either hot air or scare tactics. Still, I continued to scan the show's weekly line-up in *TV Guide* for any stories vaguely resembling mine—a task I had carelessly neglected during our Oregon ski vacation.

Kim and I headed straight for the library's periodical section, where I found the January ninth edition of the *Seattle Post Intelligencer*, turned to the entertainment page, and ran a shaky index finger down the Wednesday Evening Highlights column. "*Unsolved Mysteries*, here it is," I muttered. "Escaped murderers, priest turned child molester, lost loves, aliens."

I tossed my sunglasses and gave my wife a big hug.

"It ain't me, babe," I whispered in her ear.

Sunday, January 13, 1991: Morning brought sunshine back to the island, and no surprise guests. Our stomachs settled. We had breakfast at the hip diner by the ferry dock, picked up a paper, stopped by Totem Storage, and drove home. We were big football fans and the playoffs were on. Kim made a pizza, and we kicked back and tried to relax. Another night passed without sex in a marriage that had no shortage of passion. Even after seven years together, two nights in a row was strange for us. I knew it wasn't because of her. It was me. And no matter what emotion I was showing, it said a lot.

Monday, January 14, 1991: Five days had passed since the alleged show was aired. I awoke determined to dive back into my routine and spend the afternoon at the tennis club. By the time I finished playing doubles and volleying with Kim for an hour, I was convinced that Moon would phone to inform us he'd reviewed the *Unsolved Mysteries* tape, and my face was not on it.

Kim had two appointments to deal with first: an eye doctor, and a chiropractor. She stood in the doorway, hesitant to leave, holding her tennis bag halfheartedly. I put on the blue warm up suit she'd given me for Christmas and gently kissed her on the lips. "Go on, Meekla," I said. "Got to take care of your health." I gave her a little shove. "See you on the courts at two."

From the deck I watched as she disappeared down the lane in her beige Volvo. I spread breadcrumbs for the wild birds, then stared entranced at the broken earth where last year's garden had grown. Soon, we would plant again and sounds of mating frogs would fill the vacuum of these silent nights. Hummingbirds would hover at our bright red feeders, flowers would bloom, and barbecue grills would free island chefs from the confines of their kitchens. Our landlord Steve Wallace and his wife Cathy would invite us to sail with them. Any day now, a bouncing basketball and laughter would echo in the woods as I enviously listened to the likable lawyer Tom Brewer when he found time for his family between high profile trials. Then missing my own family, I'd cast aside paranoia, run through the gap in the fence like an Indiana kid again, and shoot hoops until Kim called out my alias: "Paul! Dinner's ready! Time to come home!"

Home. I remembered when Tom Brewer first brought pheasants from a hunt as a welcome gift to us, the quiet couple next door. We were touched. Later, I returned the favor with salmon fillets and Dungeness crabs fresh from my trap.

I loved the island, but it was changing too quickly and becoming overdeveloped. Perhaps being a fugitive magnified my Daniel Boone syndrome, but I craved elbowroom. My free and easy life had become an oxymoron. I was tired of running. I was an incurable romantic restrained by stressful circumstance, a social cat turned recluse by cloak and dagger rules, a wanna-be writer banned from the dream of publication by my own contrived invisibility. And my wife was right. There was no end or cure in sight.

I rapped my knuckles on the weathered redwood handrail. Apparently, all of my worrying since Moon's warning had been wasted energy, but I could not forget that a vengeful Indiana cop had vowed to get his daughter back. In many ways this peaceful island had been a blessing. I did not want to see it become a curse. It was a sad fact, I decided, but our days on Bainbridge were numbered.

Eleven-forty A.M.: I slipped on my lucky gold lion ring, tucked my brown leather valise under my arm and left the house, locking the door behind me. The sky was blue, the island uncommonly quiet. Two cats relaxed on the deck railing, fat and sassy in the noonday sun. I hopped into my Ford and started the engine.

Seconds later, Smokey pounced on the hood and pawed wildly at the windshield. When I stepped out and grabbed him, he rabbit-kicked my gut, hissed, and jumped to the ground. The little calico, Punkin, let out an eerie cry, catapulted from the rail and dove under the deck along with Smokey. Crouched side-by-side, eyes bulging, whiskers twitching, they screamed a silent warning for me to come and hide.

Then I heard the sounds: engines revving, spinning tires that spit gravel, heavy bodies snapping tree branches! I held my breath. The sounds grew louder.

My heart beat faster. *Fuck*, I thought. For five years the long arm of the law could not reach me. It took deputizing eighteen million television viewers to get the job done. The idea of running never occurred to me. Forget the movies. Forget dreams. This was it. Time for a dose of pure reality. Precious seconds of freedom ticked away. My heart raced. I stood straight-faced, alone, waiting, *hoping* to weather the storm.

They came through the woods. They came from behind the red horse barn—fast moving men wearing matching dark blue windbreakers lettered in bright yellow: *US MARSHAL*. A plain looking sedan slid sideways, blocking my truck, and two agents jumped out, guns drawn.

"FBI! Freeze!" screamed a raw-boned, lanky man with five-o'clock shadow and a face like Officer Barney Fife from Andy of Mayberry.

"Don't move!" warned his wild-eyed young sidekick.

I focussed on those two big guns and the surprisingly shaky hands that held them, recalled *Unsolved Mysteries'* allegedly describing me as armed and dangerous, and slowly raised my hands in the air. "Relax," I said, with all the composure I could muster. "I hate guns. What's this all about?"

The marshals' team moved in closer, giving the nervous special agents a needed shot of confidence. The FBI kid climbed inside my truck to conduct a search. The Barney Fife look alike flashed his ID and began the crucial Q & A scene: "What's your name?"

In my mind, I had been here many times before. I knew the territory and all my experience with official faces had just been practice for these few minutes. But in fact very few chess moves remained in the game.

"Paul Kelly," I said.

"Date of birth?" the agent asked.

I wrinkled my brow. "August fourth, 1964. Why do you—"

"Where?" the agent snapped.

"Where, what?"

"Where were you born?" he smirked.

"Wichita, Kansas," I answered calmly. "Why? Would you please tell me what this is all about?"

The agent frowned. His partner crawled out of the Ford, handed him my unfolded wallet, and whispered something. With one eyebrow twitching like Clint Eastwood, he asked, "What's your Social Security number, Mr. Kelly?"

For some ungodly reason, my photographic memory screen went blank. "I always forget," I said. "That's why I carry the card." I sounded like Carl Malden doing an American Express commercial. I felt like an idiot.

The government's team exchanged proud glances. Barney Fife produced some papers and waved them in my face. "I don't believe your name is Mr. Kelly, sir. I believe that you are Thomas Paul Hickey!"

I hadn't heard that name in years, but failed to flinch.

"Is this your wife?" Fife pointed to a fuzzy photostat of Kim.

Sure as hell was! And it was stapled to a collection of faxed photos, which could only have come from the infamous Phoenix raid. "Does kind of favor her," I said.

Fife was elated. "Where is your wife?"

"In Seattle," I lied.

"When is she expected home?"

"After four," I lied again, hoping to buy her some time.

"Her father's been worried sick about her," the tall agent blurted.

I didn't blink, but his remark had the effect of a hot knife being plunged into my back. And still, the questions kept coming.

"Where are you employed, Mr. Kelly?"

"Seattle."

"Where was your last place of residence?"

"California."

The cuffs appeared. Fife fingered another photo and claimed it was of me. I, of course, disagreed. "Mind if we have a look inside the house?" he asked.

Time for my last move. "Got a warrant? Am I under arrest?"

Checkmate.

"Put your hands on the truck. Spread 'em!"

Click, frisk, *busted.*

Believe me, you don't know the value of freedom till they snap on those cold steel bracelets. My farewell note to Kim was two dusty handprints on a black pickup's door. After they crammed me in the car I held my head high, but my heart sank as I stared through dirty window glass watching my cats, garden, cozy island house—the entire fugitive illusion—disappear forever.

When the feds and I crossed over Agate Pass Bridge without an escort, the outlaw in me pondered a bribe—a big one. "What would it take to clear up this misunderstanding?" I asked provocatively from the backseat.

Barney mumbled something. The Kid laughed, turned around and read me my Miranda rights.

Minutes later, we arrived at the tiny Olympic Peninsula town of Polsbo and parked near a marina restaurant where I'd dined a dozen times. They paraded me up some wooden stairs to a FBI Resident Agency disguised as a real estate office, sat me behind a cluttered desk, and attempted an interrogation.

"Cigarette?" the Kid asked.

"No, thanks," I said politely. "I don't smoke."

The ambiance of their musty headquarters, combined with their jubilant demeanors, led me to believe two things about these G-men: (A) They spent most of their time watching mold spores grow on doughnuts. And, (B) The windfall of my capture was a big coup for them.

"Where are the other fugitives?" Barney inquired.

Determined they would score no more brownie points at my expense, and with no intention of selling out my friends, I gazed silently out their spy window to the waterfront below.

Frustrated, Barney phoned his superiors, who consequently ordered my delivery via the next ferryboat to Seattle.

In the middle of Elliott Bay, in the back seat of a fedmobile with a head full of questions, I watched Bainbridge Island fade away in fine sea mist, and wondered about my wife. Would Kim be all right? Sure she would. I'd never hurt her. This was my war now. All she had to do was click the heels on her ruby slippers and head home to Daddy M. But for me, there was no Kansas in the foreseeable future. I sighed.

The legal battle was about to start.

I called upon the Lion's courage, the Tin Man's heart.

Next stop, Emerald City, Seattle—Oz.

And only one thing was certain.

I needed a legal wizard badly—if ever a Wiz there was.

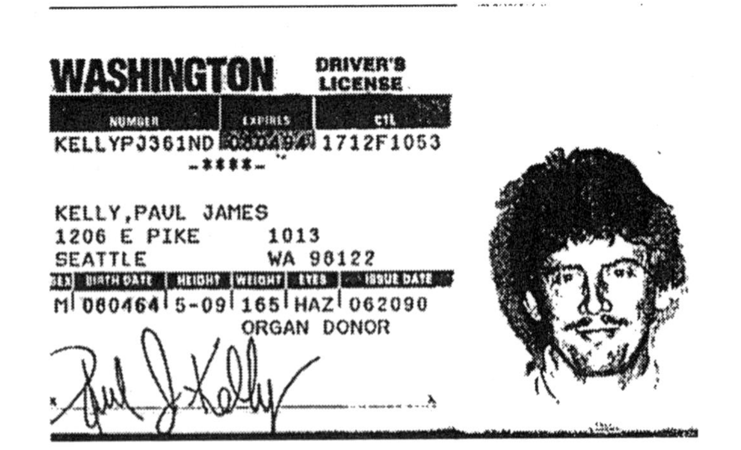

FBI Report on arrest of Thomas Paul Hickey

FEDERAL BUREAU OF INVESTIGATION Date of transcription 1/23/91

THOMAS PAUL HICKEY was taken into custody after he exited a black, 1985 Ford, pickup truck bearing Oregon license plate number PPN515. The cockpit area of this vehicle was checked for weapons, and on the bench seat of this vehicle was located a leather valise. Inside this valise was a wallet. Inspection of the contents of the wallet disclosed a Washington state driver's license for PAUL KELLY, date of birth, August 4, 1964. HICKEY was asked to furnish his name, which he gave as PAUL KELLY, date of birth, August 4, 1964, at Wichita, Kansas. Inside the wallet was a Social Security card for PAUL KELLY, but KELLY was then unable to furnish the Social Security Account Number thereon. At this point, Special Agent (SA) THOMAS A. HARNEY advised HICKEY that he did not believe that he was PAUL KELLY but that he was, indeed, THOMAS PAUL HICKEY. SA HARNEY then showed HICKEY a photostatic copy of a photograph of KIM SA HARNEY advised HICKEY that he knew that the depicted woman was his wife, without giving any name for the depicted individual. HICKEY agreed with the statement by advising that the depicted person was his wife. HICKEY was then shown a photograph of himself and told that was the picture of THOMAS PAUL HICKEY. HICKEY paused and then advised that was not he but a person who looked like him.

It is noted that the arrest was effected at approximately 11:50 a.m. at 5875 Northeast Tolo Road, Bainbridge Island, Washington.

At the time of his arrest, HICKEY had maintained to the arresting agents that he had previously lived in California and was currently employed in Seattle, Washington. He advised the arresting agents that the black pickup truck belonged to TIM BARNES and was temporarily in his custody while BARNES was in Canada.

At 12:00 noon, HICKEY was placed into an FBI automobile and transported by SAs PATRICK GAHAN and HARNEY to the FBI Resident Agency at Poulsbo, Washington. On route, he was advised of his rights as set forth in the Standard Interrogation: Advice of Rights form. After having heard his rights, HICKEY advised, "I have nothing else to say at this moment." Thereafter,

---

estigation on 1/14/91 at Bainbridge Island, Washington File # 245F-IP-159-

SA CHARLES PARDEE, SA GEOFF BICKERS, SA PATRICK GAHAN,
SA THOMAS A. HARNEY TAH:hw Date dictated 1/22/91

HICKEY refused to furnish any other identifying information. While still on route to the FBI Resident Agency, HICKEY initiated a conversation with SA HARNEY. He asked what it would take to clear up what he identified only as "this." SA HARNEY inquired of HICKEY if he meant what it would take to clear the matter up between the two of them, and HICKEY replied in the affirmative. SA HARNEY then informed HICKEY that if he were Santa Claus, he could go free, but inasmuch as he was THOMAS PAUL HICKEY, he would have to remain under arrest. At 12:15 p.m., HICKEY arrived at the FBI Resident Agency, Poulsbo, Washington, where he remained until 12:40 p.m. At that time, he was transported to the Winslow ferry, and via ferry, was transported to Seattle, Washington, arriving at the U.S. MARSHAL'S OFFICE at approximately 2:00 p.m.

On route to Seattle on the ferry ride, the money located both in the wallet of THOMAS PAUL HICKEY and in the leather valise was counted. Located in the leather valise, with a rubberband around them, were 14 $50 bills, 15 $100 bills, and three $20 bills, totaling $2,260.00. Located in the wallet in two separate areas of the back of the wallet were the following series of money: three $100 bills, two $50 bills, and seven $20 bills, totaling $540.00; one $20 bill, one $5 bill; and five $1 bills, totaling $30.00.

It is noted that at the time of his arrest, the Oregon registration for the pickup truck was located in the driver's side visor area, and this was taken into the custody of the arresting agents, also.

It is noted that at the time of his arrest, HICKEY was wearing a gold ring on which was the figure of a lion's head, in the mouth of which was a diamond. It is noted that SA HARNEY was in possession of a photograph of THOMAS PAUL HICKEY in which he is depicted holding up a glass of wine with his right-hand and clearly displayed is a ring, bearing striking similarities to the one which HICKEY was wearing at the time of his arrest. Consequently, at the U.S. MARSHAL'S OFFICE, Seattle, prior to being turned over to the MARSHAL SERVICE, the ring was removed from HICKEY. The ring was taken into possession of the FBI as evidence.

The Federal Government gave the insuring of the detention of Thomas Paul Hickey the highest priority.

I hereby certify that the annexed instrument is a true and correct copy of the original on file in my office.
ATTEST: BRUCE RIFKIN
Clerk, U. S. District Court
Western District of Washington
By [signature] Deputy Clerk

FILED
JAN 25 1991
RICHARD E. TIMMONS, CLERK
U.S. DISTRICT COURT
NORTHERN DISTRICT OF INDIANA

UNITED STATES DISTRICT COURT
WESTERN DISTRICT OF WASHINGTON

UNITED STATES OF AMERICA, Plaintiff; v. Thomas Paul Hickey Defendant.	)	NO. MOTION FOR DETENTION HEARING

The United States moves for pretrial detention of defendant, pursuant to 18 U.S.C. § 3142(e) and (f).

1. Eligibility of Case. This case is eligible for a detention order because the case involves (check all that apply):

___ Crime of violence (18 U.S.C. § 3156)

_X_ Maximum sentence life imprisonment or death

3

Looking Back

January 14, 1991, King County Jail: My refusal to cooperate and stead fast denial of my true identity earned me eight hours in a puke-stained drunk tank, a bright orange jumpsuit, and admittance to a federal prisoner holding pod. The instant the electronic steel door slammed shut behind me, every eye shifted from TV rap videos to the new commitment with the salon-styled haircut and the fresh scent of Calvin Klein Obsession cologne. It was my first time behind bars—culture shock. I swallowed hard, nodded nonchalantly, and tossed my bedroll in a vacant corner.

Shouting erupted. Two men tumbled down a flight of stairs from the upper level of the pod and rumbled on the floor. A human curtain quickly formed to block the action from a security camera's view. Fists, feet, and elbows flew. A chair became a weapon. Within seconds, the black Nigerian heroin smuggler's head hit the concrete, where he then lay, body twitching and clean white T-shirt turning crimson red.

There was silence for a brief instant in this twisted scene of violence. Then, mistakenly, the African tried to rise. "In my country, I kill the lion with my bare hands! Now, I kill—"

Crack! The muscle-bound Aryan Brother charged with armed bank robbery delivered another blow with the folding metal chair. "Welcome to America, chief," he declared.

The men cheered the victor. "Snitchin' piece o' shit!" they shouted as the African's ribs were kicked until broken.

Wisely, I fought a crazy urge to verbally intervene, pressed my back against the cold wall, and absorbed my first lesson in Survival 101: jailhouse fights were nothing like the choreographed crap where Rocky endured one hundred blows before landing his deadly hay maker. Real ones ended quickly, and anything goes was the only rule.

A goon squad burst into the pod and herded us into a line-up. "Wanna tell me what the hell happened?" one jailer asked as he checked each man's extended knuckles for cuts or redness.

"Poor nigger just slipped and fell," responded several witnesses.

"That's right, massa'," others snickered. "Uh, huh. Weak mutha' fucka' had himself a little jailhouse accident."

"And what did you see, Mr. TV star?" the turnkey asked, staring into my eyes.

"Nothing," I said, for which I received numerous nods of respect and curious glares from the others.

Not long after the brawl, television delivered the day's main event as a pitch-black sky over Baghdad exploded with Iraqi anti-aircraft guns giving hell to the first wave of American pilots. The military industrial complex unleashed its biggest and baddest high tech toys. The Gulf War was a go, and manmade Desert Storm was on the move.

Bets of contraband and smokes were made on when and where the first SCUD missile would fall. Would it carry chemicals, or nukes? How many troops would die? Prisoners in the King County Jail hailed the festivities and hollered like loonies at the top of their lungs. "Nuke 'em! Kill 'em all! Burn them sons-a-bitches! Fuck 'em up!"

A chill ran down my spine. I felt sick. They were cheering for Saddam Hussein's forces to pull off the upset and prevail, for their own people—American troops—to die. I scanned my environment and its inhabitants, listened to scar-faced, tattooed cons cursing, and unsentenced crack kids talking in rap-rhyme, all of them acting like this was cool. This was not cool. *This* was precisely what I had spent the past five years running from!

My mind whirled. Anxiety overwhelmed me. I missed my wife and hoped she'd called our emergency phone numbers and avoided arrest. I wondered if the Air Force had shipped my oldest brother, Kenny, to the Gulf conflict. How long could I continue to deny my identity? How would my mom and dad take the news of my arrest? Would the friends-turned-witness who'd found it so easy to betray me in my absence be as willing to look me in the eye at a trial, and testify? What about my money? What about the other fugitives—especially McCarthy? Would they talk? Who else had Robert Stack's media net managed to drag in?

I imagined my fellow captives sizing me up. I hadn't been in a fight since junior high school. What if one of these bastards tried me?

I took a couple of deep breaths, pulled my knees to my chest and slowly shook my head. What if the world ended tonight, with me separated from the people I loved? I'd never felt so damned alone. The present was depressing, and the future was a mystery. I stared at CNN's presentation of the largest pyrotechnics show in history and started drifting back, back into my past—land of pleasant memories, and difficult decisions.

I was born and raised about one hundred miles east of Chicago in Mishawaka, Indiana, sister-city of South Bend and neighbor to Notre Dame University. The pace of life was slow there. It was small, safe, and clean then, with plenty of woods to roam, and miles of meandering St. Joseph River to fish. I was second youngest of six children, a small outgoing boy with Dennis the Menace hair, big ears, and a freckle face like Howdy Doody's. Our family may have been large like TV's *Waltons*, but our tiny home on Berry Road did not sit on any mountain, and my old man could drink both John and Grandpa Walton under the table. Dad was never fond of punching a time clock. And when he lost his job spraying airplane parts at Curtis Wright, he became a self-employed painter.

We were poor. Mom worked full-time at Goldblatt's department store, and part-time at the Kosher Hot Dog House, from which six hungry mouths received many carryout orders donated by the kindly owner. Somehow, she always made time for her kids—miraculously managing to keep her sense of humor intact, while teaching us manners and survival tactics. There were those hard preteen summer months spent picking seasonal fruit beside migrant workers, and scavenging roadside ditches for returnable pop-bottles, but all in all I cherished memories of my *Wonder Years* in that house on Berry Road—finding the golden egg at Storyland Zoo's annual Easter hunt with help from my older brothers, listening to Elvis records with my two date-crazed sisters, then performing my own version of *The King*; scrambling for shiny pennies in itchy straw at VFW picnics, hunting box turtles in the big woods, chopping down our Christmas trees and singing carols; snowball fights, sledding the Mishawaka Hills, and sharing Choco-mint sodas for six at Bonnie Doon's ice cream counter.

On a second-hand black and white television we saw Americans land on the Moon and followed President Kennedy's assassination in Dallas. Our family survived direct hits from the infamous Palm Sunday twin tornadoes that took out our great willow tree. We also survived the competition which siblings engage in during the course of growing up. But everything did not survive the tense, crowded living conditions of the Berry Road era.

All through elementary school, I was an 'A' student who acted in plays, had artwork displayed, and poetry published. And during the last years of a dying marriage, I was Mom and Dad's comic relief, their pride and joy, their green-eyed gremlin, Tommy. Toward the end I would hear my parents argue about money from the upstairs I shared with my five siblings, and feel sick inside. Dad cursed at Mom, then left for weeks to live with his mother. Inevitably, the weeks became months. In the summer I sought peace of mind in nature. In my school classes I daydreamed it would all work out and we'd be a family again, but it never did.

After their divorce, I spent the school months with Mom and summer vacations with Dad at my Grandma Daisy's place. Grandma Daisy had a heart of gold, and a rustic house occupied by dozens of cats. She was a quilt maker and gardener who was always kind to her grandkids.

My Dad was a jack-of-all-trades who instilled the entrepreneurial spirit in me. Between summer house-painting jobs, we made decorative home address markers, which I then sold door to door. When Grandma Daisy's garden ripened, I set up a roadside vegetable stand. Each winter, I prayed for snowstorms so I could walk miles to rich neighborhoods and make big bucks shoveling driveways until dark. On the weekends I played poker with the older kids hoping to increase my savings. Every spring, my hard-earned money was sent south with trusted, driving-aged emissaries who brought back illegal Tennessee fireworks that I would sell for twice the price. Having money became important to me.

I was a driven, rebel kid, looking for a cause and an audience. At Bieger Junior High, my classmates and I collected food to send to the starving African kids my sister Judy was caring for in war-torn Biafra. It was the '60s, and I wrote poetry about preserving nature and protesting things like the Vietnam War and greed, when in truth I was already a closet capitalist. Wild dreams of traveling to exotic places and writing bestseller novels filled my head. At age fourteen—ninety pages into my first manuscript—I realized I had plenty of imagination, but was sorely lacking in life experience and discipline.

In the summer of '71, Dad lured me back to Grandma Daisy's one last time by allowing me to live in her dilapidated 1940s trailer at the edge of the property. It had no plumbing or electricity, cobwebs were everywhere, and some floorboards were missing. When night came, the cockroaches ran wild. Dad ran an extension cord from his bedroom and repaired Daisy's old outhouse for my personal use. I hung Peter Max posters on the tattered walls, and listened to James Taylor tapes until I knew every song by heart. I was fifteen. It was heaven.

Cannabis sativa grew wild in good old Indiana when I was a kid. Still does. It's a hard plant to kill off, as the government has found out. During the war to end all wars, they planted cannabis throughout the Midwest to manufacture rope, and it was this durable hemp rope that allowed Allied forces to scale the cliffs of Normandy and liberate Europe from the Nazis. Now, cannabis has become a key element in yet another battle—the endless *War On Drugs*. Many people swear it has medicinal powers, millions worldwide prefer it to alcohol, but Americans who grow or possess it go to prison and have their property taken away. In Amsterdam cannabis is legally served at coffee houses. Here it's a mainstay for countless federal prosecutors and their defense lawyer counterparts.

One sweltering August day after painting with my Dad, I was bathing in my favorite trout stream when a towering patch of weeds caught my eye. Their jagged-edged, odd-numbered leaves reminded me of the "Dangerous Drug Identification Chart" hanging in my freshman Drug-Ed Class. Curious, and buck naked, I moved in for a closer look. It was pot, *Mary Jane*, growing free and wild for as far as I could see! My imagination ran wild. I had tried cigarettes and, despite the big tobacco companies' clever advertising, failed to comprehend their fascination. I had experienced puking my guts out and being hung over from beer. Determined to experiment with all life had to offer, I picked a handful of flowering buds, put them in my fishing creel and headed back to Grandma Daisy's trailer.

The next day I enlisted my friend Bruce as a co-guinea pig. We bought a corncob pipe, and crawled under the fence of a local concrete company seeking isolation for our experimentation. We sat inside a five-foot diameter, precast concrete sewer pipe puffing and choking our way through bowl after bowl, trying our best to hold the sweet smelling smoke in our lungs.

"Highly overrated," I informed my friend between coughs.

Bruce nodded. Our eyes got watery. A summer storm appeared out of nowhere, and we became entranced by Mother Nature's power. Normally shy Bruce rambled on, disclosing his innermost fears and dreams. We shared thoughts about girls, school, and having both grown up in broken homes. When things got too serious, I shifted into my comedian routine and we laughed until our stomachs ached.

Hours later, when the rains subsided and our *cotton-mouths* were too dry to talk anymore, we raced each other to the local drugstore where we drank our fill of sodas and stuffed our smiling faces with all the junk food we could buy. The great experiment was over. I felt deceived by the anti-pot propaganda my government was pushing in school. We had smoked Devil Weed and not seen demons, turned green, nor gotten weirded-out the way our drug education teacher said we would. Not only was pot more enjoyable than beer, it was more readily available, and free.

A friend of Bruce's drove us to the resort area of the Wisconsin Dells for the 1971 Labor Day Weekend. We pitched a huge tent, hiked, fished, and swam. While smoking pot by the campfire, I revealed that I'd gotten laid at the past summer's wild gravel-pit beer bash. Both my friends confessed they were virgins. With a head full of resin and hormones-a-raging, Bruce challenged me to recruit some party babes from town.

"No problem," I said, brushing out my shoulder length hair, splashing on cologne, and slipping into my trademark red and white striped coat.

"No way!" Bruce laughed.

I disappeared down the road with my hitch-hiking thumb extended, singing Beatles songs.

About two hours later I returned triumphantly. "Right, then," I announced like Paul McCartney, straining to stay in character. "Here we are, ladies! Well done. Lovely. Welcome to Camp Run Amok."

"Are you really a foreign exchange student from London?" the perky redhead asked.

"Actually, love, I'm from Liverpool," I drawled with a wink, "but London's bloody close enough."

"I just love your accent!" she said.

"All right, where's the pot?" inquired her thin blond companion. "And where can we go skinny-dipping?"

Bruce poked his head out of our tent, aimed a flashlight at me, and did a double take.

"Ahoy, mates!" I shouted. "Set out the fine china. Stoke the fire, and fill the peace pipe, lads! We've two lovely guests to entertain to-night."

They couldn't believe it. My bag of marijuana and offbeat sense of humor had gone a long way. We all lost our inhibitions and got lucky. Three days of peace and love ensued.

By staying with us, the girls missed their ride home to Madison. In return for driving them there, we were given a tour of the hip University of Wisconsin campus and invited to their brothers' fraternity party. With the bright-eyed redhead by my side and my improv-comedy act never missing a beat, I was a hit. My pals nodded off in a corner, but I talked on about politics, poetry, and eventually about the pot patch near Granny's place.

The Wisconsin Badger frat boys were extremely interested and offered to purchase all I could bring them at thirty bucks a pound. I jotted their number down on a matchbook cover, kissed Red goodbye, and woke up my friends. All I could think of during the drive home was that a green gold mine was growing just outside my backdoor. For a poor kid from Indiana, it seemed like a dream opportunity.

The following night, I picked pot from dusk till dawn and dragged bulging plastic garbage bags through endless rows of corn back to Grandma Daisy's trailer. Mosquitoes made a pincushion out of me. My scrawny arms ached, but visions of easy money drove me on. That weekend, I bought a Greyhound ticket to Madison, Wisconsin.

"Good Lord!" the balding bus driver exclaimed as he stuffed my two fifty-pound footlockers into his storage compartment. "What do we have here, young man, books?"

"Yes sir, books," I blurted, before quickly stepping onboard. "We have books and educational materials. Mind food for my brother, the freshman college student."

True to their word, the Wisconsin frat boys paid me thirty dollars per pound for my cargo of weed, which they weighed on a fancy platform scale as opposed to the bathroom version I'd used. Pointing out that it was not entirely dry, they proposed withholding a percentage for weight-loss due to evaporation, and we settled on a figure of $2,500.

With considerable effort, I concealed my elation. $2,500! For some plants millions of people thought should be legal.

I rode the bus home with a stack of liberal reading material and a clear conscience. Having studied plenty of inconclusive research on grass, and tried it myself, I honestly saw no moral wrongdoing in the act of dealing it. Alternative university newspapers from Ann Arbor to Notre Dame were attacking Tricky Dick Nixon and the Vietnam War while simultaneously extolling the virtues of getting stoned. Movie stars like Jack Nicholson and musicians like Paul McCartney were openly smoking joints. In Merry Old England a future president smoked without inhaling THC between anti war protests and Oxford-style debates. From Harvard to Berkeley, young legal-eagles destined to soar to nests on our nation's highest courts locked lips to hookahs and heralded the same slogan as the Wisconsin frat boys and I had between tokes: "Peace, love!" Even conservative Quayle in Indiana reportedly found time amid driving and putting at Daddy's country club to puff. Ah, sweet memories of youth. But later, political correctness apparently caused them to forget both their idealism, and the truth.

That Christmas I bought my parents the best presents ever. When the summer of '72 arrived, I purchased a backpack and hitch-hiked around the country in tattered blue jeans. It was a season of discovery for a naive Midwestern boy. I saw anti-war rallies, gay-rights parades, the musical *Hair* in a park, psychedelic outdoor concerts, ghettos patrolled by inner-city street gangs, the Rocky Mountains, and the Pacific Ocean. Much of what I saw amazed me. Some things scared me to death. But one thing was certain—Mishawaka, Indiana would never be the same for me.

Homeward bound and east of L.A., a hippie couple driving a customized El Camino invited me for a stay at their ranch on the outskirts of Tucson, Arizona. The woman's tasteless health food and hairy armpits turned me off, but her man Tony turned out to be a fine musician and fellow poet.

On my last night at the ranch Tony produced a brick-shaped package from a stash panel in his El Camino, spread its sticky contents on some newspaper, and proceeded to roll a monster joint. I got so high that columns of silhouetted saguaro cactus jutting up from the valley floor started marching right up to the horizon and ascending to the very summit of Mount Lemon! For the longest time, Tony strummed his twelve-string guitar and we harmonized on Beatles tunes beneath a star-filled desert sky.

"What kind of grass is this?" I eventually asked.

"Acapulco Gold. It's good shit, huh?"

I nodded, then told him about the much weaker local weed I'd sold the guys in Madison. "How much does a pound of that Gold shit go for?"

"One hundred to one hundred-fifty dollars. Depends on the quantity. Why? Think you can move some weight?"

"Maybe," I replied.

Tony pointed to a sunken area several yards from the rear of his property. "See that dry riverbed? It's my pipeline for killer-kilos of Mexican herb. A couple times a year, some *amigos* of mine backpack a few hundred mini-bricks all the way from the Mexican border to my back door." He took a deep toke of Acapulco Gold and exhaled a curly plume skyward. "Dealing grass is not just a great paying occupation, my young friend. It's an adventure. Pot dealers live by a better code of ethics than most politicians, and believe me, you couldn't have ran across a better reefer connection if you tried."

A pack of coyotes started yipping, a roadrunner shot between us, and my host began playing another song. With my youthful writer's eye, I envisioned human mules with Pancho Villa moustaches carrying contraband by desert moonlight to Tucson Tony's ranch. I tossed and turned all night, dream-weaving a movie script with me starring in a lead role.

In the morning, I wrote Tony's number in my little black address book while he drove me to the on ramp at Interstate 10. We shook hands firmly, certain we'd see each other again. "I'll be in touch," I promised.

§

During my junior year of high school, home life deteriorated. Mom had remarried a former military man who was big on discipline. All my siblings, with the exception of my youngest brother Bill, had moved on. Kenny joined the Air Force. Judy graduated from Holy Cross School of Nursing and shipped off to Africa with the Peace Corps. Joe Ann was married-with-child, and George had joined a hippie commune in South Bend.

After helping renovate the house we'd moved to on Victoria Street, I tried working at a Howard Johnson's busing tables. One week from the day I started, the stuffy manager took me aside for a talk. "You're a great worker Tom," he said, "but you have to get a haircut."

"Why?" I asked.

He furrowed his brow. "Because I say so, that's why!"

Country singer, Johnny Paycheck, wrote a song with the same title as my response.

"Take this job and shove it," I said.

"No one's going to hire you looking like that," my step-dad remarked that night at the dinner table. "Matter-of-fact, if you can't look normal like everyone else, I don't want you living in my house anymore."

Mom's face turned beet-red. I bit my tongue. He may have been right about my employment opportunities, but the last thing in the world I wanted was to be like everyone else—partying their way through college on their parents' hard-earned money, or stuck in some damn factory for the next twenty years. Not when I knew there was an easier way.

As 1973 dragged on, the more my step-dad told me to cut my hair, the longer it grew and the more senseless the rift between us became. Rebel that I was, I even started buying my clothes at Pier One Imports instead of the local K-Marts. At Mishawaka High School, I kept up my grades, printed an underground newspaper, and formed the first political party for a student council election. My Robin Williams-style comedic campaign speech swept my cohorts and me into office by a landslide.

That summer, I lost some respect for my real dad when he refused to accept the responsibility of signing for my driver's license. My mom, whom I never lost respect for, negotiated a diplomatic resolution to this dilemma. My step-dad agreed to sign for my license and I, in return, moved in with some older friends near the Notre Dame campus for my senior year. I traded a bag of weed for a '64 Studebaker Lark, installed an 8-track tape player under the seat, and went about conducting a market study on the supply and demand for Mexican pot. What I discovered was a rapidly growing army of older consumers, and eager collegian distributors who were ready to service it. There were no "bosses" per se. Everybody bought and sold pot based on availability. Math skills, humor, hustle and supply-side connections were the keys to success. I was perfectly qualified. That fall, I gave Tucson Tony a call.

My crew was given two primary rules of operation: no business to be conducted around school, and no violence. We agreed to live by a code of ethics. If you got caught, you kept your mouth shut and would receive financial aid from your friends. My main distributors were high school grads who had decided to attend college. Most of our product went to local Universities like Indiana, Purdue, Ohio State, Wisconsin, and Notre Dame.

We all had nicknames: Lex Luthor, Bear, Clem, Zeb, Red Bud, and El Gato. Initially, I was called T-bone because of my slight build. Some hippie girl got me interested in astrology one night and told me that my long blond hair looked like a lion's mane. I was a Leo, a born leader with a warm heart, she said. She called me *Lion*. The girl moved away to California. The name stuck, and I also started collecting stuffed lions.

It was a very good year. Tony made two trips east and included me on his delivery route. Back then there was no crack cocaine or kids carrying guns. Deals were done on weekends in the privacy of customers' homes, where the product's wonders could be demonstrated—similar to door-to-door vacuum cleaner sales. The big event of the year was when the Mishawaka Cavemen's football team finished second in the state, and half of these fine athletes smoked pot.

I broke one of my own rules by hosting a graduation party at my house, which had been a low-traffic, low-profile place of business, but I wanted to treat my classmates. We had shared four great years that were truly better entertainment than most B-grade movies, and I wouldn't be seeing most of them for a while. Fortunately, a house party thrown by senior Notre Dame football players down the block diverted my neighbors' attention. My shindig was an all night affair highlighted by helium tanks, tokes, and heartfelt discussions about friendship and our futures. In the morning, I handed out surprise gifts, and we caravaned off to school honking our horns.

During graduation ceremonies, we selectively released helium-filled balloons from beneath our robes. Upon pronouncement of our independence as the Class of '74, in celebration we tossed not only our maroon caps, but also scores of colorful Frisbees toward the gymnasium ceiling. I watched the festivities, wondering what my friends would say if they knew their Student Council President was about to forsake pursuing a career in journalism for a couple of years in the pot trade. I could not tell them the truth, but would not have to lie. A week later, I relocated to secluded southern Michigan with two adorable Irish Setter pups and my high school sweetheart, Leigh.

Marijuana money made one of my childhood dreams come true that first year out of school. I bought a ticket to Africa, took two suitcases of Notre Dame T-shirts as gifts for kids, and got to spend a month with my saintly sister Judy travelling the continent.

By 1975, Tucson Tony's wholesale market had grown considerably, and he decided to stop making deliveries. At his urging, I bought an old camper truck and installed a false ceiling to transport the compressed marijuana bricks back to Indiana. The stash held nearly 300 pounds. With my quantity discount, I was paying around $70 per pound for these loads. He *fronted* me the remainder if I didn't have the cash. Within days of delivering to Indiana, I wholesaled most of it to other distributors for $110 a pound. I picked through the lot for the best looking bricks, and retailed them at $150 a pound. Life was good, and I loved the scenic trips across the American West. I took my dogs with, and eventually brought my girlfriend, Leigh. I was seriously considering moving to Tucson and attending the University of Arizona, until my luck changed.

In 1976, the Drug Enforcement Agency effectively destroyed the Mexican marijuana market by implementing "Operation Tri-Zone," during which (without regard for unlucky consumers' lungs) they sprayed our southern neighbor's perennial pot fields with a toxic pesticide called paraquat. Even the most avid Mex-tokers found the short-term side effects of that season's crop—feverish sweating, vomiting and dizzy spells—not worth the risk. The result was similar to a stock market crash. Dealers like myself were stuck with inventory they couldn't give away.

Tucson Tony reported that corrupt Mexican officials cried crocodile tears over lost bribe revenues, but before certain high-level American politicians could be swayed by Mexico's powerbrokers to renege on their international drug eradication agreement, the strangest thing happened. As if pre-informed by DEA officials, Colombian growers harvested a record crop of killer weed and shipped it north to the states onboard anything that could float or fly. By 1977, the cunning Colombians had successfully stolen the herb-market with their more expensive and more potent product.

A national scramble to reconnect in South Florida ensued, and groups from Michigan and Ohio cornered the local marijuana market. TV shows like *Miami Vice* fueled this latest gold rush. It seemed like everyone wanted in on the action. And if losing my Tucson source was not enough, I returned home to my Twin Lakes rental cottage that September to find a disturbing note on my dining room table. My elderly Polish landlords had written: *WE KNOW WHAT YOU'RE DOING. MOVE OUT IMMEDIATELY! (P.S. OUR SON IS A SOUTH BEND POLICEMAN.)*

I ran to the garage to discover my two dogs tied in a corner whimpering. A hundred pounds of weed was missing from the loft. I made a mad dash to the bedroom closet, pulled back carpeting, and frantically searched the secret floorboard stash for my money. Twenty thousand dollars was gone! My loveable landlords' Law & Order son was a man way ahead of his time. I had been ripped off—*by cops*—and there wasn't a damn thing I could do about it.

After inheriting eight thousand dollars from my great grandma, I moved back to Mishawaka, bought a rundown house on Russ Street behind the Red Lobster restaurant, and got a real job in Elkhart airbrushing artwork on recreational vans. Soon I tired of breathing paint fumes, and had saved enough money to invest back into the pot game.

Not long after I finished renovating Russ Street, Grandma Daisy broke her hip and went to a nursing home. When my dad moved in with a woman he'd been dating, I sold my first house and built an A-Frame on the former site of Daisy's trailer. Some carpenter friends helped me frame and enclose the house, but I fell in love with finishing it myself over the next two years. During the home building experience Leigh and I split up, partly because of the stress of the business I was still engaging in, but mainly because of my flirtatious nature and lack of commitment. The split was mellow, and we remained friends.

I was a happy young bachelor with a house full of stuffed lions and a faithful red dog. Working out, hitting tennis balls, gardening, and collecting antiques became my new loves.

In the spring of 1979 Bill McCarthy—a major marijuana dealer making big moves in South Bend—paid a mutual customer of ours several thousand dollars for a formal introduction to me. I had heard about him through the grapevine, but had no desire to make his acquaintance until he started dating my former girlfriend. Through Leigh, Bill learned that I moved quantities of Colombian and with the proceeds wanted to start up a small construction company.

I was digging holes to plant blue spruce trees in on the day that Bill first approached me. My normally mellow dog Benjamin barked, then growled when the stranger stepped out of a black BMW wearing fancy shoes and a gold Rolex. "Relax," I said, "he thinks you're a Jehovah's Witness."

"I'm Bill Mc—"

"I know who you are," I said, extending a hand covered in dirt. "Let's go inside and talk." He knew about me. I knew about him. He was not a man of many words. We got right to the point.

"What would you say," he began, "if I told you I could supply you with carloads of Colombian pot at unbeatable prices, and put up enough laundered money for you to start that construction company of yours by building a nice spec-house?"

What could I say? I mean, the man exuded confidence. There had been a pot drought for many months, as consumer demand had exceeded my ability to supply product. Not even my new and well-connected friends from Columbus, Ohio had been able to bring any weight north from Florida. With one more good year in the trade, I could get out and go straight in the real estate game. I had never wanted a partner in crime, but couldn't pull off the construction company dream alone. And although he spoke in a monotone and had an air of arrogance about him, I smelled green money in that air. Obviously Leigh had seen something in the guy, and I trusted her judgement.

"Ever been busted?" I asked.

"Nope," he lied, not mentioning his conviction for selling LSD at Ball State University. "Let's just give it a try."

Months later, after a gourmet dinner to celebrate our second successful pot deal, Bill chopped out a line of high-grade cocaine and again posed the question of becoming partners. "Well? What do you say, Thomas?"

The snort of cocaine—which people of my metabolism should never mix with business or pleasure—shot straight to my brain where it immediately shook hands with Mr. Greed and Mr. Champagne. "What do I say? Wh...what do I say?" I stammered. What would my friends think about me forming a business with my former lover's new beau? Who gave a damn? I thought of the bitterness that had kept my mom and dad enemies long after their divorce and made them avoid each other at all costs in the same small town. I recalled how I'd vowed to deal with any romantic separation differently.

Bill cut out another line. "Well? What do you say?"

My heart pounded. Perhaps the challenge of Bill's competitive spirit could be a healthy experience for us both. I extended my hand. "I say you have a deal...*partner*. But what will you do when the day comes that I can beat your prices?"

Bill smirked, then laughed. "If *you* can ever beat *my* prices, and deliver? Then I'll sell every pound you can get." Suddenly, he tightened the grip of his handshake. "Oh, by the way, how do you feel about Leigh and me living together?"

"You have my blessings," I said, casting aside the remnants of possessiveness which all ex's secretly retain. What the hell, I thought. With her in his camp, how could I ever get screwed?

We named it Aardvark Construction Company, in honor of the Pink Panther cartoon character, and for a prime alphabetical phonebook listing. Bill and I were the CEO's of this Subchapter-S Corporation. Todd (my best friend and marijuana driver), Bruce (classmate, friend, driver and customer, who spent that first wild weekend in Madison with me) and several skilled carpenters formed the nucleus of our crew. Bill hired two of his own men—Tim Meers and Brian Stromier—to look after his interests. These workers were also available for any marijuana driving that needed to be done. Talk about convenient.

I cut my hair, learned to estimate labor and materials, and worked on job sites with the guys. It was me who delivered our lumber in an old pick up truck with a red dog panting out the window, me who dealt with concerned homeowners at all hours of the night, and me who met and appeased the building inspectors. But I was also my own boss—highly visible in a legitimate job—and I liked that. I loved building and repairing things. I got in touch with a lot of old school friends and new women, to whom I didn't have to lie about my occupation. That peace of mind was worth plenty to me—almost as much as the illegal money I was making. *Almost.*

Meanwhile, Bill's job was juggling Aardvark's books and bringing cars loaded with bales of Colombian pot back from South Florida. When the smuggled weed was safely offloaded and stashed in Florida, Bill's college friends gave him a call and the deals were on. Our Aardvark workers were immediately flown to Florida where they rented automobiles with large trunks. Bill averaged six cars per trip. Each car carried about 200 pounds. I received two cars per trip. Bill retailed the other four. The weed was costing me about $320 a pound. I wholesaled my share for $345 a pound. I was happy, and so were our drivers.

What happened next happened fast, and just like meeting Tucson Tony when I hitch-hiked around the country, it would forever distinguish my life from that of the average man. While attending a party of friends and fellow dealers Jim and Irene on their farm near Columbus, Ohio, I casually mentioned Bill's boast about being able to move all the Colombian he could get. Irene's ears perked up. Jim whisked me out of the barn where the band was entertaining his guests and grabbed me by the shoulders.

"Hey, guy!" the smiling host asked. "How ya doin? Enjoying the festivities, are ya?"

I nodded and gazed back through the open barn door to his dazzling girlfriend, decked out in white, dancing in the straw with an elderly guest, her high cheekbones glowing. Jim and Irene were only in their thirties and had it all, I thought, as I saw the moon reflecting off their fish pond on the back forty, and the sports car parked in the drive. Twice a year they jetted off to Aspen where they owned a condo. They spent many weekends in New York seeing Broadway plays and partying at The Plaza. "Irene's a fox, Jim," I said. "Well educated, warm heart. You're a lucky man."

"She's a winner," he agreed while reaching into his pocket. "I think I'll marry this one. Life is good, Tom. You can have all this, too. That's why I wanted to take you aside and touch base with you. You know, kinda let you know what's happening. Tom, do you seriously think you can move a big load?" His head bobbed rapidly.

I had met Jim through a mutual friend who became a schoolteacher and retired from the trade. Before Bill entered the picture, Jim was my main source for hundred pound lots of quality weed. He was a hard working guy with a good sense of humor. We had a shared history of getting our first connections in Tucson, and both enjoyed fishing. I liked Jim and Irene, and trusted them, too. "How big?" I asked.

"Tons," he answered, grinning ear-to-ear. "Could you make a healthy down payment?" His blue eyes were twinkling like stars.

My mathematical mind quickly estimated the combined totals of Bill's, my own, and our regular customers' cash-on-hand. "Half-a-million, conservatively."

Jim's fair-skinned, freckled snout snapped up a capful of pure cocaine. "God bless you, Tom! A friend of mine just became Mr. Big in the Colombian trade, and I've got a sneaky feeling he's gonna want to meet you."

To say that Jim was high would be an understatement, which is why—after waking up the next afternoon—I dismissed his remarks as delirious drug-induced babble.

A month later, I sat across the table from Mr. Big at the Cornucopia, a downtown South Bend health food restaurant that I frequented on my construction rounds. I had on my contractor's outfit—coveralls, tape measure, and N.D. baseball cap. My mysterious luncheon guests looked nothing like my preconceived notions of them—no fedoras or wing-tipped gangster-style shoes. Mr. Big, a short, muscular and balding pea-headed Italian-American gent with a New Jersey accent, wore blue jeans and the football jersey of a very controversial University. His tall, dark companion—introduced as *Maui Ray*—wore a snug black turtleneck and slacks. Both men were in their thirties. I was twenty-three.

"Our friend Jimbo tells me you're smart, safe, reliable, and low-profile," Mr. Big (a.k.a. *Maui Bert*) said. Bert tested the strength of my handshake, and studied what I knew was my surprisingly youthful appearance.

Ray shook my hand, too. "It's a pleasure to meet you, mate," he said smooth and slow as he stared into my eyes.

"The pleasure's all mine," I replied while trying to pinpoint the origin of Ray's southern drawl. "You look like a ball player."

"You're very observant," Bert interrupted. "Ray played college hoops in Florida, and was quite a..."

Suddenly, there was tension in the air. Several of the other customers—along with my favorite waitress—were watching us, and Bert had noticed. I dove instinctively into my imitation of comedian Rodney Dangerfield. "Hey, I try. But yer' wreckin' my image here! Talk about no respect," I remarked, kicking Bert's foot and poking his chest with my finger.

Mr. Big recoiled with his brow furrowed. Maui Ray fidgeted nervously in his chair.

"This town lives and dies for Notre Dame football," I whispered. "We're two weeks from the home opener, and here you sit with the ultimate Fighting Irish fan wearing a Miami Hurricanes jersey. ND fans hate Miami's football team. So much for low-profile."

For a moment, there was silence. Then Bert laughed. "I like a good sense of humor, Thomas," he said with a strong New Jersey accent. "But you best be serious when it comes to business."

I folded both hands atop the table and said, straight-faced, "Believe me, I am."

"Good," Bert said. "Many great things come out of South Florida, as you'll soon see. And when my Hurricanes play your Catholic mackerel-snappers this year, be ready to put your money where your mouth is."

"Count on it," I said.

Bert proceeded to quiz me about every aspect of what we called "the mission," and was pleased with all of my answers. I was instructed to purchase a secluded parcel of land and construct a building big enough to conceal a semi-tractor trailer. Upon completion, Maui Ray would fly in for a final inspection of the unloading facility.

"Our delivery ship is on the water," Bert said matter-of-factly. "I can't tell you the exact price or amount of the load until it gets past all the payoffs, but I promise it will be the best product around at the right price. And if you take too long to move it—my young, enterprising Notre Dame fan—it will be the last load you'll ever get...*from me.* My man Ray here will escort the truck driver to your building. He'll be my representative in any weight disputes. He will collect the money and deliver it to—"

I cleared my throat as our waitress arrived with the check. "Yes, Mr. B," I said. "I'm certain that Aardvark Construction is the right company for this project."

Maui Bert smiled approvingly, and the meeting was adjourned.

We found the perfect place just over the Indiana State line near Niles, Michigan. Bill paid a county health inspector named Laird Willard to purchase the property with a small cash down payment and a bank loan so there would be no paper trail leading to us. The large, inconspicuous parcel bordered busy Highway 12, and included a small farmhouse. It was heavily wooded with no out buildings.

The plan was to have as few people as possible know about our clandestine project. And so, with a crew consisting of our Aardvark Construction Company workers who doubled as marijuana drivers, I built the ideal storage facility. I rented a dozer, and we cut our own lane deep into the woods behind the farmhouse. Paying in cash and procuring the materials from various suppliers, I assembled all the ingredients for a popular Midwest structure called a pole barn. Massive rounds of pine, similar to telephone poles, formed the skeleton of our building. Corrugated metal sheets comprised the skin. We set our trusses from the top of two rented U-Haul trucks, and the roof was covered with green fiberglass panels that blended in pleasantly with the surrounding trees. Upon completion, I flew over the area in a small plane. The sixty-five by thirty-foot structure was nearly invisible by air. It could not be detected from the ground.

Maui Ray came to town for the official inspection, which the environmentally non-offensive facility passed with flying colors. He was particularly impressed with the enormous electric garage door I'd installed.

§

Niles, Michigan 1979: On a cold winter's day, I paced a wooded lane with great apprehension, like a soldier readying for battle, like a gambler about to bet the ranch on one roll of the dice. My bird dog panted beside me, disturbed by my lack of interest in the stick he was offering me. Inside the rustic farmhouse, Bill and our Aardvarks waited nervously with the money for my voice to crackle over their walkie-talkie. They were armed with a rifle.

The mother lode was three hours late. Sweat dripped down my forehead from under my stocking cap. A newspaper article from last summer about another dealer's robbery and murder crossed my mind. This incident had prompted me to apply for a handgun permit at the county sheriff's office. Because of my clean record and request for self-defense while visiting job sites, I was granted a permit. I rarely carried my Charter Arms .38 special. In fact, I had only practiced firing it at tin cans a couple of times.

Presently, I adjusted the uncomfortable leather strap attached to my shoulder holster, felt the butt of my first handgun, and speculated as to what could or would happen to us all. Up until this time, most of my deals had been done with friends I knew fairly well. Now I was waiting on a multi-million dollar shipment from an Italian called Maui Bert that was supposedly being escorted by a basketball player called Maui Ray. I'd met them through my Ohio people and felt comfortable with that. But what about this semi tractor-trailer driver? What if he was a FBI agent? What if the guy was a hit man for the mob? As head Aardvark, I was responsible for the men and the money in the farmhouse. Again I felt the gun, and realized that this wasn't just a kid's game any more.

Suddenly I heard the hissing sound of airbrakes being applied to an eighteen-wheeler out on Highway 12. A plain beige sedan with a tall antenna whipped into the drive. Benjamin dropped his stick and started barking. My heart raced. The gang inside the farmhouse pressed half-dollar-sized eyes against steamed-up window glass, and the big diesel Peterbilt rig rolled in gracefully behind Maui Ray's escort car. I extended a shaky thumbs-up, walked briskly to the pole barn, and pressed the magic button on my remote control. The door opened, and the skillful trucker's semi quickly disappeared inside.

I reported the landing to the farmhouse, and we Aardvarks collectively sighed over our walkie-talkies. "I'm going inside," I said. My anxiety was quickly magnified when I stepped into the dark building and turned on the florescent lights.

A tall, leather-skinned redneck wearing blood-stained blue jeans and cowboy boots jumped down from the big rig's cab and gave me the evil eye. "You the boss of this outfit?" he asked as he reached behind his back.

The man looked like the bad guy from some spaghetti Western. I nodded, then noticed the scar under his right eye. The trucker whipped out a pocketknife. I considered reaching for my weapon when Ray approached me from behind me and placed an arm on my shoulder.

"I done my part," the trucker declared, picking his teeth with his blade. "I delivered this crap to your barn like I promised. Now call your boys back here and get this shit unloaded! I don't like having my rig in this building any longer than necessary." He spat a wad of chew on the floor. "I got cattle back home to tend to."

Maui Ray's laughter echoed in the barn. "Roadrunner here has a point," he said. "Let's get the show on the road, partner."

"Don't pay no mind to my mood, son," Roadrunner explained, extending his hand. "I'm wired from the road. Too many smokies and too many ag-checks for this ol' boy. What I need's a damn cold beer."

Ray laughed again, obviously relieved to have reached Michigan safely. "Bert makes the rules. He sent you this gear on credit. Fair is fair, mate. Give the man his beer and get your guys back here."

Roadrunner—a full-time Florida cattle rancher and part-time truck driver—popped the sealed side doors on his trailer, then the twist-off cap on the beer I retrieved from the pole barn's refrigerator. "Gotta screwdriver, good buddy?" he asked me in classic southern CB radio redneck vernacular.

"Sure do," I said, staring at the trailer's contents which appeared to be nothing but tropical houseplants. The thought of movies like *The Sting* crossed my mind. "Where's the pot?"

"Trust me, mate. It's there," Maui Ray said. "Call your crew back here," he added abruptly, after helping Roadrunner remove the license plates from the semi and his escort car.

There must have been a thousand plants, ficus, ferns, philodendron...and for over an hour, we unloaded them carefully. Finally, we reached a bed of cedar chips, which covered a lower layer of factory-sealed cardboard boxes labeled: Marlboro Cigarettes. Each box of fluffy, gold marijuana buds was weighed, tagged and listed on an inventory sheet. Boxes were inspected for moisture or mold damage. The average weight per box was thirty-seven pounds. When the total weight was agreed upon, I gave Maui Ray our down payment—$850,000 I'd managed to cobble together from partners and clients—and accompanied him and the empty semi to a nearby hotel where, after reporting via payphone to Bert, he and Roadrunner began recounting the money.

Meanwhile, back at the barn I packed smaller trucks with Marlboro boxes, covering each load with itchy rolls of fiberglass insulation and old, nail-infested lumber. These orders were subsequently delivered to their eager buyers at predetermined destinations by our Aardvark Construction workers, which was all part of the security measures I'd devised to minimize the number of people who knew the location of the mother lode.

By midnight, Jim Hagar had taken his share to Ohio, and only a few hundred pounds designated for my retail sales market remained. The majority of eight thousand pounds of sweet Santa Marta Gold was on the road to anxious holiday consumers. With a marijuana-dust-smeared face, and faithful Irish Setter Benjamin at my side, I sat atop a stack of product shaking my head. This deal would go down in Midwestern drug lore as *the Marlboro Load.* It was hard to believe. Bert had delivered on his promise, and Bill McCarthy had lived up to his boast.

Three weeks later, Todd and I drove the million dollar balance of my debt down to Maui Bert's waterfront rental in Isle Mirada, Florida. He and Ray counted and recounted the money, banded it in five-thousand dollar bunches, and packed it under ice in two huge fishing boat coolers for its ride to Bimini and eventual deposit in a Bahamas bank. To celebrate, Bert took us marlin fishing and hosted a gala dinner at Mile Marker 88 restaurant. He waded through call girls like candy. That night Bert even set me up with a hooker, but I sent her home—explaining that she was pretty enough, but I preferred romance.

We spent a couple of days on Miami's flashy Biscayne Bay, capped off by mooning a cruise ship. We danced with models at a nightclub in Coconut Grove. We watched speedy cigarette boats racing from marinas to massive, offshore, silhouetted freighters at sunset. It was like an episode from *Miami Vice*—which had never been on my preferred viewing list.

At the time, neither Todd nor I felt comfortable with that lifestyle. After a week in South Florida, all we wanted was to get back home to our dogs and watch the Super Bowl.

Like Kenny Rogers sings in *The Gambler*, "You never count your money till the deal is done." I never did. But when this deal was done, I cleared an average of $20 per pound between retailing and wholesaling on eight thousand pounds. The potent weed was only $280 per pound. I could have easily stretched my profit margin to $40. But like Maui Ray said, "Fair is fair." At age twenty-three, I made $160,000—more than most politicians were *reporting* on their tax returns—in one month. I had hit the big time.

By Christmas of 1982, all my friends' homes were filled with tropical houseplants. Thanks to Bert's semis and Aardvark Construction's infamous pole barn I'd also surpassed every financial goal I'd set and reset for myself in the biz. To be sure, the marijuana half of my partnership with Bill McCarthy was a hit, but the legal side, now that was a different story.

In response to high interest rates, which made new home sales next to impossible, I switched Aardvark's focus to Housing and Urban Development jobs that were tedious and time consuming. Then, like some Robin Hood of Reefer, I got in the habit of giving low-income senior citizen clients all the extras I could, often to the point of actually losing money.

Of course, Aardvark, never showed a loss. By employing a half/cash, half/accountable bank money formula for covering labor and materials, we always showed a profit. This was the foundation of our "Tortoise and the Hare" approach for cleaning up our illegal money. For example, we paid our carpenters four dollars an hour cash, and seven dollars an hour via payroll. We paid for part of our materials in cash, part on credit, and part by Aardvark checks. And when tax time came, we paid Uncle Sam for profits that didn't exist, just to surface cash we couldn't account for. There were quicker ways, but they were risky.

With this *laundered* corporate money, we acquired rental properties and pumped cash into them as well, which we'd one day launder by selling the houses at a healthy profit. Unfortunately, these properties also fell under my supervision. I had a fortune buried in plastic pipe beneath Grandma Daisy's old outhouse, but spent the construction season working seventy hours a week and living for weekends and vacations just like every other Joe.

As the construction months dragged by, I often contemplated risking a trip to Vegas and paying the Mob some juicy percentage just to claim that I'd won all my money in one of their casinos. This gambit was not a fantasy but a real option, as I had a friend who knew a friend in Vegas. But every time I grew impatient with the construction company front for laundering cash, I envisioned myself lying face down in the Nevada desert after my friend's Mob contact had taken my suitcase full of money and put a bullet in my head. I was about as afraid of that avenue as I was of falling into the latest trend of doing cocaine and harder drugs.

Fortunately for me, I had another life. I joined Dave's Gym, played indoor tennis, and became a regular patron of South Bend's exclusive Summit Club Restaurant—where the maitre d', Mr. Grant, allowed me to pay my tab in cash and sing Sinatra songs with the band. Waitresses, wines, gourmet cooking, and collecting antiques and lions became my addictions during the roaring '80s era. Taking winter vacations in Hawaii, giving gifts, and sharing my prosperity with friends and family were some of the biggest joys of being in the business. I hosted many holiday parties, and always had money in my pocket, but because of this I attracted the attention of some of South Bend's rougher crowd. I didn't like guns, but after hearing about more dealers getting ripped off, I got used to sleeping with a .357 revolver under my pillow. Thank God I never had to use it. No doubt about it though, The Kid from Berry Road was evolving into a man-about-town.

Bill was now living his version of the American dream, and doing less and less of his share of the work for Aardvark Construction. He and Leigh—happily married—were hanging with a different crowd, experimenting with narcotics, and taking too many Caribbean vacations for my liking. He bought a house he could never legitimately afford. Then, in an attempt to launder more personal funds to account for his lifestyle, he got involved in numerous harebrained schemes—among them, former TV game show host Monte Hall's *Genesis* diet food pyramid sales scam, and the *Fat-O-Meter* body fat regulation/measuring device.

One time, I saw Bill write down the license plate number of Roadrunner's semi before Maui Ray could remove it. On one of our rare joint appearances at a dinner party after I finished singing a Nat King Cole song, my business partner made a snide remark about which of us would go to jail in the event of an investigation. We almost got into a fight, and I stayed mad for weeks, until Leigh convinced me that the heroin he'd sniffed was the culprit. There were other things—not to mention my instincts—that made me increasingly nervous about Bill, but the promise of Bert's next load and my own greed kept me from dissolving our partnership.

February 1983, the isle of Maui, Hawaii: Halfway to the summit of Mount Haleakala, surrounded by a fragrant grove of eucalyptus trees, I sat inside an ornate gazebo sharing a champagne cocktail with Maui Bert. Between sips, I studied the expansive valley below which separated the island's two volcanoes. The laid back tourist town of Lahaina—barely visible on the horizon—had been infiltrated by Los Angeles' elite who seemed determined to remake it in the image of Rodeo Drive. The infinite acres of lush green sugar cane that once dominated this upcountry view had been decimated by encroaching housing developments, which now hugged the very foothills of the mountains.

Long before I met Bert, I'd come to Maui to visit former high school chums-turned surf bums, and fell in love. My first visit was in 1975, and Maui was so alive. Like an undiscovered model with a dozen different looks, she dazzled and excited me. My friends and I explored wet, virgin valleys scented with wildflower perfumes, plunged deep into her sacred pools, cruised curvy coastal highways in a rusty old car affectionately called *The Pumpkin,* and hunted pristine beaches for wanton waitress babes whose hormones were raging, much like our own. In those early days amusement was easy to find. We partook of connoisseur *Maui-Wowie* herb and consumed fabled magic mushrooms plucked from cowshit. We dove from jagged cliffs into a shallow sea to chase needle-nosed fish we knew we'd never catch, and then conducted war games with rotten guava fruit that stained our tanned skins. I used to tell my good friends that they were only delaying the sad inevitability of growing up by hiding out in Paradise. But part of me envied their carefree existence, and was desperately trying to recapture the childhood I had forsaken since that summer of the Wisconsin frat boys deal at Grandma Daisy's Trailer.

Like so many of Maui's early pilgrims, my childhood friends—unable to afford the rising cost of living in Paradise—returned to the Mainland. I, however, continued to come to the island—not to party, but to gaze in wonderment at the annual migration of mighty humpback whales, to paddle kayaks on the infinite ocean, and reflect upon the dual life I lived in far-away Indiana where Aardvark Construction, Bill McCarthy, and fears of being robbed or busted were stealing my peace of mind. Back home I was fast outgrowing anonymity in my small town aquarium, but way out in the middle of the Pacific Ocean I was still a young shrimp swimming in the waters of the rich and famous, free to relax out of sight and mind of watchful, envious eyes. In the early '80s during the winter months between deals, Maui Ray and Bert became my Hawaiian vacation connections, and mentors on my road to maturity.

"We had a good run, didn't we kid?" Bert said that day, clicking my glass.

"Had?" I replied nervously.

"That's right, had. I invited you here to announce my retirement."

"Why?"

"Lots of reasons. Gloria and I are getting married. She's pregnant, which means I'm gonna be a daddy." Bert snickered. "Gotta clean up my act."

"Congratulations," I offered, along with my hand. Leave it to a woman to break up a good thing, I thought.

We watched a massive Love Boat motor into Maalaea Bay and lay anchor beside another. The hungry sea swallowed a blood-red sun, and the two stark-white cruise ships shimmered in front of the black, silhouetted island of Lana'i.

"Our friend Jim is having a little trouble with the law," Bert said.

"How?" I blurted, nearly swallowing my tongue. "Why? What happened?"

"It's nothing," Bert said nonchalantly. "Just some worthless people talking trash and giving up names. But that's all it takes these days to catch a conspiracy indictment."

I'd never heard that word used before, except in reference to the Kennedy assassination. "A conspiracy indictment, for pot?"

"Bet your ass."

In that instant, I contemplated the prospect of prison and the liabilities of my rocky partnership with Bill. "Do you think he'll talk about us?"

"Nope. Jimbo will hold his mud. The charge is out of New Orleans. A guy couldn't ask for a more corrupt venue than that. Tons of pot comes off those shrimp boats every day, and Jim's got a lawyer who knows how to work down there. He'll get off with a slap on the wrist this time."

"This time?" I repeated, straining to interpret Bert's encrypted smile.

He folded his muscular windsurfer's arms, and leaned back in his white wicker chair. "Let me tell you a little story," he said, pointing toward the horizon. "You know the history of Lahaina Town?"

I nodded. "It was once the capital of the Hawaiian Islands, and whaling capital of the world. Right?"

"Right. For decades, wealthy boat captains and their wild crews came to Lahaina Town to get drunk and screw the whores. Naturally, the natives learned to hate them. Eventually, whale oil lost its significance on world markets, and harpooning the beasts was considered barbaric. Sailing ships found other ports, holy roller priests evicted the prostitutes, and Lahaina turned into a quiet little ghost town. But as you and I can attest to, she came back bigger and better as a tourist destination."

"So," I said as Bert refilled my glass, "what's the moral of your story?"

"Like whaling, which we both despise, the marijuana business as we know it is on the verge of extinction. A new animal has entered the scene. The public's perception of what is acceptable is about to shift for the thousandth time, and if we don't change, then you and I will go the way of the dinosaurs. For years now, gentlemen like ourselves conducted our business discretely with mature adults. We didn't sell coke because we didn't believe in the morality of the product. Right?"

"Right," I agreed. "So, what are you trying to—"

"Damn it," Bert snarled, slamming his glass on the black wrought iron table between us. "You may not see it in the mild Midwest yet, but on both coasts, ignorant punk gangsters are pushing dangerous new products on inner-city street corners, right out in the open, like fuckin' hot dogs. Smuggler friends of mine say the government is supporting its covert activities with this crap. Maybe that's what makes these new players so cocky," he muttered, rubbing his temples. "Regardless, it's bad business. They give good city cops the finger. They employ young kids who knock on passing car windows, and shoot each other over a few hundred bucks, a box of Arm and Hammer baking soda, and ten square feet of concrete turf. These kids flash what they think is big money, and misuse the miniscule power that it buys. The Nightly News reports it. The public sees it and gets scared, then pissed. Politicians hungry for voter rallying issues are proposing tougher drug laws."

"But we don't sell drugs," I interrupted. "We're pot guys. You're mixing apples with oranges."

"That's nice, Tommy, real nice. Tell it to your sentencing judge, but even if His Honerableness smokes weed every night to help him sleep, he's still gonna do what's politically correct and hammer your ass if you end up in his court."

"I don't run around giving local authorities the finger, or firing guns. I'm a good neighbor. Some of my friends and customers are cops involved with clubs and bars where shady shit goes on."

"Fuck the local authorities," Bert shouted, reverting to a rough New Jersey accent. "I thought you were smart, but you're obviously not getting my message. One of my lawyers is an ex-prosecutor out of South Florida. I pay him a lotta money to tell me things. He tells me federal drug laws will get tougher. They're forming Drug Task Forces to investigate every region of the country. And, because reefer is so bulky and hard to conceal, large suppliers will be easy targets. My friend, they are going to squeeze the pot-pipeline like a teenager's zits! Surveillance balloons and Coast Guard craft will cover the water routes, and highway roadblocks will become commonplace."

"Won't smugglers just switch to smaller cargoes of cocaine?"

"Sure they will. That shit will flood the country. There'll be a fuckin' blizzard, and domestic pot production will soar. But the feds will get their headlines, and an uninformed public will be temporarily appeased by the body count, and that's all that matters."

I thought about a recent call, which reminded me that Bert's show was not the only one in town. "I have an old friend in Tucson who says Mexican growers have improved their product, and that he can get tons across the border. He says..."

Maui Bert's muscular hands fell hard upon my shoulders. "How would you like to spend five years behind bars with a bunch of street punks?" he shouted as he shook me. "How would you like having a boyfriend named *Bubba* bunking with you? Huh? I like you, asshole! You done good, kid. Now quit."

"I'm not a kid anymore," I muttered, pulling away.

"Good! Now you're learning. This part of the adventure is over, Tom."

After Bert let go, I just sat there biting my lip. In the beginning my thinking had been that an arrest on a first offense, especially in light of my clean record and young age, would cost me very little. Spend two years writing a novel at Club Fed and come out with a healthy nest egg? Sure, I could do that. Suddenly my own words echoed in my head: *I'm not a kid anymore.*

Maui Bert's impassioned speech had struck a nerve.

We talked into the night about life after our pot distributor careers. I described the Indiana antiques dealer, Richard Miller, introduced to me by one of my customers. Miller had offered me his wholesale furniture shipping connection in Northern England, and to teach me everything he knew about the business if I provided him with financial backing.

"What did this customer of yours tell the old man about your business?" Bert asked.

"That I'd made some money gambling at one of the local cop's places," I said, "and wanted to surface it. The antique trade is an ideal way to launder money."

Bert frowned. "Be careful. If you're going to retire then cut down on the number of people who know your business. Don't increase it. Remember what I said about conspiracy," he hissed.

I mentioned my many trips to the San Francisco Bay area where one of my customers now lived. "There's a big gay market for art deco figures out there," I said. "And I know a sexy French girl who'd be more than willing to help me scavenge Parisian hot spots for them." The thought of such alternative challenges to dealing pot actually began to excite me. "There's another side of me few people know about, Bert," I announced. "I've always wanted to write a book."

"Great. Now you're talking. Go for it." He rubbed his chin with an encouraging look. "A book, huh? Just don't put any short, muscular, balding pot dealers in it. All right?" We shared a laugh. "Any moron can sell pot, Tom, maybe not as successfully as us, but the real test comes when it's time to pull away and make your money work for you. You're a big boxing fan, aren't you?"

I nodded.

He punched my arm playfully. "Think of all the champions who came out of retirement because they didn't know what to do with themselves when they quit, or couldn't manage their money."

"Or had Don King's fingers in their wallet," I quipped.

"Right. Now they're broken down men, bobbing their heads and babbling, 'Brain damaged? No suh, ah ain't brain damaged. I jus' gots caught by that las' punch. I jus' feels tired.'"

To end our evening, Bert took me on a tour of his newly completed Oriental-style palace and its manicured grounds. The electronic gate at the end of a private road, matching guesthouse, gold Buddha statues, and extensive art collection must have cost millions. "How do you account for it all?" I asked.

"It's mine, but 'I' don't own it," he said, after considerable hesitation. "It's all registered to a foreign corporation. And me? I'z jus the humble groundskeeper," he snickered.

"I don't get it."

"So I see grasshopper." Bert gestured at a moonlit path and we walked on. "People with questionable money who want to live the good life need to know how to play the same games as the Kennedys of this world. You already risked your life to earn this money, right? Don't you think it's time for your money to start working for you?"

"Sounds great," I said. "What's the secret?"

"How would you like to hear a layman's mini-course in the art of *offshore banking?"*

"Why, coitanly," I clowned, like Moe of the Three Stooges. "Go ahead, master. I'm all ears."

Bert proceeded to tell me all about the alternative to laundering money: evasion. He explained how money managers in tax havens like the Bahamas and Cayman Islands accepted large sums of cash, invested them for clients, and helped them avoid both taxes and prying eyes. As for your explanation of your cash's origin, the rule of thumb was "don't ask, don't tell." All they required were your trust and a management fee. Once your dirty money was safely in an offshore corporate account, many options were available for returning it through normal banking channels to your place of residence. You could play the stock or currency markets. Your corporation could buy a restaurant and make you its well-paid manager. Company X could buy a resort property, and rent it to you or a family member at whatever price you desired. The rental fee was paid back to your account via Company X, where it accrued interest based on the currency you kept your investments in. If you were creative, Bert concluded, anyone curious about your lifestyle would find it impossible to prove you were dirty, even the FBI.

I was fascinated. But how would I find a good money manager I could trust? And which tax havens were the best?

By the time we'd gotten to the bottom of the wine bottle he'd procured from his cellar, Bert came as close as he could to telling me where his millions were stashed. "Forget the Caymans, or Switzerland, and forget the Bahamas, too."

"I thought you sent your dough to the Bahamas," I said.

"I did. But it was just an easy place to transport the physical cash and feed the main account from. I have a tax attorney there." He paused to pick and choose his words, then imparted his final bit of wisdom. "Like the drug laws, international banking laws are getting tougher, too. Our government will squeeze these Caribbean tax havens into giving up account information. There are two tiny islands between England and France—one is Guernsey, the other is Jersey. They're called the Channel Islands." He looked me in the eye. "Are you really going to quit the biz?"

I nodded.

He patted me on the back. "Then take a trip to London and learn about shipping antiques. Look, I can't give you a name. I know it all sounds scary, but just catch a puddle-jumper over to Guernsey and do some research. You'll figure it out. Good night."

I couldn't sleep. The same powerful energy that had swept into me when I met Tucson Tony kept my mind whirling all night. In front of me I envisioned men with trench coats and stuffed briefcases stepping down a small plane's ladder in a foreign land. Secret accounts, slick money managers, and mathematical equations on interest rates and currencies were all I could think about. I decided to go to this speck of land in the English Channel as soon as I could.

Forsaking sleep, I drove to the summit of the mountain, climbed out on a rocky ledge, and sat with my legs crossed, staring at the world's largest volcanic crater in silent meditation. The air, even though it was tropical Hawaii, was freezing at the ten thousand-foot level. I tucked my head into my hooded sweatshirt, placed my hands into my pouch, and waited for a sign.

Eventually, night's stars danced their way off the celestial stage and from beyond the broken rim that framed famed Haleakala Crater, House of the Sun, a burst of color was born from the sea. As cotton ball clouds raced over my head and dawn's soft pastels painted the vast volcanic moonscape-crater's floor, I vowed with religious conviction to initiate a change in my life path. I knew it would not be easy to exit the fast lane, nor could it happen overnight; but I was a Leo—*a sun sign*. Something told me the strength would come. It was time for the Kid from Berry Road to take another uncharted step on life's evolutionary ladder.

Back home, my announcement was met with mixed reactions. My customers complained, citing the fact that they had not yet stashed enough money. "And whose fault is that?" I responded with uncharacteristic fervor. "Didn't I tell you to quit blowing your profits on toys?"

Like late night party-goers looking for that proverbial last line of cocaine, they pleaded: "Come on, Tom! Just one more load."

Although he doubted my resolve, Bill liked the idea of my pending retirement. Dealers, especially two Leos, are competitive creatures by nature. My partner saw the approaching vacuum as the perfect opportunity to surpass me in the unspoken competition between us, which he was hell-bent on winning. During my association with Bert, Bill had moved the vast majority of the weight, which allowed him to multiply his working capital many times over.

And so, on the very day of my announcement, Bill chose a different path, vowing that—with his million-dollar *down stroke* (or, down payment power)—he would lure loads from his own connections which would make Bert's dwarf-like in comparison. In the months that followed, Bill traveled to the Bahamas, Cayman Islands, and God only knows where else, supposedly pursuing his game plan. Having been enlightened by Bert's offshore banking lesson, I figured Bill was also in search of a money manager.

I spent the summer of '83 crawling around low-income housing doing HUD estimates, and spending more time with my family. On a short trip to England I met Richard Miller's wholesale antiques shipping connection in the town of Wigan. Jimmy Collins was an interesting character who was surrounded by a colorful crew. Jimmy Collins was bisexual, not my bag, but he was a classy guy I could do business with. He shipped my first forty-foot container, and back in Indiana I opened a shop with Richard Miller. I attended every estate auction I could with him, and began stockpiling a hellacious inventory from carousel horses to Carnival glass in a barn he owned in Argos.

While preparing my exodus from Indiana I began courting a local, intriguing beauty with serious intent. That fall I made the second in a series of trips overseas. Life seemed to be going very nicely. I felt as if I was being guided along some mystical, predetermined path.

In the winter of '83 I had just returned from a successful trip to Europe—successful for several reasons. I was unpacking my things, unwrapping delicate objets d'art, when someone began tap-tap-tapping on my chalet door. Bill McCarthy came in wearing a smile as big as a quarter moon.

"Good God," he said, looking at my treasures. "Do you really think this shit is going to sell?"

While picking up various bronze figurines and critiquing them, Bill came across a document relating to the offshore corporation I had just set up in the Channel Islands. It would have seemed suspicious for me to show alarm. I tried to distract his attention. *Too late.* Our eyes simultaneously fell on my Leo Investments account statement. I could see his wheels turning. A deathly silence followed.

I thought about all the time and money I'd spent to get a letter of introduction to my money manager, Blake, from my English antique dealer's weird financial guru, Keith Jones. Was it all blown because Bill now knew what I was up to? He had something big on me, and was capable of using it if he ever got in a fix where knowing the secret location of my investments would do him any good. Somewhere down the road, I would have to make changes.

"So, what brought you out to my neck of the woods so soon?" I asked. "Did you miss me?"

"Nope. Just thought you'd want to know I've got a semi of primo-Colombian on the way from the West Coast," Bill said proudly. "Six million dollars worth. I'm counting on you to help with the down payment."

That was damn near double the size of Bert's biggest load. "Where is this semi coming to?"

"The pole barn," he said smugly. "Where else would it go?"

"No way!" I shouted, slapping the tabletop. "My name's on that land contract you drew up, showing me as half-owner. It's been used too many times. Too many people know about it."

"Fuck you! What's a matter? Losing your nerve? I own half that land too, or did you forget? You should be happy for your old partner, not envious."

"Envy is not the problem," I snapped. "You're involving me with people I don't know shit about—or want to."

"Don't worry about *my* connections. Your people are the one's I'm worried about."

I was boiling mad. I wanted to tell him he was getting too greedy. I wanted to tell him to go to hell, and to give me my share of our precious laundered investment capital—immediately—so I could make our severance complete, and move West, before his house of cards fell. But I bit my tongue and softened my tone. This was not the place or time, and his newfound knowledge of Leo Investments had significantly weakened my bargaining position.

In the '70s I became a big fan of The Eagles. The first time I heard their song *Desperado*, it gave me goose bumps. In the beginning, I sang it with pride, but by the early '80s it had become a bittersweet theme song. Words like, "you better let somebody love you before it's too late," pierced painful holes in a tender region of my hardening heart. It's a known fact. We get like that, us desperado men, when we're riding high in the saddle and making too much easy money. Personally, I let a lot of fine women go during my outlaw years—smart, sexy, funny, good lookers—partly because I was against exposing them to the risks associated with my business, but mostly because I just wasn't ready. I could be the warmest, most romantic, gentlest, entertaining gentleman a lady could hope to meet. But when she got too close? I'd hop right back over my side of the fence and ride on out of her life.

Big Cindy's was *the* salon to get a stylish haircut in South Bend. It was an entertaining place with happy gay employees. It was also where local dealers came to be seen and swap stories. Not only was Cindy a talented stylist, but she had the prettiest receptionist in town, thus my business. Kim was a tall brown-eyed blond, with a centerfold figure that she didn't flaunt. She drove a four-wheel drive truck and had a wolf for a pet. Word was, she didn't like men, and hung out at a wild club called the Seahorse Lounge. I wanted her and she became a challenge. She had a rebel spirit, a Hungarian temper, and gypsy blood that longed to travel—this I learned while reading magazines near her work station, nursing on her captivating scent, and waiting on the countless haircuts which were key in courting her.

Eventually I lured Kim to my chalet for a taste of candlelight gourmet cooking. A torrid affair followed. We were inseparable for weeks, enjoying the same food and music, dressing in vintage clothing and driving my 1950 Oldsmobile into the country, laughing like kids, sweating and cuddling night after night. And like her beauty, it was all so natural. She was mature beyond her twenty-one years, and different from any woman I had dated. Like me, she saw life as an adventure, and talked about her willingness to take on the world alone. She mentioned being bored with Indiana, and wanting to travel. In her I saw that rare combination of compatibility and passion which could sustain the relationship I craved. I was considering cohabitation, until a business associate approached me with the news.

"Don't you know? Her dad's an undercover narc. A real son of a bitch, too! My people say he owns a lot of property for a cop. Didn't she tell you?"

My biggest fear was of being betrayed by a beautiful woman. I worried that our affair might not be a coincidence. After a month of heaven, I avoided her like the plague.

Dazed and confused by my withdrawal, that gypsy blood led Kimberly on a magical mystery tour of the American West. It was a journey reminiscent of my own, and one she had to make. She'd call once in a while to give me road reports. There was a brief sojourn with the Rainbow

People, and the Grateful Dead concerts. She lost her wolf, then her truck. Every time I heard her voice—even though it was long-distance—I was aroused and reminded that no one else came close. The mere thought of her ruined my pleasure when making love with other women.

Eventually we lost touch, but not long afterwards her girlfriend gave me the disturbing news of Kim's nosedive into cocaine with an abusive musician's crowd on the shores of Lake Tahoe.

She was working hard by day as a lift operator at Tahoe's North Star Resort, her girlfriend reported, and trying to get ahead. But Kim was living in a crowded house with a bunch of losers who partied all night, and couldn't afford to leave.

"Tough shit," the desperado side of me responded.

Maybe it was just timing in my life, but the more I thought of Kim, the more I longed for her, body and soul. It wasn't her fault that her dad was a cop, and I didn't detect a sting. She may have been a lot of things, but she damn sure was no fake. I found myself having conversations about her with myself. I had all the symptoms of a man in love, and by the winter of 1984 I'd had enough of Bill McCarthy's surging ambition, and Indiana as well.

My plan was to stay with her a few weeks and get her a car and an apartment. I took a westbound flight to Lake Tahoe for a search and emotional rescue mission that was more or less accomplished. Standing at my boarding gate in Reno on the night I left for South Bend, I looked into her glassy eyes and said the words I'd refused to say to any woman until that day. "You know I love you, don't you?"

A few months later we were riding together in the cab of my camper truck, towing a U-Haul trailer filled with stuffed lions and furniture and doing seventy on Interstate 80—destination California.

October 1985, Truckee, California: From the deck of my antique store, *The Lion's Share,* I scanned the wooden Wild-West sidewalks of historic Commercial Row, feeling good about the changes I'd made in my life. We were California residents now, Kim and I, and the store was really starting to catch on. Together we had taken a rundown turn of the century building and breathed new life into it. Together we explored the surrounding Sierra Nevada Mountains on our free days, and the powerful magic of love and lust every night. The gypsy woman had passed all my tests.

Between silk sheets, we shared precious secrets. Neither of us cared about the details of our pasts. All we were concerned with was living in the present and building a future. She knew through the grapevine about my former business. But before we moved West, I promised her that my dealing days were behind me. She knew I had money too, but no idea how much, and never asked. She said she loved me because I was kind, and funny, and smart—not because I had money.

Like me, Kim had a warm heart, but all too often she hid it behind a facade of toughness. I figured she'd developed this coping skill to survive a troubled childhood brought on by her father's heartless desertion of an all-female family, which might have accounted for Kim's distrust of men in general. She had a short temper, lacked patience, and kept important feelings to herself. I, on the other hand, admittedly kidded too much, was a terrible flirt, and needed to work at becoming a better listener. Yet, after one year together, I knew that between the two of us there wasn't a thing we couldn't lick.

Before we left Indiana for good, I made an effort to meet Kim's family—her mother, Grandma Wheezy, two younger sisters and one brother. We even paid a brief visit to her dad's place. He had left the police department, supposedly because of a neck injury, which accounted for his disability pension. Kim's mother told me there were other reasons why her ex-husband had to leave the department. Regardless, Kim's dad offered to drive my car out to Tahoe after we were settled in. Being a good diplomat, I accepted.

My future father-in-law stayed with us for several days in late summer, 1985. He was a huge man with unruly, curly blond hair and an untrimmed red beard. He carried a gun and dressed like a lumberjack. Kim said that he'd maintained that look since the days when he did undercover work. He had a way of staring right through you. I wondered if he knew anything about me, or cared. But Kim swore they never talked about it and I believed her.

I was wary, but never caught him snooping around the basement where I hid the money. I felt uneasy during his visit, yet kept an open mind. The man was good with his hands, and helped me repair some furniture and clocks. He was also a hard drinker, and one night after failing to keep up with him, I found him on my living room floor with a local lady he'd hustled. The room smelled of reefer, but it would have been the ultimate act of hypocrisy for me to complain. He was still living in South Bend with the younger woman he'd left his family for, yet none of his actions seemed to faze my future wife.

Before her father flew back to Indiana he shook my hand and gave me a hard stare, which Kim said signified his silent blessing. I'd heard enough about him to know he wasn't dumb. An ex-narcotics cop had to be curious about where I got my money. But he was also the proud father of a beautiful, rebellious, young lady who apparently had found a solid man. I assumed he saw how much in love we were, and decided he could live with that.

"Dinner's ready, honey!" Kim called from an open window of the Lion's Share. "Come uncork the wine."

"Just a second, Sugar-B," I answered, still lost in thoughts.

The store cat Jagger lunged for the door. My Irish Setter's tail started wagging. A fellow downtown Truckee business owner walked past me and waved. I returned the gesture and sighed. Funny thing, life.

The normality I'd shunned more than a decade ago now seemed more appealing every day; and I finally had someone to share my hopes and dreams with, as well as the fruits of my outlaw labors. Dreams. For the first time in ages, I had dreams again: of writing books, and playing a white baby grand piano while kids—my kids—played happily at my feet. I hoped it would be advantageous to have a lady schooled at evading her cop-father's nosy eyes on my side, for there was still the matter of money to be laundered. Perhaps, in time, her father would become my ally and friend. Regardless, I wanted a special partner and lover, and I wanted that person to be Kim.

On the night I proposed, Kim told me the prediction that the girls from Big Cindy's had made for her: "You'll make a great mother, Kimberly, but you'll never be a good wife."

"Nonsense!" I replied. "I promise not to become a sexless, fat-ass couch potato who never puts out and orders you to bring his beer. Can you promise not to nag? Come on! Let's play it by ear. Two things I guarantee. I'll never leave you, and our life will never be boring. And once the antique business gets rolling, you'll be Cinderella at the ball. I promise."

She accepted, and we set a wedding date.

We planned a very special ceremony, and invited less than twenty people. Kim's mom, Donna, wanted to come, but was afraid to be anywhere with her ex-husband. When Kim's dad announced he would not attend our wedding if his ex-wife were there, it was a relief for everyone.

I couldn't have written a better movie script for my life, I decided that sunny October day as I opened the door to the Lion's Share. Indiana and my past were two thousand miles away, and I had six military ammunition boxes containing nearly one million dollars buried in the basement. I'd committed a passive nonviolent crime, and gotten away clean.

"Yeah," I sighed with a clenched fist. In my mind I had made it, but only in my mind. I had yet to discover that a drug conspiracy is a very unforgiving mistress who, once scorned, remains venomous for years to come.

"Honey, there's a phone call for you!" Kim shouted.

"Tell them I'm busy. Tell them we're horny. Say the shop is closed and—"

"He says he's an old friend of yours. He told me to tell you it's *Smiley*, and that it's very important."

My jaw dropped. It couldn't be. No one had heard from him in months. Rumor had him in Mexico. The man was a hot potato.

"Tom?" Kim asked. "Is this some kind of practical joke, or what? Do you know someone called Smiley, or not?"

I most certainly did. After serving a few months in a halfway-house on his New Orleans smuggling charge, Smiley Jim Hagar had come home to his Ohio farm only to be slapped with a new federal indictment on conspiracy charges. Rather than face a second offense in a tougher district, he'd decided to flee. Jim Hagar was a fugitive from justice—*a wanted man!* What in the world did he want with me?

I yanked on the door handle, heart pounding, stomach churning, feeling that old familiar paranoia. Unfortunately it was justified, as I found out when I picked up the phone.

"Tom?" he asked eagerly. "Hey, guy! Good to hear a friendly voice. How ya doin? We need to touch base and have a talk."

I could hear the tension in Jim's perennially happy voice.

Smiley didn't talk long. He was doing seventy miles an hour on

Route 66. He was afraid of giving details on his cellular phone, and hinted that my line might be unsafe as well.

Two days later he showed up with his wife at the Lion's Share. They parked six blocks away. They waited until my customers left, then walked in with the hoods of their ski uniforms over their heads. They were wearing scarves and dark glasses. Kim had gone to lunch with a friend. I hung the CLOSED sign on the front door.

"Sorry to be the bearer of bad news, Lionman," Smiley announced. "But your name's come up in a Regional Drug Task Force investigation in Ohio. Todd, Bert, Ray, your ex-partner Bill...the FBI's been asking everyone about all of us."

I shuddered. "So what, let them ask. I quit. It's over. The IRS even audited our books last year."

Smiley bobbed his head repeatedly. "They did? That's the beginning of the investigation. They're looking for the money."

"Right," I said. "Well they couldn't find it, 'cause we passed with flying colors. They didn't catch me in time."

His wife, Irene, closed the curtains facing the street.

Smiley pulled off his glasses and massaged the dark area beneath his tired looking eyes. "Sorry, Lionman," he sighed. "I'm afraid the rules have changed. Trust me, I'm your guardian angel. I'm here to save your ass."

Irene gave him a nervous glance and tapped her watch.

"Gotta run, guy," Smiley said. "A friend's rented us a cabin nearby." He handed me a piece of paper. "Give me a ring at this number tomorrow. And don't call from here."

I closed the store early that day. I isolated myself in my office and told Kim I had bookwork to do. I never ate dinner. My mind raced for hours until I felt sick, then I simply shut down. I went to bed at three A.M., tossed and turned until dawn, and refused to wake for work. I told my wife I was catching something.

One week later I held Kim in my arms and told her about the news that had tossed me into a mini-depression. Her face lost all color. She did not believe I would be indicted. "Don't worry about it now," she said with surprising nonchalance. "Whatever is meant to happen will happen, and we'll deal with it when the time comes."

"Honey," I said, "don't mention this to your dad. All right?"

"Don't worry, I won't."

Her reaction only strengthened my love and respect for her.

January 5, 1986, South Lake Tahoe, Nevada: Three stretch limousines pulled up to Harrah's Resort entrance, picked up a jovial wedding group dressed to the nines, and glided away. In the lead car I leaned back, took a deep breath, and collected my thoughts and emotions.

The preceding days had been hectic. Over the holidays, I'd rented a condo for family and friends who harbored reservations about our marriage and Kim's intentions. "She's a gold digger," some whispered. But with each remark I rose staunchly to Kim's defense, not just because I loved her, but also because only Kim knew that what she could conceivably inherit was no woman's—not even a gold digger's—dream. Eventually, after deciding that I'd been around the block enough to know what I was doing and finding Kim adorable, everyone jumped on the bandwagon. But there was more.

My mom, who'd been staying with us for weeks, was going through a painful divorce and the only thing I could do for her was give her my company. My sister Judy had invited her depressed girlfriend. Judy herself was a wreck, having just parted ways with her seven-year live-in lover, in part because of the French girl he'd met during an art-buying trip to Morocco with me. While slick managers were rumored to skim millions from Uncle Sam's IRS coffers in Tahoe's casinos' counting rooms, I was about to willingly pay taxes on tens of thousands of dollars of inflated antique profits to surface some more of my cash. But there was more.

My best man Todd and I were under investigation back east, I was about to exchange vows with a vindictive ex-cop's daughter, and the car behind us was transporting two bona fide federal fugitives, whom I was technically aiding and abetting by inviting to this affair. As if this weren't enough, I was being strongly advised to create alternative identities for Kim and me—*just in case.* Truly life is strange and love *is* blind, I thought as my wedding hour approached.

The motorcade crawled along a narrow, icy, access road, and skidded to a halt at Heavenly Valley Ski Resort's main lift shack. "We're here," I announced, giving my nervous bride's—as well as my mother's—hand a reassuring squeeze.

"Th-that's a cable car! Where's the chapel?" Mom asked.

"This is our chapel, Ma," I said. "And it's called a gondola."

"Oh my God, Thomas! How romantic," exclaimed Kim's hip mother Donna.

"Cool," muttered Kim's bridesmaid Rachael.

"Righteous," said my younger brother, Bill.

My best friend Todd, who towered above the others like a bodyguard, folded his huge hands in front of him and grinned.

The surprised passengers were quickly ushered into the warm and waiting gondola. The doors closed, all worries disappeared, and we began climbing high above the majestic Tahoe basin. It was a smooth ascent, during which everyone whispered, smiled, and held tightly to their leather ceiling straps, awestruck by the glorious scenery. And glorious it was. But I swear, no snowcapped mountain, no shimmering lake or sun splashed sea ever looked as good to me as Kim did that day. Something old, something new, something borrowed, something blue. My gypsy bride had been transformed into Cinderella at the ball, and as I'd hoped, our *chapel* delivered more spirituality than any church could have mustered. I studied the wedding party's faces. They studied mine. None of us were faking that happiness, or imagining those vibes. It was pure bliss. If you could bottle that emotion, the world would be at peace tonight.

The Heavenly Valley operator played the cassette tape I'd brought—George Winston, Windham Hill Records Pianist—and we recited our version of the sacred vows. The pastor of a small South Lake Tahoe church officiated. It was perfect. My girl and I held hands, got goose bumps, and saw smiling souls through each other's eyes. The ceremony was short. We dropped the word obey and kept, "till death do us part." I can't describe the feeling inside me, but I will say—having avoided such commitment until age twenty-nine—that I took those words to heart. We kissed. The gondola clicked to a halt at the top of the mountain. Doors opened, cold winds blew, and a waiting, all-girl ski lift crew showered us with rice while friends and family encircled us. Tears of joy fell all around. It was beautiful. I'll never forget the day. It was beyond a doubt the happiest moment of my life. Then we descended—two of the most unlikely holders of the titles husband and wife.

k at our reception suite, we opened presents, posed for pictures, drank Perriet Joet Champagne toasts until our heads got dizzy. At the height of the celebration, Jim and Irene called us into our bedroom and promptly closed the door.

"Surprise!" Irene announced, handing Kim a cocaine-covered mirror. "A special present for the blushing bride and groom."

I furrowed my brow. It had been a long time since we'd been around cocaine. I had no desire to alter the natural high I was enjoying, but the ladies quickly powdered their noses and passed the mirror to me.

"Listen guy," Jim said, "the wife and I gotta run, but before we go I wanted to give you this and some parting words of wisdom in private."

He handed me a booklet and I read its cover out loud. "*One Hundred Ways to Disappear and Live Free,* published by Eden Press. What nut wrote this crap?" I snickered.

"I think the author's name is anonymous," Smiley said. "It explains different ways of changing your identity. In the underground it's called paper tripping. It's no Pulitzer Prize winner, but it gives you an idea of what we're talking about. Or did you think the wife and I were just cruising around the country under our real names, waiting to get busted?"

"Isn't the right to free speech wonderful?" Irene sighed.

I grinned and pleaded, "Come on, Smiley, not tonight."

"Come on nothing. Talk is cheap," he blurted. "It's time for action. Time for you to cover your ass, because when the shit hits the fan back east, all your good friends will go cut deals with the feds—just like my own brother-in-law did against me."

"I still don't believe that, but if they do I'll go to trial and—"

"You'll lose. You stand a better chance of beating a murder charge in this country. And when you lose, you'll do more time than a murderer. The feds are like pit bulls. Once they sink their teeth into your ass, they never let go. Take my advice. Do it. And forget about the movies where some fat biker supplies you with the whole ball-o-wax on a moment's notice. Good paperwork takes time. We leave for Tucson in three days, and that's where we're meeting our ID man. What's your decision?"

I took a deep breath and turned to my young bride. "Honey?"

"I told you, Tom," she said with cocaine confidence. "Whatever it takes to stay together, we do. Screw the government! Christ's sake.

You're an ex-pot dealer, not Al Capone."

I pecked Kim's cheek and listened to my drug affected heartbeat. I doubted the validity of Smiley's warning, and regretted getting high on my wedding night. *Love, honor, freedom, money...* these were things that people had taken drastic measures to preserve throughout history. "Guess we need to place an identity package order," I said. "Just in case."

Suddenly the bedroom door opened. Jim jumped up, and the photographer snapped a couple of shots. Kim shoved the coke mirror under the bed and smiled. "Bring on the bride and groom!" someone shouted from the living room.

"We'll be right there," I answered, waving away the cameraman.

With my wife's hand in mine, I escorted the Hagars to the exit, where we exchanged kisses and hugs.

"We love you guys!" Irene said with teary, tired eyes. "It was wonderful."

They turned and walked away.

"Thanks for letting me wear your pearls," Kim called after her.

I watched them disappear into the dark shadows at the end of the hall, sensing their loneliness, and wondering if they were as happy as they led me to believe with their glorious life on the lam.

"Thanks for coming," I whispered when they rounded the corner.

My wife and I rubbed our ring fingers together, performing what had become a standard ritual since the arrival of two fugitives in our life.

"*Shazamm*!" we said when the gold metal clicked. "*Shazamm*! Whatever it takes—even a paper trip."

And *we* turned to face a warm room filled with life's greatest treasures—love, family, and friends.

4

The Paper Trip

Three days after our wedding, Kim and I arrived at the Hagars' secluded Lake Tahoe rental for our initial fugitive photo-shoot. As instructed, we came prepared with numerous clothing changes and the names and information we had painstakingly selected for our alternative identities. They greeted us with open arms. Jim put a log on the fire. Irene made strong drinks, and the four of us sat down at their kitchen table where we were shown the most popular identity "starter" kit in the underground world for 1986.

"This is the Nebraska driver's license," Irene whistled through the gap in her front teeth. "It comes from an actual Cornhusker State license branch, and some underpaid government employee."

Jim produced another document. "This is the birth certificate. Of course, it's official, too. Go on, pick it up and give it a feel."

I ran my fingers over the crimped area at the bottom—bearing the emblem of the Sunflower State—and read, "James Blackwell, born this day in the city of Wichita, in the state of Kansas."

"Did you read that booklet I gave you?" Jim asked.

"Yes," I said. "Most of it."

"Great. Then you know that these are the two cornerstones on which your identity is built, and that both of them will be requested at every step along the path to obtaining real, registered paperwork, like Social Security numbers and passports. By the way," Jim added, "a birth certificate isn't worth the paper it's printed on without that embossed seal."

"Why?" Kim asked.

"Because it's the first thing some curious passport agent or Social Security clerk will look for while pretending to listen to your story," Irene said. "A weak identity change is worse than no identity change."

"So, lesson number one, class," Jim said, drumming his fingers on the tabletop. "Kansas birth certificates and Nebraska driver's licenses.

A good match, geographically. Don't ya think?"

"Straight from the heartland!" Irene whistled. "You can't beat that. Right, honey?"

I noticed with concern that our hosts were exchanging cryptic glances. They were talking fast. I detected some negative energy, some clashing of egos in the air. I considered how little I actually knew about them. Before our wedding we had only done a few deals, skied Tahoe, and dined together five or six times. Now we were facing the possibility of sharing a bizarre adventure, and trusting them with our future. Were they really the good-hearted, fun-loving couple they appeared to be? Was it only their situation that filled me with some deep sense of foreboding? Suddenly, I questioned my decision to come here.

Outside we heard the sound of a car engine approaching the cabin on the narrow lane. Everyone looked toward the window.

Kim sipped her cocktail nervously.

"Relax," Smiley said. "We're not being raided by the FBI. They're probably driving to one of the other cabins at the end of the road."

Irene ran her hands through her husband's curly blond hair.

Jim bobbed his head, emptied the contents of his billfold, and continued his presentation. "These pieces are the mortar in the foundation of the ID pyramid." He spread Blue Cross, Blue Shield, Metropolitan Life, Voter Registration and other documents, like so many playing cards upon a poker table. "They call this dime store ID, or filler. It gives you a full wallet, which will look normal to nosy eyes. Here." He tossed me a laminated Texaco Oil Company employee ID badge. "This is the most important one of this group. Texaco, IBM, Whirlpool...you can be a trusted worker at whatever Fortune Five Hundred corporation you want. These employee cards also provide an instant answer to the number one most-asked, annoying question, 'Where do you work?' We can even get reporter's or cop's ID."

"I see you're wearing a suit and tie in this one," I said. "Very nice. You've sure gained some weight since your disappearance. You really look like a bum in the Nebraska driver's license photo."

"That's the point," Jim replied. "Variety, my boy! That's why I asked you to bring all those clothes. The employee ID badge requires a formal business look, and the driver's license is more casual, kinda laid-back. *Capice*?"

"What about getting dead people's birth certificates the way it was described in the booklet," I asked, "or using an institutionalized person's paperwork?"

"A loony bin person's paperwork is hard to come by," Jim said. "Buying the basic documents makes more sense. This is easier, and you get to create your *new* self from scratch."

"What name did you choose, Kimmy?" Irene asked in a condescending, Connecticut-bred accent.

"Diane," my wife replied. "Diane Kay Moore. Tom and I stayed up half the night deciding. It was kind of exciting, like picking baby names."

"Diane. That's pretty." Irene squeezed Kim's hand. "What about you, Tom?"

"Timothy Alan Barnes," I answered. "And don't ask me why. It just has a nice ring to it."

"What about your new man's vital statistics?" Jim asked.

"I listed my weight as 155 instead of 168, called my green eyes hazel, and switched my brown hair to blond. It felt best to stay close to my actual birthday of July 24, so that *Timothy* would still officially be a Leo. I did, however, change my age from twenty-nine to twenty-two—because I look so much younger when I shave off this moustache."

"Good man," Jim said. "I knew Tom would do well at this, honey," he told his wife. "I see you read the part about altering your profile slightly in case some FBI computer whiz-kid is flipping through files in the future, trying to find you. Beyond a doubt, you, my friend, have the ideal mindset for this fugitive game."

I nodded, still hoping this madness was indeed just that—*only a game.* Then I thought about going to prison. I needed to cover my ass, and after scanning the underground booklet I was already starting to think like them—and beyond them—for ways to master this paper trip challenge.

"I have to admit that I changed my age slightly, too," the forty-ish Irene said, her face flushing pink. "Oh, all right! Considerably. Eight years, to be exact. But what woman wouldn't, given half the chance?"

"Eight years, eight inches—every woman's dream," Jim joked, pinching her ass. "What about the information on your birth certificate, *Timmy*? Is it the kind of stuff you won't forget if you need to recall it in a situation?"

“I think so,” I replied. “My father’s name is Kenneth E
and his employment at the time of my birth was a lawye

Irene snickered. “How apropos.”

“My real dad’s name is Kenneth Eugene Baker,” I explaine
for my mother’s maiden name, I wrote down Daisy Mae Lynch.” I fought back a tear and knocked on the table. “God rest her soul,” I added, hoping somehow my dear, deceased Grandma Daisy could hear me and understand.

In the moment of silence which followed we watched gray clouds enshroud the mountains as an oncoming snowstorm rolled in over the Tahoe Valley. My hosts hung a plain white bed sheet on the knotty-pine wall and stretched it tight with stickpins. Jim loaded a Polaroid camera with a fresh film pack, while Irene wet my hair and combed it back. Smiley Jim Hagar lit a joint and offered it to me. I passed, explaining that I didn’t want my eyes looking glassy and red on my new ID. “Let’s get started then,” he said.

In my flannel woodsman’s shirt, sporting a hair-do like Ted Danson had on *Cheers*, I stood erect, shoulders pressed against a wrinkle-free white sheet, awaiting my first outlaw mug shot.

“The Nebraska driver’s license has a blue or red background, depending on the day of issue,” Jim said, with the joint dangling from his lower lip. “But our ID man can work with white.”

“Say cheese!” Irene whistled, and we were off and running.

Dozens of pictures, many costume changes, and hours later, we spread Polaroid snapshots on the living room floor and selected the best for the three ID packages I would order. Jim had convinced me to create a second identity. This other me, John Paul Simms, would be a disposable person that I could use to establish mailing addresses or *mail drops* where sensitive documents and communications could be sent.

“We haven’t taken the paper trip to the next level ourselves,” Jim admitted.

“You haven’t?” I said, somewhat startled and beginning to question my judgment again.

“Well, not exactly,” Irene muttered.

“Underground press publications like *The Social Security Agent’s Manual, The Passport Agent’s Manual, The DEA Agent’s Manual* and others are of particular interest to us all,” Jim continued. “We want you to uire these before you disappear and the feds start flashing your picture around."

"You mean *if* I disappear," I said.

"Whatever. I'm a realist. Just be aware that if you order this kind of revolutionary shit your name is placed under an FBI magnifying glass."

"In other words," I groaned, "Timothy Alan Barnes can be my long-term project if I choose to run him through the system, but poor Mr. Simms will be a sacrificial lamb?"

"Precisely," Jim said between sips of his beloved *Crowny*.

Fifty times we wrote our selected names in various sizes on unlined sheets of paper, in a styie unlike our normal signatures but one we could easily reproduce. *Timothy Alan Barnes, John Paul Simms, Diane Kay Moore,* we signed with odd slants. These were then folded into three envelopes with the corresponding photos and information, which we sealed with a sense of bittersweet relief.

"The ID man likes to have a good selection when he shoots the signatures for the different documents," Jim explained. He tucked our paperwork in a briefcase and cleared his throat. Irene led Kim into the bedroom and closed the door. "Money time," Jim said.

Like me, Smiley had made over a million dollars in the trade. His healthy financial status was a major factor in my decision to consider sharing their company in this endeavor. As I saw it, there was no reason for a rich fugitive to make desperate moves. Consequently, I was surprised when he asked to be paid up front for our paperwork.

"The ID packages cost me twelve hundred apiece." Again he cleared his throat. "I'm a little short on pocket cash at the moment."

I had no idea of the going price in the ID market, but it seemed like a reasonable sum to pay to avoid going to prison. I reached into my jeans, pulled out a five thousand-dollar bundle of hundreds and removed five of them. "Here's forty-five hundred for the three sets." The extra is for your expenses."

"God bless ya, guy," Jim said, handing me a business card. "This is the number of my Houston attorney. Like I've told you, he's a *real lawyer*—with balls—and a personal friend of mine. You can trust him. He's expecting your call. Make an appointment, talk face-to-face, and when you see him, tell him the wife and I are fine."

"Will do," I promised. "Anything else you want to say in private before I leave?"

"Yeah. What exactly have you told your friends and family?"

"I told my friends to be careful, trust no one and stay clean and clear of business, like I've been doing. I haven't told my family—"

"No! I mean about us, the wife and me."

"Nothing. Relax," I said, surprised to see his hands were shaking and his perpetual smile had faded. "No one knows you're fugitives."

"What about your wedding photographer? What do you know about him?"

"Nothing. I hired him out of the phonebook. Why?"

"Do me a favor. Make sure you buy *all* of his pictures and the negatives, too. I can't have anyone holding recent photos of us. Understand?"

I nodded.

Jim pulled back the drapes, removed his thick spectacles, and took a swig from the Crown Royal bottle. "Listen, guy," he whispered. "Are you still in touch with that old friend of yours down in Tucson?"

"Why?" An uneasy feeling stirred in the pit of my gut.

Suddenly the women returned. We stood in silence watching wet snow paint white stripes on giant Ponderosa pines through the sliding glass door. Irene wrapped her arms around Jim. Kim gave me a big hug. I sensed some kind of weird chemistry brewing between the aging beauty queen and my gypsy bride.

"I was just telling *Diane*," Irene said, pausing to smack her lips like someone who'd just licked a cocaine mirror. "I was just telling her how lucky she was to have landed Thomas for a husband. I was telling her how ironic this entire fugitive thing has become for us. You know, nothing like the movies! We wake up every day beside the person we love with no responsibilities, and do whatever we please. Isn't that right honey?"

Jim Hagar scraped his nails across the frosted window glass. "You know," he said, "I was just telling *Timmy* here the same thing."

The next week Kim and I flew to Houston for my first experience with a criminal defense attorney. When I entered his office, the lawyer bounded up from his chair like a quarterback breaking from a huddle. We shook hands. Jerry Patchen was a stout Texan with powder-blue eyes who lived and breathed law. He specialized in drug conspiracy cases, and confidently claimed he was one of the top trial lawyers in the country. His office was on the second floor of a refurbished historical home that reminded me of the Lion's Share. Navajo rugs, legal degrees, and memorabilia from Houston's professional sports teams were prominently displayed. Pictures of his family and pets dominated his desk. He had a pretty wife, beautiful children, dogs, horses, and a smooth southern style I found refreshing—along with strong references from fugitive Jim Hagar. Jerry had a firm handshake and a straightforward, no-nonsense approach to the process of assessing a client once the office door was closed and the billing clock was ticking. Twenty minutes after we met, I wanted to hire him.

That afternoon he took us to see his horses and in the evening we had dinner with his wife. Kim got the same good vibes as I did from the Texan.

Indiana pot dealer, the President, O.J. Simpson, the Menendez Brothers...it made no difference who you were, every client's defense team wanted the real story before forming a strategy. That's what I learned during my second day in Houston. Unlike my offshore money manager, who did not want to know the facts that had brought me to his office seeking his services, Jerry demanded them.

"Thomas," he said with a smooth Texas drawl, "it is my understanding that the government has set in motion a sequence of events which require our candid and immediate assessment. The Department of Justice is gathering information from Jim Hagar's drivers in Ohio, and other men you've worked with over the years. They will parade this information before a grand jury in the Northern District of Indiana with the intention of indicting you. It is called a historical investigation. As your lawyer, I need to have your total trust. I also need to be prepared."

"How can I help you prepare?" I asked.

He tilted back his chair and clasped his hands behind his head. "Stop talking in rhymes and codes. Tell me your story."

It's one thing to know how many times you have broken the law, because after a while it didn't even faze you. It was quite another to recite those acts verse by verse to a total stranger. Facing the facts was a roller coaster ride that covered the good times and the bad ones from the

Wisconsin Frat Boys trip in 1971, to the Maui Bert years. It forced me to reflect on how much of my life had revolved around a damn plant. Once I got started, I couldn't stop. This debriefing was a draining, cleansing process that went on for hours. I sat in my chair and fidgeted nervously, reliving several close calls. I paced the floor, occasionally laughing as I recalled humorous stories. At times, I felt like I was talking to a priest.

As a criminal attorney living and working near the Mexican border, Jerry had heard stories like mine before. But through it all, he sat attentively writing page after page of notes on his yellow legal pad. Occasionally he'd nod or laugh. Once or twice he chewed his pencil and asked for more details. But for the most part, he simply listened.

At the conclusion of my debriefing, Jerry reaffirmed that everything I'd told him was protected from the government's investigation by attorney/client privilege. He then forcefully clarified the drug conspiracy laws that Maui Bert had first brought to my attention back in 1983. For over an hour he made me fully aware of what I had gotten myself into. When he finished, my hands were trembling. This was no longer gossip over champagne cocktails at Maui Bert's palace. I was shook.

Assuming that my associates—who had continued working with Bill McCarthy after my withdrawal from the conspiracy—were on the verge of being subpoenaed for pending grand juries, Jerry proposed a fact finding mission: go to Indiana, conduct interviews, and inform my friends of their constitutional options. He advised me to wait for his assessment of the situation before making any rash decisions.

I gave him the go ahead, and a ten-thousand dollar retainer, with the understanding that there would be another thirty grand if my case went to trial. Before departing, I passed on the message from Smiley.

"Give Jim and Irene my best," Jerry said. "Tell them to call sometime." He curled his lip. "And tell them that as an officer of the court, I advise them to come in and deal with this mess."

Two days after we flew home to Truckee, Kim stayed to mind the store and keep my mom company while I took another trip, alone. For the first time in a long time, I returned to Indiana on a whirlwind tour. I wanted to let my former associates know that Jerry would be coming to town to listen to their concerns and offer legal advice. I needed to conduct some business, too.

Rumors of investigations and pending arrests were rampant. It seemed like every dealer knew the feds were in town for their regional house cleaning of the dirt that local cops refused to bother with. A friend of mine on the Mishawaka police force confirmed that my name had been mentioned. I could taste tension in the Hoosier air. Paranoia prevented me from visiting my old familiar public haunts. The Kid from Berry Road—former man about town—crept from house to house, undertaking various, long neglected and unpleasant tasks.

I closed down my Midwest antiques outlet with Richard Miller—who knew a good deal about my money laundering—and asked him to liquidate my $75,000 furniture inventory. I met with Dan Morissette—owner of a local music and video store—who had been my main marijuana customer since high school days, and had a heart to heart talk. He was an overweight, self-proclaimed tough-guy who spoke with a lisp, swore he'd never sell me out, and said the government could go to hell *if* I donated $40,000 dollars to his defense fund. My promise of offering legal aid funds to fallen comrades was a long-standing one. I compared Dan's legal fees to liability insurance, and gladly paid them.

Bruce Pratt, childhood pal who'd smoked his first joint and gotten his first piece of ass with me in Wisconsin, was now the owner of my old A-frame house on Oakside Avenue, and a full-time employee of my former partner Bill McCarthy. I informed him of my attorney's planned visit, and advised him that his current employer could help with any legal fees. Bruce was scared to death. When he asked what my plans were, I told him I was going to play it by ear and hope to keep living my new life with Kim in California. I felt for him, and briefly thought about inviting him on the paper trip, but knew that Bruce had neither the social skills nor scruples to survive as a fugitive, should the shit hit the fan as hard as Jim Hagar was predicting.

My best friend, former right-hand man, and biggest liability, Todd Maher, was nervous, but dedicated to the same causes as myself: staying free and not helping the US Government put more people in steel cages for selling pot. When Todd asked what his options were, I told him to listen to Jerry Patchen's advice, then plan on an extended vacation out West afterwards if he felt uncomfortable. I decided not to tell him then, but smart, polite, compassionate and compatible Todd would be welcome on my paper trip if it came to that. I gave him payphone numbers in Truckee for us to use in the coming months, and my hand in friendship. As things heated up, I would count on Todd's opinions and his inside knowledge of Bill McCarthy's activities when formulating my own moves out in distant California.

Bill McCarthy and I had problems. After two years of nagging him for my share of our corporate assets, he still hadn't delivered. When I invited him and Leigh to my wedding they did not come, claiming that their infant daughter Shannon was too young to travel. Through Todd, I discovered the real reason. Bill was involved in his biggest pot scam yet and having some serious friction with his suppliers over the timeliness of his payments. Because of my constant nagging, Bill had finally sold our infamous Michigan pole-barn property and established a new stash house through his right-hand man, Tim Meers, and a local restaurateur.

Deciding that Bill's continuing involvement had no bearing on me, I settled for calling him insane for still dealing. He called me a worrywart, and we got down to business as we always had done. Bill was convinced he could hold things together, get everyone to lie to the feds, and keep right on rolling the reefer-dice—*same old Bill.* Even though I knew he was out of touch with reality and addicted to the very same business high that I had pulled away from, I wanted desperately to believe he could do it. I made him an offer of free legal consultation. Having not yet hired a lawyer, Bill gladly agreed to host my Houston attorney upon his arrival in South Bend. In return, Bill promised to immediately sell our rental properties, and finally pay me my money.

Satisfied that I had done all I could, I visited my dad, brother and sister, then caught a night flight back to Reno.

Two weeks later at a Lake Tahoe restaurant, Jim Hagar handed me a manila envelope with three sets of IDs and more underground press publications. One booklet, *Directory of Mail Drops in the United States and Canada*, listed hundreds of locations that could be acquired over the phone. Smiley told me that Bert was considering the fugitive option as well, and had already sent his right-hand man Ray on a world tour to keep him out of the reach of any Federal Grand Juries that might want to subpoena him. Jim also disclosed that he was helping others disappear besides me.

"Remember my friend Sonny?" he asked. "Sonny got indicted up in

Aspen and has decided to go underground, too. Sonny's good people. There's a lot of good people taking the paper trip."

We talked about many things, including my trips to Houston and Indiana. Jim advised me to set up a communication system and start getting some experience with my new identities. "Get a pager," he said.

"I hate those things," I replied.

"Then go through that list of mail drops and select one or two that offer answering services. Get me the numbers of some clean payphones, too. Things are gonna heat up for you, and I'm not comfortable with calling or stopping by the Lion's Share anymore."

I asked him how he felt about getting Todd some paperwork. My friend's criminal exposure to Bert and himself were of great concern to Jim. He agreed that Todd was a prime candidate for a new identity.

"How are you and Kim holding up under the strain?" Jim asked.

"We're okay." I paused to think about my mother, who continued to stay with us while the wounds from her divorce healed. "The worse part is not knowing for sure. I hate uncertainty."

"Don't worry. You'll know soon enough. Till then, just keep playing happy shopkeeper, be a good son, and wait until you get the phone call from Houston."

In February of 1986 I made my final visit to the Houston office of Jerry Patchen. A pretty Latino secretary escorted me to my chair and closed the door behind her, and a hospital-room silence set in. The stocky, dark-haired lawyer stared at me expressionless, hands folded atop his desk. The twinkle I'd seen on my previous visit had vanished from his powder-blue eyes.

We shook hands and I sat down. "Give it to me straight Doc," I said, like some terminally ill cancer patient seeking a second opinion.

Patchen proceeded to tell me about the grand jury process that was underway in Indiana. "They will conduct several rounds, scare some people into cooperating, and catch the rest lying. Basically, it is a rubber stamp for the prosecution, because if they want you indicted—son, you *are* indicted."

"What about the good old days," I asked, "when people stuck together, kept their mouths shut, and beat the rap?"

"The current harsh sentencing laws," he replied, "have made it easier for the government to convert tough guys and former friends into witnesses when the rubber meets the road."

Jerry gave me a play by play of the trip to Indiana. He was accompanied by his private investigator. Bill McCarthy met them at the airport and offered an overview of the situation, conveniently omitting his own major and most recent dealings. Patchen rented a suite at the South Bend Ramada Inn and conducted interviews. Each of my associates told the Texan as much as they felt comfortable with, and were informed of their constitutional options during grand jury appearances, such as taking the Fifth Amendment.

One by one Jerry described their strengths and weaknesses in amazing detail that confirmed Jim Hagar's high regard for his skills. Todd impressed him the most: a sensitive, articulate gentleman, with a good heart. He described Bill McCarthy in entirely different terms. "Bill scheduled several of his own people for appointments with me, tried to get me to cross the line, control his guys, and catch an obstruction of justice charge for him. I can see how you two had disagreements," Jerry said. "You're warm and emotional, and Bill is... Anyway, I could not believe it. The man even wanted me to buy his dinner. Old Bill thinks he is extremely clever."

"What do you think?" I asked, resting my chin on my hand. "I mean, what do you really think?"

Patchen's barrel chest expanded, then—unblinking and in that smooth Texas drawl of his—he painted a very clear picture. "Tom, the old black cast-iron frying pan is on the fire. The grease is getting hot. The feds are shopping around, and soon all the necessary ingredients will be located in the government's kitchen." He curled his lip. "Remember, we are talking about an extremely conservative Midwest state."

"But they haven't got any evidence!" I shouted, pounding his desk.

"Tom, we've been over this," he said, surprised at my ignorance. "One of the saddest results of the war on drugs, is that *they* don't necessarily need any evidence."

"Just what are my chances?" I asked, squirming in my seat.

Patchen slowly shook his head. "Tom, I think there is going to be a run on the courthouse up there in Indiana, and you will wind up being the main course for a media dinner. Picture the front page of the *South Bend Tribune* reading, 'Former Housing and Urban Development contractor from Aardvark Construction led secret life of crime.' It will make good headlines, and unfortunately, the prosecutor and a news hungry public are going to love it."

I slid down lower in my chair, heart sinking, mind racing, struggling to maintain my composure. "So, what's next?" I muttered. "I mean, what can I expect?"

He predicted the grand jury process would run its course, and my friends would fall like dominoes. Local lawyers would negotiate guilty pleas for their clients, build up their credits in the US Attorney's favor bank, and help ensure the indictment of the major players targeted for prosecution, namely Bill and me. My clean record and good nature would have no bearing on my punishment.

"Tom," Patchen said. "As I see it, there are only two options. You can either prepare to go to trial, or approach the government and cut a deal." Patchen fixed me with an impenetrable look. "There are two kinds of clients in criminal cases. There are fighters, and there are quitters. At this time I must tell you that I refuse to represent men who cut deals and send their friends to prison. Which type of client are you?"

I thought of all the dealers who had crossed my path over the years. Some had made it and retired like I'd tried to, some couldn't quit. Most of them I considered friends. "I'm a fighter."

The Texan nodded. "Tom, it may be one month or six months, but you will eventually get subpoenaed for a grand jury appearance. Government agents will come to your store, hand you a piece of paper, and request your presence in South Bend for fingerprinting, photographs and handwriting examples."

I looked him straight in the eyes. "Jim says the feds have been known to grab people right at the grand jury and never let them go. Is that true?"

"Not likely, but entirely possible," Patchen sighed.

"Shit! *Prison*," I mumbled between deep, irregular breaths. "Damn if Jim wasn't right all along." I cursed above the strange noises coming from my stomach. My face felt flushed. The room started spinning. I was flooded with emotions, flashbacks of my life, and *flash-forwards* about life on the lam. "Jesus fucking Christ, Jerry! Tell me what to do," I begged in a voice I didn't recognize as my own.

"Tom, as an officer of the court and your attorney of record, I must advise you to go in with me when the time comes, and face this thing like a man."

"Fuck that!" I screamed, rubbing sweaty fingers intensely at my temples. In that moment of insanity, with blurred vision, I searched my attorney's blue eyes for dollar signs, determined to vent my anger and frustration on him when I found them. But to my great surprise, all I could see was genuine concern. I rested my head on the desk in front of me. "Jerry, this is not what I wanted to hear," I whispered.

"You didn't hire me to tell you what you wanted to hear," he said, rising unceremoniously from his leather chair. "Did you?"

In silence, I watched him plunge his huge hands into deep pockets and pace a familiar stretch of worn flooring. I watched his poker face contort in ways that depicted a man wrestling with his own conscience. I bit my lip and watched him walk—as if before some invisible jury—until he sat back down across from me.

"I don't agree with the laws and punishment for your offense," he said, "any more than you do. You have a beautiful young wife. I was impressed by her maturity the night we had dinner together. You are a sharp, likable, young man. I could see in your faces how much you two are in love." He formed a clenched fist to emphasize his point. "Kim is a strong woman and I sense that she will stay with you, as Irene has with Jim."

I half-smiled, warmed by his words. "There is a third option," I said, "one that would preserve my marriage, and spare me from the Purgatory our government has planned."

He paused to loosen his tie. "Tom, I encourage you to step forward and face these charges, but also understand your reluctance to do so."

"Jerry, part of me wants to buy a little cabin back in the woods and wait this thing out."

"Wait for what?"

"Our politicians to come to their senses and stop trying to prove how goddamn tough on crime they are by over-punishing nonviolent, productive citizens who've grown up and moved on," I replied, "over what we both know from experience, is nothing more than prohibition politics."

I'd been fully informed of my situation. My mind was set, and I assumed Jerry knew it. Any further insistence on his part would have merely alienated me. He literally would have had to tie me to a chair and called the DEA to stop me from running.

Patchen sighed, then reached into his pocket. "I've got an extra ticket to the Rockets' game," he said. "Why don't you come with me tonight. We can talk again tomorrow."

"Thanks," I said, "but I miss my wife."

He smiled. "I understand."

We shook hands. "I really appreciate your advice," I said. "When Uncle Sam hands me a subpoena I'll give you a call. I'm sure lucky to have you in my corner."

In spite of everything I left Houston a new man, dedicated to tackling the mission at hand—just as I always had been during my dealing days. There would be no looking back. I would begin liquidating my antique business assets, arrange our escape into the underground world, and be ready to go. The race was on. The freedom-clock was ticking. When the feds came to serve me with a subpoena, I'd evade them and skip their invitation. My game plan was clear. I would take the paper trip, pray for public opinion on pot laws to shift back to a *'60s mentality* in support of decriminalization, call Houston from time to time, and hope to negotiate a fair settlement with the United States government when the fire beneath their frying pan died down. And in the event of my untimely demise due to arrest, the legal wizard from Texas would represent me in a trial.

In the month that followed, life got even crazier around Lion's Share Antiques on historic Commercial Row in Truckee—especially after I advertised our clearance sale on cable TV, and offered free deliveries. My mother, Kim, and I would drive to the store from our rental house on Donner Pass Road, eat at a hip diner a couple of blocks away called the Squeeze In, and entertain customers for the rest of the day.

Displaying trademark manic hyper-energy, I attacked shoppers the instant they stepped through the front door. "Good afternoon, ma'am. Have I got a deal for you! Who's yer buddy? Who's yer pal? It's me, Mr. Lion, isn't it? We got it, you like it, you want it. Don't you? *Sold American*!" I would bark like an auctioneer; then I'd send them to my lovely wife at our brass-keyed cash register and pick another victim from the curious crowd.

Furniture flew out the doors. Art deco statues sold like
Racks of vintage clothing found new closets in which to hang.
had more fun in that one wild month than at all of her ann
sales combined. Good deals were plentiful at Lion's Share, and word got around fast. But behind my happy salesman's smile, it all made me sick.

Day after day I watched the post-marijuana-dealer master plan, designed to help me become a respectable citizen, disintegrate. Even my taste in books took a twisted turn. I stopped reading writers I admired for their literary talents, and stayed up late with titles like Ingo Walter's, *Secret Money—The Shadowy World of Tax Evasion, Capital Flight, and Fraud.* Part of me was dying, and I could only pray for the existence of an afterlife.

Having always been a packrat, I inevitably fell in love with each item I'd bought. There were many prized pieces at Lion's Share which I had never intended to sell, so late one night while studying the Yellow Pages from my new *pending-fugitive* perspective, I decided to start taking steps to preserve them—and the million bucks buried in the basement. The next morning I told Kim and my mom that I had deliveries to make in nearby Reno. Instead, I drove to the state line area's Boomtown Casino, rented a room with my Timothy Alan Barnes identity, and started paging through phone books.

My experience in the legitimate world had taught me the value of conducting telephone interviews instead of face to face ones. Not only did letting my fingers do the walking in the Yellow Pages save time, it enabled me to be serious and forceful when questioning business owners about their services. With my discerning outlaw's eye, I discovered that needful things abounded; like self-storage facilities, alternative mailing addresses, and secretive safety-security boxes. The mere wording of their ads made shopping for my privacy demands simple.

For example, the standard requirements for obtaining an address at nationwide chains like Mailboxes Etc.—as well as their independent counterparts—were a driver's license and your signature on a contract which gave the establishment permission to receive your mail from the United States Post Office. In less than a dozen calls I clearly understood why the underground press called private mailboxes "one of America's best kept secrets, from the privacy conscious citizen's perspective." I selected two mail drops, which were so liberal that they didn't even ask ɔ see my face. All they wanted was a postal money order for six months in advance.

In Los Angeles on Wilshire Boulevard—sight unseen—I rented a street address for John Paul Simms. Next, I called Loompanics Press in Port Townsend, Washington, ordered several sensitive research books, and had them sent to Simms' L.A. *apartment number* on Wilshire Boulevard. I also sent a postal money order to Paladin Press, requesting a booklet called *Paper Tripping Overseas*, by Tony Newborn. California-based Eden Press got an order from Mr. Simms as well. In Reno, I acquired a second address for him and a twenty-four-hour answering service at The Postal Depot.

My next assignment was locating a new home for all that money buried in the basement of the Lion's Share. Like mail drops, most major cities have independently-owned businesses that provide the same services as banks. Many times Kim and I had dined at a small Japanese sushi bar in Reno's Meadowood Mall and watched a vast array of classy cars come and go from a place called The Vault, located across the street. Their Yellow Pages ad and an exploratory phone call fueled my curiosity. The Vault was more secure than banks, more expensive, and much more discreet. Whatever identification you provided was proof enough to them of who you were. They did not care about verification. The Vault's main concern was renting thousands of steel boxes and scores of climate-controlled rooms (for rare artwork and wines) at prices ranging from hundreds to thousands of dollars annually. It was a million-dollar business idea, and it made perfect sense to me.

Timothy Alan Barnes left his Boomtown Casino hotel room carrying a briefcase full of earthy-smelling currency and gold coins. His hair was slicked back to match the picture on his fraudulent driver's license. He was wearing a three-piece suit and a pair of gold wire-rimmed John Lennon glasses. Tim had a lilt in his step, places to go, and people to see.

At The Vault, Barnes introduced himself to an armed security guard as a successful young businessman from Nebraska who was new to Reno, traveled a lot, and had inherited a very nice coin collection from his father. The guard gave Timothy a tour. Tim filled out a form, paid one year's rent in cash, and was issued an access card to an electronic door, a secret code word, and a safety deposit box key. No further questions were asked. Mr. Barnes and his heavy metal box were escorted to a private, windowless room, and the guard disappeared, leaving Tim to attend to his business.

An hour later I left, empty briefcase in hand, feeling satisfied with my selection of The Vault. It was sure as hell secure, and open twenty-four hours a day, just like everything else in a gambler's city. Now the kid who had once hid all his money under Grandma Daisy's outhouse in plastic plumbing pipes had entrusted his nest egg to an Englishman five thousand miles away in the Channel Islands, and a private safety deposit box business in Reno, Nevada. At least if the feds busted me tomorrow, I thought, they wouldn't get all the money.

My next stop was a self-storage facility. Finding the place to my liking, I selected a 10 x 20 unit far from the entrance and unloaded my first cargo of antiques under the curious, watchful eyes of the elderly owners.

My last stop was back at the office of a Truckee real estate agent. Not long after we renovated Lion's Share, the agency had approached me with an offer from an interested local buyer. At the time I politely refused and informed them that I planned on staying around for a while. Reluctantly, painfully, I made an arrangement with them to discreetly entertain offers, with no advertising or *For Sale* signs. The reason I gave for my desired secrecy was my mother's failing health.

"If she knew I was planning to move back east to be with her," I told the realtor, "she would have a heart attack."

Of course, the real reason for my ploy was I did not want the feds to catch on and suspect I was preparing to make a run for it.

My mother, kind hearted, good-natured professor of common sense—God knows I love her dearly. One by one she raised her six kids under tough conditions, and nudged them from the nest to fly. And my how they had flown. Judy went from Peace Corps nursing to a respected position at Johns Hopkins in Baltimore. Bill became an environmental scientist, Kenny an officer and teacher in the US Air Force, George a successful real estate agent, and Joe Ann a conscientious homeowner and mother. Mom always said I would become a famous actor or writer, but while my siblings traveled the long, hard road to success, I took the fast lane. Now, I was preparing to become a fugitive from justice! I could not simply disappear and leave Mom hanging without a clue. It was time to tell her.

That winter of '86 in the snow-covered woods across the street from our Donner Pass Road rental home, I carved out a half-mile cross-country ski track. Many mornings before work, my mother and I would ski our way around that track with my old Irish setter slipping and nipping at our heels while we stopped frequently to feed the wildlife and talk. Initially I devised this routine to help her deal with her divorce, but as the months went by and Mom regained her strength, it became more of a stress-relieving ritual for me. On a crisp, clear mountain morning in March, she and I skied our nature trail together for the last time.

In snowy woods, beneath a Ponderosa Pine, I told my mother about the grand juries convening in Indiana and the meetings with my attorney. I told her about my fugitive friends Jim and Irene Hagar, admitted my guilt, and told her what my options were.

"Why?" she asked me. "Was it because we were so poor? Wasn't I a good mother?"

"The best," I said. "You are the best mom." I gave her a hug.

She gazed at me though misty green eyes and said, "That lawyer is wrong. This can't happen to you. There are too many *real* criminals in this world—rapists, murderers, child molesters—for the government to waste valuable prison space on people like you."

"I wish you were right," I whispered, "but that's not the way they see it, Ma."

"Then why don't you just go back and tell them what they want to know?" she pleaded.

"Because you didn't raise me that way!" I shouted, thrusting my ski poles into the snow at my feet. "Selling souls to save my own skin would only send good friends to prison and rob me of my own integrity for the rest of my life. Don't you understand?"

She did not. How could she? In sixty years of living, *she* had not engaged in one damn criminal act. To her, the outlaw code meant nothing.

I saw Mom recoil, and in the ensuing silence regretted raising my voice to her. I watched her stare at that azure blue High Sierra sky, and recalled the good times we had shared: sledding together on the Mishawaka Hills; me singing Frank Sinatra songs for her at South Bend's Summit Club; rowing her across Diamond Lake in a little green rowboat with a red dog nose-to-the-wind at the bow; watching autumn leaves turn and blow, planting flowers together every spring. *What would life be like without her?*

This was it. After twenty-nine precious years, I was sharpening the tip of a knife that could forever sever the tender strands of invisible umbilical cord remaining between us. I put my arm around her shoulder and squeezed. "You raised me to be a survivor, Ma. Always remember that."

"Please! Don't be so melodramatic." My mother the eternal optimist forced a smile, fighting back tears. "If the choice is seeing my little Tommy miserable behind bars or missing him every day, knowing that at least he's free and with the woman he loves, then the choice is easy. You do love Kim, don't you?"

I nodded. "But I love you too, Ma."

"I know. I know," she sighed.

She asked many questions: When would Kim and I go? Where would we live? Would we be safe? Would we take our animals? What did Kim's Mom think? What about her father the ex-cop?

I told her that I didn't have all the answers and then, I did the hardest thing I'd ever had to do—*I asked her to go.*

"It's for your own good Ma," I explained. "There are things I have to take care of, and I don't want you to get involved."

"But who is going to watch the store?" she asked.

"It's probably already being watched," I said. "By the feds. The phone is probably tapped. And when you get home again, assume that yours will be, too. But I promise you, no matter how long it takes to work this out, we'll stay in touch. I'll send you messages and when it's safe we'll meet somewhere. Just like—"

She pressed a finger to my lips. "Just like in the movies?"

"Yeah, Ma. Just like in the movies."

That Sunday afternoon I drove my mother to San Francisco's international airport. We arrived late intentionally to avoid a long goodbye. I double-parked and carried her bags to the counter. I asked her to do me three favors. "First off, don't worry about me—live your own life. Secondly, cut out this self-doubt crap brought on by your divorce. Don't kid yourself, Ma. You are one unique, special lady. Some guy is going to be damn lucky to fall in love with you. And lastly," I said, my voice starting to crack, "please stay healthy, Ma."

"Better hurry, Ma'am," the clerk at the ticket counter said. "Your flight has already begun to board."

We embraced like there was no tomorrow. I pecked her on the cheek.

"Be careful out there, Tommy," she whispered, choking on her words.

I exchanged *I love you's* with the woman who until that day had been the most important person in my life, and then I watched her walk away, wondering if I would ever see her again.

Without saying one word to Kim, I drove my camper-truck like a madman far away from concrete-covered San Francisco Bay to the rugged coast, seeking solace in an infinite oceanic horizon and keeping misty eyes on winding Highway 1. Somewhere past Pillar Point I pulled roadside and watched the setting sun, all the while soul searching and weighing circumstance against common sense and consequence. Then, when darkness descended on the shimmering sea, I lay my head on the dashboard and cried like a baby.

My last recollection of that night was of my young wife—who had never seen me break down—massaging my temples and whispering, "It'll be all right, it'll be all right," as if to let me know that she was both ready and willing to fill the vacuum my mother's departure had left in my heart.

At daybreak after making soft love, Kim and I watched slick brown sea otters in the frothy waters below, resting on green kelp beds, cracking abalone shells, floating on their backs—free as the soaring birds above. A light rain began to fall. A sense of urgency filled the salty air. We rubbed wedding rings and whispered our battle cry. *"Shazzam!"*

Suddenly possessed by the kindred spirits of a modern-day, but kinder, gentler Bonnie and Clyde, my gypsy bride and I jumped in our camper-truck and stepped on the gas. A thick fog rolled in at our backs. The Bay Area disappeared into the mist. The sun broke through due south, and we headed that way, where the prospect of a new life lay before us like some sinful, mysterious promise. We moved fast, and did not stop until we hit Los Angeles where I made a brief appearance at a Wilshire Boulevard mail drop as Mr. John Paul Simms.

By nightfall we had secured mail drops for Timothy Alan Barnes and Diane K. Moore, and settled into a hotel room just north of Ventura,

California—intent on acquiring one of the key ingredients in the identity recipe. According to their training manual—now in my possession—Social Security Administration employees were not the police, nor did they have the authority of law enforcement officers. What they did have, was a *profile outline* that alerted them to pressure suspicious applicants for further information. As Jim and Irene Hagar had feared, the older you appeared to be, the odder it was for you to be a first-time Social Security applicant. If the clerk did not buy your story, he or she could require you to write an essay detailing your employment and residency histories while warning you of the penalties for perjury. If there were still doubts after reading your essay, a private interview with a supervisor could be demanded. If you found yourself in those shoes, you were screwed. Might as well trash that identity and go back to acting school—if you weren't already being detained, that is.

For days we studied Social Security branches from Long Beach to Oxnard. We racked our brains to come up with a practical plan of attack and decided on a winner, which employed Kim's hands-on experience from Big Cindy's hair salon. I have always looked much younger than my age. Mom always said this would become a blessing some day. As usual, Mom was right. In the spring of 1986 I was a healthy twenty-nine year old heterosexual male, but with a clean shave and some creative thinking, twenty-two year old first-time Social Security applicant Timothy Alan Barnes' desired image was easily achieved.

Inside our camper parked at the Ventura Social Security Administration building, Kim put the finishing touches on my costume: clip-on earring, dainty heart-shaped locket dangling from a gold neck chain, rouged cheeks, mauve lips, screaming floral blouse and hot pants. She also gave me pointers on walking and talking. "Hold your leather satchel like a purse. Here, cradle it like this." She demonstrated while I drank my second confidence-building beer.

We skipped the good luck kiss, not wanting to mess up my lips.

"If I don't come out that front door when the place closes at five," I said, "stash the money and IDs and go home to the Lion's Share."

"Good luck," she whispered, wearing a face like my mother had for my first day of school.

"Fuck luck," I said. "See you in an hour."

I paused at the front entrance to psych myself up for the role. "Show time," I muttered. "Get serious. Walk feminine. Play the part." It was four o'clock. The place was packed. I pushed open the door and swished my tail right up to the counter, winking twice at a macho-looking male clerk en route. Then—after eyeing the conservative-looking lady in plaid pants whose line I would wait in, whom I'd watched working the day before, whom I'd spoken to on the telephone to get a feel for—I took a number, took a seat, crossed my legs and started filing my nails with an emery board.

Timmy Boy was blatant! My opening act was brilliant. But then I waited for what seemed an eternity, stomach churning, pre-mission beer-buzz wearing thin, staring down at my pink tennis shoes and straining to stay in character while the whispering among clerks behind the counter became more frequent and obvious.

Miss Plaid Pants went through dozens of wetbacks with dime store IDs, trying her damnedest not to acknowledge the apparent homosexual waiting for her help, but at twenty minutes before five o'clock her luck ran out. A hush fell over her co-workers and finally, she called my number.

I jumped up off my chair, heart pounding, palms sweating, inner-voice preaching the gospel of *The Paper Trip*: "Remember, Thomas, you are who your paperwork says you are in America and no one knows any better but you! *Think*, Thomas. Think of being in a very small cell with your prison roommate *Big Bubba.* Think survival *Mr. Desperado."*

I cradled my satchel, sashayed to the counter batting my eyebrows and said the words I'd practiced with my wife in front of our bedroom mirror that morning. "Good afternoon hon, I'm afraid I need a Social Security number. Have I come to the right place?"

Miss Plaid Pants—who resembled Miss Hathaway from *The Beverly Hillbillies*—lowered her wingtip glasses to the bridge of her nose and glared. "Could I see some identification please?"

Bingo! Testing, one, two, three. With a steady hand I placed my Kansas birth certificate, Nebraska driver's license and American Life Insurance card on the counter. "Here you are Miss," I said, tapping my painted nails nonchalantly.

Jane Hathaway rubbed a fat thumb across the embossed seal on my jive birth certificate—just like the book said she would. *Check.* She wrote down the information, returned the American Life Insurance card and scrutinized the driver's license. "So *Mr. Barnes*...you've never had a Social Security card?"

I tugged at my hair coyly, slowly shaking my head. "Pretty silly of me, huh?"

"Mr. Barnes. May I ask what brought you all the way from *Lincoln, Nebraska* to sunny Southern California?" She paused to attract the attention of her co-workers.

Fortunately, I was prepared for her question. "A-actually," I stammered, with a distinct lisp. "I left the family farm in 1984. Lived in San Francisco ever since—*in the Castro District.*" I made a sad face. "My *boyfriend* finally passed away last week," I mumbled, leaning toward her. "It was a terrible illness. He never had a chance. *No known cure.*"

The conservative clerk took two steps back.

"Anyway," I continued, fighting back a smile, "I just couldn't stay in my City by the Bay. I-I needed a change of scenery," I sobbed. "Then, this great guy offered me a place to stay close by, and a job doing nails at his hair salon! I know this is a big step," I added, nodding and biting my lip. "But I promised my William I would fend for myself once he was gone."

That did it. Jane Hathaway's face turned crimson red. She cleared her throat and handed me my fraudulent ID. "I see," was all she could manage to say. Even then, AIDS was getting plenty of press down in sunny Southern California.

No essay was requested. She quickly typed forms and I carefully autographed my first document as Timothy Alan Barnes—exactly the way I had practiced doing—to match my Nebraska driver's license signature. Upon providing her with my local mail drop address, she assured me that I would receive my card within two weeks. I had no reason to doubt her.

I walked briskly across the parking lot, removing homosexual *props* along the way. I could see Kim at the wheel of the camper-truck, watching closely behind her dark glasses. I gave her a worried look. She cranked up the engine.

"Problems?" she asked, as I jumped into the passenger seat.

"Let's go," I said.

"Tom, what happened?" She tapped my shoulder.

A broad smile broke across my face. "Nothing, honey. She couldn't process my application quick enough! She thought I was a kept man. It went like clockwork."

Kim sighed. We kissed. And while she drove we decided that my success had cleared the way for her own performance the following day in the role of *Mistress Di* at another Social Security office, where she could work with an older male clerk, wear a low-cut sundress, and show plenty of...*charm.*

Our hotel room was a ways up the coast. It was rush hour in sunny Southern California. Desire called our names and we could not wait to answer. We parked beside the ocean and pulled down the blinds. We were overjoyed, oversexed and overconfident. No doubt about it—*we were good together.*

Two days later in San Francisco, our mission continued. Kim had a conspicuous tattoo on her left shoulder which she'd gotten one wild teenage night. The blue butterfly stood out in swimwear or low-cut tops, and though the law would primarily be looking for me, we both agreed the butterfly had to go. Kim located a laser surgeon who specialized in tattoo removals and scheduled an appointment for later that month.

I rented another mail drop and began implementing my two-pronged fugitive financial game plan. My biggest phobia was that the government would change US currency and accelerate the march toward a cashless society in *One World Order* fashion. Part of me believed this would inevitably happen, resulting in chaos for the underground economy and ultimately rendering my hard-earned million dollars worthless. Another part of me believed that there were far too many crooked politicians and law enforcement officials with metal boxes full of dirty money in places like The Vault to ever allow such changes to occur.

My answer to this quandary was to collect certified checks for amounts under IRS reporting limits, and mail them overseas to my offshore Leo Investments account. I also bought gold coins to stash in my box at The Vault and various self-storage facilities—the intent being to keep assets geographically convenient and convert them to the new US currency at a future date. While working with several gold coin dealers, I cultivated two interesting relationships: one as Thomas Paul Hickey with a downtown San Francisco metals and currency dealer, and another as Timothy Alan Barnes with a silver-haired Greek gentleman from the old school who shared his customers' fears of a *One World Order* cashless society. Instinctively sensing that we would become good friends, I used all my charm on him while continuing to perfect my role as Timothy Alan Barnes.

March 1986, Sacramento, California: Based on my lawyer's opinion of my friends' strength under Justice Department pressure, I had to presume no one could be trusted to know what I was driving post-flight. Come D-Day, we would have to dump all our vehicles at one of those *Cash for Cars* places. The bottom line was clear—Tim Barnes needed to stash a clean vehicle to make his getaway in.

For two days we toured Sacramento's Auto Row to test drive pick-up trucks. We found an '85 four-wheel drive we liked. They wanted $10,500 for the black Ford F-150, but I knew its color was not popular with Sacramento drivers who each year endured scores of scorching 100° days in bumper-to-bumper traffic. It was, however, the perfect machine for the cool, green Pacific Northwest, which I had fallen in love with during that teen-age summer of hitch-hiking back in 1972, and was now considering as a target destination for flight.

Kim and I performed our tag-team *newlywed couple with an attitude* act. The overstocked dealership needed cash. The horny salesman couldn't keep his eyes off my wife's breasts. We stole the truck for seven grand and the ensuing paperwork session turned out to be another enlightening pre-fugitive training experience.

In California, auto buyers must provide a Social Security number prior to transfer of title. *Big problem.* Tim Barnes didn't have his Social Security number yet. Flustered, but not panic-stricken, I informed the salesman that we were going to a local bank to get the money and would be right back. "Hold that paperwork," I said, index finger in his face.

After feverishly paging through the underground research books I kept in the camper, I located a listing of Social Security numbers as issued in sequence, by date and state. Then I concocted a number corresponding to what would have been an approximate date of issue for Tim Barnes at age sixteen in the state of Nebraska.

Back in the tiny office of the starving car salesman, I recited the Social Security number, then placed forty one-hundred dollar bills and a certified check for the balance on a cluttered table.

"Sign here, Mr. Barnes," the man said. "Oh yeah, this dealer plate is good until the end of the year," he added.

"Such a deal," I said.

The black Ford episode only underscored the need to get plugged in to the system with real insurance and real paperwork if indeed we were to survive. Common sense told me that a State Trooper yanking me over to the side of the road for a faulty tail-light, would not be as easily snowed as some hungry used-car salesman.

We dropped Tim Barnes' truck off just south of Reno for some conversion work, returned to Truckee, and resumed the clearance sale at Lion's Share Antiques.

Weeks later, Todd Maher walked into our store wearing a disguise. Normally calm, clean-cut, Todd was visibly shaken, unshowered, and sporting a five o'clock shadow. He had driven non-stop from Indiana after narrowly avoiding a grand jury subpoena by hiding in the basement of his South Bend home for a day and a half.

Todd told me things were quickly deteriorating on the home front and he wasn't going back. Bill McCarthy was finally showing outward signs of stress, and Todd suspected my ex-partner was in deep shit with *both* sides of the law. "Bill even mentioned some hair-brained scheme about getting fake IDs and leaving the country," Todd said, studying my face for a reaction.

"And does that sound crazy to you?" I asked, matter-of-factly.

"Christ! It all sounds crazy," he said, shaking his head. "Nothing's been the same since you left Indiana, Bud. I know you. I know you too damn well. You've got a game plan, don't you? Come on, Tom. Tell me what it is."

I stared out the window at a mountainous horizon and wondered what to do. Todd wasn't a minor player in the plot that was unfolding. His testimony could sink me, Bert, Ray, and many others. Taking him along on my trip could be stressful and costly, but he was my best friend. I had to trust him, for if he betrayed me I would lose all faith in humanity. But what was best for him, for both of us? I felt like one of Ann Rice's conscientious vampire characters about to execute *the bite.* Would I be offering my good friend eternal life, or some terrible curse? I sought my own reflection in the window glass, then chewed my lip.

"Todd, my friend," I said, "let me tell you all about the paper trip..."

We took a long walk on the shores of Lake Tahoe. By the time the sun was setting over the mountains, my best friend stood beside me shaking his head. That trademark rosy glow from his cheeks was gone. He looked like he'd just seen a ghost.

"Its insane," he said. "I'm not as outgoing as you. I'm not an actor like you. This is crazy. I can't do it."

I tossed a stick of driftwood into Lake Tahoe. We watched the rings it had formed until my Irish setter jumped in and retrieved it. "You can do it...if you want to," I said. "Who's yer buddy? Who's yer pal? Who's yer best friend? Think of the options."

"How do we even know this paper trip can be done?" he asked.

I took a deep breath. "Oh, it can be done all right. Trust me. I'm doing it."

The following day I tucked an envelope containing Todd's first fugitive photo-shoot pictures in my coat pocket, and gave him the number to my John Paul Simms answering service in Reno.

"Call twice a week," I said, shaking his hand firmly.

"Will do," he replied. And with that he drove off toward San Diego to visit some golfing buddies.

I got three interesting phone calls in the days following Todd's departure. The realtor had a buyer for Lion's Share, and we met to iron out some unusual requests on my behalf. I had devised a plan to prevent the government from seizing the money from the transaction, even if I was a fugitive, and I needed their help.

Then Bill McCarthy and I spoke payphone to payphone. He inquired about Todd's disappearance from Indiana, and asked if I had any connections in what he referred to as "the fake ID market." Possible replies flooded my head. I thought about Bill's wife and my ex-lover Leigh, and their little girl Shannon. I thought about what a liability Bill would be for me if he negotiated a guilty plea with the government and painted me as the heavy. We were no longer partners. We were hardly even friends. For all I knew, he could have been calling from a tapped payphone line. I had no intention of tipping my hand to him in advance of his probable grand jury appearance.

"Have you sold our rental properties yet?" I asked, still waiting on the money he owed me.

"Not yet," he replied nonchalantly. "What about getting IDs?"

Bill's request posed a difficult problem. How could helping him to disappear hurt me? I thought. Especially if he never came to where we lived, or knew my new name? I decided to keep my options open, and gave him the number of my disposable John Paul Simms answering service. "Keep in touch and I'll see what I can do," I said.

Then Maui Bert called about an intriguing dilemma. Having moved his millions to offshore accounts in the Bahamas and Europe, Bert now had a working man's problem—he was *cash poor.* He needed green money to employ a legal gambit, which to me smacked of *Justice for Sale.* He also needed cash to keep Ray on the road. He was willing to wire a cool quarter million to my offshore account—which would spare me the tedious task of getting scores of certified checks—in exchange for the same amount in moldy-smelling twenty dollar bills. It sounded good.

From a payphone I called my English banker collect to ask about making arrangements on his end. By this time, I had made three trips to the Channel Islands and entrusted Mr. Tim Blake with a third of my wealth. On the last trip, he'd taken me under his wing in a way that reminded me of my relationship with Maui Bert.

"No problem," Blake said.

Then I asked a question which had been bothering me since the day Bill McCarthy saw that document on my desk back in Indiana exposing my account: *Leo Investments, Fort Group Trust Limited, Guernsey, Channel Islands, U.K.*

"Mr. Blake," I began after clearing my throat.

"My God, you've been a client of mine over two years," he said in his proper English accent. "You've slept under my roof, and dined with Judy and I. Please call me Tim."

"Tim, is there a way to make Leo Investments disappear after this transaction, and leave no paper trail?"

"Many ways," he replied. "Is that what you want?"

"Yes," I sighed. "As soon as the quarter of million arrives safely in my account from the London bank."

"Say no more. These transatlantic phone lines are suspect. Consider it done, and ring me back in a fortnight."

Somewhat relieved, I hung up. But only somewhat. Life was becoming increasingly complex.

Either I was getting overly paranoid, or Lion's Share was under surveillance. This same guy kept coming in every other day. He drove a green Ford LTD, was dorky-looking, and never bought any thing. One thing was certain, Todd's great South Bend subpoena adventure meant my first encounter was not far off.

Feeling edgy, Kim and I phoned our Ventura mail drops and asked the owners what we had in our boxes. Bingo! Social Security cards had arrived for Timothy Alan Barnes' and Diane K. Moore. Employing yet another popular service provided by private mail businesses, we instructed Ventura to forward our letters to my latest mail drop just off Union Street in San Francisco.

When paper trip time came again, we drove east toward Reno with a load of furniture as if making Lion's Share deliveries. No one followed us. We traded our delivery vehicle for Tim Barnes' stashed black Ford F-150 and headed due west to the City by the Bay.

While my wife was having her tattoo removed downtown, I met Maui Bert at Fisherman's Wharf. The area was alive with tourists. We leaned on the seawall watching white swarms of sea gulls circle in a clear blue sky above dozens of charter boat crews who were cleaning their catches. Large, hungry sea lions begging for salmon scraps began barking loudly. "The money's sealed in plastic underneath the ice, same way you used to send it to Bimini," I told Bert, referring to the contents of the blue cooler on the concrete between us. "It's all there."

He smiled. "I've trusted you for a lot more than a quarter mil. What about your man, Todd?"

"I'm taking him along," I said.

Bert breathed a sigh of relief. "Too bad things turned out this way for you, but if my window of opportunity closes before I make my move, I'll be out there with you by the end of the year. By the way, how are Smiley Jimbo and Irene? Have they quit snorting dust since dis..."

Two men in dark suits appeared out of nowhere walking quickly towards us. My heart raced. We froze in place. The two suits broke into a run, shouting at two black kids jogging just a head of them: "Police! Freeze!"

One of the kids tossed a plastic bag into the water.

Maui Bert wiped imaginary sweat from his brow, then shook my hand firmly. "Good luck, kid," he said. "It's been a trip." That was it.

He grabbed his blue cooler, and we parted ways.

"Fuck luck," I whispered to myself as I watched him disappear between the fishing boats. Bert had been a fair businessman, a teacher, and a friend. I hoped he appreciated my loyalty, regardless of how the dice tumbled in the coming months.

The time had come to acquire the most coveted piece of fugitive paperwork—*a United States Passport.* "Why do you want these so badly?" my tattoo-less wife asked as our jetliner ascended from San Francisco International Airport. "Can't they wait?"

"I promised you I'd show you the world, honey," I answered, pecking her cheek. "I want to get this out of the way now—before they're looking for me—so we can just kick back by some mountain stream for the first six months."

I saw her relax. I watched her smile. I felt her trusting head fall on my shoulder and decided not to tell her how much the thought of Jim Hagar's ID man knowing our driver's license numbers bothered me, or how wary I was becoming about letting anyone compile blackmail ammunition against us—like Bill possessed. And though I had remedies for these ailments, I knew right then that in order to maintain any semblance of peace of mind or normality in our underground lives, I would have to stow a lot of heavy baggage in my stomach lining in the months and years to come.

Spring, 1986, Omaha, Nebraska: The nature of our paperwork convinced me that the heartland was the place to pursue the crown jewel of fugitive identification. Jim and Irene planned on going directly to the San Francisco or L.A. regional office and requesting a *rush issue,* claiming they were leaving on an impromptu trip to Europe. I didn't like the approach. To me, it seemed logical that the best-trained government employees would be encountered at the regional level; which is why I chose to go to the US Post Office in a fair-sized Midwestern city and deal with a regular postal worker who doubled as a passport agent.

Our first act in our downtown Red Lion Inn hotel room was to telephone two suburban Omaha mail drops. Next, we studied our copy of *The Passport Agent's Manual.* Once again there was a need for some creative thinking. The following morning we had passport photos taken at two downtown studios. I, *Timothy Alan Barnes*, wore a suit and tie.

Kim, *a.k.a. Diane K. Moore*, wore a very conservative floral dress.

As Thomas Paul Hickey, my last well-used passport had been applied for in South Bend, Indiana, and issued from the Chicago regional office. Our research revealed that all northern US applications from Omaha to the West were processed in Seattle. Wary of having my face on two Chicago files with different names, I decided that Tim Barnes, local boy, should apply in Omaha.

Kim had never owned a passport, and I wanted her first one to be issued from a different region than mine. This same line of thought kept us from making our last names the same, thus separating our paper trip paperwork and avoiding a married fugitive couple's profile. So for Kim, the Chicago regional district would do fine; and all she had to do was take a cab across the Mississippi River into Council Bluffs, Iowa, to accomplish her task.

At lunchtime I walked to the central post office, filled out an application in the busy lobby, went to the appropriate window, and was directed to the passport man. The minute I saw him I relaxed. What luck! The mighty passport agent looked like television's Captain Kangaroo—a mellow, kindly fellow in a knit sweater who had to be nearing retirement age.

I displayed my Lincoln, Nebraska license, previously tested Kansas birth certificate, and brand new—but crumpled to look worn—Social Security card. This time my Texaco employee ID badge also made the starting line-up.

"I'm getting married," I told Captain Kangaroo.

"Congratulations," he said, studying my paperwork.

"Yes sir," I announced, proud as a peacock, "found myself a nice California girl and we're going to Paris, France for our honeymoon."

"Lucky you," the passport agent responded. Then, while simultaneously inspecting my application, he proceeded to tell an interesting tale which had occurred during the closing days of World War II in the countryside of France—a tale of a young Captain Kangaroo, a pretty French mademoiselle, and true romance.

"When did you say you needed this by?" he eventually asked, apparently not suspecting my motives.

"The wedding is on the coast next month," I said. "We leave for Paris the following day. I guess three weeks would do."

"Don't worry, young man," he grinned. "You'll have a passport within two weeks. Just you make sure your future wife gets hers on time, too."

"Thanks! I will," I said with a wink. Then I walked away—right past a stack of Wanted posters hanging from the wall—hoping Kim's mission had gone as smoothly as mine, and feeling guilty about having lied to Captain Kangaroo.

Hours later I found myself alone, pacing the carpet in our room at the Red Lion Inn. My stomach churned. Kim had not returned. There were no phone messages. Speculation tormented my mind. In this moment of doubt I realized what she meant to me—*everything*. I phoned the front desk for a taxicab to Council Bluffs, Iowa, downed a double-shot of Finlandia Vodka, and put on my black leather bomber jacket.

Suddenly a key slid into the lock and the door swung open.

"Seventy-five bucks for a damn cab! Can you believe it? All because we got stuck in commuter traffic on that stupid bridge! I swear I almost punched the driver's lights out! Honey, I need a drink." My wife let her conservative floral dress drop to the floor, revealing Victoria's Secret's latest sexy lingerie. "And that's not all I need," she cooed. "Come here, Mr. Lion...can you say *horny*?"

We drank together, and made whoopee, and I never mentioned in words how much she had worried me. But later, as I stroked her spun-gold hair afterglowing, I knew that like my love for her, my confidence in her was also growing stronger every day.

During the flight back to California I reflected on how easy the paper trip was turning out to be. With Social Security cards and passports we were two-for-two, and I had a plan for new driver's licenses as well. Life was good. The world was a big place and we would do fine once we got lost in it. But then, after deplaning at busy San Francisco International Airport, we ran smack-dab into an Indiana friend's fiancée at the baggage carousel.

"Well hello, Tom!" the bubbly airline stewardess announced. "What a coincidence meeting you here. Small world, huh?"

"Sure is, Cheryl," I said, scrambling to cover the Tim Barnes name tag dangling from my suit bag. "Sure as hell is."

§

That very same pleasant May night, I was unpacking on the second floor of the Lion's Share when an unmarked fedmobile parked in front of the store. "Honey, I think it's them!" my wife shouted from the bottom of the stairs.

"Battle stations!" I replied. "Follow plan A."

Kim answered the door. I ran to the closet, climbed atop a crate, pulled my body up into the attic and closed the access hatch behind me. In total darkness, through gaps in turn-of-the-century wood siding, I watched and listened as events unfolded on the front porch below.

Even though this evasion was a planned, logical move, I felt like some two-bit punk hiding up there, shaking in my boots. What was I exposing my wife to? I wondered. A charge of lying to government agents? Undoubtedly they had been watching the place and knew I was inside somewhere. I heard one G-man say, "Subpoena," but not the word warrant.

According to the gospel of Jerry, the grand jury process had yet to run its course. *"Christ's sake, what are you?"* I whispered. *"A man, a lion, or a mouse?"* I took several deep breaths, dropped down from a splintered truss board to the closet floor and dusted myself off.

With feigned casualness I strolled to the front of the store. "Good evening gentlemen," I offered, peering over Kim's broad shoulder through the half-open door. "Is there something I can help you with?"

My wife's jaw dropped. Her long neck became spotted with a nervous rash.

The feds flashed their genuine government ID, and I invited them into the Lion's den. "How about bringing our guests some tea?" I suggested to Kim.

Shortly thereafter we sat on antique parlor chairs sipping from Wedgwood china. After all the months of anticipation, I felt surprisingly calm, like my old self—cool under pressure. "Now then, what's this all about?" I asked.

They handed me a piece of paper.

"We're here to serve you with this subpoena for the Northern District of Indiana," one fed said.

"Mr. Hickey," injected his stern-faced partner, "you are the target of a historical grand jury investigation."

"What does that mean?" I inquired naively, simultaneously recalling the Texan's thorough definition.

They told me it meant I was in a heap of trouble, informed me I was accused of selling tons of marijuana once-upon-a-time, and advised me to help them get to the bottom of things by giving them names and information.

"Marijuana?" I said, straight-faced. "I don't smoke the stuff."

They set down their Wedgwood cups and snarled.

"Mind telling me more?" I asked.

"Sure, if you're willing to cooperate with us," the two suits coaxed. "We want to know about all of your co-conspirators."

Silence, eerie silence, ensued. It was the moment of truth and everyone knew it. The sound of six clocks' pendulums tick-tick-ticking atop the fireplace mantel pounded the message into my brain like some kind of moral metronome—*put-up or shut-up, Mr. Desperado, Mr. Lion!* I pulled the business card of my Houston criminal defense attorney from my pocket and placed it on the marble tabletop in front of my guests.

The two suits read it. One curled his lip and nodded, the other smiled. Both rose up slow and easy. "You're making a big mistake, son," one said, straightening his tie.

"Maybe we'll get to talk about it all one day," I said, walking them to the door. "By the way," I added, "does the government pay for my plane ticket to this grand jury?"

They shook their heads and smirked.

"You can afford it," one said.

"I can? Guess I'll see you there, then."

"Seen Todd Maher lately?" the other agent asked me.

"Sure haven't," I lied.

"Tell Todd we're looking for him," they said in stereo, before unceremoniously tramping outside and slamming their car doors.

I watched them sit in that fedmobile for some time, making notes and smiling occasionally through the windshield at me like Cheshire cats. And each time they did, I smiled back. It was a chess match. I could see how much they got off on the challenge of breaking guys like me who were such easy targets, sanctioned by Drug War laws. In a strange way, I was enjoying the confrontation I had feared for so long. Why don't you earn the taxpayers' money by capturing spies and terrorists? I wanted to shout as they drove off. But instead I did the smart thing, said nothing and bit my tongue.

That night I nosed-dived into another mini-depression. I had been strong and cocky during the live performance with the feds, but as the mental tape was replayed through another restless sleep, my confidence was shattered. I could sense how much they wanted to slap the cuffs on me and drag me out of the Lion's Share in front of my wife. But like Jerry had said in Houston, "They have to go through due process first."

After that day, I no longer had to wonder when I would hop into Tim Barnes' black Ford F-150 packed with camping gear and cash, and disappear. I now had an invitation to the government's little party back in Indiana on July seventh of 1986, and had no intention of attending.

June 1986, the Arizona Border: We needed a peaceful place to unwind and strategize before the impending run, so we rented a houseboat on scenic Lake Powell with Jim and Irene Hagar. This time, they seemed more relaxed. For seven days it was Woodstock-on-Water. We bonded and shared a special week which reminded me of my early hippie days. We got back-to-nature-naked and stayed that way. We walked beneath Rainbow Bridge, studied ancient petroglyphs, rode cool-running streams down smooth rockslides, and soaked in sacred mineral pools tucked in secret, shaded places. We fished each morning and enjoyed our catch every night with a crackling campfire echoing off canyon walls and curious coyotes serenading us from cliffs above. After dinner we'd share a smoke, count shooting stars, and talk about how great fugitive life was going to be compared to prison.

On the last night, we agreed to meet at Lake Tahoe on the Fourth of July with Todd, then regroup as a *fuge community* somewhere on the California Coast. I gave Jim the envelope from Todd's photo-shoot, and mentioned Bill McCarthy's most recent and urgent plea for identification, as well as my reasons for considering it.

Jim snorted half a vial of cocaine and wheezed, "Mr. Barnes, what we ought to do...is hire someone to cut the tongues out of the government's witnesses against us."

"What are you saying?" I asked, wondering if he were testing me.

"Nothing, guy," he muttered. "Just forget it. Don't you know me well enough to tell when I'm joking?"

§

July Fourth, 1986, Lake Tahoe, California: Sitting on a beach blanket drinking beers, my well-medicated mind reviewed the past twenty-nine years of life. Beside me sat the brown-eyed beauty I'd made my wife. Above me—just beyond reach against a silhouetted mountainscape backdrop—pyrotechnic spiders mirrored on pristine waters exploded across starry Western skies and disintegrated within my eyes. Before me, boaters' running lights fanned out over the bay like swarms of fireflies.

Between illumination and darkness I saw strobe-lit faces destined to accompany me on the mysterious journey about to unfold: Todd Maher, fellow Hoosier, best friend, former right-hand man in my marijuana endeavors; Mr. and Mrs. Blackwell, formerly the Hagars of Ohio who were little more than business associates not so long ago; and others whose names were yet to be revealed in the months ahead.

Between deafening bangs from each firework's report, an old red dog wearing a dirt-stained bandanna barked in my ear, and from a nearby ghetto blaster I heard '60s singer Janis Joplin belting out a befitting Independence Day tune. "Feeling good was easy, when Bobby sang the blues! And feelin' good was good enough for me."

I sat there on that surrealistic night, pondering the past that had brought me to this crossroad. The '60s were gone forever, and the country was marching to a different tune. I wasn't such a bad guy. There were thousands like me. Why couldn't the government just let me complete my metamorphosis from pot-smoking, hippie rebel kid to tax paying, apple-pie eating American citizen? What was to be gained from sending me to prison for a long time? In my mind, it wasn't fair for them to dig up my past. But fair or not, I had been discovered, and didn't want to face the government's music. Smiley was right. It was easier to simply get stoned and disappear.

"God bless America!" Jim Hagar (alias Mr. Blackwell) sang out with his beloved purple *Crowny* bag in hand. "Land of the free!"

"God bless America!" whistled his gap-toothed wife, Irene.

"God bless America," I whispered, echoing the wish. Come tomorrow, I'd be gone. In three days, I would officially be underground. *But for how long?* I wondered. *How long?*

And Janis sang the song.

"Freedom's just another word for nothing left to lose. It ain't nothin'! Ain't nothin', hon, if you ain't free!"

January 1991, Seattle, Washington: "Lights out! Party's over," shouted the jailer in the King County federal prisoner pod.

My recollection of that summer night in Tahoe disappeared.

The image of rockets exploding over Baghdad faded from the television screen, and the guard tossed me a tattered gray blanket saying: "Here ya go, Hickey, John Doe, Kelly, Barnes, or whatever the hell your name is. That concrete floor gets mighty cold this time of year."

The seriousness of reality engulfed me. A shiver ran down my spine. I had to believe the media attention I'd received would considerably raise the stakes in this game—for all the players. I shook my head and wondered why I hadn't heeded the warning signs a long, long, time ago.

5

The Cliffs of Mendocino

Late January, 1991, Seattle's King County Jail: A rumble rose like rolling thunder around the television screen where a big black guy was channel surfing for some rap-video relief from Gulf War coverage. At first I thought it was another fight, but then I heard that hauntingly familiar tune. The theme music from *Unsolved Mysteries* faded, and the smooth voice of host Robert Stack filled the uncommonly quiet confines of the federal prisoner holding pod. Beneath a bright orange jumpsuit, my white skin crawled. Suddenly, I felt even sicker.

"Yo, Kelly!" the biggest black man demanded, clearing a wide viewing path for me. "Check this shit out. You one bad mutha-fucka! Why didn't you say you was a goddamn movie star?"

I shrugged my shoulders as news of Bill McCarthy's capture in Canada filled the screen. "Idiot," I muttered when they showed footage of my former business partner covering his face and walking fast. Hadn't Moon called to warn him? Why didn't he run? I wondered how long it would take for Bill to turn on me.

When Robert Stack announced my updated status—accompanied by a mug shot—cheers rang out around me, then applause. And my crash course in *Con-World Mentality 101* continued. In their eyes any media coverage was cool, but getting caught on *Unsolved Mysteries* was tits. None of this was cool to me, but common sense told me to take my newfound celebrity status in stride and reap whatever benefits it afforded.

Ever since my arrest I had remained a mute curiosity to my peers, huddled in a corner, hugging paper and pencil, writing the first wave of heartfelt love poems to my wife. After a few days, no one seemed to even notice me. Now, I was the talk of the pod.

"Ya know Kelly, it's hard to picture you being the armed and dangerous type," the resident Aryan armed bank robber remarked.

"Maybe it's just hype," I replied.

"You guilty of all that shit, like TV say?" asked a thin black kid.

"Nope. I'm innocent," I answered with a smile. "Aren't you?"

The older guys laughed.

"Did you really sell tons of pot?" a skinhead quizzed.

"That's what I'm *accused* of," I said.

"Yo! Lemmee ax ya somethin'," said the young crack dealer, tugging on the sleeve of my jumpsuit. "Where all the money go?"

Suddenly I felt uncomfortable about coming out of my shell.

"Shit! I know why my man Kelly's been so qui—ette," the crack kid chided, poking his finger in my chest. "You too damn cool to be locked up with us po' niggers, ain't ya? You a fuckin' millionaire, ain't ya?"

I shook my head, struggling to hold my tongue. For days I had endured the afternoon ritual of this kid's posse playing rap-videos at full volume. I had crammed toilet paper in my ears and tried to envision sounds and scenes from my travels to block it out, but it was beginning to get to me.

The kid poked my chest again. "You too cool to talk to us po' niggers, ain't ya?"

"You ignorant, ain't ya?" I blurted, grabbing his finger.

"Fuck you, honkey! I'll cut you a new ass—"

"Thas' enough, nigger!" demanded the pod's old black orderly from Arkansas. "Get out the man's face!" He yanked the kid's collar. "Don't pay 'em no mind, Kelly. They's jus' crack babies. Their brains been pipe-fried from suckin' on that glass dick too long. They thinks bein' in jail is fun-n-games. Reality ain't set in yet. Jus' wait till they gets them-selves a shit-load of time."

One of the rappers snarled at my new friend.

"Thank you, sir," I said, shaking his huge hand.

"Please, call me Buck." He led me toward a quiet corner while con-tinuing to watch my back. "Can't believe them peoples put yo' ass on the TV fo' sellin' weed. Man, you a mutha-fuckin' dinosaur, *for real.* Rock and tar are where it's at today, Kelly. Where ya been anyway, in one-a them damn time capsules?"

"Yeah! Where ya been, you white dinosaur?" rapped the school of crack babies behind us. "Don't-cha-know that weed ain't King no more? Rock rules the block! Rock rules the block! Don't-cha-know, don't-cha-know, don't-cha-know, you white dinosaur? Weed ain't the shit no more."

Unceremoniously they returned to video-worship services at the TV altar.

When the rappers cranked up the volume of their hate music, I cringed. "I guess maybe I have been living in a time capsule, Buck," I said. "I certainly haven't ever heard any music that irritating. And I never heard the 'N' word used so often, especially by a Negro to another Negro."

Buck nodded. "The music's not my bag either, Kelly. But they controls the TV. And in here, you learns not to sweat the dumb shit. As fo' this nigger business, there's a difference, especially in the city. Them boys is niggers. I'm a black man. You dig?"

"Yeah, I guess so."

"I been watchin' you fo' days now, Kelly. Been meanin' to ax ya about that writin' you be doin."

"It's for my wife," I said, suddenly feeling shook by my near-rumble with the rappers. "Poetry, mainly. It used to be a hobby of mine."

"Uh, huh. Been meanin' to ax ya fo' a favor, Kelly. Could ya help me write a poem for *my* wife?"

His big hands were trembling. I saw sincerity in his misty brown eyes, and realized he'd just saved my ass. "Sure."

"Could ya help me to write a letter, too? Ya see, she ain't got no phone, and I can't..." Buck stomped his foot down hard on the dirty concrete floor. "Damn it, Kelly! I can't read or—"

"No sweat, Buck. Let's sit down and talk about what you want to say to her. And by the way, my name isn't Kelly...it's Thomas."

That night I made a decision. It was time to end the identity game once and for all and get on with the legal battle back in Indiana. I desperately needed to see my wife as well, and had devised a way of doing it. Comfortable with my decision, I relaxed slightly. Later, when the pod's crack babies began the nightly ritual of mimicking their TV rapper-heroes by tapping on metal-pipe rails and rhyme-talking, I surprised a captive audience with my own little ditties in the dark.

"Used to think that outlaw life was just a breeze," I blurted, pausing to make some rap-percussion sounds, "until they put my ass on *Unsolved Mysteries*!"

The entire pod erupted with laughter, and for the first time since my arrest—*I laughed, too.*

"That you, white-weed-man dinosaur?" the crack kids asked.

"Ten-four," I said.

"White men can't rap, and you can't deny it. You can't rap, so don't even try it!"

"Even if a man can't dance or sing, any fool can do this crazy rap thing. Remember *Disco*?"

"Disco dead, for real, dinosaur!"

"Ten-four. Disco dead and that's the way that rap go! Don't-ya-know, don't-ya-know, don't-ya-know? *For real.* I'm just telling you how I feel, so don't get violent. But before I go silent, let me sing you some merry old Nat King Cole. Now that man had talent—*and soul.*"

"You one crazy dude for real, Thomas," Buck said.

"Yeah, wild and crazy. That's me."

But when the last laugh died, snoring and crazy-talk from sleeping men with tormented minds reverberated off the walls of our concrete cage—like a jack-hammer jamming on my brain—and heart-felt pain from missing my wife returned.

The Public Defender I had been assigned by the authorities as pauper persona, Paul James Kelly, was an amicable, competent, open-minded lady lawyer. During my first week of confinement she was contacted by Houston attorney Jerry Patchen, who informed her he was tied up in a Texas trial and could not immediately pull away. On Patchen's advice, I confided in my public defender and put her in touch with Kim through the Houston attorney's office. The next day, I was apprised of my wife's situation.

Kim had come home that fateful afternoon, only to find handprints on the fender of the Ford F-150 and my keys hanging from its ignition. She asked the neighbors to watch the pets, grabbed our birds, packed a suitcase, and hit the road. She made all the right moves, phoning Patchen in Houston, our English banker Blake and fugitive associate Moon, to inform them of my demise. When she told Todd in person at his Hood River, Oregon, home, my old pal broke down and cried. Kim stayed with one of her island tennis friends a couple of nights, then drove south of Seattle on Interstate 5, settled into a low-profile hotel, and waited for a sign. Like mine, her nights were lonely, restless and nauseous.

§

Kim's sign came the day after Bill McCarthy's capture was announced on *Unsolved Mysteries.* Washington State had no judicial interest in me, but the Northern District of Indiana was chomping at the bit to get me back. I had been fighting extradition. The feds didn't want to waste funds on my extradition hearings; but regardless, it was only a matter of time and money. Which is why—via my public defender—I made a painless offer the feds would not refuse: A) Let my wife go back to Bainbridge Island, collect our belongings without harassment or fear of arrest, and allow her to return to Indiana. B) Allow Kim to visit me at the county jail. In exchange, I would sign my real name on a waiver of extradition. Insisting on this protection for my wife provided me with the illusion that I was still capable of controlling the outcome of things from inside. I had a lot to learn.

"Sounds good," said my lady lawyer. "I'll see what I can do. Anything else?"

I produced several crumpled sheets of paper from inside my sock. "Could you give these to my wife?"

"What are they, Thomas?" she asked.

"Love poems. And a note telling Kim to trust you."

The note also instructed Kim to call her mom, Donna, in Buffalo, New York and have her fly to Seattle to lend her support. It said it was safe for her to return to the house, pack up the pieces of her tattered life, and go home. I instructed her to rent a U-Haul truck big enough to hold all of our home's furnishings and the contents of our Portland, Oregon self-storage unit. The latter included choice inventory from the Lion's Share and a sizable nest egg of gold coins. As soon as her mom arrived, Kim was to inform my public defender, who would then arrange our visit.

Later that day, Kim drove to downtown Seattle dressed like Jackie Onassis in dark shades and a stylish hat. She slipped into the Public Defenders' Offices, picked up her note, and disappeared.

On visiting day we made our way to a narrow room divided into small cubicles by half-walls. The guard locked us inside, and I selected the end stall for optimum privacy. And there I sat like some dog-pound mutt waiting to be adopted, wearing the frozen, impish grin of a kid in front of a family photographer waiting on the camera's click.

When she shuffled in on the *free-side* of the thick glass, my heart melted. I was glad. She looked good. We just stood there for the longest time, studying each other and showing nothing but strength until we were both satisfied. Then we lay both hands upon our respective sides of the filthy glass that separated us as deeply as the Grand Canyon. Carefully, we aligned our fingers, touched, felt, fought off tears, and mouthed three words simultaneously: *I LOVE YOU...*

Oh, how I wanted to hold her in my arms.

She bit her lip and almost lost it.

"Don't," I said softly through a perforated glass circle. "I'm doing all right, honey. Really. How you holding up?"

"Fine, honey," she said, while that telltale red rash spread like wildfire on her long swan's neck. "Miss you, my green-eyed gremlin."

"Miss you too, Meekla," I said, using my most sentimental pet name for her.

Suddenly the black rapper kid in the stall next to mine stretched his brillo-pad head around our partition, pointed at me, and waved at my wife. "Dude is white, but he can rap all right!" he blurted. "Uh-huh, uh-huh."

Kim laughed. Three big black girls crammed into the tiny free-persons space beside her laughed. Everyone in the visiting chamber lightened up for a second, then leaned in closer to the perforated glass to whisper private things that needed to be said.

And the turnkey's clock started ticking.

"Forty-five minutes, people!" yelled the guard through a wire-mesh window. "Use it or lose it."

When the guard walked away to smoke a cigarette, my wife got right down to business and gave me the latest news.

Our island self-storage unit had been hit, resulting in a loss of forty grand, but revealing no sensitive documents. Feds tore the house to shreds searching for buried treasure. The pets were frightened, but okay. Only her mother's companionship made returning to Bainbridge bearable. And sleeping in that rustic home without me? Being on that small island when practically everyone knew? It was paradise lost. She'd given most of our plants and the aviary we'd built—filled with finches—to her girlfriend at Island Pet Store. It had been a rough two weeks for her, and wear showed below her sad brown eyes. For five years she'd lived a fantasy life *somewhere over the rainbow* and now, like Dorothy, she just wanted to go home. But before that journey, she was going to attempt to rescue our Portland stash from the asset-hungry jaws of the government.

Fearful that the room was bugged, Kim chose her words carefully—as I did mine. "What about Bill and Leigh's arrest?" she asked.

I shrugged my shoulders, opting not to share my concern about McCarthy affecting my legal case.

"What did they say when they busted you, honey?"

I recalled the Barney Fife-look-alike FBI agent saying, "Her father's been worried sick about her," and bit my tongue. "Not much," I muttered. "What about Blake?"

My wonderful wife pulled a paper from her bra and pressed it against the glass.

I quickly read her report. 1) Called Blake. Told him you were dealing with your past and to be prepared for an IRS investigation. Blake was sad, but said to tell you that you had a true friend and "a very good poker player" in the Channel Islands. 2) Told Arnie, who moved immediately. 3) Rented a twenty-four foot U-Haul for rescue mission. 4) Sold the Volvo at Cash for Cars.

"Good girl!" I exclaimed.

"Ten minutes to go, people!" shouted the guard.

"*Shred that paper*," I told my wife.

With all the secret stuff having been discussed, Kim waved her mother in from the wings where she'd been waiting. They clasped hands, turned to face me, and stood speechlessly exchanging intermittent glances. Suddenly the demeanor of my outlaw partner changed drastically as she shed her veil of strength, allowing the suppressed little girl inside to surface. Kim started hyperventilating, which in turn led to sobbing. Soon, tears were falling on both sides of the glass.

Her statuesque blond mother handed Kim a tissue. "Hi, Tom," she whispered, forcing a cheery smile from wet lips.

"Hi, Donna," I said. "Thanks for coming."

"My big girl and my son-in-law needed me," she said, squeezing Kim's hand tighter.

I listened as she assured me that she and all her children were behind me one hundred percent. She denounced the laws that depicted marijuana smokers and dealers as worse than murderers. "By God, I'm a '60s mom," she proclaimed proudly, proving beyond a doubt where her daughter's spunk originated, "and I know better!"

"Five minutes remaining, people!" boomed the voice of authority over a speaker box. *"Wrap it up."*

The wise-crack-kid beside me rattled off a responsive, rhyming riff of obscenities.

I started talking fast and told them Jerry was flying in from Houston to review the case and our strategy. Soon afterwards, I would be transported back to Indiana. Until then, I would call collect twice a day to our Bainbridge Island house. "Send a bouquet of flowers to my public defender," I said as the seconds wound down on our time together. I heard the telltale clicking of keys, then the door swung open. My heartbeat quickened as the guard began clearing out my side of the visitors' chamber.

Donna swallowed hard, hugged her daughter, and wiped the wetness from the corner of her eyes.

I placed my palms against the glass and blew them a kiss. "You were the one thing I could not give her...*family*," I whispered through a warm smile.

The turnkey repeated his order. *"Let's go! Visit's over!* Time to leave."

In that moment of tenderness—oblivious to the world—my wife and I locked eyes, instinctively rubbed wedding rings against the grimy glass, and whispered, *"Shazamm."* Our shivering spines were injected with sorely needed strength, for we both knew what this meant. We'd find a way. We'd see it through.

I envisioned us making love in tall grass atop the rugged cliffs of Mendocino. And by the look I saw in her big brown eyes, I thought she must have, too.

"You there! Let's go," the lion-tamer commanded, like I was a wayward child.

Being fresh from the wild, new to the zoo, I snarled.

"I'm talking to you—move!"

We all had jobs to do. There was nothing to prove.

"Love you," I said. "Stay strong." And she was gone.

Back inside the pod on a concrete floor, I suffered severe mood swings, loss of appetite, and cravings to be with my mate—all symptoms of what I would eventually come to call *Post-Visit Syndrome.* I became drowsy and sought to soothe the painful present by reliving my memories. I pictured Kim's face, and wondered if America's married soldiers in the Gulf War gained much strength in their strange surroundings by knowing somewhere out there—away from the madness—people who loved them were on their side, praying things would work out right. I wondered if the time had come to call my mother, now that I had admitted my identity. And as my eyes grew heavier, I thanked the heavens above for having a soulmate like Kim.

Shazamm! Love, even without lust—*powerful stuff.*

In my private hell, I blocked out the raw reality around me, and conjured up poetic moments from the days of fugitive-past. I heard Pacific Ocean waves caressing smooth-rock shores. I slept long and fast, and dreamed of her and me on that first official day as fugitives—on the cliffs of Mendocino.

July 7, 1986, The Medicino Coast: The cliffside vacation rental was everything its owner advertised it to be in the *San Francisco Chronicle's* classified section. The big bay window's panoramic views of the wild, windswept Northern California coast alone were well worth $1200 a week. Following a wonderful home-cooked meal, we sat on the big bay's sill with our gray cat Jagger and Irish setter Benjamin, sipping cabernet and watching the sunset. A mysterious mist descended at dusk and hovered on the horizon. Strings of light belonging to the Pacific salmon fleet broke free of the fog bank, came into sight, and cruised slow and easy up the coast in pursuit of aquatic gold.

We walked outside. The air was fresh. We felt so good, so amazingly relaxed after all those months of anxiety and stress. That first fugitive night reminded me of graduating from high school, then moving away to a Michigan lake-cottage with Leigh.

I opened my wallet, glanced at my Timothy Alan Barnes ID, and breathed a sigh of relief. "Well, we did it," I said to Kim. "What do you think?"

She took one more look at her Diane K. Moore passport, and handed it to me. "I think it'll be nice waking up together tomorrow, and not having to worry about who's watching us."

"So, Lady Di," I whispered, slipping my arms around her slender waist. "Would you entertain a summer affair with a green-eyed stranger such as I?"

"Excuse me, sir," she said, weakly attempting to escape my embrace, "but I am a married woman."

I bowed my head and made a puppy-dog sound. I kneeled on a grassy spot of ground and gazed skyward. My wife untied her robe enticingly and wrapped its cotton folds around me. My senses were engulfed by her scent. My hands explored the goddess-like curves of her firm young body.

"Excuse me," she sighed, "but what did you say your name was?"

"Bond, my lady," I muttered between nibbles and hot breaths. *"Just call me Mr. Bond."*

Jim and Irene arrived on the morning of July eighth. They'd bought a brand new compact pick-up truck, and were towing a pop-up tent camper. "Hey, guy!" Smiley called out. "How the hell are ya?"

"Let's just say I feel like a new man."

"Told ya so. Welcome to my world." He shook my hand.

"What a lovely house," Irene exclaimed. She pecked my cheek, and hugged Kim.

I stared at their matching Banana Republic baggy khaki hiking clothes while they dug through camping gear for sundries. "What gives with all the stuff?" I asked.

"*This,*" Irene whistled, with both hands placed on her shapely hips, "is the latest in fugitive-fashion wear."

"We're going to camp our way across the great American West this summer in search of a sanctuary," Smiley announced. "It's something we always wanted to do, and a perfect way to blend in with the masses."

"Makes sense," I said.

We spent the day on the beach, and dined out down the road at a quaint, white, wood-sided restaurant high atop a lofty ridge. At sunset, we watched a river far below ramble to the glowing sea through tangled stacks of driftwood. We toasted freedom, and wondered about my friend Todd, who had been expected around noon, but never showed. Back at the house we played Trivial Pursuit until midnight, at which time Kim and I retired to the master bedroom for romance.

My guests romanced a cocaine mirror until the wee hours.

I slept light, woke at dawn, and crept out of the house with my dog—like a kid hunting an Easter basket—hoping to find my old friend's blue Volvo parked in the driveway. No such luck. *Paranoia.* Had Todd changed his mind, or met with some surprise when stopping by a mutual friend's (and marijuana growers') ranch in the foothills east of Sacramento? Were the rest of us already in jeopardy? I recalled the long running television series *The Fugitive* with its one-armed man.

"Shit! The show's just begun, Big Red," I told my canine friend, "and we're already in danger of being cancelled."

The large Irish setter barked, cocked his head, and gave me a crooked smile.

"If Todd doesn't show up by dark, we might as well bug out," I mumbled as we descended a winding, rocky trail to the beach. "Then there's the problem of my buddy, Bill McCarthy, and all his dark secrets."

The peace the previous day had brought quickly disintegrated. My stomach churned. A covey of quail crossed our path and took flight on a Pacific wind at the sight of my furry sidekick. My old bird dog half-heartedly lunged toward them, and pulled up with a limp. *One more tough decision*, I thought as I massaged his hindquarter, uncertain of how demanding the road ahead would be or what was best for Ben.

He was thirteen then—quite old for a setter. I remembered the day I brought him and his sister, Poppy, home the month before my graduation from Mishawaka High School. Miss Poppy got hit by a car three summers later but Ben survived to see it all: The face of the South Bend cop who robbed my cottage of money and weed, my many mini-romances, business ventures, and crazy annual Hawaiian luaus at Diamond Lake. Big Red had sat atop mountainous bales of Colombian pot and barked like a royal marijuana mutt. We'd been coast to coast together, camped in restricted bear-inhabited areas of our National Parks, and played fetch the stick from Tampa to Tucson. Ben shared my zest for life. How then, could I leave him behind? For the longest time, I stared at the hazy horizon while cool tides tugged at my feet.

Morning sun burned through an ocean mist. My gray muzzled friend's growl broke the spell and brought me back to our Mendocino beach. He tilted his frizzed-out head to one side and gave me a concerned look. I took the stick of driftwood he had found from his gentle jaws and rubbed the velvet inside of his ear until he laughed, left leg twitching the way it did. I loved that dog. I looked straight into those glassy brown eyes and made a promise. "Wherever I go, you go. Period. Even if I have to get you a new set of American Kennel Club fugitive canine papers. Got that, pal?"

Ben wagged his wet tail.

"I'll shave your red hide so short, you'll look like a damn poodle! Then no one will recognize you."

He barked and dipped his nose defiantly beneath a breaking wave.

I pitched the smooth piece of brown driftwood into a frothy sea.

He pranced through shallow water like a show-horse, glancing back occasionally as if to say, "Look at me." He swam into deep water, displaying youthful energy, and retrieved that stick for me.

We played our game. I tossed, the stick floated. Ben plucked it from tidal currents and ran along the shoreline while I chased close behind. He growled when allowing me to pluck the foam-coated wood from his bird-dog grip like a baton from a relay-running partner, never breaking stride. Then side by side he pursued me, aggressively pawing, snarling, and nipping at my heels and the wood. Only with me could he be this way. Small, obnoxious children could tug on those sensitive gold-plumed ears and old Ben would never protest.

But this was *our* game. And though we played it well, we had not played it in months—two pacifists who possessed plenty of heart should we ever find our backs against the wall. We played hard that day. I sensed Red wanted to prove his mettle for the road his canine instincts must have told him lay ahead.

But I loved that animal. He had nothing to prove to me.

She watched, waiting...waiting until boy and dog panted breathlessly beneath her, where tidal pools filled and wet sand met algae-covered rock upon which reddish-green mussels clung to life above the California kelp beds at low tide. Then Kim called down to us from the Mendocino cliffs above. It was something about Todd, and there was a sense of urgency in her voice.

Once again, my dog and I ran.

It happened at a marijuana growers' ranch in the country west of Auburn, California. The feds had been there the week before hunting a friend of ours, hoping to invite him to an Indiana grand jury. Todd was just leaving for Mendocino—driving slowly down a narrow dirt lane—when a suspicious-looking white sedan squeezed by his blue Volvo. He nodded cordially at the two suits behind the wheel and they returned the gesture. He watched in his rearview mirror as they pulled up to our friend's front door, then started knocking. Just before he rounded a curve, he saw them run back to their car. He increased speed as sweat poured down his forehead.

The feds' sedan appeared in the blue Volvo's rearview mirror.

My friend's size thirteen tennis shoe flattened the gas pedal. Tires spun. The chase was on! J. Todd Maher was a stick of flesh the feds desperately wanted to fetch back home to their superiors, and this was not a game.

Two Indiana-based G-men on strange Western turf tried like hell to stay with the wily golfer, who had come to know the Sierra foothills all too well in the spring of '86. They fishtailed on shoulders of dry dirt side roads, roared through rocky canyons, and raced over rickety one-lane bridges. The bewildered feds flicked their headlights on and off the entire time.

"Finally," Todd said, sucking air between giant gulps of cold beer, "I lost them in a cloud of dust, then watched them wander aimlessly out of sight from a nifty wooded vantage point." He paused to wipe his flushed face with a wet rag. "I sure hope you've got my IDs, Bud, because I think those guys will be pissed if we ever meet again."

"God bless 'em, guy!" shouted Jim Hagar-Blackwell, flashing that broad shit-eating grin which had earned him the nickname Smiley. He popped the locks on his briefcase, pulled out an envelope, and handed it to Todd.

The golfer opened it and inspected his new identity papers.

"Welcome to the gang, *John Boy,*" we proclaimed in concert.

J. Todd Maher was history, and John Paul Morgan was just beginning life as a thirty-something fugitive.

That night we barbecued fresh salmon over mesquite, speculated about grand jury proceedings back home, and played "the name game." According to the Blackwells, formerly the Hagars of Ohio, we three Hoosiers needed to become as comfortable with our new names as they had.

At first it was crazy. We practiced for days over dinner tables, at grocery stores, on public tennis courts, and in the pro-shop of a local golf course. I never once called my wife by her alias in private, instead preferring any one of my many pet names for her. As for the others; I dubbed Jim, *Smiley*; Todd, *Arnie*—for golf legend Arnold Palmer; and Irene, *Lizzy*. I asked our fugitive instructors to call me Tim.

On more than one afternoon, the men went golfing with the resident pro Arnie while the women shopped or shared feline secrets at the beach in our absence. But every night without fail, the five of us gathered around the big bay window for after-dinner drinks. With the exception of my wife, we were all well read and politically opinionated. Todd and I were news junkies, and Jim and Irene were voracious novel readers. We all were blessed with a sense of humor. Our after dinner dialogues ranged from discussions about Teflon President Ronald Reagan and his scandalous advisors like Attorney General Edwin Meese III, Ollie North and crew, to opinions about the religious right and the great Drug War which our omnipotent nation had been losing for years. Sometimes I sensed that my wife felt out of place during our serious talks, and so I would switch to a combination of politics and comedy.

On one such occasion, I did a routine featuring Jim Bakker and Tammy Faye, which was representative of our collective view on the marijuana issue. The skit's imaginary setting was one of the holier-than-thou Bakkers' oversold condo timeshares, and it began with their butler serving them a magnum of chilled bubbly. "Jimmy, 'ah cain't stand it! I jus' know it," my version of the rotund savior screeched.

"Stand what, Tamma' Faye? Know what, my dearest?"

"The fact that somewhere in this fair city, someone is having oral sex at this very minute!"

"My God, Suggums! Why, the mere thought of it sours the sweet taste from this two-hundred dollar bottle of our parishioners' sacramental champagne."

My stoned fugitive audience applauded. My wife seemed relieved to see her uptight husband acting like his old self.

Minutes later I concluded. "Their own off-camera lives are so damn boring that they become obsessively concerned with what's going on behind closed doors across town." I paused to take a puff. "Such as mature adults smoking pot. And so they crusade to pass the time. Yet all the while, these televangelists give testimony to street-corner prostitutes in the backseat of their clean, white limousines. Why? Because all tutes in the backseat of their clean, white limousines. Why? Because all the makeup and facelifts in the world, and all the faithful's mishandled funds can't provide a fountain of youth capable of retrieving their old ladies from the land of past-prime. That's what's wrong with America," I declared, rapping my knuckles on the bay window's sill. "We're fast becoming a nation of hypocrites, too concerned with other peoples' private lives, and always busy championing the moral barriers that illegality creates."

After a gourmet dinner, cocaine is like a deadly dessert tray. You're all liquored-up, licking your lips, on the nod; then your pals produce a mirror and spill-out the magic dust. It's a known miracle how 'toot' extends an entertaining evening. Pop music star Eric Clapton summed up the illogical rationale behind ingesting a harmful drug into your system best by singing: *When your day is done and you wanna ride on—cocaine!* Comedy great Richard Prior put it another way: "Cocaine is God's way of tellin' a mutha fucker he has too much money!"

Kim didn't smoke pot but had a bad history with cocaine. Todd tried to stay away from coke. Cocaine and I never got along too well. We had a love/hate relationship because—during each affair—after the initial orgasmic rush, it made me paranoid, then physically and mentally impotent. Consequently, I eventually learned not to keep a toot stash around the way most dealers did. This was not the case with my fellow fugitives from Ohio. To them, cocaine was their American Express card—and they *never* left home without it. Which is why, during those Mendocino nights, I became convinced that—like "part-time" alcoholics—they had a serious problem.

Cocaine is a truth serum. Somehow, after a while, it always loosens the tongue, allowing those you are tooting with to know most of what is on your mind. Case in point: one particular binge night near the end of our first week at Mendocino. I was extremely concerned with the goings on back home, but had managed to hold these thoughts at bay—until the toot-monster invaded my brain. Then, duly wired, I disclosed the contents of my latest disturbing payphone conversation with Bill McCarthy.

He had informed me that during a second round of Indiana grand jury hearings, numerous people were caught perjuring themselves. My main customer Dan and old friend Bruce were babbling like brooks to country and was certain that by now they'd passed on my misinformation to the law. Fearless Bill McCarthy had finally bugged out, and was hiding at a friend's place in Indianapolis, waiting for me to send him some identity papers. "I just couldn't hold it together," he explained nervously over the payphone.

Apparently, Bill's right-hand man, Tim Meers, had snorted a vial of cocaine with a government informant who was wearing a body mike; then bragged on tape about beating the first grand jury by lying out his ass. What Bill didn't say, was that he then asked this Tim to minimize the McCarthy involvement in the marijuana conspiracy, and maximize mine. But those weren't Bill's only secrets. Through FBI documents, I eventually learned that he was running from *both* sides of the law. Over the years I would discover more about my ex-partner Bill, but there are mysteries surrounding him, his money, and the United States government, which for me remain "unsolved" to this day.

I paused mid-speech on that medicated Mendocino evening, pondering the decision of bringing Bill McCarthy into our underground world, and struggling to stuff my concerns back inside the Pandora's Box from which they came.

"What's on your mind, *Timmy*?" Smiley asked, noticing my distance.

"That's Tim," I snapped. Reluctantly I slapped the photo-shoot envelope Bill had sent to my Reno mail drop on the windowsill.

"Sorry, Tim," Smiley said, thumbing through the stuff.

"Penny for your thoughts," whistled a sniffling Lizzy.

"I'm just not happy with their selections for new names. That's all." I paused to grind my teeth nervously. "I explained in detail about avoiding old patterns, but Bill ignored me. His wife, Leigh Ann Taylor/McCarthy, is listed as *Anna Leigh Fisher*, and their daughter Shannon is still *Shannon.* At least he switched William to *James.*"

"Not very creative, is he?" Smiley noted.

"Nope." One more reason to worry, I thought.

The Blackwell's testimony under truth serum was entirely different, but equally revealing. They congratulated us on our successful missions securing Social Security cards and passports, yet also appeared to be envious. Not to be outdone—and in the true competitive spirit of pot dealers—they announced their pending acquisition of a rare "institutionalized person's paperwork" for a mere pittance of five grand. I'd read about these in the underground press. They consisted of the birth certificate and Social Security number of someone locked up in a loony bin who wouldn't be getting their walking papers for a while.

Smiley had learned that his ex-partner, retired smuggler Maui Bert, was preparing to battle his conspiracy rap in the courts. After waffling between fighting and *fugin'*, Bert finally concluded that with all of us conveniently on the lam and his own right-hand man Ray safely on a world tour, time was ripe for testing the waters. Consequently, he paid a former Miami prosecutor big bucks to help him attain a survivable outcome by any means available. Years later, I would be amazed and mystified at what big money and former federal prosecutors could accomplish.

Both Blackwells were bitter about recent developments back in their beloved homeland of Ohio. They gave sharp-tongued harangues on *rats*, often muttering the word *retribution*. One person in particular "wasn't holding his mud," as Smiley put it. This person was Jim's second partner, Gary Ankerman, who had married Irene's sister.

"Rat!" the spouses snarled. They were irate about the family snitch selling out, and offered a shocking solution.

"It would be so easy," Smiley said, his eyes half-closed and sinister. He rolled a crisp hundred dollar bill tightly, snapped up another long white line lightning-quick—like a human Hoover vacuum cleaner—then continued. "I know these bad-ass Colombians, friends of *The Glove* down in Tucson.

Lizzy, a competitive cocaine tooter, cleared the remaining powder from the mirror and mumbled, "Yeah. Glad we kept our Tucson people..." She paused to lick her lips. "Like *The Glove, Shorty Bob,* and *No Show*, secret from our no good brother-in-law. Rat!"

Smiley scowled at his wired wife, as if she'd just made a major slip up. He rose from the table and plunged his hands into his pockets.

Arnie glared at me and shook his head.

Smiley paced the carpet with unchopped cocaine flakes falling from his flared nostrils. "Anyway, I know these Colombians. And it wouldn't cost much, maybe twenty-five grand a pop." He gulped some Crown Royal while watching for my reaction.

My wife's face turned red, then white.

They had my attention, and I listened closely.

"Think the feds would throw this kinda time at us for fucking pot if they didn't have any witnesses?" Smiley snarled, slapping the table.

His anger surprised me, and aroused me from my stupor.

He spilled more demon dust onto the mirror, hands shaking. His wife chopped it, formed lines in the shape of a peace sign, and gave me a courtly smile. When she asked if we three Hoosiers wanted more, I waved her off.

"Maybe we could get a package deal on these friends of yours and our family rat, Gary," Smiley proposed. "*Seriously.*"

That's when it hit me. I couldn't believe he'd said it. "Listen to yourself," I said, shaking my head. "I've never heard you talk like that. Maybe you'd better lay off those lines."

"Shit, Timmy! These people could make us serve more time than murderers for fucking marijuana, just to save their cowardly skins! *That* drives *me* to consider taking drastic measures. *They* made us outlaws."

Arnie gave me a worried look, grabbed his beer, and stood. "I'm going for a walk," he announced.

I felt my wife's hand clutching mine beneath the table.

"No one *made* me anything," I said. "Freedom of choice, remember? This was *our* choice. You're talking about taking family and friends." I felt a sharp pain in my gut. "No, fuck that. You're talking about taking human life!" I felt nauseated. "I couldn't live with that anymore than you could." I drew a deep breath, then exhaled.

Smiley stared down at his haggard image in the drug-stained reflection glass.

Irene kept chopping powder with a blade.

"I thought a big part of this was about being able to look at our selves in the mirror years from now with pride," I said.

Smiley slowly dropped his head, nodding. He removed his thick glasses, rubbed his temples, then grabbed Lizzy's hand.

"Nothing, and no one, will *ever* lower me to that level," I said, walking toward the door with my wife and dog in tow. "I know you, man," I declared, pointing a finger. "It's the fucking coke that makes you talk so crazy. Think about it. *Screw the government. Screw the laws.* Inanimate objects, pal. That's as far as my militancy goes," I whispered, as the door closed tightly behind me.

And Smiley never mentioned it again.

During our the second week at Mendocino, I came to realize that the two people who had invited us on the paper trip were not the same ones we'd skied with on the snowy slopes of Tahoe, nor were they the ones we had communed with in Lake Powell's peaceful canyons while believing their promise of compatibility in the forthcoming fugitive world. The Ohioans and I had clashing agendas, and would have to go our separate ways. Getting high on coke daily was bad enough, but Smiley demonstrated all the symptoms of retaining marijuana dealer's fever as well. Several times, I watched him pump coins into public telephones and talk in conspiratorial whispers.

Finally, one day on the golf course, he told me what I already had guessed.

"Hey, guy. I'm planning on doing a little business down South when the next crop comes in, and—"

"Why?" I asked.

Smiley told me he had sunk most of his cash into real estate, only to have the feds freeze his assets.

"The farm?" I asked. "The condo in Aspen?"

"Gone. I'm not a millionaire anymore," he groaned, slicing his golf ball off the ninth tee. "I was kinda' hoping you could touch base with Tucson Tony for me. I need to work."

"I sympathize with your situation," I said, before swinging away with my driver, "but I went cold turkey. I broke the fever a long time ago."

"You're an outlaw, aren't you? Perhaps I can tempt you?"

"I don't need money, just peace of mind." I shouldered my golf bag and stepped onto the fairway.

"But..."

"But nothing. I'm not a dealer anymore, Smiley. I only went underground to be free."

Kim and I retired early that evening to the master bedroom, and there we spent hours, studying maps of the Pacific Northwest in our *Rand McNally World Atlas.*

"Honey," she asked, "why don't we move somewhere warm and sunny?"

"We're exiles, dear. Exiles don't get to live in resort cities on the Black Sea. Exiles go to Siberia."

"Honey...where's Siberia?"

"Never mind," I sighed.

"Honey," she announced right when I was about to nod off. "I think I should to fly east to Buffalo and visit with my mother before we disappear."

We were to vacate our Mendocino vacation rental by Sunday noon. On Friday after dinner, Irene suggested we go out and hear some music. We drove to the nearest bar and found it half-filled with friendly bikers and Rainbow People who were the local pot growers. Jim stuffed an old neon jukebox in a dark corner with his precious payphone quarters. We listened to rock n' roll, reminisced, and drank shots of peppermint schnapps.

We three Hoosiers shot pool together, talking between turns about out hometown, South Bend and good times had there. The Blackwells, who'd sworn their cocaine stash was gone, hit the bathroom every fifteen minutes to powder their noses. Every person in that crowd knew why, but Northern California was friendly turf so their public charade was acceptable.

Back at the table, Smiley told me they were headed down to Tucson on Saturday, and would search for a home site in Arizona or Colorado by autumn. I'd already announced my plan to take my team north for the summer to Oregon, where we would acquire new driver's licenses. "We'll keep in touch by answering services, and play the rest by ear," I explained.

"The wife and I were kinda' hoping to have some playmates this winter," Smiley said longingly.

"What about Sonny and Missy?" I asked, artfully changing the subject.

"Sonny's convinced the crowded city theory is the way to go. So, he rented a place in L.A."

I saw sadness in Smiley's blue eyes. But then the music played, and it and the elixir of his pending road trip seemed to rejuvenate him and jumpstart his trademark grin. I sighed, sincerely relieved. Irene returned from her twelfth journey to the ladies room, simultaneously patting her hair and wiping her nose. The Boss, Bruce Springsteen, blasted from the jukebox.

Smiling Jim Hagar hailed his wife. "Come on, Lizzy, let's dance! Come on, Timmy. Get on out here, Di," he coaxed.

But I had too much on my mind, and respectfully declined.

We Hoosiers watched *Smiley* and *Lizzy* dance wildly across a wooden, peanut-shell strewn floor while an old favorite played on the juke. "Glory days!" Smiley shouted as he swayed side to side. "In the wink of a young girl's eye."

"Glory days," I muttered. "Don't let 'em pass you by."

I watched fat bikers knock back longneck beers, watched my young bride biting her lip, pondered the madness of the paper trip, and heard my heart pounding above the volume surrounding my senses. I held Kim's hand tightly and told her things would work out right. I gazed into my good friend Todd's face, and gave him the thumbs-up sign.

Soon every foot in the joint was jumping, including mine.

Saturday came and the Blackwells went. We waved with mixed emotions as they pulled away towing their pop-up tent. Smiley tipped his Banana Republic safari hat. "See you in sunny Arizona after you've had enough Pacific Northwest rain," Irene whistled through those gapped teeth.

Don't hold your breath waiting for us, I thought.

For Kim, some serious questions arose during those initiation days at Mendocino. Ever since retiring from dealing, I'd made her the center of my universe—even surpassing my mother. Now she had caught a glimpse of the old glory days group mentality and witnessed her pillar of strength—*me*—in rare moments of cocaine-induced weakness and doubt. Her pedestal shaken, she became paranoid and sought reassurance from me.

After the last Mendocino dinner, Arnie cleaned his golf clubs and played with our cat, Jagger. Kim and I went alone to the cliffs, where we stood in tall, golden grass tossing stones to the sea, a red dog by our side. I thought about the idea of her visiting her mom and remembered the old proverb about setting something you love free and how *if it did not choose to return, it was never meant to be.* The possibility of her leaving me was deeply disturbing. There were many reasons why she might not return, but I had faith in our love and marriage. Feeling it would be an insult to both these bonds, I decided not to mention it.

"Within a few weeks, the Lion's Share closing will be final," I said.

"As soon as the title company confirms the transaction, we'll head to Southern Cal and I'll rescue another hundred thousand from the feds."

"Are you sure your plan will work?"

"Yes, dear. But when *I* do it, you'll be on a night flight back to Buffalo to see your mother. By the way, I want you to have her compile a list of payphone numbers at restaurants and shopping malls while you're there, for future communications. Set up some times and dates that are convenient for her to receive your calls."

Kim nodded. "Honey, where are we going to live?"

"Oregon," I answered without hesitation. "It's an easy place to create ID. And forget Irene's remark. Contrary to public opinion, the Pacific Northwest is not one big rain forest. There's a high-desert region with plenty of sunshine and very little rain. I'll find a perfect house in the woods. We'll have the pets and plant a garden. It will be just like before."

"But what will happen to us?" she asked, grasping my hand tightly.

We embraced. Ocean winds blew. Tall grass swayed around us. "I don't have all the answers, Meekla," I whispered, massaging her shoulders. "But one thing's for sure."

"What's that?" she sighed.

"It will be much harder to get used to this name game and all the rest of this crap, than being rich and alone with you."

We kissed, with eyes misting. She did her little closed-mouth mime thing and mumbled, "Yes, but do you love me?"

"With all my heart and soul."

A song by Fleetwood Mack played inside my head. The sun turned fiery red as it penetrated the sea. We rubbed wedding rings and said, *"Shazamm."*

Pastel clouds claimed the horizon. The song inside my head grew louder: *Won't you lay me down in the tall grass, and let me do my stuff.* And down we went—my bird dog beside us—with tails wagging and noses to the wind. Down through warm, wet grass, to hard ground with hands clenched and wedding rings click-click-clicking on the cool, refreshing cliffs of Mendocino.

Shazamm.

§

January, 1991, Seattle's King County Jail: I felt someone tugging at my sleeve. The poetry of Mendocino faded, and an animated black face came into focus inches from my own.

"Yo, Mr. Movie Star!" the strange voice said. "Wake your white ass up. The man wants to see ya. I think your high dollar mouthpiece is here."

RCMP Documentation on Arrest of Bill McCarthy.

OCCURRENCE REPORT/DISPATCH TICKET DISPATCHED
91JAN15
CRIMESTOPPERS **Occurrence No. 91-00155**
VCP offices

Investigator: Sgt. Al Campbell
Type of event: Intelligence Info. **91Jan10**
Crimestoppers tip on person seen on T.V. Show—
"Unsolved Mysteries" 91Jan09

SUMMARY OF EVENT

Report #V2250-1 received from Cst. ZIMMERMAN of CRIMESTOPPERS Section from an informant who stated he had viewed the TV program on the 9th January, and feels that one of the subjects aired on the show was enrolled in a tennis course for "Advanced Strokers" which commenced on the 13th November 1990 at the Oak Bay Rec Centre and held Tuesdays and Thursdays from 10 to 11 a.m. Stated that he knew...the person by the name of "Scott" approx. 35 years, 6', 180 lbs. average build, with brown curly, short hair. Attended with his wife.

Continuation Report **Occurrence No 91-00155**
Item Date Time Action Taken
91Jan15 Writer checked with "Holly", Racquet Co-ordinator at the Rec Centre and she supplied the names of the participants in this particular class, two of them being a husband and wife team by the name of Scott and Laura DALEY, of 1460 Oliver St., phone 592-7476. She thought it rather odd a young couple should be enrolled in a daytime class, but stated they were an average charming couple. They have been enrolling in tennis classes since Oct. 90. Writer checked at Oak Bay Municipal Hall and learned that 1460 Oliver is obviously rented out but it cannot be established to whom. The phone book was checked and it shows an ALLEN DALEY living at 1460 Oliver St. phone 592-7476, the same as that given to the Rec. Centre. It was learned a C.P.I.C. message was received from Cpl. Jim POWERS of the Federal Enforcement Branch H.Q. Ottawa, their file #89HQFP14909. This Message stated that two fugitives, namely William Charles McCARTHY, B: 54-08-16 and Thomas Paul HICKEY, B: 56-07-24, and associated to an Anna L. FISHER. B:

58-02-24 alias Laura Lee MATHEWS, B: 64-02-22 with infant daughter Shannon McCARTHY MATHEWS, were featured on "Unsolved Mysteries". Subjects were indicted on 43 criminal counts stemming from drug trafficking. They both fled prior to sentencing. R.C.M.P. Vancouver investigation confirms McCARTHY using the alias, of M. MATHEWS, along with Mrs. L.MATTHEWS, and an infant, S.MATHEWS, arrived in Vancouver from Hong Kong on the 1st May 1989. The C.P.I.C. message also stated that photograph and further details will be forwarded for our assistance.

91Jan17 1000 Writer and Cst. Bryant observed a car in driveway, garage door open at 1460 Oliver St...

91Jan21 1130 ...FBI member familiar with case stated the name "Scott" that suspect used at Oak Bay Rec Centre had been used by him several times in the past. Also his wife has always maintained the name of "Laura" or similar in past transactions, and they have never used anything else but the name SHANNON for their young daughter.

91Jan22 0905 It was decided to attend house and arrest suspect. Members FOWLER, McKAY, SYMES, PARKER G., GAUDET and writer surrounded house. McKAY/SYMES attended front door. Suspect opened door and was arrested on Immigration Warrant, Chartered and warned. Suspect who identified himself as Scott DALEY was cuffed and brought to Oak Bay P.D. Wallet seized with several pieces of identification, three Ohio drivers licenses, phony B.C. Identification card, AFS (American Fleet Service) card, and numerous other pieces of identification in the name of Scott A. DALEY, and Michael C. DOHERTY seized. It was noted immediately that photo identification on the Ohio drivers licenses matched the photo in the wanted circulars on Wm. McCARTHY. He also appeared to be one and the same person except that he had no mustache and was clean shaven. At the Oak Bay P.D. writer spoke with DALEY and advised him that it was suspected he was one and the same as William Charles McCARTHY. Also showed him warrant from U.S. District Court outlining charges and warrant for his arrest issued by Canadian Immigration. He was asked if he was McCARTHY to which he replied that fingerprints would have to determine that. He was printed by S/Sgt. FOWLER who made a tentative identification. FOWLER presented this evidence to him to which he replied he was William Charles McCARTHY. FOWLER then took fingerprints to RCMP Victoria Sub/Div...

U.S. DISTRICT COURT indictment against McCARTHY to us plus his affidavit outlining the reasons to suspect McCARTHY was and still is living off the proceeds of his drug distributions in the U.S.A. He also advised that the McCARTHYS should be in possession of several passports all fraudulent, plus other identification and also a large sum of U.S. currency. Once this info was received Cpl. CLARK prepared an Information to Obtain a Search Warrant outlining the writer's findings thus far and included the FBI member's affidavit along with the U.S. Indictment

91Jan24 1215 Writer i/c with Cpl. CLARKE, S/Sgt. FOWLER, Cst. WOOD and Sgt. McNEILL attended at 1460 Oliver St. and executed search warrant. There was no one at home and copy of warrant was left on table in front hallway. House was methodically searched and a number of documents seized and retained by Cpl. CLARKE. In suspect McCARTHY's brief case was found another safety deposit box key, location unknown. A large envelope was found containing documents to indicate that McCARTHY, his wife and child were about to obtain new identification from the Province of Alberta, birth certificates, etc. This was probably the reason for their intended trip to Calgary this week. In the master bedroom was found a brick, approx. 6 oz. of good black hashish. Hashish smoking paraphenalia was also found…

1902 End of interviews and they departed office. DONALDSON did ask if it was my intention to lay same charges on Wm. McCARTHY. I replied yes.

6

A Hanging in El Reno

Late January 1991, Seattle's King County Jail: Unlike Kim's highly anticipated visit, I approached the arrival of Houston attorney Jerry Patchen with great apprehension. The guard escorted me down a long hallway. I wore no cuffs. We turned a corner, and there was my counselor. "Here's your client sir," said the smiling turnkey, showing a courteous side I had yet to see back at the holding pod.

We entered a tiny, private room furnished with a small wooden table and two folding metal chairs.

"Just knock if you need me," the guard said, before closing and locking the door.

It had been five long years since I first met him after Smiley advised me to be prepared for bad times. I studied his familiar face, seeking strength. We shook hands firmly. "Long time, no see," I said.

"What happened to the little cabin in the woods?" Jerry asked.

"Guess we got bored. What can I say? We were lonely, needed to belong somewhere, and couldn't stay away from tennis clubs." I took a deep breath. "At least we did some living."

In the hour that followed, I scanned a copy of my indictment for the first time. It was thick as a book and I didn't like the title page: *The United States of America v.s. Thomas Paul Hickey*. Fingering through the text, I found the government's accusations to be hauntingly familiar, but amazingly vague. There were scores of "counts" and over one hundred "overt acts." Count Seven read, *The Grand Jury further charges: In or about July 1982, the exact date being unknown to the Grand Jury, in the Northern District of Indiana, William C. McCarthy and Thomas P. Hickey, defendants herein, did knowingly cause Daniel Morissette to travel in interstate commerce from Winimac, Indiana, to Niles, Michigan, with the intent to promote, manage, establish, carry on and to facilitate the promotion, management, establishment and carrying on of an unlawful activity, namely a business enterprise involving the possession and distribution of marijuana...* The indictment book was not a page-turner. It had too many long sentences, the plot was predictable, and I already knew the ending.

"Well, what do you think?" my attorney asked.

"Poorly written, too much sensationalism, but scary as hell. I feel like Saddam Hussein." I put down the document. "The entire US of A against one pacifist guy? What are my chances?"

He clasped his huge hands behind his head and tried to paint a positive picture. "Tom, you are not a violent person," he said with eyes unblinking and that smooth, soothing Texas drawl sinking into my psyche. "You have no prior record. The government knows this. And although their snitches painted a dark portrait of you during your absence, I strongly believe your personal charisma and character will be valuable assets in defusing that negative image." He lowered his powerful voice to a weak whisper. "Speaking of assets..."

Money, Jerry assured me would be a key element in the shaping of a just outcome for me. When I informed him about Blake in the Channel Islands and Kim's initial phone call there, his eyes grew wider, his whisper softer still. "How much are we talking about?" he asked.

My offshore account was a touchy subject. It was the one thing I did not disclose during my pre-fugitive meetings with Jerry. Hesitant to answer, I scrutinized the room, ran my fingers under the table and chairs, then took his yellow legal pad and wrote: *Over one million.*

He rubbed his chin, then asked about my arrangement with Blake.

I said it was friendly, informal and personal, and made it perfectly clear that the Englishman would only respond to Kim's voice, or mine. He suggested finding me an expert on such sensitive banking matters. "Like Bert got in Miami?" I asked, thinking of my Maui smuggler buddy whose millions had apparently bought him a dandy slice of American justice.

The look I got in reply worried me. Had the government actually bugged the sacred attorney-client chamber? Later I learned that it was not unfounded paranoia. I watched him recoil, then was promptly informed as to why he was gun-shy.

"When it came to light that you had fled with the beloved daughter of a South Bend narcotics officer," Jerry said, "I was placed under immense pressure to assist the authorities in locating you. There was a law enforcement agenda to rescue Kim, and the government believed I was the only person who could be convinced to assist in the manhunt."

"What happened?"

"I was given two choices by the government: help find Tom and Kim or get indicted for obstruction of justice."

"What did you do?"

Jerry took a deep breath, then continued. "The thought of betraying you, my client, never crossed my mind. I spent tens of thousands of dollars in legal fees and expenses and weeks of my time resisting a federal investigation and a target grand jury subpoena. I prepared myself to be indicted and to face the prospect of incarceration," he said proudly. "And narrowly escaped indictment."

"I'm sorry," I said. "How do you feel about going to trial?"

"I wish your case was in less hostile territory, like N'Orleans, or South Florida, where large pot cases are a dime-a-dozen." Jerry cleared his throat. "Tom, to be perfectly honest with you, I am just not on good standing up there in good ol' South Bend, Indiana. You'd be better served by another attorney."

My heart sank. He was a fighter, and I didn't want to lose him.

"Don't misunderstand me," he said, "or think I'm searching for an out. On the contrary, I am itching to have at them and test their trial skills." He grasped my shoulder and gazed into my eyes.

Our time together was rapidly waning. I watched him closely, drumming my fingers nervously atop the table. He furrowed his brow, clicked his ballpoint pen and proceeded to formulate our game plan on his yellow legal pad. "We'll need local counsel up there," he sighed. "Someone connected that I can work with."

I smiled, relieved, and listened carefully to his every word. He proposed having his private investigator locate government witnesses claiming to have bought pot from me in the early 1980s. The P.I. would show pictures of me, McCarthy and others; then ask these witnesses to pick me out of the lot. Most of the snitches—lying their amoral asses off for reduced sentences—would not be able to recognize me. Each test's results would be documented. Patchen could talk with my old pals—long since paroled—and determine where they stood in 1991 on the issue of testifying in open court.

He was concerned about Bill McCarthy—currently behind bars in

Canada, where he was fighting extradition—and promised to contact his Indiana attorney, Rick Kammen, and attempt to coordinate defense strategies. Another problem was the government team waiting for my return: same judge, same persistent prosecutor, same pissed-off agents I'd served herbal tea to at the Lion's Share back in 1986 on the day they subpoenaed me. These were the mad chefs in the government's kitchen, getting that old frying pan good and hot again, with seasoned, personal grudges for their freshly captured *Unsolved Mysteries* celebrity. Then, there was the wild stepfather card.

There came a knock. The door swung open. "Five minutes more," said the guard.

"What's next?" I asked Jerry.

He told me I'd be moved very soon, either by a combination of vans and buses the BOP (Bureau of Prisons) called Diesel Therapy, which was designed to encourage defendants to break-down and cooperate; or by their ever-popular carrier line Con-Air. Upon arrival home, I'd get thrown in some hellhole local county jail that would make Seattle's look like a Holiday Inn. I would be paraded back and forth from the federal building for days, face an arraignment at which we'd plea not guilty; then attend a bond hearing where I'd be denied bond because I was a flight risk potentially facing life in prison. We would seek local counsel. Preliminary motions would be filed. Then, I'd be shipped off to Chicago and housed inside a high-rise federal facility called the Metropolitan Correctional Center. Months would pass, the feds would try to find my money and threaten me with tons of time, all while we turned down plea after plea and prepared to go to trial.

The Texan's barrel chest expanded. "It's gonna be a rough ride, son. Get mentally prepared."

"Will media coverage be a problem?" I asked.

He breathed deeper yet, then said stern-faced, "If and when an *Unsolved Mysteries* camera crew catches up with you, keep your head high and your opinions to yourself. Understand?"

I nodded, noting that the former was easy, but the latter was something I'd have to work at. "Can you meet with Kim again before your flight back to Houston?" I handed him my latest collection of crumpled love poems.

"Sure." He gathered his things.

"Funny, isn't it Jerry," I said, swallowing hard. "Here I am in a hell of a fix, caught pants down, facing major prison time, possible loss of finances...and she's the most important thing in the world to me." Moisture filled my eyes.

"She is a strong woman," he said reassuringly. "Trust me. Most of the marijuana men's wives, ones with half the man Kimberly has, are still out there waiting when all is said and done."

I fought off surging emotions, gathered my courage, and asked about a mystery which had haunted me for over two years. "What really happened to Jim and Irene, Jerry?"

Jerry jotted something on his pad, then pounded his fist on the table. "Ever since that debacle in Arizona and the senseless act of violence, Jim has never been the same." The Texan rubbed his temples and stared at the wall like a zombie.

"But what did he tell them before…"

The door swung open before I could finish my question.

"Ready, counselor?" asked the guard.

Jerry closed his briefcase and stood. We shook hands. "Stay strong. Don't talk to anyone about your case. You won't get many telephone calls en route," he added, handing me his business card and my indictment, "but catch-as-catch-can." He started for the door. "Study that document, and note the inaccuracies," he ordered over his shoulder.

I nodded. "Will do. Thanks for coming."

Senseless act of violence, I thought as my lawyer disappeared. The picture conjured up by that phrase sent a chill through me.

Back at the pod, I traded my dinner tray for some extra phone time. My first call was to Kim on Bainbridge Island. Her mother's boyfriend had flown out to drive their oversized U-Haul back home to Indiana. If they weren't being followed, they would swing by our Portland self-storage unit and salvage the treasures. Kim had sold her beloved yuppie-Volvo to Cash for Cars and would be driving Tim Barnes' black Ford pick-up packed with plants and pets back east. It promised to be a long period of separation. We wished each other safe passage, and strength.

My second call was an emotional one to Mom. I told her I'd be home soon, and not to worry. She said my capture was front-page headline news, and on the TV, too. She was saddened by my arrest and angered by some lies being put out by the press. "The whole family is behind you. And your friends..." Her voice was cracking. "You have so many friends who care. Love ya, Tommy," she said.

"Love ya, Ma," I replied.

That night I slept uneasy, thinking that negative publicity being leaked to the press by the government was a bad omen.

At four o'clock the following morning, they came for me. "Grab your bedroll, Mr. Unsolved Mystery, your limousine is on the way," quipped the guard.

Buck, the old black orderly from Arkansas who had befriended me, helped gather my things; then he, a young black rapper, and the Aryan armed bank robber accompanied me to the door. "Good luck, Dinosaur," they said, extending their closed fists.

Fuck luck, I thought, because that had always been my approach to life.

"Good luck," I said, tapping my closed fist to theirs.

"Let's go," ordered the guard.

Downstairs at the property room, I traded the county jail's jumpsuit and flip-flops for the blue jogging suit and Nike tennis shoes I was captured in. I cherished the feel of familiar clothing, recalled Kim saying she'd been sleeping in my shirts, and sought her scent in my freeman's outfit. They tossed me in the drunk tank where a puke river flowed to a rusty floor drain. I sat on cold steel in a corner. Two derelicts asked me for smokes. I shook my head, read my indictment, and waited.

The arrival of the United States Marshals' prisoner transport team was announced by rattling waist chains, clanging leg-irons, and clicking handcuffs. When they finished with me, I felt like Harry Houdini, who'd claimed to be able to escape from anything. I wondered how Harry had done it. We took the elevator down to the basement. I'd been there twice before. It was where the government's motor pool was kept, but there was not a US Marshals transport van in sight.

My two escorts donned dark shades and suspicious smiles. They straightened their ties and combed their hair. Something wasn't right. I sensed danger in the air. One guy grabbed a 12-gauge pump shotgun off a rack. The other shoved me forward from the middle of my back. The big overhead door to their high-security Bat Cave opened wide, revealing a bustling downtown Seattle street at rush hour. "Ready, Mr. Movie Star?" they asked. "Move out!"

I stumbled over a steaming sewer cap into a frosty cityscape, unaccustomed to the shackle-feet-shuffle. Confusion and fear engulfed me. According to the media, I was armed and dangerous—a regular Al Capone. Why then, were they disregarding their own security procedures? Weren't they afraid "my gang" would make a daring attempt to rescue me? I closed my eyes and envisioned Moon and his Hell's Angels friends driving over the curb in a bulletproof van, jumping out, disarming the marshals and taking me away.

"What gives?" I asked.

"Just walk," said one marshal, grinning.

"I couldn't find a decent parking spot for the van," blurted the other.

Out of the corner of my eye, I spied a slow moving vehicle edging unusually close to the sidewalk. Its passenger rolled down his window and aimed a video camera my way. A long boom microphone was extended within inches of my face. It was an *Unsolved Mysteries* camera crew, filming update footage. I held my head high and kept walking, all the while thinking about the SCUD missile that had just struck a barracks in Saudi Arabia, killing scores of American soldiers. *Why the hell was one ex-marijuana dealer's arrest such earth-shattering news?* The rebel voice in me felt like shouting: bring our troops home alive, let the oil companies fight their own damn wars! But I remembered my attorney's advice, bit my tongue, and said nothing.

They stuffed me inside a wire-windowed van beside two tattooed skinheads, and seconds later we were speeding south for Portland, Oregon on familiar Interstate 5. "What's with all the media coverage, dude?" they asked. "Yeah, what's your charge?"

"Accused marijuana dealer," I said.

They busted a gut laughing. "That ain't shit!" they shouted, bobbing their heads briskly and tugging hands that were cuffed tightly to thick waist chains. "We kill niggers," one said proudly, pointing his scarred chin at their bleeding wrists. "Even the man knows we're bad," he bragged. "That's why they make us wear these black boxes."

I studied the ebony blocks between their wrists which they wore in addition to handcuffs, taking particular notice of the sharp-edged half-moon indentations pressed against their skin and how they grimaced painfully with each attempted movement of their hands or arms. "What did you call those?" I asked.

"Black boxes, dude. High-impact ABA plastic restraints, designed to immobilize potentially dangerous prisoners li—"

"Like us," added his associate, proudly.

I nodded and leaned back against the van's window, feigning sleep. We arrived at PDX, Portland's airport, in record time. The van was waved off the main boulevard past a large electronic gate into a special section where a small army of men with guns wearing dark shades and bulletproof vests surrounded us. Soon another van appeared, then a bus.

"Da' plane! Boss, da'—plane," screamed the black-boxed skinhead beside me in a voice like the midget's from *Fantasy Island.*

"There's our ride," said his friend. "Con-Air, dude. If you're not indicted, you're not invited."

Con-Air's well-worn craft shimmied and skidded to a halt nearby. Scores of convicts streamed from the bus toward stairs at the rear of the plane, their hot breath shooting plumes into the crisp morning air. Along the way, chains were tugged and cuffs tightened by a US Marshals' receiving line. Eventually, our van unloaded and we fell in line, stumbling up steel steps like stiff, arthritic penguins.

"Piece of shit pig," said the skinhead next to me, referring to a young black fed escorting us down the aisle. "I never forget a face, Tobey."

"Yeah. And if you ever set your black foot in Idaho," added his tag-team partner, "you're gonna regret the day you signed up for this gravy job with the federal government."

We were seated three abreast, second row from the bulkhead, behind three big female prisoners. Several men jeered and made crude sexual remarks. I started feeling sorry for the women, until they turned to flash decaying smiles, as if they were enjoying the attention. A tall silver-haired man in a wrinkled captain's uniform limped up the aisle, whispered to a marshal, and lifted the green, tattered army blanket separating cabin from cockpit.

"Fuck you, Captain Gimp!" one con shouted.

"Hope your weak-ass instruments fail," added another.

"Send me a big-titted stewardess with cocktails!"

The cargo of lost souls shared a brief moment of laughter.

Seconds later we ascended; after which I kept my face glued to scratched Plexiglas, my thoughts to myself, and watched soothing cotton clouds and familiar mountains—as opposed to my murderous traveling companions inside the ratty aircraft.

Con-Air made stops at prisons in California. Passengers were herded on and off like livestock. It was a flight from hell, lasting forever. Finally, we touched down at Sky Harbor in Phoenix, which triggered flashbacks of the nearby Camelback Road incident that had done in Jim and Irene Hagar. Two buses transported us north of town to a federal correctional center nestled in the foothills. Once we were all secured inside, they removed our restraints and sent us through a maze of rooms where questions were asked, pictures taken and papers signed.

"Ever testified against anyone in a criminal investigation?" a heavy-set woman in thick glasses asked me.

"No," I said proudly.

"Any noticeable scars or tattoos?"

"Nope."

"Next!" she shouted. "Move 'em out, guys. My break was supposed to be an hour ago."

It took two male guards a good half-hour to count and document all the skinheads' tattoos, after which, I never saw them again.

At 1:00 A.M., I waited in my last line, listening to a grouchy voice on the other side of a steel cage ordering me to give him my clothing. "Tennis shoes, too! Hand 'em through the window." A grabby white latex glove shot out to take them.

I moved slowly, hating the idea of giving up my personal stuff. The second I had stripped down to my underwear, someone tossed me a pair of khaki pants and a T-shirt.

"Put 'em on! Christ's sake, we ain't got all day," shouted the guy inside the steel cage, eyeing my expensive, blue warm-up outfit. "You want this crap sent home, or donated?"

His words cut like a knife. For the first time in my life, I didn't have a home.

I pulled Jerry Patchen's business card from the waistband of my skivvies and showed it to him. "Here, send them to Houston." The latex glove handed me a piece of paper, which I read and signed. Then came another. At the top of this page was written: **Inmate #00071-522—me!** I was officially the property of the Bureau of Prisons, with an apropos, spy-like ID tag: **Triple-O-7**—close enough. No need for fugitive name games anymore. They'd given me a number, and taken away my names.

Seconds after I'd settled on the floor of a large bullpen to consume the contents of a small paper sack, the disturbing sounds of clanging chains and clicking keys returned. The marshals transport crew was back. They called us out by number. It was all new to me. They had to call 00071-522 twice. That was at 2:00 A.M.

By 4:00 A.M., we were onboard Con-Air, headed east. This time, I was seated between a greasy-headed biker wearing a blackbox, and a distinguished-looking Italian with a styled haircut similar to mine. The first hour was quiet; then a conversation began.

"Flown much?" the Italian asked in a deep and gravelly native New Yorker's voice.

I nodded. "England, Spain, Greece, Africa—"

"Great," he said with a gracious smile. "I lucked out this time around. They slipped up and let me sit next to someone sophisticated, someone else who's been around the block. I've been starving for some decent conversation, kid."

For the longest time we talked of our travels, sighing and nodding, eyes drifting into wondrous glory-days-dementia as we reminisced. We even discovered that we had both vacationed at the quaint Greek village of Lyndos on the isle of Rhodes. "Small world," he said. Eventually, he asked what I was charged with. When I told him, he laughed, too. "What are ya worried about, kid? We got a saying for guys in situations like yours. Ya won't even have to take your shoes off. You'll get a skip bit!"

"Excuse me?" I said, not recognizing the lingo.

"Ya say it's only marijuana? The shit should be legal. It's just prohibition all over again. I mean, how long can ya get?"

I described how politically conservative Indiana was, and—for the first time with anyone—expressed fear about my father-in-law influencing the agents, judge and prosecutor in my case.

"You married a cop's daughter? Boy, do you have balls!"

I shrank down into my seat, recalling the time Kim's father physically threatened my mother in our first weeks as fugitives. "My balls don't feel so big lately."

"Mmmm..." my seatmate muttered, scratching his cuffs across his chin. "On the other hand, maybe the guy will do the right thing, and call in his markers for you."

It was certainly something I intended to suggest to my wife.

"But if ya can't get a decent plea-bargain, ya know, one that preserves your integrity?"

I nodded, encouraging him to continue.

His face contorted. His shoes slapped the floor. "Then by God, fight 'em all the way, kid! That's what's wrong with this country today. We're a nation of quitters. That's why the feds get all these convictions and the military can't finish our wars."

I waited for him to unwind, then asked his name.

"Sal," he said.

"I'm Tom," I replied. Unable to shake hands, we tapped cuffs. "What are you in for, Sal? If you don't mind me asking."

"RICO, and I got a dime—ten years. Had a good legal team." He flashed a cryptic smile.

"What's a RICO?"

"Racketeering. In 1988, they changed the Organized Crime Act to RICO."

"Married, Sal? Any kids?" He nodded twice. "How's your family taking it?"

"Which one?" he replied with a wide-eyed smirk, and a pause for my reaction. "Fine. They're both taking it fine. How 'bout yours?"

"Me? I'm an independent operator," I snickered back. "Where you headed, Sal?"

"We're all going to El Reno, Oklahoma—a notorious clearinghouse for the Bureau of Prisons. But don't you worry, my friend. As bad as they want you up in South Bend, I'm certain your stay will be brief. No more than a week or two, I'd say."

"Where have they been keeping you?" I asked, wondering why a guy with a thick Brooklyn accent was coming from a West Coast location.

"Obviously, I'm from New York, ya know..." His dark eyes drifted, then narrowed. "I've been down four years now, all at a new joint in Sheridan, Oregon." He took a deep breath, then exhaled. "Only had two visits in four years. That's because the feds like to send us organized crime figures as far away from our regions as possible, so's we can't get favors from the local guards, or continue a life of crime from behind bars." He broke out laughing. The laugh became a cough. "Since the start, I fought 'em hard to get closer to home on a hardship. Finally won one," he sighed. "I'm bound for Loretta, Pennsylvania where my wife can come visit twice a month." He paused a moment, with a faraway look in his eyes.

I wondered how many thousands of miles away from the people I loved I'd be kept in the coming years, and for how long.

"What's El Reno like?" I asked.

"Ancient," he replied. "And the joint can be intimidating, if you let it. Fortunately, my people get good service there. I'll get real food, extra bedding, an occasional nip, and clothes that fit."

Big deal, I thought. For a guy who came off like a bona fide heavy hitter, how could such trivialities bring that broad smile to his face? Little did I know how much I would soon yearn for the very same things, and more.

"I got good friends there," Sal continued. "They already know I'm coming...through the grapevine. Matter of fact, Gene's awaiting my arrival." Sal cleared his throat, then glared at me. "Gene Gotti."

I nodded, instantly recognizing the Dapper Don's family name, but wasn't particularly impressed.

Sal underscored his remark. "John's brother is expecting me. He's head of the laundry there, and—"

Suddenly the plane was jolted by a blast of air turbulence. The Fasten Seatbelts sign flashed on.

"What a joke," I said.

Sal shrugged his shoulders. But the face of the greasy biker who sat on the other side of me turned white. He fidgeted in his seat, eyes closed tightly. Obviously, the big guy was afraid of crashing in chains.

Funny, I thought. A quick and fiery death didn't worry me as much as wasting my prime years in prison where my mind might turn to mush, or losing my wife.

When calm returned, Sal signaled a marshal and was escorted to the restroom.

My biker neighbor elbowed me. "That guy, Sal, is straight-up, man," he said, taking the Italian's absence as an opportunity to educate me. "I did two years with him in Sheridan. There were a lot of unsolved murders in his case." He lowered his voice to a whisper. "You might be sitting next to the guy who offed Hoffa! These guineas run most of the joints.

You should show more respect, man. This is your world now."

I cringed instinctively. There it was again, that sickening, irrational statement. This is *your* world, I thought. *It'll never be mine.*

Sal returned, and before long we landed in Oklahoma City where two buses were waiting on the tarmac to take us to the penitentiary at El Reno. En route, Sal told me what to expect. There would be hundreds of road-weary men. They'd strip us, dress us, fingerprint us, take mug shots, ask the same stupid questions; then herd us like cattle to our assigned cellblocks. Like all unsentenced inmates, I would be confined in *the hole*—a decaying segregation wing of the pen better known as Arkansas One.

As our bus lurched to a halt on a circular drive, gray dawn revealed a four-story granite and brick structure. Three giant steps led to enormous, barred-steel double doors, above which was what appeared to be the date, 1922, etched in stone. I swallowed hard. My tough-guy facade crumbled. The joint looked like Frankenstein's Castle! My eyes wandered across the way to an old brick house where a warm, inviting fire flickered through a frosty window. I imagined being an extra in an old black and white James Cagney film...*wearing zebra stripes.*

"That's the warden's place," Sal said.

We were called off the bus and ordered to stand between two tall fences topped with concertina razor wire. "Lean forward, gents," said an obese guard with a big shotgun, "and place your palms against the fence in front of you."

A hard snow started falling. One of the hacks brought Sal a parka, draped it over his shoulders, and walked away. "Sorry I couldn't get you a coat, Tom," Sal said. "But people are watching us now. You understand? I'd have to explain where we met and how long I knew ya." Snow accumulated on the sleeves of my T-shirt. "Ya got class, kid," he said. "I can tell. I wish you well. Ya want I should have a carton of Marlboros sent to your cell?"

"D-don't s-smoke," I answered, teeth tapping from the frigid air. "But in case I never see you again, thanks for the civilized conversation."

Sal nodded. "Ya never know, kid. It's a small world, especially in the BOP. Maybe we'll meet again."

Forty-five freezing minutes later, we shuffled inside. People shouted greetings, exchanged war stories and scrounged smokes. It was like some demented family reunion. Stout, tobacco-chewing Oklahoma farm boys-turned-prison-guards tossed bag lunches into our bullpens, and us hungry cons wolfed down the stale cheese sandwiches they contained. The last time I saw Sal, he was exchanging traditional salutations with some of his people, being given extra bedding, and digging into a large paper sack with McDonalds' golden arches on the side.

"00071-522! Front and center," shouted a guard.

Once again, my presence was demanded for the most degrading portion of processing. Standing stark naked in a small cubicle with a grown man who appeared to derive great pleasure from eyeing my nutsack and probing my anal cavity, made unpleasant memories of my junior high school physical seem like a cakewalk. Next, I mounted a wooden pedestal, where someone else scanned me with an electronic device.

They took me to fabled Arkansas One, tossed me in a musty cell with a plastic mat, plastic toothbrush, and a roll of sandpaper-grade toilet paper, then told me the program.

"One shower per week. No phone calls."

When my steel cell door slammed shut, furry mice scurried across cold concrete in all directions and cockroach armies rejoiced at the sight of another warm body. I found myself confined with a foul smelling, wild-eyed cellmate who grunted, covered his face with a towel and turned toward the wall beside his lower bunk. Staring through rusty bars to broken glass windows, I watched snow-snakes slither out of view down a long dark corridor. I was dog-tired, had no blanket and no desire to talk to my cellmate. I studied my surroundings, climbed onto the top bunk, tugged a tiny brass chain connected to a swinging light bulb, ran my fingers over crumbling brick mortar, felt wall carvings, and read words like *Rocky, 1937* and *Moe, '36.*

"This is not my world," I whispered, shaking my head. Unable to focus on the text of my indictment, I tried imagining I was on a primitive camping trip in the Cascade Mountains. But soon depression settled in like a thick fog bank—and with it came annihilating sleep.

July 1986, Northern California: Tim Barnes' black Ford roared away from the Mendocino Coast through ancient redwood groves, over raging rivers, and into mountainous North Central California. My best friend Todd, now Arnie, drove ahead of us. Every campground, every rest area, was filled with happy vacationers. It was a fine season for *fugin'*, and my mind—strangely at ease—meandered back to the summer of my sixteenth year, when I'd hitch-hiked throughout this country and yearned to see more.

A loud meow drowned-out the James Taylor tape we were listening to as we descended the Trinity Mountains on Highway 299 toward Redding. "The animals are roasting to death back there," Kim said, opening the window between the Ford's cab and bed. Mr. Jaggs instantly dove onto the seatback, meowing at the top of his feline lungs, which was his trademark—and precisely why Kim named him after rock-n-roll icon, Mick Jagger.

"It'll be hotter than hell down in the valley, honey," I said. "Check the map for someplace in the cooler elevations north of Redding where we can let them run. And while we're..."

My Cobra radar-detector alarm sounded. A California Highway Patrol cruiser appeared two cars behind mine in the rearview mirror. My pulse rate increased. I scanned the pavement ahead for Arnie's blue Volvo, which the feds had rendered radioactive following their Sacramento foothills chase scene. *Arnie was going too fast, and the Highway Patrol was gaining on me!* I signaled him with my brights, closed the gap between us, and resumed our pre-designated traveling formation—leaving no room for nosy troopers to see those hot Indiana plates of Todd's.

That trooper trailed me all the way to Redding, across Shasta Dam, and along the shores of the expansive blue lake of the same name. I kept one eye on my rearview mirror, and one eye on my speedometer while my mind recalled the vital statistics of my fugitive identity. Eventually he passed us, engine roaring and lights flashing, headed due north on Interstate 5.

After climbing higher still into the Shasta National Forest, Kim pointed out a roadside tourist trap which caught her eye. At Railroad Park we stopped for pet-recreation and lunch in the shadow of Castle Crags, near the town of Dunsmuir.

"Hey, Big Red," I said to my seasoned traveling companion, who waited patiently for me to free him while drooling puddles on an old blanket. "How was the ride back there with Jagger?" The instant I lowered the tailgate, the little cat shot forth like a furry gray cannon ball and scrambled beneath the nearest of many antique railroad cars comprising the restaurant there.

"Jagger! Come to momma," Kim pleaded in vain. Seconds later, she was on her knees, trying to coax her nervous pet from his hiding place.

Meanwhile, Benjamin jumped down, watered a tree and lapped up half a small creek. With Jaggs refusing to return from the dirt crawlspace beneath an old red caboose, I decided to tie Ben to a nearby shade tree while we ate lunch.

"He'll come out," Kim promised. "You know I have magical powers over animals."

"Yes dear." I couldn't argue with that.

Arnie walked over from the other side of the parking lot, and the three of us disappeared into the railroad caboose diner.

Six hours later, as the sun slipped behind sharp, craggy peaks, I tossed a rock into the stream and resumed calling that gray cat. We'd combed the grounds for hours, but Jaggs was nowhere in sight. I was concerned about the attention we were drawing to ourselves, but I would have stayed all night.

"For Christ's sake, he's just a cat," Kim hissed, showing her tough side. "We're giving up our families for this, aren't we? Get real, Tom."

And so I had a talk with the restaurant owner. Normal people would have left an address and phone number in case the family pet turned up, but not us unsettled fugitives. "We're on summer vacation from San Francisco," I told the pleasant female owner. "But I'll call you every other day from the road. Jagger is friendly," I assured her. "He's bound to show up looking for affection."

"Don't worry, Mr. Barnes," the owner said. "When Jagger returns, we'll feed him well and wait for your call."

A large turkey buzzard swooped down from the cliffs above Railroad Park and started circling. "Thank you, ma'am," I said.

Our fugitive journey continued quietly toward mighty Mount Shasta, which shimmered in alpenglow on the horizon. As we pushed on past the town of Weed and cruised down desolate Highway 97, lost-pet depression and fatigue took their toll. It had been a long day, and we had suffered our first casualty. Eventually, I flashed Arnie's blue Volvo with the brights. Enough adventure. We spent the night in our little dome tents, deep in the heart of the Klamath National Forest, minutes from the Oregon border, knocking on the door of the vast Pacific Northwest.

We broke camp early and hit the road cheerfully, but the morning's peace was instantly shattered when we rounded a curve and encountered an agricultural inspection station. Fruit checks are no cause for alarm among normal travelers, who see them serving their self-described purpose of preventing diseased fruit from entering their state; but when I saw those inspectors wearing official uniforms, my stomach knotted up. Suddenly I recalled the long-ago teachings of Tucson Tony. "Always avoid ag-checks, Tom...especially in the Southwest. They may appear harmless, but those employees are trained to look for nervous drivers, ask pointed questions, and poke inside coolers and car trunks, hoping to discover something that will get their name in a local newspaper."

It was too late to pull out of line, and not my nature to panic. All I could do was watch Arnie closely, while keeping one hand on the gearshift. A lady officer leaned into his car, reviewed his cooler's vast array of fresh fruits and juices, smiled—charmed by his graciousness—and waved him through. We followed without incident.

Oregon was beautiful and inviting. In between the border and our planned pit stop farther on, my eyes panned miles of snowmelt flooded grasslands sweeping across the valley floor to the boundary of the southern Cascades. Wildlife was abundant. The fresh air of freedom filled my chest. Gazing at the blue bowl of sky above, I felt like a sport fish who'd just shook a hook and was swimming in a sea of mirrors. But—like spawning salmon—I was a fish on a mission.

At a diner in the logging town of Klamath Falls I bought newspapers from every corner of Oregon and scanned them for pertinent information. The Central Oregon ski town of Bend was most intriguing, but acquiring new driver's licenses called for visits to the state's two biggest cities, Portland and Eugene. I planned our route accordingly.

We drove north out of Klamath Falls into Central Oregon's High Desert region, making several lengthy exploratory excursions along the way. The resort community of Sunriver had an exceptionally well-designed layout, year-round recreational activities, countless vacation rentals, and a continual influx of tourists. These advantages did not elude me.

The city of Bend, whose size and ambiance reminded me of my

hometown, Mishawaka, had enough grocery stores, restaurants, and movie theatres to keep three Hoosiers from getting cabin fever, should they choose to winter in the mountains nearby.

We took scenic Route 20 east through Sisters, and up into the high country. Kim and I read every roadside information sign like excited children. I was amazed by all the lava fields, and fascinated at how volcanic activity had shaped the region.

"Look at the way the shades of purple change behind those snowcapped peaks," my wife said, almost in awe. "And the green shadows in the valleys. I've never seen so many trees. We could get lost in darkness on this two lane highway!"

"Getting lost would do just fine," I said, trying hard to keep darkness from my mind. I had chosen the remote Northwest for fugin' rather than a major city because, by nature, I felt better with space around me. But now, as we wound down a steep grade, crossed a bridge over the McKenzie River—big radials hissing beneath our black Ford—I became eerily mesmerized by the curving, swerving waterway playing hide-n-seek in green folds of wilderness engulfing us. The river turned blue in a deep channel, and rippled golden-white where the strong current carried it over submerged rocks. I dreamed of rafting the river. There were places on it that would be dangerous. There could also be other treacherous areas for strangers to these mountains. The movie *Deliverance* came to mind.

A loaded logging truck blew by us. I tightened my wet hands' grip on the wheel, focused on the pavement, and hoped I hadn't chosen the wrong place to hide out.

In the black gulf of an Oregon night, we camped near a spring-fed tributary of the McKenzie River. This serenading creek, this trickle of clean, cold water, which slipped down a slope of the Cascades, also served as a nursery for native trout. And as these salmonids snapped at insects that evening, a passion simmered inside me second only to my sexual desire for the woman beside me with the green bandana on her head.

"Quit dreaming of fishing, Tom, and help me wrap our dinners in tin foil," Kim said.

It was the end of our second day in the great state of Oregon. We three Hoosiers cooked hobo stew in a crackling fire, watched shooting stars, speculated about the legendary *Bigfoot* said to patrol the wooded shores of local alpine lakes, and savored friendship, freedom, and love.

Eugene, Oregon's second largest city, and home to the University of Oregon, was our next stop. There were bike paths everywhere. Joggers and picnickers filled every park. We bought fresh fruit and New Age music tapes from a graying hippie couple, then scouted out mail drops and Department of Motor Vehicle branches.

"If there's 100,000 fugitives in this country, I'll bet a few dozen of them are hiding around here," I said jokingly to Lady Di and Arnie. All day we had encountered nothing but friendly faces and liberal attitudes.

As it turned out, there was more truth than humor in my remark. Among others seeking refuge in the Eugene-Corvallis area was Alice Metzinger, alias Katherine Ann Power, a '60s radical bank robber who remained on the FBI's Ten Most Wanted list longer than any other woman in American history. If I'd known about it at the time, we would have dined at the restaurant she'd opened under her new name and asked her for some advice.

Before we left Eugene, Arnie and I decided he would claim the college town for his paper trip, and Di and I would secure our Oregon IDs in Portland.

We headed north, stopping just south of the city to register at a KOA campground that accepted pets and had two good payphones. Phone calls from here to Portland were local, which was a necessity. I could not conduct my tele-research to city DMV clerks and mail drop owners, and have conversations interrupted by long distance operators asking for additional change.

"Why don't you two make a day of it tomorrow," Arnie suggested that evening, as I cooked our dinner on my Coleman stove. "I'll stay here with Ben and do some reading."

I nodded, both pleased and relieved by his offer. Kim and I had not had a day to ourselves since becoming *fuges*, and we needed one. My friend's name may have changed, but thankfully, his powers of observation remained astute.

We toured the City of Roses the following day, and fell in love with it. Cosmopolitan Portland was diverse and vibrant. Within her boundaries we discovered natural beauty, culture, fine cuisine and—amazingly enough—small-town friendliness and accessibility. We browsed the creaking floors of the biggest bookstore I'd ever seen—a terrific barn of a place called Powell's City of Books. We bought a map and strolled the streets. They were a feast for the senses. We watched street-mimes in Pioneer Courthouse Square, ate oysters in Old Town, walked the riverfront, and explored Knob Hill's restored Victorian and Georgian mansions that had been turned into a unique shopping mecca.

"This is wonderful, honey," my wife squealed in delight when she jumped into the taxi I'd just hailed. She squeezed my thigh and planted a wet kiss on my lips. "I keep thinking about the first time you showed me around San Francisco."

"Where to, buddy?" asked the cabby, catching an eyeful of heavy petting in his mirror.

"Barbur Boulevard," I answered, slipping on my wire-rimmed glasses. "The ninety-eight hundred block."

My goal was to secure a permanent suburban address for Mr. Timothy Alan Barnes; and as we ascended the hills of Southwest Portland high above the scenic Willamette River, I sensed I had chosen a winner.

"Good luck," Kim whispered when we parked beside a small white house which had been turned into an alternative mailing services business.

"Fuck luck," I said, straightening the sleeves of my sports coat. "Start thinking about what you want for dinner."

When I entered, the lady owner was on the phone giving her standard pitch to a potential customer: "And we provide each of our box renters with a front door key for twenty-four hour access to your mail and phone messages..." *Less personal contact.* I liked that. A Volvo pulled up out front and its conservative looking driver checked his mailbox. *Classy clients.* I liked that, too. The lady hung up the phone. I introduced myself, and asked to see one of her rental agreement forms.

The phone rang again.

"Excuse me, Mr. Barnes," she said politely. "The Home Office, may I help you?" she answered professionally. "No, Mr. Davis is not in. Can I take a message?"

Ten minutes later, The Home Office had a new client, and Tim Barnes had a permanent Portland address to build the balance of his identity around—9875 Barbur Boulevard, Apartment #11. I loved it. Eleven just happened to be one of my lucky roulette wheel numbers.

"What are you hungry for?" I asked Kim, upon jumping into our waiting taxi. She whispered a wet response in my ear. "Driver, can you recommend a classy downtown hotel?" Kim pinched my inner thigh. My trousers got tight. "Someplace with antique beds?"

"The Benson is what you're looking for," the cabby answered. "If you can afford it."

"Take us to the Benson," I said.

A couple of hot showers and a couple of hours later, I wrote my alias Tim Barnes a letter on the hotel stationery, then mailed it at the front desk when we checked out. "Honey," I said, "I need to explore a place called The Columbia Coin Exchange."

"Cool," she said. "I want to explore that department store we saw called Nordstroms. Remember the Japanese restaurant next door—Bush Gardens?"

I nodded and pecked her cheek. "Get us a place at their sushi bar. I'll see you in an hour."

My wife's independence was another pleasing surprise during our initial days in the Northwest. She didn't need to hang on me, and kept herself entertained by exploring the parts of the city that appealed to her.

That night, back at our KOA base camp, Kim and I shared our Portland experience with Todd. Afterwards, I reviewed Jim and Irene's recommendations for converting our Nebraska driver's licenses to our chosen state of residency. Their plan was to go to New Mexico, which like Oregon, Washington, Connecticut and Florida did not require a valid Social Security number or a fingerprint to issue a driver's license. Their first step was to get a blank apartment rental or lease agreement form from a local realtor to "look-over," type in their information, and take it to a license bureau as the document that proved their local residency. My worry, based on research, was that after turning in an old Nebraska license, as required, it could be mailed back to the state of issuance for destruction, and possibly show up as a forgery. There was no way of knowing if our Nebraska licenses had actually been registered as Smiley's ID man claimed.

"These licenses we turn in might end up in some FBI file on *fuges*," I said, "and cause them to start a follow-up investigation."

"How can we avoid that risk?" Arnie asked.

"Simple," I said. "I'm going to claim I never had a license before. I'll say I lived in San Francisco and used public transportation all my life. And now that I've relocated to the great Pacific Northwest, I'm going to need wheels. I'll show my US passport, Kansas birth certificate, and cancelled mail from my new Barbur Boulevard apartment as proof of identity and residency. I'll take the road test and act like a worried teen. You know...pop the clutch, slip off the break pedal, and parallel park like shit? I'll be polite though, and barely pass. By going this route," I closed in an animated tone akin to Dr. Frankenstein, "I will have created Timothy Alan Barnes from scratch."

"I like it," Arnie said.

Before crawling into our sleeping bags, I called Railroad Park in California to check on Mr. Jagger. He hadn't been spotted yet. It was the end of our third day on the run in Oregon, and I felt surprisingly relaxed. I studied the Oregon driver's test booklet in our dome tent by candlelight, Kim scanned fashion magazines, and a red dog snored contentedly at our feet. Arnie read *Clan of the Cave Bear*, one tent away.

I spent the next morning memorizing Oregon's road signs behind the wheel of the black Ford while listening to National Public Radio's *Morning Edition* and watching neighboring campers vacate the park. Around noon, Kim drove me to Southeast Portland's Powell Street DMV branch and parked across the road as per my instructions. I did not anticipate any problems, but as always, advised her to stay clear of danger and evacuate the scene in case I encountered any.

My San Francisco story was so convincing that while breezing through the written exam, I began to worry about how easy it was becoming for me to lie. After passing the test, I tried smooth talking my way around the next hurdle, which I had learned of during my phone research. "Is there any way I can take the driving test today?" I asked the lady in charge.

"Sorry, Mr. Barnes," she said, "but we've got two weeks worth of high school Driver Education Class graduates to wade through. We try to keep things fair at this branch."

"I can appreciate that," I said.

"Sign here please," she said, handing me a form. While she told me about bringing my own test vehicle, I almost signed Thomas—instead of Timothy—as my first name. And when she said, "Be sure whoever loans you their car provides you with proper registration and proof of insurance papers," I nearly swallowed my tongue. I hadn't figured on that. First time driver, Tim Barnes, certainly couldn't take the test in his new Ford truck with California dealers plates, and Arnie's blue Volvo—still registered to Todd Maher in South Bend—was not an option. As fate would have it, the two-week gap between Timothy's written and road tests turned out to be a blessing.

On the way back to Camp KOA, I felt compelled to call the title company in Truckee, California, and inquire about the Lion's Share transaction. "Ah, Mr. Hickey. I've been expecting your call," answered the likable, liberal British lady who had been a valued customer of my former antique store. "It's certainly been an interesting week here."

"How so?" I asked.

"I'm afraid the authorities have been sniffing around our offices making inquiries about your whereabouts and such." She cleared her throat. "They've also made some rather difficult-to-believe accusations about you and your wife..."

She said the transfer of title would be finalized in two days, and swore that, "Barring a court order freezing my assets, my special instructions concerning the transfer of funds would immediately follow." Nervous adrenaline surged through my system, but I also felt a sense of relief. For the mere fact that the sale was proceeding led me to believe I had not yet been indicted.

"Don't worry, love," the Englishwoman said proudly, "when D-Day comes round, rest assured—our title company will perform its duties!" She lowered her voice to a curious whisper. "What exactly are your plans, Mr. Lion? If you don't mind me asking."

"My wife and I are leaving the country tomorrow," I lied with ease.

"Very well, then. Mum's the word." She sighed like a mystery fan who'd just been made privy to a juicy secret. "Best of luck to you both. Keep a stiff upper lip. Bye-bye."

"Bye-bye. And thanks," I said sincerely. I suspected the feds had told her about my past and tried to sway her by claiming I was dangerous, but the former Lion's Share customer seemed sympathetic and trustworthy. Apparently, not everyone thought marijuana distributors were dangerous thugs.

Driven by the urgency of my Lion's Share gambit, I cancelled our exploration of the Northwest and initiated another game plan. We would drive to Reno where I'd withdraw some road cash from my private safety-box at The Vault. Then we'd head back to San Francisco so Kim could visit her tattoo removal surgeon for a required check-up and Todd could dump his Volvo at some Cash for Cars place, leaving no Oregon trail for the feds. We made Reno in record time.

All details were taken care of neatly. Then as promised, I booked Kim on a red-eye flight to Buffalo, one-way, under her new name, D.K. Moore. I gave her enough cash to treat her mom to a vacation in Toronto, Canada, and catch a return flight to Portland at a predetermined date. "Go on," I said, prying her hands off my three-piece business suit disguise. "Give Mom my love."

We rubbed wedding rings together and whispered, "*Shazamm.*"

Watching my wife disappear down the boarding ramp gave me goose bumps. Right in the middle of vanishing into another dimension, she was revisiting the old one. It was risky business. And even as she turned and said her last, I love you, over those broad shoulders, I wondered if I'd ever see her again.

July 24, 1986, Southern California: Thirty years earlier, to the day, I was born into a poor but decent, loving family and raised with strong moral values in a small Midwestern town where I was blessed with good friends and showered with praise for my creative endeavors. Now I was a damned fugitive-outlaw, looking over my shoulder, feeling lonely, and searching for an isolated phone booth a few miles from the beach where I had left my two best friends, Todd and Benjamin. The security I felt when my wife and friends were with me was noticeably absent on this trip.

Sweat poured from my fingertips as I dialed the Mishawaka phone number. I knew the line would be tapped and our conversation would be brief, but I needed to talk with her.

"Hello, Ma," I said.

"Tom? Is that you?" she asked, stunned.

"Yeah, Ma, it's me." Her voice sounded tense. I pictured her familiar image in the phone booth glass. "How's your health?"

"Fine. Are you okay? Where's Kim? Is she going to stick with you? You're not alone on your birthday, are—"

"Ma, Ma...don't worry about me. I can't say too much on this phone, but everything is fine. Kim and I are getting along good. We're going to leave the country tomorrow. What about your divorce?"

"Pat was here yesterday. We talked about selling the house. It's too big for me to live in by myself. I..." She paused.

She didn't sound good. The thought of her living alone after all these years worried me, but there was nothing I could do. "Has anyone talked to you?" During the ensuing silence, I pictured her biting her nails down to the bone. "Well, have they?"

"Yesterday," she mumbled.

"Who?" I asked, stomach churning.

"Kim's father. I was in the garden when he whipped into the driveway and charged through the gate, cursing. He had long hair and a beard, smelled like booze, and was driving an old Corvette. I had no idea who he was. 'Where the hell are they?' he yelled. 'Tell me!' He actually screamed at me. 'I'll have this fucking marriage annulled. I'll find them. I know plenty of powerful people who owe me favors. I have friends at Interpol! This won't last long. I'll get that son of a bitch! Your son should have never kidnapped my daughter. Tell me where they are!' I was scared, but I told him his daughter was with you because she loved you and knew you were a decent man."

My mother sobbed, nearly out of breath.

"Then what?" I asked. "What did he say to that?"

"He grabbed my shoulders and shook me. He—"

"Bastard," I said, seething. "That macho asshole. Kim's mother said he's gotten away with plenty of questionable conduct for years, and has quite a few assets for an undercover cop. When his daughter was sniffing cocaine in Tahoe and really needed him, who came to her rescue? Me, Mr. Dangerous Marijuana Man, that's who! He's embarrassed," I hissed. "His little girl chose the honest outlaw over the undercover cop, and his ego can't take it."

Someone walked past my phone booth and I strained to regain my composure.

"Did he hurt you?" I asked. "How did it end?"

"Pat pulled up in the middle of things and threatened to call the Mishawaka police. The minute her father heard that, he marched off to his hot-rod in a huff. Then he pointed his finger at me and yelled, 'I *am* the police, lady. And mark my words, I'll get even with that boy of yours!' Then he squealed his tires and sped away."

Silence followed. I heard strange crackling noises on our phone lines.

"Are you sure about Kim?" she asked.

"Yeah, Ma," I muttered. "Ma...I wish I could be there for you."

"It's okay. I have all my friends. I'll visit Billy in Alaska, Kenny in Southern California, and Judy in Baltimore. What about you? Will you *ever* come home?"

"Yeah. I'll come home when this hypocritical government offers a reasonable punishment that fits the crime." I said it loud and clear into Big Brother's electronic deaf ear. "But until then, always remember, Ma...you raised us to be survivors."

"Tommy, how will we keep in touch?"

"We will," I said, choking on the words. "We just will. They're probably tracing this call, Ma. I have to run. Love ya."

"Love ya. Be careful. Happy Birthday, son. Tell Kim I love her, too."

I hung up the payphone, hung my head, then thanked God I had work to do.

In the city of Thousand Oaks, California, on the designated day, I walked up to the counter of a coin shop wearing a blue United States Air Force jacket and said two words, "Mickey Mouse."

"Welcome to the Magic Kingdom," said the owner.

He handed me a sealed box containing fifteen pounds of gold, and I was gone.

"Where did you get those?" Arnie asked while I took inventory in our Ventura hotel room.

I smiled smugly. "When the Lion's Share sale was final, the title company carried out my orders and wired most of my equity to precious metals dealers in downtown San Francisco. Deak Perrera converted my money to one ounce Chinese Golden Panda coins and immediately shipped them to an Indiana coin shop. A man there took six Pandas—his commission—and instantly shipped the balance to an old friend's coin business in Thousand Oaks. I strolled in wearing the right outfit, said the right code word, and bingo! I just beat the feds out of another hundred grand."

"Won't the feds trace the coins to Elkhart?" Arnie asked.

I nodded. "They're probably there now. And my friend's probably already told them how Kim and I picked them up in person."

"Where do you come up with this stuff?" Arnie shook his head.

I shrugged my shoulders. "Truth is stranger than fiction, huh?"

"I guess. But if most of the money went to Deak Perrera, what happened to the rest?"

"Kim said her mom wants to open a custom lampshade business in Buffalo. I plan on helping her out. I like to see independent women go into business for themselves."

I paused to gaze out the window toward the eastern horizon.

"You miss her already, don't you?"

"Sure do," I mumbled. "Sure as hell do."

Late July 1986, San Francisco's Mission District: I was no stranger to San Francisco, but in my pre-fugitive life my haunts were the Wharf, North Beach, Union Street, and Embarcadero Square. Now I parked six blocks away from my destination on Valencia Street because I was nervous about exposing my fugitive wheels. I felt uncomfortable walking past a dilapidated housing project in a three-piece suit, but I didn't show my fear with body language to the gang kids tossing dice. The first time I came to the Greek's place, I'd wondered why he did business in such a tough neighborhood. But after my first afternoon with him, I understood. For guys like him from the old school, matching wits with street-wise hustlers was more than a game—it was their life. Buying gold, coins, and jewelry for the lowest price, and selling them at the highest price was how he scored his goals. And in order to play the game he had to have the nerve to play on inner-city turf.

I stood at the door of the Greek's place, hoping the handle on my briefcase would not break from the weight of Chinese gold. The Mission District's sidewalks were alive with panhandlers. The smell of ripening fruit from the Mexican family's stand next door to the Greek's place filled my senses. A wino bumped me and I instinctively reached for my back pocket to confirm that my wallet was there.

The Greek's coin shop was in a former bank building and had a walk-in, time released vault in back with three walls of private safety deposit boxes. Security was extensive. Video cameras were visible everywhere except at the privacy booths where safety box clients reviewed their treasures. His box business was just a smaller version of The Vault in Reno. I pushed my John Lennon glasses up to the bridge of my nose, gazed into a security camera lens, and rang the buzzer.

The Greek ruled his kingdom from behind a bulletproof shield that separated him from his clients, who were required to ring a buzzer in the entry foyer. There was a pass-through slot in the shield where clients placed their goods for the Greek's inspection. He was surrounded by display cases filled with inventory. His personal bathroom featured a glass toilet seat with gold coins embedded in it. A panic button at his feet could bring the cops to his place within minutes. No one entered the kingdom until he had screened them.

Through the shield, I saw the Greek on the phone, talking and gesturing with his hands. His curly silver hair glistened beneath the florescent lighting. His French dress shirt was unbuttoned halfway, and his sleeves were rolled up. I stared at all of the collectors edition trains, dolls, old toys and junk that he kept like trophies on the shelves around him. When he glanced at me and nodded, I nodded back. A minute later he hung up the phone and wiped his brow with a silk handkerchief.

I unbuttoned my suit coat, and pressed the buzzer again.

"Good day, sir," he said, sizing me up through the shield. "I can't recall your name, but I never forget a face. Come in, buddy."

"I told you I'd be back with my coin collection," I said.

We walked toward the rear through a second secured door where his son sat manning a computerized device resembling a prop from *Star Trek*. "What's that thing?" I asked.

"That's how we identify our box renters. Like I told you the first time you stopped in, we don't use names here, only numbers and codes which you enter yourself. Times are changing, kid. It's not the good old days anymore. In this age of greedy divorce attorneys and too much government invasion of privacy, confidentiality is important. Don't you agree?"

"I guess that's why I'm here," I answered, nodding naively.

We walked past a row of classy natural wood booths just outside the vault—private places provided for clients from policemen to politicians to fugitives, so they could sort through and fondle their sacred stashes. I noticed a pair of expensive Bally loafers exposed at the bottom of the last booth. Yeah, I liked this. It was a taste of financially secretive Switzerland in the heart of San Francisco, for two hundred bucks a year.

I followed the Greek into his vault. He slid his master key into my box. I slipped in mine.

"Here ya go, buddy. I'm going back up front," he said. "Just step into one of the booths with your father's coin collection, and take care of your business. Buzz me if you need me."

After carefully arranging my treasure, I walked to the thick glass partition separating the coin shop from the depository and paged the Greek. In the air, I detected the unmistakable aroma of moldy greenbacks wafting from one of the privacy booths.

"What should I call you, buddy?" he asked as we went back and re-entered the vault.

I placed my heavy box on a small table and flipped open the lid for a final look. "My friends call me, Tim," I replied, allowing the silver-haired gentleman's eyes to scan the upper layer of rare coins I'd recently purchased, hoping this would kill his curiosity. Below my numismatic props lay 205 hibernating Chinese Pandas who'd begun a strange journey several blocks away, only to return home to their city by the Bay.

"Where ya from, Tim?"

"Chicago, originally," I said, cautiously. "How 'bout yourself?"

"I've lived all over, Tim. I was a gunner on a battleship in World War II. Been a Californian for more years than I want to say. But I was born in the Midwest...so I know Chicago."

"Really?" I asked, breaking a sweat. "I haven't been back since my dad died, but I have plenty of fond memories, like trips to Brookfield Zoo, buying cracker balls in Chinatown, marching in the closing ceremonies parade at Riverview Amusement Park..."

I gazed at my reflection in the wall of shiny steel boxes and recalled those carefree summer days spent with Ma at Grandpa's row house on Belmont Avenue in Chicago.

"Those were the days," sighed the Greek. "Some greedy politicians let 'em tear down Riverview to build a goddamn industrial park."

"That's sad, " I said, sliding my box into its slot. "Where did you say you were born?"

"South Bend. South Bend, Indiana. Ever heard of it?"

Heard of it! I nodded nonchalantly, but nearly shit my pants. "Isn't

Notre Dame University there?"

"That's the place. I used to sell hot dogs at the stadium on game day when I was a kid. They had the Four Horsemen then, and the Gipper," he sighed nostalgically. "Are you a Notre Dame fan, Tim?"

"Grandpa got me hooked early. I'll always be a Fightin' Irish fan." Nervously I remembered all the exciting N.D. home games Todd and I had attended on those crisp autumn Indiana afternoons... *Todd!* I stared at the Greek's platinum Rolex and realized I was late for my rendezvous with Arnie.

"You know, Tim," he said, resting one hand on my shoulder, "grading is everything in the numismatics field. One guy sells you an MS-65 Shield nickel for five grand, ten years later some shoe clerk convinces you it's only MS-63, and you lose thousands of dollars. Know much about grading, Tim?"

"A little," I said, suddenly anxious to get on my way. "My dad was teaching me before he died."

"How about taking some lessons from me? I do appraisals for insurance companies, and I'm a licensed coin grader. Maybe we could look over your collection next time you stop in. You don't strike me as the type to turn down a chance to gain some knowledge." He suggested it with a twinkle in his eye. "My wife and I appreciate good company. I'll cook you a real Greek meal with choice tender lamb and retsina wine. Whatta ya say, Tim?"

What could I say? How much exposure should I risk so soon—especially in San Francisco? I was wary of him, and knew how the coin game was played. Was he the kindly, curly silver-haired professor he appeared to be, sincerely seeking a student? Or some con man smelling a mark? I had, after all, embarked upon a quest for unique knowledge, and the coincidence of his being born in South Bend of all places, could be considered an omen. "Yes, I'd like that," I said, deciding to trust my instincts and continue cultivating a friendship with the Greek. "But I've got to run. Time's up on my parking meter and my old Irish setter's probably roasting in the back of my truck."

"I understand," he said with a firm handshake. "Next time, you can park in my private lot, even bring your dog in if you like. Take care, Tim. And be careful out there...driving."

Something about the Greek bothered me. I couldn't quite put my finger on it, but for the first half of my drive across the city I kept picturing the old man opening my box with an extra key and handling my gold and coins. I hadn't eaten all morning though, so I wrote off my paranoia as part of the normal hypoglycemic mania such neglect induced.

As my frustration with finding a parking spot near the waterfront grew, a new concern came to mind. My relationship with Todd since moving from Indiana and getting married needed to be refreshed. Todd wasn't just an acquaintance. He was my best friend and confidant, and had been for quite a while.

During my junior year I fancied myself a part-time hustler at games like pinball, air hockey, and pool. Todd's father had leased the vacant building that once housed the legendary Klines Drugstore and its '50s-era soda fountain, and opened a controversial pool and pinball palace across from Mishawaka High School called *The Cave.* His capable son Todd was put in charge. And there—after battling to numerous draws that never failed to impress promiscuous young girls—we earned each other's respect and became friends.

We were perhaps the only players who did not curse and smoke cigarettes in The Cave. Instead, we practiced improv-humor skits, discussed politics and poetry, and smoked weed when the doors were locked and the day was done. Todd read all my early creative writings and became a trusted critic. He got his personal stash from me, and eventually—long after The Cave was closed—employment as a marijuana driver.

Presently, the ringing bells and slapping flipper buttons echoing inside a game room at Fisherman's Wharf were music to my ears. In the late '60s and early '70s, I spent my share of adolescent nights beneath the neon lights of neighborhood pool halls and closed down arcades in local shopping malls en route to becoming a pinball wizard called *Tommy.* It was, in fact, our mutual love of games that brought Todd and me together back in 1973.

"Arnie!" I yelled in the direction of a noisy machine he was dominating. His young multi-ethnic San Francisco audience glared at me in my businessman's disguise, like I was some alien.

Arnie roughed an Asian kid's hair and gave his free games away.

Outside on the sidewalk the biggest kid with the receding hairline said, "It's about time you showed up. I was getting worried."

"Yeah, I could see," I quipped.

At our next stop, a car lot on the outskirts of Sacramento, Arnie bought a compact pick-up truck, employing the knowledge I'd learned when purchasing Tim Barnes' black Ford. Arnie had craved another Volvo, but heeded my warning when I said, "A Volvo is part of your profile now, and *exactly* what the feds will be looking for."

We raced north in two trucks with California dealer's plates, stopping only once in the Golden State to check on Jagger the cat. After finding Railroad Park's restaurant closed, we pushed on past midnight, eventually pitching our tents beside the Rogue River near Grants Pass, Oregon.

In the following days Todd and I renewed our friendship while simultaneously experiencing both great joy and rejuvenation of spirit as we journeyed together on the Oregon Trail. We spoke honestly about our legal concerns and laughed at ourselves for having ever feared the theory of wives coming between male relationships, oftentimes destroying them. "Only when those friendships were weak from the start," I told my friend with a handshake and a wink.

The Three Sisters Wilderness Area, with its desirable high desert climate and the renowned Deschutes River brought thousands of summer tourists to raft, hike and fish in Central Oregon. But there was also a mountain called Bachelor, and when summer died and autumn faded, skiers flocked to the coveted, fluffy, dry-powder-snow—rare in the wet Pacific Northwest. Mount Bachelor was what brought me to Bend. Just as Lake Tahoe had helped to season Jim and Irene, I figured we three Hoosiers would blend well as ski bums wintering here, get our bearings, and perfect the art of being *fuges.*

My house-hunting mission called for a short-term vacation rental with a phone, where my inquiries to classified ads could be returned. I located a townhouse in Bend whose owner, Elroy Prosh, lived on the coast and asked few questions. "My wife and I and her cousin Johnny drove up from California looking for real estate," I explained.

"That's nice," Elroy said with a twang. He cleared his throat. "I'm going through a rather ugly divorce. Would you mind paying me in cash?"

"No problem," I said. "No problem at all, sir. I'll stop by the bank today."

In between nature hikes, dog walks, tennis matches, and golf lessons with Arnie, I searched diligently for the ideal long-term rental house. I knew precisely what our situation required, and when the Sunday paper hit the stands, I left well thought-out messages on selected advertisers' answering machines. The timing was right. The dog days of August were at hand, and summer rental season would soon end. The following nights while Arnie, Ben and I watched old *M*A*S*H** reruns, responses from curious landlords slowly trickled in. Problem was, most of them wanted references, or did not allow pets.

But I had an answer for that.

I was feeling a little low from missing my mate as I stood in a phone booth punching the numbers to my Reno answering service. The Deschutes River rambled within sight and I'd much rather have been fishing in it, but had promised the other fuges I'd check in. I also had to be certain my rental references idea would work.

"The Postal Depot, may I help you?" asked the cheery female voice.

"This is Mr. J.P. Simms," I said. "Do I have any mail or messages?"

"One moment please." She ruffled through notes, then read my messages verbatim, "Number one; Call Mr. Fisher about the paperwork..."

Quickly I flipped through the phonebook to find out where the area code Bill McCarthy had left was located. It was a Connecticut number with no extension, and no set time to call. That meant he was at a vacation rental, like us.

"Number two; Darryl and Lizzy called three days ago. Wondered how things were going. Sent Fish his tickets. Call our service if you want to talk. God bless you, guy."

Christ, I thought, couldn't they leave normal messages? Thank God they were phoning my disposable Simms answering service. I sure as hell didn't want to expose Tim Barnes' new Portland address to such suspicious calls. This poor girl probably thought I was a terrorist or something. "Is that all?" I asked her.

"No, sir. There's one more. A *Lady Di* called. She left her hotel number not more than an hour ago."

I couldn't hang up quick enough. Seconds later, I nervously slipped quarters in the coin slot, recalling that old saying again, 'If you set something you love free, and it comes back to you…'

Her mom, Donna, answered the phone in their Toronto hotel room.

"Tom!" Donna exclaimed in an animated tone. "Oh, my. This is so exciting. She showed up at my door in the middle of the night, then we—"

"Motho…please," a familiar voice pleaded in the background.

"She's right here, Tom," Donna said, surrendering the receiver.

"Hi, honey," Kim said in a highly-accentuated, sultry, wanton whisper. "*Motho* and I are having a great time, but I miss you—all of you!"

"Even my sick sense of humor?"

"Yes, even your irritating sense of humor. Are you ready for *me* yet?" she cooed.

My heart fluttered against its ribbed cage. "I, I miss you too," I stammered. "More than I can say in words." We talked for fifteen minutes. My wife told me about her Toronto shopping spree.

"Lots of leather, and lacy lingerie," she assured me. "*Motho* is so supportive. She says I have a healthy glow on my face."

The two women giggled for a moment.

"Does she know our plans, or where I'm calling from?"

"No way," Kim said. "She only knows I'm safe and happy with my outlaw hubby. *Right, Motho?* Any interesting developments out there?"

I decided not to mention her dad's incident with my mom. Instead, I told her about house hunting, and we reviewed the plans for our Portland rendezvous. I didn't talk about Jagger the cat, nor did she ask. We said our *I love you's,* and I left that steamed-up phone booth feeling lighter than air. An hour later, I sent two dozen peach-toned gladioli, our wedding color, to the Toronto hotel room of Ms. D.K. Moore.

Two days later, Arnie and I left Bend, drove the northern route across Central Oregon's high desert, toured Mount Hood and the Columbia River Gorge, then got a cheap motel room on the Southeast end of Portland. Early the next morning, Timothy Alan Barnes took his first ever driver's road test in J.P. Morgan's shiny new truck. Mr. Morgan served as my licensed driver chaperone, and showed his fake Allstate insurance card to cover that requirement. Tim Barnes appeared nervous, acted nerdish, and drove Morgan's truck herky-jerky, but he was polite, and so the friendly female inspector passed him.

I exited Portland's Powell Street DMV branch with a broad smile and a brand new, real, clean, Oregon operator's license. From that day on, I no longer had to worry about whether the Nebraska license from my original ID packet was registered, or if information on me was being held in someone's blackmail files. Tim Barnes Nebraska license would only be used for mail drops and hotel room registrations.

"To our man, Barnes!" I told Arnie at dinner as we clicked our longneck Rainier Beer bottles. "May his identity pyramid be complete."

"Live long and prosper," Arnie proclaimed, giving me the Vulcan hand sign.

After the first beer, I broke to the payphone for yet another call to Northern California.

"Railroad Park Restaurant," answered the woman owner. "How can I help you?"

"I'm calling about that lost gray cat," I said.

"Yes, Mr. Barnes. Jagger showed up two days ago. He's charming," she sighed, "just as you said. Matter-of-fact, we're already growing attached to him. Where are you now, and what do you intend to do?"

Decision time. It was seven o'clock in the evening, and Kim's plane was due the following morning. Railroad Park was a six-hour drive. I returned to the table, pushed away my second beer, and told Arnie, "There's two days left on our Bend townhouse rental. Please take Benjamin and go back there. I'll call you early morning or late evening tomorrow if there's a problem. If you don't hear from me in two days, hit the road and call Smiley's pager and my Reno service."

All that night I wondered if any Wanted posters on me had been circulated in California yet.

I slept soundly in the black Ford's cab alongside the banks of the soothing Columbia River, within sight of Portland International Airport, gray cat purring on my lap. My alarm clock beeped on the dashboard. Big planes soaring overhead slowly came into focus. Anticipation built inside me. I spotted a jumbo jet with United Airlines' colors descending against the glacial backdrop of Mount Hood.

Touch down. Time for action.

Fifteen minutes later, I drove through the passenger pickup area. It was crowded. The Red Lion Hotel courtesy shuttle bus was crammed with business travelers, but none had the broad shoulders and long blond hair I sought. A car honked behind me. A cop waved me on. The black Ford raced ahead of the bus to the Lloyd Center Red Lion. The plot thickened. I had reserved Kim a room there under the name, D.K. Moore. The shuttle arrived. My heart raced faster. The last passenger off the bus wore a fancy hat and filled a floral sundress like a model...*like my soulmate.*

She was flawless, never once scanning the lot for me. I watched with admiration as she snapped at the short bellboy who'd been staring at her perfect ass. Then she lugged her own luggage inside to the Red Lion's lobby—my sign to depart to our real rendezvous point.

On the northern end of town in the lot of the Delta Inn, I listened to National Public Radio, pretended to read *The Oregonian* and petted Jaggs the cat. Each time a car pulled in, I peered through the pinhole I'd made in the newspaper. Soon a taxi stopped under the canopy and I caught a glimpse of that sundress again. And still, I watched and waited like a hungry lion, heart pounding, adrenaline pumping, a million and one emotions flooding my logical mind. Her wild father's words to my mother echoed in my brain. "I'll get even with that boy."

Don't move too fast.

Slowly, cautiously, I drove around the perimeter of the parking lot, looking for suspicious cars. I pulled up to the hotel's back door as it swung open...*bingo!* She emerged, her surprisingly short-cut golden hair glowing in the bright sunshine, and a broad smile beaming my way. I wrapped my arms around her slender waist, and grew weak in the knees, intoxicated by her scent. We kissed. I tossed her bags in back, and we bugged out like two impassioned teens skipping school, intent on losing their virginity together.

I drove fast and far. We held hands so tight that our knuckles got white, and just when I'd parked in the lot of the Columbia Gorge Hotel, my wife heard clawing on the sliding glass window behind her long swan's neck. "Jagger!" she shouted, showing rare emotion, then shedding even rarer tears.

That picture was worth a million bucks.

And the next twelve hours were priceless——*shazamm*!

§

February 1991, El Reno, Oklahoma's Federal Penitentiary: The wife and I are consumed by the sweet, burning fire of sensual desire—the carnal embrace. Bone-to-bone, face-to-face, harder, faster we race toward the goal of consummation. Fingers interlocking, an antique bed rocking, eyes rolling back, back...a shuddering sensation. My head spins, the room goes black. Her warm, quick breath blows across my chest as I stroke her liquid gold hair and stare beyond to where a blue bird appears and squawks out a warning: "He's coming! Fly!"

Anew, I break into a sweat. The metal bed is wet. My stomach is sticky. I hear voices...strange voices. "Nothing lasts forever. Life is full of choices."

My wife pulls away from our union. She rises off the bed, shaking her head. She cries. She waves goodbye with sad brown eyes. The little blue bird flies to my fingertip, a tiny tear forms and rolls down its beak. My soul mate passes through solid steel bars, blows me a kiss, and disappears in a fine white mist. Then the blue bird flew, and my happiness, too.

I feel myself falling hard and fast, as if having been body slammed. I see the haggard face of my cancer-stricken father for a fleeting moment. His hand reaches out for mine, then he fades away into a long, dark, dank corridor.

"No! Don't leave! Stop. I'd rather die than—"

"Wake-up, dude!" my cellmate shouted, shaking me. "You already slept through lunch and dinner. I had to eat your fucking swill," he added with a sick laugh. "And while you're up there fucking some damn dream cunt, you're missing the real show."

Dream cunt, huh? You're talking about my wife, you greasy punk. I fought a primitive urge to pounce on him. I sized him up as he sidestepped away, grabbed the bars, and stretched his tattooed neck toward the corner of our cage to get a glimpse of something. I noticed the matching suicide scars on his bony wrists, and relaxed my fists. An overpowering odor of defecation slapped my face and brought me back to this Godforsaken place in the middle of a cold winter's night. Fight or flight? Prison guards were everywhere. I felt impotent.

"What are you staring at, goofy?" a big guard blurted at my cellie.

"Mind your own business," another guard ordered, glaring our way.

"Hey, Joey, get a body bag," the big turnkey said, spitting chew down the hall. "We got us a stiff." The face of the young hack beside him lost all color; then his muscular arms went limp.

Later we heard through the grapevine there had been a suicide hanging just three cells down the range that night in El Reno's infamous Arkansas One cellblock. The men in the block said he was a young black crack kid, like the ones I encountered in Seattle's county jail. A nonviolent first-time offender, like me. Couldn't stand the pressure. Took the ultimate paper trip—escape from judicial overkill. One less mouth for "tough-on-crime" politicians, and their Christian Coalition constituency to bitch about feeding.

A hanging in El Reno just three sliding steel doors away from mine produced what I believed was my only out-of-body experience. I hoped, I prayed, these were not omens. Regardless, one thing was certain. My wife and I were separated now. I was in this alone, and even *shazamm* might not save us. "I" was in prison. It was slowly sinking into my psyche. Prison. Real prison, with bad people on both sides of the bars. It was viciously depressing, and I was lonelier than I had ever been before.

"But you are a Leo," I whispered to myself, "rich with memories. Wrap yourself in their warmth to ward off depression. This is not your world. This is not *my* world. This is not happening...to me."

But it was happening. Like anyone who broke the law and got caught, I was falling into another dimension. The book on my life was about to take another turn, from rags, to riches, back to rags. I knew I was facing great loss, but had no idea how hard and fast my fall would be. Surprisingly, in those initial days and nights of confinement, this uncertainty became my biggest tormentor. From the very beginning of my journey, I tried to analyze what was happening.

The mental disruption caused by imprisonment, and more especially by solitary confinement, has come to be known as sensory deprivation. During waking hours, the brain only functioned efficiently if perpetual stimuli from the external world were received. My strong relationship with the environment and my understanding of it depended upon the information I gained from my senses. In El Reno's notorious Arkansas One cell block, the stench of urine and mold and the visually depressive surroundings caused me to employ a defensive strategy: sleeping sixteen to eighteen hours a day.

Only in sleep were my perceptions of the gloomy external world reduced. Only in sleep could I enter the fantastic world of my dreams, a world governed by my previous experience, my wishes, my fears, and my hopes. Inevitably, these dreams always led me back to the surrealistic fugitive life with my lovely wife, in the woods of the Pacific Northwest. And for many days, I lived in this dream world.

The FBI was putting the heat on Hickey's attorney. Special Agent Hanis, a friend of Kim's father, was in charge of the investigation.

FD-302 (REV. 3-10-82)

6.

FEDERAL BUREAU OF INVESTIGATION

1

Date of transcription 8/20/86

DAVID SMITH, Manager, RAMADA INN, 52890 U.S. 33 North, South Bend, Indiana, telephone number 272-5220, was served with an administrative subpoena on August 11, 1986, for all records pertaining to the stay of a JERRY D. PATCHEN at the RAMADA INN between March 1986, and June 1986. SMITH then made available a duplicate of a RAMADA INN registration receipt indicating that JERRY PATCHEN, 1400 Congress Street, Houston, Texas, 77002, was registered in Room 183 at their hotel on March 12, 1986. Their records reveal that PATCHEN stayed overnight and paid for it with American Express Credit Card number 372881793911002-1. SMITH advised that during the overnight stay of PATCHEN, he placed four long distance telephone calls; however, the area code of the call was not recorded. The long distance telephone calls were placed to the following numbers:

973-7650
526-0621
222-2000
973-7650

SMITH advised that PATCHEN checked out of the motel on March 13, 1986, and his total bill came to $70.12. SMITH advised that Room 185 adjoins Room 183 but without a name, the records would have to be hand searched to determine the occupant of that room on March 12, 1986.

Investigation on 8/11/86 at South Bend, Indiana File # IP 12F-409

by SA ROBERT J. HANIS -mjk Date dictated 8/14/86

7

The Octagon

August1986, Central Oregon: A fugitive's home is like a vampire's coffin—not only a sanctuary, but also a place of great vulnerability—for if a trail leads the hunters here, a stake through the heart will surely follow. Or so I thought as a freshman fugitive in the summer of 1986. Accordingly, I had narrowed my short list down to the rural areas near Sunriver Resort, feeling we were not yet ready for community living, and should settle on the fringe of civilization and tap its amenities from our tranquil, magnificent isolation. Moving from vacation rental to vacation rental with Arnie and our pets was not a palatable solution. I wanted a place where we could settle in for the winter, and had promised such quasi-normality to both Arnie and my wife.

"What makes you so sure this is the one?" Kim asked as I turned off hot pavement into a maze of dirt and gravel roads.

"I just have a feeling," I said, watching red clouds of dust rise off the road behind us. "The lady lives in Seattle, far enough away to eliminate surprise visits. She's coming down tomorrow to interview renters, and if it's anything like she says, we'll be first in line."

"If it's anything like she said, other people will want it, and we'll be—"

"We'll be the ones she picks. Trust me, my wild Hungarian gypsy," I said, gently pinching her thigh.

"There's our turn, Solar Drive," Kim said excitedly.

I set the odometer and slowed to a crawl. Five tenths of a mile later, we parked the Ford beside a locked gate and slipped beneath it.

"What if this isn't the place?" Kim quizzed, as we tiptoed down a long shady lane. "We could be trespassing. We could be—"

"Shhh! Listen." I inhaled the invigorating scent of pine. A breeze roared through the tunnel of limbs above us, then died. We walked further, and heard a river flowing. A duck quacked, then took flight from some tall green reeds below. "Look," I said, pointing to an octagonal building nestled in the trees. "This is the place. Let's take a peak through the windows."

It was an eight-sided, two-bedroom, rustic house with a big bathroom and a modern kitchen featuring plenty of cabinet space. In the center of the living room sat a circular metal fireplace. Outside, on the huge wrap around deck, was an empty Jacuzzi. Fifty feet from the house was an old woodshed, an ideal place to hide IDs and cash. Rickety redwood stairs led down to an overgrown riverside landing where two marmots scavenging for food stood attentively returning our gaze. Fish broke water up around the bend. A bald eagle soared overhead. It was like a live scene from *National Geographic*. But best of all, there was a small studio apartment situated above the garage, right behind *The Octagon.*

"Arnie's new home," I said, raising my eyebrows in that direction. "Now, maybe we can get back to the honeymoon. Right, Meekla?"

"Maybe," she sighed, unable to contain her elation. Her brown eyes—showing specs of mood-induced gold—scanned the grounds. "And maybe you'll get lucky this afternoon in the back of the truck."

"Maybe *you'll* get lucky," I laughed, taking her into my arms.

That night, at our Twin Lakes campsite southwest of Bend where we had relocated when our townhouse expired, Kim and I rehearsed our lines for the coming morning's charade. We wanted that house badly, and long after she had gone to sleep with a gray cat purring on her chest, I stared up through our tent screen at a million stars, hoping we could make it happen.

The short white-haired woman stood on the deck of the Octagon, elbows resting on the rail, watching the driveway like a hawk. She observed the freshly washed Ford truck bearing California plates, and nodded approvingly. She ogled the two young lovers coming toward her—dressed in matching Lake Tahoe T-shirts, hands clasped tightly, genuine newlywed glow radiating from us—dropped her arms to her sides, and smiled.

We were given a friendly, thorough tour. "My son bought this place so he could ski Mount Bachelor, but he got bored and moved down south," Marguerite Shell explained at the conclusion.

"Where to?" my wife asked, making conversation.

Marguerite cleared her throat. "The Caribbean. Kenneth has a sailboat there that he charters out."

"How nice," Kim said.

Oh boy! What if her kid's a Caribbean smuggler, I thought, and this house has a bad history? At least he's not a cop.

"So then, you're thinking of relocating from California?" Mrs. Shell asked. "If I decide to rent to you, can you give me any references?"

I handed her a business card that read: J.P. Simms, Property Management Specialist, Reno, Nevada. "As I told you earlier, Mrs. Shell, my father left me several commercial buildings in San Francisco. Do you know the city?"

She shook her head. "Been there once or twice, though."

I nodded, relieved. "Simms is a busy man, always on the run, but leave a message on his answering service, and he'll get right back to you. Feel free to ask any questions you need to about my income." I placed my palms upon the deck rail, watched the Deschutes River flow, and went into a trance.

Mrs. Diane Barnes took her cue. "Money is not Tim's problem, Marguerite. You see, after his dad's death, the family doctor advised him to get away from San Francisco for awhile."

I hung my head lower.

Lady Di continued. "We both hate crowds and love to snow ski."

"I see," said Marguerite. "Well, Bachelor is certainly the place to be."

When I told her about Benjamin, she frowned. "I'm a cat lover," she said. "The last couple who rented here had a Doberman. I don't like dogs. They're destructive," she hissed.

We heard a frightened mewing. I saw a saucer of milk beside the door and serious lines of concern on the old woman's face. The snow-white kitten clinging to a branch above the deck mewed again. Kim and I exchanged glances. I climbed the tree. "Come here, *Whitey*," I coaxed.

"Those irresponsible people left the poor thing behind," Marguerite exclaimed, misty eyed, when I placed the purring creature in her arms.

I made her an offer. We'd adopt her orphan kitten if she'd allow my Irish setter, Jaggs the cat, and Diane's cousin, Johnny. Mrs. Shell wanted to get back home to Seattle. My money was the right color. I plunked down a thousand bucks for first and last month's rent, and added two-fifty for a doggy deposit. "I'm good with a hammer, too," I said. "I'll fix these loose boards and help Johnny finish the studio apartment over the garage. Might even get that hot tub working again."

"Sign here," she said, smiling ear-to-ear. "Do you have furniture and dishes?"

"Oh, yes," Lady Di replied, rocking on her heels. "Tim's dad was quite an antique collector. We can get our things and be back in... *Tim?*"

"Three days, honey," I said. "Three days."

"I'll stay here with Kitty until you return from California," Marguerite said. "And if you leave me your Social Security number, I'll switch the utilities over for you, too."

Time to test Tim Barnes' identity in the system, I thought, showing her my Social Security card. "Thanks," I said. "See you in three days. You won't be sorry you chose us, Mrs. Shell. Goodbye, Whitey-Whitey-Whitey," I whispered affectionately to our new fuge family member.

Like most landlords, she never checked my references. But if she had decided to, Arnie or Smiley Jim Hagar would have been enlisted to return her call and assume the role of my property manager, Mr. Simms. I wished my legal problems could be handled so easily.

Two days later in Reno, Nevada: While packing our U-Haul trailer with familiar furnishings—like Grandma Daisy's spoon carved oak dresser—and securing our ten speeds to the bike rack on the Ford's front bumper, I felt extremely uncomfortable about being in Reno, so near to Truckee. I decided to grab plenty of cash from The Vault, make no more southern visits until after Christmas, and move my stored items to Oregon. The last thing I did in Nevada was acquire $300 in quarters from the Peppermill Casino.

"Good luck, sir," said the cashier.

Fuck luck, I thought, tossing the payphone feed into my leather satchel.

From the Donner Pass tourist information center on Interstate 80, I phoned Smiley's pager and punched in my location codes. While waiting the customary fifteen minutes for his return call, I called Bill McCarthy's Connecticut vacation rental.

"It's about time," Bill answered, sounding irritable. A baby was crying in the background. "Where the hell are you?"

"San Diego," I said. "Just rented a beachfront condo for the winter."

"Don't suppose you want our company," he said. After a brief silence, he told me they had acquired Connecticut driver's licenses by employing Smiley's technique of turning in their Nebraska licenses, and were headed to Florida. "It's familiar territory," he explained. "Sandy beaches and warm seas ought to help us feel relaxed."

"Uh, huh—sounds good." Arrogant bastard, I thought. Spend years working pot loads in Florida, and now you want to be a fugitive there? Clever, Sherlock, but decidedly better than testifying against me at a grand jury. I was tempted to give him my Exiles go to Siberia, not Disney World sermon. Instead I gave him a new biweekly check-in schedule for my disposable Simms' answering service, and brought up the subject of the fifty grand he owed me.

"I wasn't able to sell our rental properties," Bill mumbled. "The feds will probably seize them anyway."

"What? I managed to sell my store in four months, and you couldn't—"

"Listen, Leigh wants to talk to you. Why don't we wait until we get together in person, then go over the math and settle up? You act like I'm gonna rip you off or something."

Sooner or later we would have to meet, and something in his voice told me it wasn't going to be pleasant. "Sure, put her on," I replied.

"Hello, stranger," Leigh said, sounding uncharacteristically sheepish. "What do I call you?"

"How about Tom...*Lerta*," I said, referring to her by an old pet name. It was good to hear the voice of my former lover even though she sounded sad. She told me how strange taking the paper trip felt, and repeated Bill's request to get together. "Trust me, it's better this way for now," I said. "Next time you and Kim can talk. Okay? I'm running low on quarters, *Lerta*. Sorry. Gotta go. Take care."

I held the receiver in my hand, fondly remembering my years with Leigh. How many hours I'd spent staring at her long dark hair and gentle features in high school classrooms. All the Sundays we'd walked home from her family's church hand in hand, the day we moved in together, and the day I read the eulogy at her father's funeral. She was a decent, kind-hearted lady, undeserving of any images the word fugitive conjured up.

The second I put down the payphone, it rang. "Barnes residence," I said.

"Hey, guy! What's the word?" asked Smiley Jim Hagar.

"Just talked to the Fisher family. They accomplished step number one, and are moving to Florida. Spoke with my English antique dealer friend last week. He's going to France, and will send my parents postcards to Indiana from there so the feds will think I'm in Europe. What's new with you?"

"The wife and I rented a little farm near Durango in southwestern Colorado, and we're waiting for the harvest season. There's an outrageous ski resort twenty minutes away called Purgatory, and plenty of good trout fishing, too. Had enough Pacific Northwest rain?"

"No. Matter of fact, we found some sunshine." I told him about the Octagon, and my driver's license success. He bet me I'd be ready for Arizona by spring. "Anything is possible," I said.

"Got a home phone number for me?"

"Nope. Don't plan on getting one for awhile, either," I said.

"You will, when you settle down. Want mine?"

"Sure. Shoot." While scribbling down the number, some guy in a dark suit grabbed the phone next to me. He was probably just a San Francisco businessman, but his attire made me squirm.

"Maybe we can get together for Christmas," Smiley said.

"Sounds good to me. I have to run though. I'll give you a call. Goodbye."

Suddenly I felt paranoid. I bought a *USA Today* newspaper, headed back to the Ford, and hurriedly filled in the crossword puzzle in the purple *Life* section with a series of strange letters.

"How's everyone doing?" Kim asked.

"Fine. Bill and Leigh are moving to Florida. Jim and Irene found a house in Colorado, and want to get together for Christmas." I circled a couple of environmental articles with a magic marker, then asked Kim to address a manila envelope to my younger brother, Bill, who worked for the Environmental Protection Agency. "Put this down for the return address." I showed her the information on my brother's former college roommate. "I don't want my handwriting to stand out if they're watching his mail."

"What do all those letters in the crossword puzzle stand for? What's this all about?"

"It's a code I showed my brother when he came to our wedding. It's going to be risky to call my mom, so I'm setting up a call with Bill around Thanksgiving. Those letters stand for numbers. He'll know what to do."

We coasted down from the High Sierras and stopped in San Francisco, where I introduced Lady Di to the Greek over dinner. We spent the night at his place, and in the morning he and I strolled a couple of miles of sidewalks together.

"My son is seeing a nice Greek girl from Chicago," he said. "They might get married. He might move there." The Greek slid his thumbs under his suspenders and took a deep breath. "If he does, would you consider working with me?"

I stopped in my tracks and nearly swallowed my tongue.

"I've got a good feeling about you, Tim. You have an eye for coins. I could see that last night. And your wife, Diana! *Morea*, where did you find such a fair-skinned goddess?"

"She's good in the kitchen, too," I snickered, straining to ascertain if his flattery was sincere or masking a hornet's stinger. "Say, what does *Morea* mean anyway?"

"Friend," he answered, extending his hand.

"Listen, we're looking at real estate up north, and we're going to spend the winter there skiing." I scratched my chin as an idea formed in my head. "We're basically country people. We've got pets and like to garden. Diane doesn't feel comfortable in big cities with all the crime and traffic, but I might consider your offer come spring. I'm your friend, right? We'll definitely keep in touch."

When September arrived in Central Oregon, summer people re turned to their city homes again, and we three Hoosiers settled into our routines at the Octagon compound. Arnie golfed every course within a hundred and fifty-mile radius, battled me twice a week on Sunriver's deserted tennis courts, and helped repair all those rickety deck boards. Nights, after dinner, he'd disappear to his studio above the garage to watch classic black and white movies on his new VCR. Old Ben and Mr. Jaggs adopted Marguerite's white kitten, which we quickly fattened up on fish fillets. Kim bought a dozen cookbooks, and set her sights on becoming a gourmet chef—with Arnie and me for guinea pigs. I turned into an exercise fiend, rowing, jogging and chopping firewood five mornings a week. On football Saturdays, we'd make the pilgimage to the local sports bar to cheer for Notre Dame's Fighting Irish. On Sundays, Kim served brunch on the deck, where we all admired Mother Nature's beauty and listened to Garrison Keeler's *A Prairie Home Companion* on our Bend public radio station. Our reality was not the picture being portrayed on Indiana's weekly *Crime Stoppers* TV spot. We were one happy, woodsy fuge family, for which staying busy was the key.

Kim and I fished and canoed every lake, river and stream in the area. On one outing to Crane Prairie Reservoir and osprey preserve, she landed the biggest brown trout I'd ever seen. Another day after reminiscing about South Bend's annual 4-H Fair, we drove to Redmond and took in the Deschutes County Fair where we discovered that lovable, pet-able llamas were the stars of the livestock pavilion—as opposed to pigs and cattle back home. I won her a stuffed raccoon on the rifle range, and she started a new hobby, collecting and cultivating African violets, after a substantial purchase at the horticulture building from a lady resembling her mother. We let a carney try to guess our altered ages. He could not, and insisted on seeing our licenses before giving us our prize. We rode the Ferris wheel at sunset, and fed each other soft, salty hot pretzels and sweet, pink cotton candy with llama wool scented fingers. We walked hand-in-hand for hours, dressed in vintage Wild West costumes for a photo shot, and finally felt relaxed in public.

On that simple day in Redmond I rediscovered the other side of Kim, the soft, feminine side she often tried to hide. I felt lucky to be in love with a lady who was so passionate, playful, and practical. Seeing normal families at the fair also touched a soft spot in me.

"We could have a llama ranch, honey," I said on the drive home to the Octagon. "I've been reading about them in *The Oregonian*. They're going to be very popular in the future. Them and ostriches, you'll see."

My wife drew her knees to her breasts, and rested her head. "The future, what's that?" she sighed.

"What we can share, like everyone else," I exclaimed with confidence and drama. "Something to get involved in, to hold on to. I...*we* can make it happen. We can buy a business through an offshore corpora-

Bert did it on Maui. Blake's a master at this financial spy stuff."

"And what would we call this low-profile business venture—Barnes' Double-Bar Fuge Llama Ranch?" she sneered, simultaneously slapping her palms on the dash. "Whatever happened to your becoming a writer? Uh, huh. Can you say *dreamer?* Be real! You're such a dreamer, Tom. Just drive," she muttered, shaking her head. "We're lucky to be together."

Were we? For the first time, I wondered. Who in the hell did she think she was talking to—some bum? Her mood swing shocked me. Maybe the day had stirred painful memories, but her words hurt. How was it possible for her to express such coldness and negativity without feeling the same emotions deep inside? Would these feelings grow like a cancer, or subside? I bit my tongue, tamed my roaring Leo ego, and focused on the white line in front of the black Ford that divided two dark forests. This was not an easy task. I had waited twenty-nine years and experienced much living before marrying this gypsy woman. "She is young and moody. Marriage requires great understanding, patience and compromise." These words, given me by my mother, were my self-talk as I ground the gears, found second, and turned onto Solar Drive.

"The world is full of dreamers," I said sternly in the driveway of the compound. "But you married a rare breed. I am a *dreamer-doer,* and don't you ever forget it." I reached for the truck's door.

Kim fidgeted for a moment, then nodded. "Today was special, honey," she whispered, pecking my cheek. "Don't pay attention to my PMS attacks. It's not you." She lowered her head to my lap.

I cradled her head and stroked her hair.

Minutes later the garage light came on, penetrating the darkness. A screen door slammed. Kim jumped up. Arnie lumbered toward us, beer in hand, with Benjamin panting beside him, smelling of river muck. "How was the fair?" he asked.

"Wonderful," Kim sighed, catching her breath.

"Got a mail drop in Eugene today," he announced, pawing pine needles and gravel with his size thirteen sandals. "Guess I'll take the written test there next week and turn in my Nebraska driver's license, like the others did." He paused, straining to decipher the expression beneath my furrowed brow in the dim light. "Let's face it, Bud, I'm not as good an actor as you are."

Fleeting shivers of ecstasy flew out the window and were immediately replaced by quivers of insecurity. I considered bitching about this breach of policy, but knew it was not my role or desire to push or dominate him. That kind of thinking died with the business when I left Bill McCarthy and South Bend behind, and it had no place on this journey. If I was in fact the leader of this little *fuge colony*, I didn't want to flaunt it, but lead with a laid back style and avoid exposing my own inner fears about our insane underground adventure. "Good job, *John Boy*," I said.

Eventually, Kim and I took trips to Portland where she too acquired a mail drop, then an Oregon driver's license from scratch. "We've both gotten good at being devious, haven't we?" she said, after deceiving the Department of Motor Vehicles staff. We were sitting on the colorful tile steps of Portland's Pioneer Courthouse Square. She wore a sundress and stared at a bunch of giggling little girls who were dangling bare feet in the square's fountain.

"It's just what we have to do," I said, wondering what the woman beside me—who like myself had grown up too fast—was thinking.

At First Interstate Bank I opened a non-interest-bearing checking account that would not attract the attention of the taxman, and got *real* State Farm insurance for Tim Barnes' truck. Because I'd heard local residents from gas station attendants to waiters express disdain for snooty Californians migrating north into the Beaver State, I registered the Ford to my Barbur Boulevard "apartment" and ditched its California dealer plates.

In accordance with my financial strategy of dividing my assets between overseas stocks, hard cash, and gold, I continued to collect the latter at every opportunity. In the City of Roses, I found a place owned by a Chinese family who like me favored Pandas and American greenbacks. In only my third transaction with the Asians, I was able to trade fifty grand in moldy bills for shiny Panda Proof coins. It was to be my last purchase from them, for unlike the Greek, they were not cautious enough about accepting cash above the required IRS reporting limit. What if I had been an undercover agent? I did not want to worry about random surveillance, and possible FBI heat.

Later that day, while Lady Di attended worship services at her newly adopted fashion temple—Nordstrom's Department Store—I read an *Oregonian* article describing the man who had just profited from my pot money as "a pillar of the Portland community." Why did I worry so much about the use of cash disappearing or changing drastically in this country? I laughed. But then I saw another article that was not funny—"Drug Laws Stiffen." I scanned the column with sweating palms.

"So much for a return to the '60s mentality," I muttered after pitching *The Oregonian* in the trash. "Good thing I'm retired."

In the glow of Indian Summer, we celebrated Kim's *real* birthday. I had commissioned Hans' Pastry Shop in Bend to bake her favorite cake and adorn it with a gingerbread raccoon representing one of my earliest pet names for her—given for her wild streak and the white rings around her eyes created from wearing oversized sunglasses on Tahoe's ski slopes. In icing were written the words from one of my favorite Neil Young songs: *Twenty-four and there's so much more.* A good thought at that tender age.

Long after Kim's candles cooled and Arnie went to bed, she and I sipped champagne buck-naked in the hot tub beneath a million Pacific Northwest stars, then we slid dripping wet between silk sheets...and the world did not disturb us there. The heat of our bodies, the elixir of our scents, our tastes and squirming limbs, all shielded us from troubling truths.

Eventually, my young raccoon slept. Yet on that night, like so many others, I lay awake watching the ceiling fan swirl and the fireplace flicker, counting nail heads on cedar wood, wrestling with the fact that my country—or at least some element of it—was at war. And I, who fancied myself a good man, was considered the enemy.

Why must America always have a war? Nothing lasts forever, I thought. Maybe they won't indict me? Then I turned my focus toward my wife, fit myself into the svelte curves of her figure, and fell fast asleep.

Northern District of Indiana, 1986: The *historical investigation* that would eventually lead to my indictment for marijuana distribution, tax evasion, and conducting a continuing criminal enterprise marched on.

> Memorandum of July 25, 1986 FBI 302 Interview with Timothy Michael Meers: "McCarthy had called him the previous Saturday at his residence wanting to know what was going on. Meers told him that he, Stromier, Pratt,

Yukovic and Kowalewski were talking with Federal authorities. McCarthy said he was sorry to hear that, as he hoped that only he and Bruce Pratt would cooperate so that information could be "kept to a minimum." McCarthy said he had been in contact with his attorney and was going to try to work a deal with the government in the near future. McCarthy described some of his attempts to hide his assets. McCarthy sounded as if he was not going to come back. He was setting up phony I-Ds. He thinks that McCarthy has already made plans to obtain this identification from Thomas Hickey, who supposedly had a contact in the California area. It is his feeling that Hickey has left the country and possibly may be residing somewhere in Europe or Africa. McCarthy's wife, Leigh, knows all these involvements.

Tim spoke at length on McCarthy's pre-grand jury advice, and offered his version of attorney Jerry Patchen's visit that spring. After Meers was indicted for obstruction of justice and perjury in June, he said McCarthy asked him to minimize his own involvement and the fact of the semi trailers coming to the pole barn, then offered to pay his legal fees and $1,000 to $1,200 per month for any time he had to serve. In August, the FBI gave Meers another chance to come clean.

Memorandum of August 13, 1986 FBI Polygraph of Meers: He pretty much clears. He mentions the additional name of John X. He also says he talked to Paul X a few days before who told him that Bill McCarthy's sister-in-law had visited McCarthy in the Toronto, Canada, area.

On September 22, the FBI interviewed Meers again. Tim brought in a revealing six-page letter he'd received from Bill McCarthy.

Dear Mr. Tim,

Hope this letter doesn't make you extra nervous, as this will be my last planned communication for a while. I understand things have gotten much worse. This is why I left. You guys have been so talkative that the feds don't even want to deal with me (unless you consider 10 years in prison a deal). Its not much fun dealing with the government, is it? Grimmer is out for headlines and numbers, too. You must play this game by their rules from here on out. That means being remorseful, damning the day you met me and generally just kissing ass...

The law's changed quite a bit. My lawyer

tells me that 2 or 3 years ago the feds wouldn't have bothered with a case like this, too expensive and too much time. Ah, but for Ronald Reagan. You'll find the prisons are overcrowded with drug people—they are the ones you'll get along with. Do not be afraid. You have gone though the worst part. I think the worst part is the uncertainty of the future. Mine is very uncertain right now, but at least I am away from all of this and that is worth something. While I am not a fugitive yet I have been living the life of one and it is somewhat lonely—with no friends and no one to talk to (hence the long letter)...

Well I know you were thinking I forgot your birthday, but I didn't. Not much use in wishing you a happy one though. Following is a present, only use it if you have to to get your prison time reduced (remove this page and burn it if not). Hickey has over $500,000 hidden in the Channel Islands off England under the name of Leo Investments. Money is still there... If presented to the feds in right way it should get your deal back. Obviously I don't want it known I told you this and am only telling you because you got yourself in trouble trying to protect me. I appreciate it. That's all for now. Be cool. Your friend, Bill.

Documents showed that after pleading guilty in Detroit to marijuana violations in the Western and Eastern Districts of Michigan and the Northern District of Indiana, co-conspirator David Neddeff gave a detailed debriefing to the FBI, describing over ten years and tens of thousands of pounds of pot deals. Neddeff described a deal in the spring of 1985 that began when a ship was offloaded to the New Orleans dock areas, then concealed in a fleet of tractor trailers. There was a problem getting it unloaded, and additional security had to be paid off. One trailer tractor, containing 33,000 pounds of Columbian marijuana costing approximately $400 per pound, was delivered to his main customer Bill McCarthy in Michigan. Neddeff told agents that in late 1985, McCarthy informed him that he was not paying any more toward a debt of nearly one million dollars. McCarthy was apparently in trouble and planning to leave. In early 1986 Ron Maloney met Neddeff in a mall. Maloney, an Italian built like a boxer, was acting on behalf of his employer and told Neddeff that his boss wanted his money or action would be taken against Neddeff. About a week later Maloney and others visited Neddeff's home and requested to see his business records. At the conclusion of their meeting, by request, Neddeff gave Maloney a picture of McCarthy, a list of McCarthy's associates, and telephone numbers for McCarthy and his associates.

The Octagon Compound, October 1986: Central Oregon's highly-touted 263 days of yearly sunshine dwindled down to a precious few. Indian Summer rode in hard on a Chinook wind, like a rejuvenated medicine man emerging from the tribal sweat lodge, ordered area Aspens to carpet the forest floors with gold leaf, then mysteriously disappeared—only to be replaced by those infamous Northwest rains our fugitive friends from Ohio had warned us about.

Halloween came to the Octagon, and deep in our pine-scented woods we could smell it in the air. Driven by memories from our Midwest childhood, we paid to pick pumpkins from a farmer's patch, then held our first annual "*fugitive* jack-o-lantern carving contest." After I, the democratically elected judge, declared Kim's creation the winner, we retired our Chicago Cutlery, roasted pumpkin seeds, and watched—sagging spirits lifted—while a rare parting of gloomy skies revealed another pristine sunset performance.

Todd lit a joint and passed it to me. The tacky feeling between my thumb and index finger, and the sweet familiar, pungent aroma triggered pleasant memories of Halloweens-gone-by as I pondered getting high. Part of me feared the paranoid fugitive mindset my role as leader required I maintain might rush forth uncontrollably from my sub-conscience, detracting from the relaxing qualities of the herb. But, for the first time since Mendocino, a bigger part of me wanted to partake.

"Ah, what the hell," I said, sucking a sizable dose of THC into my lungs. "One day, the government might succeed in catching our asses, but we can't ever let 'em imprison our minds—especially out here."

Arnie nodded. Kim, who'd been nursing a cold, coughed and concurred.

Getting high was weird. I had managed to create our own little Oz world and block out any Midwest memories of family and friends that attempted to invade it. My altered state eroded such discipline.

Autumn clouds reassembled over the Deschutes River. A formation of boisterous waterfowl descended at dusk, and their elongated silhouettes brought to mind visions of prehistoric pterodactyls hovering over erupting volcanoes. Our pets scrambled down the muddy bank to intercept the incoming squatters. Kim's laundry billowed on a line against the evening breeze like a family of dancing ghosts.

"What would we be doing if we were back home?" I asked, exhaling a connoisseur's curl of gray-green smoke skyward.

Arnie sighed longingly. "Shooting pool and drinking beer at Bridget McGuire's, Nickie's, or Corby's, just blocks away from Notre Dame's golden dome."

"For sure," I said. "And visiting our parents,"

Our screeching cats bounded onto the pier gnashing their teeth, old Benjamin dove into the river, and the pterodactyls—who now resembled the Wicked Witch's flying monkey warriors—abruptly resumed their migratory journey.

"Why don't you two go to Sunriver and play a few games," Kim suggested, as if sensing a need for some male bonding.

"Sounds good," Arnie said.

"Want to come along, honey?" I asked. "You're as good a player as we are, and—"

"Go," she whispered, pecking my cheek and winking. "I'll be okay."

The rustic sports bar at Sunriver's Business Park was packed with a local crowd. In the lull between summer and ski seasons, they had slowly taken back their territory from the tourists. We'd noticed the lack of outsiders weeks ago—at Sunriver's grocery store, Bend's movie theatre, Grover's Pub, Mexicali Rose Restaurant and other places we frequented—which is why we had been keeping a low profile lately. All three tables were occupied, so we put down a coin on the green felt, got a beer, found a corner pinball machine and entertained ourselves, oblivious to the tension-filled air.

When our quarter came up, we beat two intoxicated Indians, then defeated two drunken cowboys. After our third victory, we played each other in singles Eight Ball. Eventually, my stoned gaze drifted from green felt in front of me to a side table, where a big man—looking fresh off the set of a spaghetti Western—was watching us.

He wore a ten-gallon hat, leather vest, and Tony Llama ostrich-skinned boots with silver spurs. He had a .357 long barrel revolver strapped to his waist, a Bowie knife sheathed just below one knee, and was chewing on an oversized toothpick. The man—who resembled TV's *Paladin*—was also playing partners. His sidekick was a scrawny dude with a scraggly billy-goat beard and half the hat of his apparent idol's—a hat that might have been squashed by angry hands a time or two.

Instantly alarmed, I tuned in to numerous conversations within earshot—a talent and a curse of mine. No one was talking about golfing the North Course, bragging about what a great resort Sunriver truly was, or taking guesses as to when ski season would begin. There were mostly conversations about tracking, weaponry, rewards and such.

Someone slammed down a shot glass at the bar and declared, "Fuckin' faggot Californians oughtta all be hung by their damn nutsacks!"

"Eight ball, side pocket," announced Arnie cheerfully, followed by a belch.

I swallowed hard and nodded. A quick scan of the room brought the image of a sheriff's posse to mind. There were lots of long coats dripping rainwater from where they hung against a wall, and everyone was carrying guns...*except us.* My stomach tightened.

"Great costumes these guys are wearing, huh, Tim?" Arnie remarked while chalking his stick. He tossed me the plastic triangle like a Frisbee. "Rack 'em, Clem," he ordered, sounding like one of the many cowboys surrounding us.

"Listen," I said. "We drank two beers, had some fun...manly shit, just like old times, right? What say we retire undefeated? Don't want the *wives* to start worrying about us, do we?"

My friend looked at me like I'd just lost my mind. He studied the contortions on my face, and watched me gesture with my eyes toward the weird crowd behind me, which had grown uneasily quiet. Suddenly, the years of sub-culture experience and chemistry between us clicked.

"Yeah...*the wives,*" he said.

Two footsteps from the door, I felt a tug on the back of my black leather bomber jacket. It was the little drunk from the other table. I turned to face him.

"Hey, stranger," he said with a shrill twang. "Wanna shoot a game fer beers with me an' ma' pardner?"

I shook my head, leery of the little guy's attitude, and wary of dealing with a potential sore loser, which encouraged him to enlighten me.

"Don't cha know who the big feller is?" he asked.

I took a good look, thinking *movie star*. The toothpick-chewing cowboy tipped his hat and smiled. His dental work was terrible! *Definitely not Hollywood*, I thought, shaking my head.

"That thar's a human bloodhound!" his sidekick snorted defiantly.

"Scuze me," I said, not catching his drift.

The billy-goat-bearded-babbler spat chew in an empty beer can. "Why, he's only the best damn *bounty hunter* in the entire Pacific Northwest!"

Arnie's face lost all color. A shudder ran down my spine. "Bounty hunter? No shit?" I said, with all the calmness I could muster.

"Serious as a heart attack. That man can smell a fuckin' fugitive twenty miles away! We've caught plenty of them vermin." He poked his concave chest with a crooked tobacco-stained finger. "And it just so happens there's a murderer loose in them there woods tonight." He pointed his scraggly chin to the picture window where Spuds McKenzie's neon paw rested on a red-flickering *Bud Light*. "Yessir. Scum escaped 'round suppertime from LaPine." He paused to put another pinch of Redman between cheek and gum. "We'll be stalking him soon's them rains stop. And smart money says we'll have his ass by morning—*dead or alive!*"

I didn't blink, but my heart started pounding so hard that all I could hear was that and the rain beating against the tavern's window.

"Well, little mister? Wanna shoot a game fer beers with me an' ma' pardner? Or are you two a couple a yeller-bellied chicken shits?"

A chuckle echoed in the gallery. Arnie's knuckles turned ashen white against the polished brass exit door handle. Butterfly wings churned up a bad mix of pumpkinseeds and beer in my gut. We all exchanged glances.

"Sure," I said, stern-faced. "Rack 'em up, Hoss."

Before our reefer-buzz faded, we fugitives shot our finest pool and whipped them rednecks fair and square, struggling to keep straight faces the entire time. When Arnie sank the eight ball for the win, *The Human Bloodhound* slapped his ten-gallon hat against the rail. "Lucky shits!" he said, spitting out the toothpick and telling his furry sidekick to fetch us two beers.

"Keep 'em," I said, laying down my stick and heading for the door.

"What's yer hurry, stranger?" bellowed the bloodhound. "Stay fer one more game...*or is there something wrong with our beer?"*

"Sorry, guys, but we gotta run," I said, walking backwards. "Gotta pick up the girls. Right, John-Boy?"

Todd-Johnny-Arnie nodded, then jerked open the door.

"You boys wouldn't want me driving drunk," I said, seeing that the big cowboy was coming to a slow boil. "Might accidentally run over that killer of yours," I mumbled, breaking for the door and leaving the posse scratching their chins.

Outside in the parking lot after exchanging high-fives, we busted a gut laughing, leaned against the black Ford and caught our breath. Steam rose from a sewer cap. A full moon peaked through breaking clouds. Hunting dogs started baying in the back of a camper truck. We jumped into the cab and hit the road.

Somewhere on Solar Drive I pictured my wife alone in the Octagon, and another kind of fugitive—the kind any sane citizen should really fear—ogling her through our windows from the dark, wet woods.

"Damn it," I muttered, slapping the dash and silently second-guessing my decision to keep my old guns in storage hundreds of miles away. Then I stepped on the gas and headed for the Octagon.

The weeks that followed saw us retreat deep into the safety of our isolation. We bought satellite dishes and installed them by the river bank to receive Notre Dame and Chicago Bears football games—thus avoiding Sunriver's sports bar. We became early fans of the Fox Network's, *The Simpsons, Married With Children,* and *The Tracey Ullman Show. LA Law, Hill Street Blues, China Beach* and *M*A*S*H** reruns also made the evening lineup. After three months without a phone, I had one installed so we could check in if late coming home, call in an occasional takeout order, and let the landlord think we were normal. I bought a second car for Kim—an old, orange Volvo she named Pumpkin—that provided her an extra measure of freedom she needed.

Just before Thanksgiving, we drove to Portland to pick up our organic turkey. I hit the payphones and paged the Ohioans. Jim promptly returned my call, from Tucson. The autumn harvest had begun, and Mexican pot was trickling over the border. Smiley was sending what he could afford back east. Once again, he asked if I had contacted my old friend, and inquired if Tucson Tony was working. I had talked to my Arizona pal—who was working—but only about old times, his relationship with a woman from Australia, and whether Tony could get his paws on some Aussie identification for Kim and me. Not one word of this did I mention to Jim, because life was tranquil for our Northwest fugitive colony and I intended to keep it that way.

"You'll get bored," Smiley predicted, reading between my pauses. "Every gambler needs a game."

Irene grabbed the phone from him and invited us to their Durango hideout for Thanksgiving. Without hesitation, I declined. Heavy snow had fallen on Mount Bachelor, we'd bought season passes, and the skiers were back in force. My troupe was not about to budge—especially to the Business Zone.

"But what about Christmas, Timmy?" Lizzy pressed, reminding me of my prior commitment to a holiday gathering. When she paused, I heard whispering between sniffles with her hubby. "We're even willing to come up there, since your mountain has snow already, and ours doesn't. Sonny wants to come, too. Well? We're all family now, right? What do you say?"

"Sure. Look forward to it."

Smiley's post-flight involvement in the Arizona marijuana scene may have seemed insane to me, but he was right about one thing—every gambler did indeed need a game. Which is why my next call—placed collect from another phone—was to the Isle of Guernsey, located between England and France. It was high time to fill the gambler's void in my life.

"Ah, Thomas," my money manager, Blake, said cheerfully. "I've been expecting your call for quite some time,"

I sighed. When you entrust your secret money to a man half-a-world away, believe me, you feel relieved every time you hear his voice on the other end of the line. I sighed again when he announced that he had changed the identity of my account from Leo Investments to a more British sounding trust—*Aldershot*—leaving no paper trail for the feds or potential blackmailers like Bill McCarthy. "I'd love to hear the details of that little trick—in person, of course," I said. "One more thing. Did you set up those feeder accounts for my certified checks?"

"Certainly." The Englishman cleared his throat. "Now then, precisely how do you wish to invest these funds?"

"As we discussed," I answered, referring to his advice to keep most of it in *sterling*—the British Pound—which was paying a world-leading thirteen percent interest rate at the time. Thirteen percent on nearly $400,000! Fifty-two grand a year tax-free. A safe and conservative move, especially for a retired marijuana dealer on the run.

"Well done," Blake replied. "Lovely. Is that all?"

"I've been watching the London market on our *Financial News Network*. Oil prices are rising. Inflation is raising its ugly head. Gold shares look like they're due for a run. Got any hot tips on mining stocks?"

"Interesting you should ask," Blake said, sounding impressed. "As a matter of fact, I do."

If he was breaking his rule against dispensing direct advice to investors, I knew the tip had to be a good one. I listened attentively.

After business and before signing off—as always—he asked me to come for a visit, and to bring the wife. "Judy's been asking when my mysterious young American client will be returning for a stay with us."

My last trip over, before my marriage, I'd spent a week at their estate. *The Coppice* was a sprawling piece of acreage situated on a green hillside where animals roamed free and winds caressed the senses with the aroma of the sea. We played tennis, rode his prized horses, and ate at his centuries-old dinner table in our T-shirts—destroying the preconceived cold image I'd had of such secret-money people. I liked Blake and his Australian wife, and wanted to maintain a personal rapport and continue building trust—so I would feel confident about shifting more cash to his care.

"We'll try to come next spring," I said, wondering when I'd feel comfortable enough to travel under my new Tim Barnes passport—and how I would explain my name change to the Englishman.

"Lovely. Look forward to it then," Blake said. "Bye-bye, Thomas."

I called my youngest brother, Bill, in tiny Bethel, Alaska, at the time we had prearranged by code via the *USA Today* crossword puzzle back in August. He gave me the update on family matters: Mom was divorced, but doing okay. She'd asked me not to worry about her. None of my siblings had been quizzed by the feds, or knew if they were being watched. Bill himself had settled into his assignment with the Environmental Protection Agency in his chosen field of groundwater management, and was dating an Eskimo woman. He was my favorite brother, my fishing buddy. We'd shared a lot of good times. We were tight.

"Maybe you can sneak up and do some salmon fishing," he said.

"Can't think of anything I'd rather do," I replied. "But you and Ma will be the ones they'll watch. This is serious shit. I'm going to stay isolated."

"Where?"

"Don't ask. Just know that I'll be doing lots of fishing, and thinking of you. Tell Ma I'll send her a sign. Have fun in those igloos. Don't melt 'em."

"Take care out there, *Blood*."

I phoned Bill and Leigh McCarthy's high-dollar condo near Tampa, Florida, where they were living as the Fisher family. Leigh sounded down, and spoke at length about religion. They both invited us to come and offered to visit. When I tactfully declined, Bill took offense. "Thought you wanted to settle up so bad," he said snidely.

If it wasn't for Leigh and my sympathy for her situation, I could easily have cut off all contact right then. The money Bill owed me wasn't worth the frustration he caused, but the longer this adventure went on, the more our wives would crave female camaraderie. At least this is what my instincts were telling me. "We'll meet somewhere before spring," I said.

Bill ended on a sour note, saying he'd "found out" we were officially indicted now, and that our pictures were appearing on a weekly Crime Stoppers show back in South Bend. "You finally got your wish to be a TV star," he snickered.

I broke into a sweat. I wondered *whom* he was in touch with in Indiana. Suddenly, I had no regrets about keeping them away from our holiday gathering. "The feds must think I'm going to waltz right into the Summit Club one night for dinner and sing some Sinatra with the band," I said, trying to sound unshaken. But I was shaken. I swallowed hard, said hello to their daughter in a funny cartoon voice, promised I'd call for Christmas, and hung up.

That's when it really hit me. I, me, The Kid from Berry Road was on some local TV cop show like a common thief, or some murderer! All over selling pot. And so much for the statute of limitations running out. Once an indictment was issued, it was like getting a prize from Vanna White on the *Wheel of Fortune*—yours to keep forever and ever.

For us, it was a solemn Thanksgiving spent watching football games, swirling snowflakes, migrating pterodactyls, and thinking of our families.

Seven days before Christmas they arrived—the Blackwells and fellow fugitive, Sonny. Starved for company, we welcomed their arrival. I'd agreed to invite Sonny, but vetoed his common law wife Missy, feeling only fugitives should attend our reunion. I'd met Sonny years before, but had never done business with him, since he was a protected interest of Jim Hagar.

Sonny was sharp witted, had a great sense of humor, and could ski circles around the rest of us. He'd been a member of the highly regarded Aspen, Colorado Ski Patrol, and a talented pilot/smuggler who tried to retire to a hi-tech Rocky Mountain music recording studio business. He had been a lot of things, had tons of potential—like all of us—until the feds indicted him and froze his assets. Now he was a desperado-fugitive pushing forty, lacking confidence and cash, and teamed up with Smiley to transport pot back east from Tucson in customized vehicles. Like the Blackwells, he had hardly any family and was starved for company. Sonny drove an old Caddy equipped with secret stash panels for carrying money and weed, which he affectionately called *The Jew Canoe.* I housed him and all his fancy ski gear in the guest cottage with Arnie. The Blackwells moved into the Octagon with us.

The first week was fabulous. We reminisced about the past. We decorated the tree, made cookies, skied Mount Bachelor by day, and toured crowded local restaurants at night. And to my great surprise, we were early to bed, early to rise, keeping healthy, happy and wise. Having no true family to shower with gifts, everyone sneaked into town on not-so-secret shopping trips. Everything was kosher.

On Christmas Eve, we piled a mountain of presents around the tree,

On Christmas Eve, we piled a mountain of presents around the tree, donned brightly colored apparel, crammed into Sonny's Caddy, and motored through a winter wonderland smoking Mexico's finest herb en route to Bend's Mexicali Rose Restaurant. The Rose was packed, but the hostess recognized me as one of her better tippers and seated us immediately. The restaurant's music selection featured Jimmy Buffet singing about Caribbean smugglers in *Banana Republics*, Billy Joel crooning *Piano Man*, and Eric Clapton's *Cocaine*. It was like a *Big Chill* soundtrack for us Baby Boomers, and the magic of our reunion continued.

After a mouth-watering meal, many margaritas, killer conversation and belly-busting laughter, I felt like I was back in the high life again. Good food and good friends gathered for holiday cheer made me feel great about going through with our reunion, then Lizzy raised her glass and popped the question in that condescending Connecticut-bred tone of hers. "Have you Oregonians been good?"

"Too good," giggled Lady Di.

"Do you want to have a white Christmas?" Lizzy whistled. "Well, do you? Santa needs to know!"

Kim and I exchanged glances. My fingers got sweaty. A drunken, devilish voice inside me said, *Give in*. We nodded.

Lizzy took Lady Di to the powder room, where the heretofore-secret stash appeared. Fifteen minutes later, Sonny and Smiley went to powder their noses, too. Giving in to the holiday spirit, I took a *bullet* handoff from Smiley under the table and headed to the john with "Cousin Johnny". Inside a locked toilet stall which was showing four legs, we gave "last rights" to my Mendocino-invoked "just say no" policy on cocaine consumption.

"It is Christmas, Bud," John Boy said. "And we have been awful good."

"No doubt, dude," I answered, imitating Bart Simpson. "We're already drunk, and I'm not driving for a change. Ah, what can it hurt?"

Twenty minutes later at our boisterous dinner table, we were enjoying the peace/love euphoria associated with the initial toot high, toasting freedom and officially proclaiming each other to be dear adopted family, when I heard a loud *beep-beep-beeping* sound. People's heads three tables away turned in our direction.

the tablecloth for his pocket-sized pager.

"No, man. It's mine." Sonny looked down at his little device and shook his curly head. "Shit. It's my driver, Sarge. Hope he didn't have any problems."

Both of them broke out rolls of quarters wrapped in Harrah's Casino paper, cracked them on the table's edge, and beat a path for the Mexicali Rose's twin payphones.

Perhaps it was only my nose-candy-cane-medicated mind, but the cheery music seemed to fade and people started staring at us. I pictured myself an actor in one of those E.F. Hutton commercials where everyone froze in place to listen. Today there are over thirty million pagers in use, but in Bend back in December of 1986, having a pager meant one of two things to me. Dope dealer, or…

"Those damn doctors!" I said, loud enough for inquiring minds to hear. "How on earth did you end up marrying one, Lizzy?"

Underneath my forced grin, I felt both paranoid and angry. But it was Christmas Eve, so I bit my lip and kept on talking to Lizzy. During the half-hour they spent phoning business connections I boiled. A good dinner went bad while I wondered whom they were calling. What if the lines were tapped? What if their hot calls led the feds on a fishing trip to tiny Bend, Oregon, flashing photos of some Midwestern fugitives long after my friends had gone? My guess was that I'd probably make as good as catch as any on some elated G-man's mantel. Before going home, I took Jim aside and asked how he'd like it if Kim and I came to his turf to call our parents.

"I get the message," Smiley said. "No need to get all bent out of shape at Christmas time. We'll hold the calls and stash our pagers. Okee-dokey?"

The Jew Canoe drifted out of town with six shit-faced *fuges* on board. I sat in back with my clan, biting my nails all the way to the back roads, searching for the speed cop who hid behind Sunriver's entrance sign, realizing how vulnerable we were, and worrying about going down over a DUI violation. The feds depended on stupid mistakes like that. Suddenly the Canoe slid into a snow bank and plowed right through it, jolting me forward.

"Yee-ha!" shouted Sonny as he hit the gas. "More power!"

"Aye, Captain! Ramming speed," snickered Smiley, staring at my furrowed brow in the rearview mirror. "Relax, Timmy. Where's that trademark sense of humor of yours?"

I did relax—long after locking the Octagon Compound's gate behind us, popping one of Sonny's Valiums, and downing a couple of stiff drinks, at which time I toasted, "To our safe return."

"Here-here," echoed Smiley. "May your isolationists' conservatism give way to seasonal spirit! God bless ya, guy...each and every one of us," Smiley slurred, knocking back his beloved Crown Royal and wiping his chin. "More liquor," he declared.

"And longer lines!" whistled Lizzy, as she cleaned the English wall mirror which was resting on her lap.

Twelve bells tolling on an antique Session's clock marked the arrival of midnight, and a very white Christmas. Colored wrapping paper piles climbed toward the Octagon's cathedral ceiling. Jagger and Whitey wrestled and played with bright discarded bows after snorting their catnip gifts. Benjamin tore open his package and ate the T-bone steak inside. And as golf balls, ski boots, sweaters, Gore-Tex gloves, Pendleton blankets and wine bottles got buried in the maze, a decadent pattern emerged. A present was opened, the mirror was passed, and more powder was snorted. Lengthy conversations filled the intermissions. Lips smacked and liquor flowed. I described how fifty grand wagered on two gold mining stocks had more than doubled due to a corporate merger—providing me with a new and legal gambler's rush.

"Sons of Gwalia and GM Kalgourlie were their names," I said proudly.

"Were?" Jim asked, his curious blue eyes blinking rapidly.

"Sold them last week," I announced. "Sold 'em, took the profit, and put my entire wad into British Sterling at thirteen percent interest." I exhaled. "Felt great! Almost like doing a reefer scam."

"How nice," Lizzy whistled through clenched teeth. "We've had a good run, too. Let me tell you all about it."

Sometime around three that morning, I thought I noticed Sonny—who'd been a total gentleman—ogling my wife. A scene from the movie *The Big Chill* flashed before my eyes. I remembered the guests for the funeral screwing each other's mates. For the first time in years, I felt a tinge of jealousy. Instinctively, I passed when Sonny offered me the cocaine-covered mirror, then glared at Kim who was helping me stoke the fire.

"Just one more line, honey," she said, studying my face.

I shook my head. "Don't ruin your appetites for Christmas dinner," I suggested to my wired guests, before excusing my wife and myself for the evening. Inside our bedroom—which like all of the Octagon's rooms had no ceiling, only sidewalls—we listened to our stoned-out visitors attempting to be quiet as we disrobed. I heard coded business speak about current drug activities in Tucson, and tales from the glory days. As I lay in bed regretting my cocaine use, the ancient, ragged Teddy Bear on the nightstand entranced Kim.

"What do you see in that ratty old thing?" I asked, tongue-in-cheek, attempting to break an unhealthy silence. It was Christmas, and I regretted the remark the minute it left my lips, just as I'd regretted my decision to leave all of our family photos in our storage building. I knew that Teddy Bear was her sole connection to her childhood and family.

"The same thing you see in that filthy old dog of yours," she snapped.

"Don't be cruel to Ben. It's Christmas. Merry Christmas, *Meekla*," I whispered.

"Yeah, Merry Christmas."

The hurt look forming on her face was killing me inside.

"Hold me, honey," she cooed with pouty temptress lips. The sound of a wineglass shattering sent our cats scrambling up a cedar wall to their perch overlooking our bed. "They're *your* friends," Lady Di said.

I filled my mouth with holiday liqueur and redistributed it on her lips.

"What if they hear us?" she whispered, grabbing my hair.

Someone switched my Christmas music to the Rolling Stones, and cranked up the volume.

I shrugged my shoulders and licked more nectar. "Merry Christmas, Meekla. Love ya, Raccoon," I whispered.

Around noon a gray snow-filtered light descended from the pines into our bedroom window. We stumbled into the living room, hung over, with hungry pets nipping at our heels. No one was in sight. The house was unearthly quiet. We tiptoed into the kitchen.

"Surprise!" shouted the guests from hell, still dressed in last night's dinner attire. Lizard-lips-Lizzy greeted us with Christmas kisses, gifts in hand. "Here, Di," she whistled. "Here Timmy, open this one."

They were like that damn Ever Ready Bunny—still going and going.

Several hours later—after a madcap group cooking effort in the kitchen—surprise number two unfolded. I was in the woodshed uncovering the metal ammunition box that contained my spending cash and IDs when I heard a car engine. Their dark sedan slid to a halt behind Sonny's Cadillac. They slammed their doors, looked at the cars in our driveway, and then glanced at each other. The man—quite tall and wearing a cowboy hat—unbuttoned his suit coat, tucked one large hand inside it, and escorted the lady to the Octagon. I covered my stash box with kindling and walked quickly to the deck before they knocked on the door.

"Hello, Tim," said my landlady. Merry Christmas."

"Merry Christmas, Mrs. Shell," I replied loudly enough for my wife to hear. "Honey!" I shouted toward the kitchen window.

When Kim opened the door, our curious new visitors instinctively stepped inside. "Merry Christmas, Diane," she said, handing my wife a fruitcake tin. "I spent Christmas Eve in Bend with friends. Thought I'd stop by and..."

My landlady's mouth dropped open as she scanned the living room floor, where over-partied fugitives blanketed by bits of wrapping paper lay curled up between empty booze bottles and Advil containers, trying to focus on a fuzzy TV screen while waiting on their duck dinner to get done.

"They're ski bums up from California," I blurted, simultaneously kicking an ashtray under the sofa. "They're in the music business."

Marguerite Shell shook her head and beat a hasty retreat. She smiled and waved as her handsome cowboy drove her away from our compound. I bit my lip and waved back, but I knew damn well that our *cute-couple* image had been irreparably tarnished.

That night I dreamed the Blackwells got busted doing business, and left us at risk with no source for new IDs. I decided Todd and I should get another back up set. My third identity would be *Paul James Kelly,* age twenty-one. Todd picked *Patrick O'Hara*, the name of the USC quarterback who helped beat our beleaguered Fighting Irish football team that year. We took pictures the next morning and sealed them in separate envelopes, which Jim mailed to an address on Speedway Boulevard in Tucson, Arizona. Reluctantly, I gave him my Barbur Boulevard apartment number as the place to mail them back to when he returned to Tucson for his next load.

"Listen, guy," Smiley said. "We're having so much fun visiting you that we might just stay on a couple more weeks. But you have my word. These IDs will get to your Portland mail drop within a month."

"Make sure my Portland address isn't left laying around," I said.

"Come on, Timmy." Smiley scowled. "What do you take me for, some amateur?"

Two more weeks with the guests from hell and their bottomless coke bag? The thought was unnerving. I needed a diplomatic game plan to achieve my New Year's resolution. January fifth was to be our one-year wedding anniversary. What a year. I'd already taken Kim's ring to a Bend jeweler under the pretense of repairing the setting, but now was inspired to make the event even sweeter. Intent upon keeping my promise to show my gypsy-blooded woman the world, and to ensure our return to quasi-normalcy, I made some secret travel arrangements.

We celebrated New Year's Eve at the Inn of the Seventh Mountain's *El Crab Catcher* restaurant. Most of the other diners wore casual ski clothes, but not us fuges. Feeling New Years was a rare opportunity to do it; we came dressed to the nines. During dinner a snowstorm slammed into the mountain and we stared through a frosty window to where families skated on the Inn's ice rink like some living Currier & Ives' lithograph. I loosened the knot on my bright orange salmon fish tie, draped my arm around my wife, and offered a toast: "To families."

Smiley stood—allowing his rainbow trout tie to swim in a fine béarnaise sauce. "To Timmy and Di, our gracious hosts. God bless 'em!"

Before we regressed, I made an announcement. "This was supposed to be a surprise, but I wanted you all to know that our wedding anniversary is on the fifth and I'm taking Lady Di to Hawaii on the second." I cleared my throat. "Waiter, more champagne, please," I said.

Halfway home to the Octagon in a blinding whiteout, I stopped staring in the rearview mirror for state troopers who were not there, parked the four-wheel drive Ford in the middle of Forest Service Road #45 and—in two feet of freshly fallen powder—relieved myself in front of the headlights, forming a yellow heart with *KIM* in the center of it. My finely dressed comrades went crazy, piling out into the winterscape playground, pissing on tires, making snow angels, and tossing snowballs at each other like kids.

"That's the old Tom we all knew and loved," whistled a wet Lizzy.

Knew? Loved? I wrapped my suit coat around my wife and tried reading between the lines of Lizzy's remark. Was this charade changing me to the point where I was no longer fun, or was I just being a careful fugitive?

"I still love you," Kim whispered. "You planned this evening perfectly."

"I'm tired," I told her, warmed by her words. "You were wonderful tonight. Why don't you drive this beast home through the storm?"

"Hop inside my truck, Big Boy," she squealed with delight.

It was the perfect ending to a perfect night.

We were thirty thousand feet above the seemingly endless Pacific Ocean surrounded by senior citizens in polyester suits who were trying to guess the DC 10's air mileage, and naïve newlyweds who were getting so wasted on complimentary Mai Tai's that their first act in the honeymoon suite would be hugging a porcelain throne. I was enjoying the other passengers' energy. I sat in a window seat staring at the wing engine, remembering a dozen other Trans-Pacific flights, and anticipating our arrival on familiar turf. Kim was napping on my lap, purring like a kitten. I pictured her face that morning at Mrs. Beasely's Country Restaurant in Redmond, when I gave her the new and improved wedding ring over bacon and eggs. She had glowed all the way to Portland International Airport, and hadn't quit glowing since.

Presently, lush green islands appeared, and I woke her gently. "Look, Meekla," I said. "There's Maui's twin volcanoes. And off in the distance there is Kauai—home of the wettest spot in the world."

"Wanna bet?" she grinned, pinching my butt.

We deplaned in Honolulu where two beautiful Hawaiian girls displaying Pleasant Hawaiian Holidays cards placed floral leis around our necks. "We're the Barnes," I said, smiling as our hostess checked our names on her list and asked us to stand to one side with the others. "That's okay," I said politely, slipping on my sunglasses. "My wife's camera shy, and were on the self-guided package. We'll just catch the *Wiki-wiki* bus over to our inter-island flight if you don't mind. *Mahalo*," I added, skillfully avoiding the group photograph.

When we arrived at Kona's airport, I snatched our baggage from the outdoor carousel, flashed my driver's license at a rental car booth, and drove us to our condo. "How did you manage all this without a credit card?" Kim asked.

"That's one reason I booked us through Pleasant Hawaiian Holidays, prepaid by certified check in Bend. Confirmed reservations and a rental car would have been tricky otherwise."

"What's the other reason?"

"I wanted us to blend in with the crowd." I sighed, drinking in the spectacular view from our lanai. "Feels great to be back," I whispered to the familiar sea. "See, Meekla, just because we went underground, doesn't mean we have to quit living."

Unlike Maui, where there was a good chance someone would recognize me, I didn't know anyone on the Big Island of Hawaii, which was just what the doctor ordered. We celebrated our anniversary at a seaside grill listening to Hawaiian sunset music, sipping our wedding champagne, watching humpback whales breaching on the horizon and local surfers dancing on softly breaking white-tipped waves. Together we explored black sand beaches, collected seashells, hiked to secluded waterfalls and went shopping. We toured the Big Island by air, hovering over her active, burning volcano. We took a snorkel-cruise on a giant catamaran to Captain Cook's Cove and spent hours in the water. I stuffed Kim's floral bikini with a stash of bread, and laughed when the swarming fish fed. We slid moon-eyed down the ship's waterslide, sipped piña coladas, and talked to two porpoises hugging the bow. We were the happiest honeymooners aboard the *Fairwinds*.

"Them people knows how to live," mumbled a sunburned, melancholy young bride from Kentucky beneath the brim of her *haole* tourist's palm frond hat.

Those solitary, medicinal Hawaiian mornings were a godsend. Feeling the influx of energy the islands had always given me, I played tennis, kayaked in the bay, and gradually cleansed my mind and body of holiday poisons. Kim thought I was reliving some premarital, Leo-bachelor, glory days ritual with my solo health routine, but with each dig of my curved kayak paddle, each swing at those yellow tennis balls, I pondered the answer to our questionable future as fugitives and always came up empty. Be thankful for the present and the magic of each moment,

I told myself every time I got out of my rhythm. After all, I was living the good life I had grown accustomed to, and she was lost in the *Lifestyles of the Rich and Famous* fantasy she had so greatly anticipated. We were young, deeply in love, and free. What could go wrong?

It was our second to the last day, predawn. We made sandwiches, drove to Honokohau Harbor, watched the sunrise, and motored off on a deep-sea charter—just us, the captain, and his big *moke* deckhand. I'd arranged it that way to avoid uncomfortable conversation in close quarters with strangers.

Not many marlin had been landed that season. It was a slow morning. We had several lookers, but no takers. Hours passed. We took in the scenery, appreciating yet another perspective on paradise afforded us by our unique nautical position. The majestic dual volcanoes Mauna Loa and Mauna Kea rose from an infinite sea, sprawling green carpeting spilled over jagged ridges through rainbowed valleys to black lava-rock shores where tepid light blue sun-drenched waters quickly turned cool, dark and deep, forming the aquatic homeland where the famed blue marlin lurked. Around eleven, broiling beneath the Hawaiian sun, we resigned ourselves to defeat and popped the tops on two ice cold beers.

"*Da' beeg one, skeepa*!" screamed the stocky, no-neck native deckhand as he scrambled to the stern.

"Take the chair!" shouted the captain, increasing the speed of the bait.

"Take the chair, honey," I said. "I've caught more than my share of trophy fish." The kite connected to the outrigger above us riffled in the breeze. A huge sail fin broke the surface close to the bait, sending a shiver down my spine.

"But... *Tim*, I've never—"

"Take it, Meekla," I insisted. "You can do it. "Just follow the captain's orders."

I strapped her into the angler's chair. The mate passed her the stiff rod from its holder, and the monster's blue bill appeared.

"Come on. Come on!" I whispered under my breath.

Splash! Rip! Water exploded. Line snapped taut. The battle began.

"Fish on!" shouted the captain. "Let it run, dear."

And run it did, with the captain shouting instructions to Kim the entire time, which she followed to a tee. I kept my hands on her broad shoulders, steadied the swivel chair, wiped her sweating forehead, and fed her swigs of beer. Meanwhile, the mate manned a mini-camera behind us, and although it made me nervous, I said nothing. I enjoyed watching her tangle with that monster more than any fish I could remember. For more than an hour the battle raged. Each time it saw the back of the boat, the big fish ran for deep water. Its final run jerked Kim forward, momentarily freeing one firm breast from its teeny-bikini-top restraint. Even the marlin—whose gender was an unsolved mystery up to this time—broke water for a peek.

And the cameraman captured it all. *"That one beeg mama!"* he noted correctly.

Caught-up in the excitement, I secured the stray breast and made crazy improv comments into the mini-cam's mike, which made all of us laugh hard. Eventually, she hauled that spent beauty to the surface as we men applauded both fish and girl's performance. Then, as the mate pawed at the long handled gaff wedged against the fish-cooler with one claw-like foot, I whispered into my wife's ear...and she nodded.

"I want to release him," Lady Di announced.

"No can do," said the captain, gesturing to his mate. "There's a marlin tournament going on, and this fish could be the lucky winner."

I watched sadly as a great, sleek, sporty creature who had circumnavigated the globe, felt the moke's metal gaff and swinging club again and again and again, until all 362 pounds, all eleven and a half-feet of him lay bloody and still across the stern—one glossy eye staring up at us, leather-scaled skin losing its luster, drying fast in the noonday sun. Unlike Hemingway, I saw no thrill beyond the hunt. My heart sank.

Static crackled over the ship's radio. "She's the biggest blue caught so far this year!" the captain reported proudly. "They're expecting us at Kailua Pier for a weigh-in and pictures. Local press, too!"

My heart pounded. *Karma. Kill a marlin...get caught on a fluke.* "That's nice," I said, "but we really don't—"

"Nonsense," said the skipper. And that was that. We headed to Kailua Pier for a potentially fatal public spectacle.

Pictures were a no-no. I pulled Kim into the head below deck for a quick strategy session. "Here, put on this T-shirt," I said. "The scar from your tattoo sticks out like a sore thumb! Now, listen closely..."

The boat pulled up to the dock. A big crowd gathered. Cameras clicked as the men hoisted her catch with a chain and pulley. We were registered as Mr. and Mrs. Barnes, but Kim demanded that her maiden name, D.K. Moore, appear on the placard. When the newspaperman asked for her island address, she said, "We leave tomorrow morning, back to Nebraska," then gave him a fake address.

I stayed onboard, blond hair tucked beneath my Isle Mirada, Florida Keys, fishing cap, dark glasses hugging cat-green eyes, silently admiring her handling of the incident at Kailua Pier. En route back to Honokahau Harbor, I became concerned about the video, and bought the only copy.

The entire next day was spent in our condo. We even cancelled our dinner reservations. I kept thinking about my indictment, and wondering what kind of manhunt the government was conducting.

We definitely did Hawaii in style. But once again, we discovered how small a world we lived in. It seemed like every time we relaxed, something came along and shook us back to reality.

8

The Oregon Trail

A smart fugitive lived a quiet, simple life ninety percent of the time—like Unabomber Ted Kaczynski did in Montana—and conducted his business on the road. I had money to move out of the country and a second paper trip to complete, so traveling was a necessity for us—and part of the promise to my gypsy bride. In late February of 1987 we traveled to a place I'd never seen before—New Orleans, for Mardi Gras week. The *Big Easy* was selected as a destination for a multitude of reasons and proved to be another educational experience for us, in more ways than one.

We flew down from Portland body-packing a hundred and fifty grand and several sets of ID, registered near Bourbon Street at a midrange, low profile place called Hotel Dauphine, and explored the crowded French Quarter on our first night. Following a quiet dinner at The Court of Three Sisters, I decided to keep my latest alias, Paul James Kelly's paper tripping far away from Hotel Dauphine, just in case I failed. That night, I studied the phonebook. In the morning I went to work carrying a large plastic shopping bag.

"Stay around the room and baby-sit the money, honey," I told Kim, scratching my unshaven face.

The Social Security branch I selected was miles away. It was raining, and I needed a car. Once again, I had to deal with the "no credit card" quandary. Aware that U-Haul required only a driver's license and a cash deposit, I rented their smallest truck and motored off to the suburb of Metairie with my AM radio scratchin' out Cajun tunes, sweating up a storm. Mail drops in metropolitan New Orleans were hard to find, so I settled for a place in Metairie called Pasternack's Mini Storage, which also provided mailing addresses. I paid six months advance box rent and left forty dollars for their all-important mail-forwarding services.

Fifteen minutes later I parked in a lot, climbed into the back of my dingy little truck, and tore open a plastic trash bag containing molding, unlaundered clothing. I put on my outfit, wrapped Paul Kelly's Nebraska license and crumpled Kansas birth certificate in a brown paper sack smelling of wine, stuffed them in the waistband of my underwear, and shuffled into the Metairie, Louisiana Social Security building, arms dangling at my sides. Heads turned. Noses twitched. I put my elbows on the counter and acted out the part: Paul James Kelly, age twenty-one. "Worked on my parents' farm outside of Lincoln all my life. Never been on one of them fancy city payrolls. My, my parents died in a car, car wreck," I stammered, scratching and staring down at my tattered tennis shoes. "After the bank seized the farm, I figured I'd move south for warm weather, work, and I guess...to forget."

The entire clerical staff went silent for an instant. Heads bowed sympathetically for the homeless Nebraska farmboy. The woman attending me—her nose having been tortured to extremes by my smell—merely asked that I sign a form stating I'd never had a Social Security card.

"Thank you kindly," I said, shuffling toward the exit with the assurance that Paul Kelly's Social Security card would be mailed to 3220 North Arnoult Road, Pasternack's Mini Storage, ASAP. Pasternack's, upon receiving my call two weeks later, would in turn forward it to 1850 Union Street, Apartment #219, San Francisco, California, where I would pick it up in the wee morning hours with my 24-hour access key.

Fifteen minutes later, after observing the Metairie Post Office's passport agent, I pitched my costume in a dumpster and sped back to Hotel Dauphine to lunch with Lady Di.

"Don't touch me until you take a shower!" she demanded. "And whoever told you that you could grow a beard was a damn liar," she added, laughing. "You'll never fill those holes in your cheeks."

Following lunch—sporting my clean-shaven fugitive look—we selected some bright pastel-colored clothing for Paul Kelly's passport pictures, and I went back to Metairie to complete my mission. By dinnertime, I'd returned the U-Haul and secured a second passport in yet another region of the country.

That night, as I lay in bed feeling the rush of energy that the day's paper tripping had given me, I wondered anew why the entire nation wasn't crawling with terrorists. The second passport had been easier than the first.

My recent success with stocks, combined with surging British interest rates, enticed me to fatten up my offshore bank account. In it and Mr. Blake I saw my financial future, and if my finances were secure I could concentrate on my marriage and freedom. I could have flown to London or Zurich, loaded down with cash. Many people took that route. I had done the same on a smaller scale to buy art and antiques, but that was *before*. Now, one random customs search at London's Heathrow Airport could turn into a critical mistake. Carrying over ten thousand dollars without reporting it was a violation. Anyway, I was not mentally prepared to leave the country on my new ID, and so my predicament called for a more conservative game plan.

It took months to get into the mindset of changing cherished stacks of greenbacks into paper receipts, then shipping them off to someone else's care, which was the primary reason for this trip. I had told Blake I didn't want "Aldershot" (my new offshore corporation) appearing on dozens of certified *smurf* checks leading to my clean new trust fund. Accordingly, I was given a series of *feeder* accounts with names like Island Management, Basingstoke Investments and Sloane Nominees. These feeders were established at London banks with Blake's old cronies to service secretive clients from Capetown, South Africa, to tiny Mishawaka, Indiana. Cash or checks were mailed to a London flat, deposited in London banks like Barclays, sorted out, and credited to their rightful owner's trust funds in the Channel Islands—sans paper trail. Suddenly I knew how dirty politicians kept their cash from curious investigative journalists.

There was a MO for every mission, great or small. Kim and I pulled the curtains and put the Do Not Disturb sign on the door of our room at Hotel Dauphine. Then I dumped hundred dollar bills on the bed and started breaking rubber bands off five thousand dollar bundles. I handed her a stack of plastic bank deposit sleeves, and a list with feeder account names and corresponding figures.

"Four thousand, five hundred and five dollars, $4,775, $4860...I don't get it," she said. "Why are these totals so low? It'll take us a couple of days to—"

"Tough shit," I said, counting money like a veteran bank teller. "I want to keep the amounts way under IRS reporting limits so we don't attract any attention. That all right with you?" I snapped, unaware of attract any attention. That all right with you?" I snapped, unaware of how mechanical I became when the outlaw in me took over. For a second I considered apologizing, but noticed that gleam of excitement she seemed to get when seeing my often-dormant business side. "And another thing, always list the remitter as John Paul Simms. That way, if there's any problems down the road, I can use my disposable Simms ID to straighten them out."

She nodded, and smiled coyly.

"Sure you want to do this?" I asked softly.

"Uh, huh," she said, removing her robe and pulling me down into the money. *"After this."*

An hour later we emerged into bright sunshine, dressed in business attire and carrying briefcases. "We're going to the Business District," I said, flagging a cab. "We'll work the same street, and I'll always be across from you watching your...*back*. Never look into the monitor camera or remove your sunglasses. If you feel uncomfortable with a teller's line of questioning, leave and go to the next bank. If one place is especially easy, make a mental note of which feeder account you used there and I'll do it the next day with a different one. Got it?"

"Got it," she said.

As expected, the banks were packed with Mardi Gras tourists. Moving money in New Orleans that spring of 1987 was like the city's nickname—*Easy*, too easy. I had a great partner, and by Friday afternoon we were done. After mailing $150,000 in certified checks to a residential London flat, all that remained of my greenback stash was a pile of pink bank receipts.

Feeling the need to celebrate, I slipped into my silk-lined Italian pants and a ruffled French shirt. "Put on your red dress, Meekla," I said while snapping on a pair of suspenders. "We're going somewhere special."

We waded into the human sea of Mardi Gras madness that was Bourbon Street, and soon we were standing before a massive carved mahogany door. Two brass lanterns burned dimly on either side. A brass plaque above them read: Private Club.

"This is the place," I said, rapping twice on the door.

A brown eye peered through a peephole. "You have reservations?" inquired a raspy-voiced black man reminiscent of comedian Jack Benny's Rochester.

The Bombay Club, doors opened. A proper Englishman with graying temples and half-moon glasses escorted us to an old-fashioned piano bar. The balding black entertainer tickling the ivories wore matching black armbands and a visor. There were no electric lights, only candles. It was like a scene from Casablanca, dark, smoky, mysterious, my kind of place.

We dined on Italian cuisine and drank a great Barolo wine. I was contemplating singing Sinatra at the piano when a guy in the corner caught my eye. He was smoking a big cigar, wearing sunglasses, a dark suit with a white tie, and a pinky-ring rock that reflected in the flickering candlelight. He was in his late '50s, had football player's shoulders, and was seated beside a heavily jeweled attractive platinum blond in a knockout evening gown. He gave *my girl* the once-over, then nodded approvingly.

An hour passed. I watched the staff spoil him. The piano man granted his every request. People came to his side between songs to kiss his cheeks and wish his father, Carlo, well.

"Good night, Mr. Marsella," they would say. "If you ever need a favor...just call."

I noticed two stern-faced suits watching this guy intensely from a nearby table. They looked like feds. That's when I placed the name Marsella from a book I'd read about the Mob. Was this mystery man the son of the boss of New Orleans, accused of plotting on tapped phone lines with Florida boss Traficanti to kill J.F.K.?

Surveillance. Neither blessed nor cursed with my astute powers of observation, my wife sipped her liqueur, undisturbed. Knowing that feds, mobsters, and fugitives were not a good mix, I paid our bill and quickly disappeared with Kim into the steamy New Orleans night.

Next came my meeting with William Charles McCarthy. He had tried like hell to get us to travel to Tampa. "We're going to New Orleans for the final days of Mardi Gras," I'd told him. "It's a neutral site. Midway for all." And though he had grumbled vociferously, he agreed to come.

Saturday around suppertime I downed two preparatory vodka and tonics, cradled my bottle of vintage red wine, and we strolled across Rue Dauphine and Rue Royale, back into that roaring river of rowdy flesh on Bourbon Street, feeling relaxed and looking forward to seeing Leigh and the baby. When we came upon two mounted police on drunk-patrol, I was inspired to pet their white-ankled horses and ask directions to McCarthy's hotel.

My wife's eyes bulged when I also asked the kindly cops for a photo-op, and handed her the camera. "Are you nuts'?" she hissed.

"They're nice guys, Meekla," I whispered. "Relax. Remember, this fuge thing is all in *your* mind, not theirs."

It was a wonderful photo.

We found the Fisher Family going "low profile" in a deluxe Four Seasons Hotel suite, pacing the floor, waiting on a professional black nanny/babysitter who came highly recommended to Bill by the hotel concierge.

"Damn niggers! Never on time," Mr. Fisher fumed, gulping his standard gin and tonic.

"Oh, Bill! Be patient," Leigh said, blushing. "She sounded so sweet on the phone."

Bill and I shook hands stiffly—as always—studying each other while we held the grip. The initial eight months of fugitivity had not taken away his arrogance, but his curly brown hair was rapidly receding and going gray. He had put on some weight, too, and the jowls on his tanned face were plumper. I pecked Leigh on the cheek, glanced into her misty brown eyes and gave her a heartfelt hug for old time's sake. She was not the same olive-skinned, raven-haired beauty with whom I'd once lived, but a pleasant sight, nonetheless. "How ya been, *Lerta*?" I asked, as always wondering what in the hell she saw in Bill.

"Okay, I guess," she said meekly. Kim complimented her outfit, and she returned the pleasantry. Anna Lee Fisher introduced us to her darling daughter as *Uncle Timmy* and *Auntie Diane*—we never told them our last names—and little Shannon stole our hearts. From that moment on, each time I saw her I felt saddened by the situation she was growing up in.

While waiting on their nanny I decanted the wine and served it with trademark style. Always the entertainer in the right company, I shared some tales from our freshman year on the lam. Leigh and Kim, keenly aware of the tension in the air, laughed freely. But Bill, who rarely made eye contact with me, maintained a fixed gaze through the room's sheer curtains to the Mississippi waterfront far below.

At dinner, after belting down more gin, Mr. Fisher bragged about some of the legitimate debts that changing his identity had allowed him to leave behind, like a large construction loan. "Did you ever collect that hundred grand from Ken Fara?" he asked.

I shook my head, acutely bothered by the thought of another one-time friend and Hoosier marijuana customer who found it so easy to ignore his debts. Ken Fara, former yardman for Mishawaka's Wicks Lumber Company, was the guy who had introduced me to my Indiana antiques connection. Ken had asked to borrow the money he owed me from his last marijuana deal to buy a farm where he could grow some weed until his divorce was settled, and had been dodging me ever since. I threatened him before going underground, but my renowned nonviolent, nice-guy nature never instilled the fear of God in such wayward clients. With no *Vinny* knocking at his door on my behalf, I had to figure my dough was going, going, *gone*. I pictured the semi-pro quality baseball player's black handlebar moustache dipping in a bag of cocaine, one Roman nostril snorting up my money with a silver straw—the last information I'd received about Ken.

"Waiter!" I said, steamed at the thought of being ripped off by friends. "Hit me again."

Bill—never one to under-salt a wound, especially *my* wounds in front of my ex-lover/his wife—continued. "And what about, 'Honest Richy', the pig farmer from Argos? Did he auction off your antique inventory and pay you your seventy-five grand?"

I slammed my glass upon the cocktail waiter's tray. "Make it a double," I added. "You know damn well people like to kick you when you're down, old pal."

"Sure do," Bill said, smiling ear to ear.

Leigh, who'd been biting her nails and blinking, asked, "How's, Ben?"

I bit my lip and nodded.

"And, Todd?" she inquired opportunely.

We saved *the discussion* for later, when the ladies slipped away into a tourist trap. "How's Leigh holding up?" I began, itching to cut to the chase.

Bill shrugged his shoulders and turned to face me with narrowed eyes. "Let's pass on the bull and talk about money."

"Fine," I said, changing to my confrontational mode. "Between my share of real estate holdings, construction equipment, and the sale of the pole barn, I figure you owe me at least fifty grand."

Bill erupted in forced laughter. "What a crock of shit! I told you there wasn't enough time to sell. Not only that, but while you were out west being a beach boy, I put every bit of twenty-five thousand into those damn rentals for repairs."

"Repairs? Repairs, my ass! You're talking to the head Aardvark who actually used to work. Remember? I know repairs. What did you do, install gold plumbing fixtures for the pimps on Williams Street? I've been asking you to settle up since 1984, plus I paid for your IDs!"

I was hot. We were shouting. A squad car cruised past slowly, and we nodded to the cops inside. I stared at the man beside me, trying to figure him out. Here was a guy, a self-confessed millionaire who had handled over 30,000 pounds of pot *after* my exodus from Indiana, wanting to pinch me for my legitimate interests. It was worse than I expected. There was something sinister in those blue eyes, something I not only found disturbing, but dangerous. I recalled how relieved I felt the day I officially severed ties with him by moving west to Truckee. "Fuck your weak-ass fairy tales," I said, turning to face him. "Where's my fifty grand?"

"Honey, look," Kim said excitedly, emerging from the shop with a porcelain Mardi Gras masque face pin. When she saw my expression, her smile quickly faded.

"We could hear you inside," Leigh told Bill. "What's wrong? What are you mad about?"

"Me?" Bill grinned, tapping his chest. "I'm not mad."

"He's not the one getting screwed," I muttered, flagging a horse and carriage. "Driver, carry us back to Bourbon Street, and take the longest route possible."

Bill and Leigh caught another coach and followed close behind.

"What's wrong with you two?" Kim asked as we rode alongside the water. She pried my fingers free from the fists they had formed. "I thought you were such a good diplomat. I thought you two were friends."

I spat into the street, then kissed her hand. "More partners than friends. I only put up with him for the money. You see, we men can be whores, too."

"What's that supposed to mean?"

"Nothing. It's Bill, sometimes he brings out the devil in me."

"Well, what about Leigh?"
"What about her?"
"Do you still love her?" Kim stammered.
I laughed. "No, but funny you should ask. Maybe that's what's under old Billy-boy's skin. Knowing that she lost her virginity during lunch hour from Mishawaka High School in the basement of my parents' house on Victoria Street. Knowing that I'm the only other guy who's made love to his wife, night after night after night."
"You told me she didn't like to do it that often," my wife said angrily.
"Oh, she didn't. Don't worry, *no one* does it like you do, dear. That's why we're married and Leigh's a good friend."
"Yes, but do you love me?" Kim asked, mumbly-mouthed.
I heard the sound of a street musician. I saw this black jazz-cat jammin' on a shiny brass sax beneath a dark brick archway, in front of a weathered pink door. "Driver, pull over, please," I said.
Kim was tugging at my heart and my sleeve. *"But do you love me?"*
"Heart and soul, baby," I said. "Heart and soul. Just listen to the melody."

Bourbon Street was wall-to-wall people. A parade came clamoring through. Singing and laughter erupted. Every curbside seat was taken. I spotted a foursome leaving from a restaurant balcony above us, whispered in Kim's ear, and ran inside. Twenty bucks later, we were sitting comfy on that balcony sipping cold, strong cocktails. The booze helped me forget how much I disliked the way the man in the wrought iron chair across from me could effect my demeanor. Soon the gracious liquor gods made me oblivious to my old nemesis. Feeling playful again, I dashed into the bathroom, bought some condoms, and brought them back to our table. Kim, now wearing a sexy black beret she'd pulled from her purse, joined me in blowing up my *latex balloons* and tossing them to the crowd below which responded with resounding howls.
"Show your tits! Show your tits!" the street savages chanted.
Kim was drunk, so was I. Her wild raccoon side was calling her. We were a fun-loving couple, but marital jealousy must have showed on my face as my gypsy-woman considered flashing them.
"Show your ass!" my wife shouted back. And the street boys obliged her by mooning the balcony.
James Mark Fisher, (Bill) who hadn't said two words since our talk,

finally had enough. He grabbed the drink from his boisterous Anna Lee's hand and called it a night. "The nanny will be worried, dear," he said.

Leigh rose reluctantly with a concerned expression on her face.

"Call you tomorrow noonish, *Lerta*," I slurred, petting her wrist.

No one pushed my buttons like Bill did, but I was determined not to let him get to me during our stay in New Orleans. After they departed, my wife and I continued to paint the town.

At the urging of the ladies, I endured two more days in New Orleans. Bill, realizing he had pushed me to the edge, humbled himself enough to ask my opinion on passports and banking matters. He admitted being worried about his right-hand man exposing his Cayman Islands bank account to the feds. But of course Bill never mentioned the letter he'd written to Mr. Meers, authorizing his friend to reveal my Channel Islands account to the government in exchange for leniency. "I'm going to go to Switzerland carrying a few hundred grand, and open another account," Bill announced. "Then I'll transfer the Cayman funds there."

Maintaining my silent-mode with him, I only shrugged my shoulders.

On Monday, we took in the parades from curbside on Canal Street. People on floats tossed colorful plastic cups, balls, beads and medallions. *Star Trek's* William Shatner—portraying Bacchus, God of wine—winked at my wife. Shannon squealed with delight every time a catch of Mardi Gras treasure was made, bringing out the kid in each of us. But the tension between Bill and me never faded.

That night at their hotel suite, I announced I'd had enough of the party. "We're flying home a day early," I said. "Fat Tuesday morning, to avoid the final madness."

Leigh lobbied hard for another get-together. "Maybe by the ocean somewhere this summer," she suggested, bouncing that beautiful baby on her knee.

Kim and I exchanged glances. I gave Leigh a hug, and nodded to Bill.

"Let's play it by ear," I replied.

§

Spring brought a string of distressing events to light. The Boston Celtic's first round draft-pick, Len Bias, died from an overdose of crack cocaine in House Speaker Tip O'Neill's district. Politicians watched the nightly news which filled the senses of frightened voters with inner-city scenes of drive-by shootings, addict-looters, and gang-bang-losers blowing people's brains out for a few lousy bucks. It was Maui Bert's 1983 pre-retirement warning come-to-pass. It was a bad scene, and it even scared me. America's ever-evolving pot laws were about to change again.

More so than ever before, drugs were all "hard" to an uninformed John Q. Public. People with no personal experience did not distinguish between marijuana and paranoia-inducing cocaine, or soul-destroying heroin, let alone scores of new drugs arriving on the streets. In a knee-jerk reaction, nervous politicians scrambled to pass unrealistic sentencing laws, without conducting proper research, which placed nonviolent, first-time drug offenders behind bars for more years than most child molesters, rapists, and murderers. This "New Sentencing Guidelines" law gave birth to a booming *Prison Industrial Complex* whose financial and psychological costs would eventually become unmanageable. It was a media-mandate to the courts that took the power of making sentencing decisions away from seasoned federal judges, and placed it in the hands of statistic hungry prosecutors. Obviously, unlike for Vietnam's draft dodgers, there would be no amnesty for fugitive pot dealers.

On the Octagon Compound, my exercise cravings increased considerably, and with each mile ran, biked, or cross-country skied, with each pull on the rower, I began to think longer term. In the beginning the idea was to survive long enough to stash some money, then negotiate my surrender. Now other ideas would have to be pursued aggressively—like paying taxes under my assumed identity and creating a history that would allow me to safely relocate to another country.

In Tampa the fugitive Fisher Family had a frightening experience. A month after our Mardi Gras rendezvous, I phoned them. They'd been dining at an expensive restaurant when the table beside them was seated with some familiar faces from the past; people from South Bend where our mugs were appearing on the weekly *Crime Stoppers* show. The tone of Bill's voice made me think it had been something more serious than a casual run-in. He and Leigh were scared. She asked how I felt about them moving near us. If Bill had been straight with me in New Orleans I might have broken weak for her and the baby.

"Not wise," I said.

"Fine," Bill declared. "Then we'll move to Colorado."

Jagger, the Lion's Share store cat rescued from abandonment at California's Railroad Park, kept coming home with fur missing from his little gray behind. Then, one day in early April, he just disappeared. Night after night I called him. Every morning, Benjamin, Whitey, and I went further into the snow-covered forest searching for a sign.

"Give it up," Kim said sharply one day while scrubbing a blackened skillet. "He probably found a normal family to live with." Changing the subject, she added, "This hard water is ruining our clothes. And my hair! How about moving closer to Portland?"

When Chinook winds brought seventy-degree temperatures back to sunny Central Oregon I scrutinized the forest floor once more, wanting and not wanting to confirm my suspicions about the disappearance of Jaggs. My red dog discovered the puff of gray hair, several large feathers, and a feline hind leg jutting from a clump of dirty snow.

Later, when burying the remains with Kim, I attempted to put things into proper perspective. "Maybe this is an omen," I said, uncomfortable with the thought of surviving another off-tourist season in Sunriver. "Stay in unfamiliar woods too long...and you eventually fall prey to the hawk."

"Please," Kim replied, choking. "Gag me with a spoon! He was just a stupid cat. Now that you know he's dead, can we move?"

Once again, her cold side struck a nerve in me. "Maybe," I said.

The last straw came one day while spring skiing on Mount Bachelor. We were going up the chair lift over the black diamond Outback Run, when a Hoosier couple from South Bend paused to rest on the moguls beneath us. There was no doubt in my mind because one Indiana summer I had dated the redhead, Sharon. She didn't see me, but it didn't matter. To me, the Halloween bounty hunter episode, the look on my landlady's face at Christmas when she discovered my guests from hell passed out on the floor, the loss of Mr. Jaggs, and seeing Sharon were all omens.

It was time to mosey on down the Oregon Trail.

It was our second summer on the lam. I longed to be by the sea, and so—like the 19th Century explorers Lewis and Clark—I followed the flow of the mighty Columbia River there, where I combed Oregon's rugged North Coast for a new refuge. I combined fishing expeditions with house hunts, scanned Vacation Rental columns in local papers, and called potential landlords from rented hotel rooms—never leaving a trail to the Octagon's phone number. What I sought was a seasonal base camp whose natural setting would infuse us with the strength I knew we'd need for the journey ahead.

After studying Tillamook Bay, Cannon Beach, and Seaside, nothing seemed to fit our needs. Then I discovered Manzanita, with a hidden, wonderful white-sand beach half a mile off busy Highway 101. Bike paths, blackberry patches, public tennis courts, wildflowers, free-roaming pets, piles of driftwood, cool tidal pools...all in the protective shadows of majestic Cape Falcon. Manzanita was a laid-back summer haven, seven hours from the Octagon and Bend, but a convenient ninety minutes from progressive Portland should we find ourselves bored.

The quaint red cottage reminded me of my childhood summers when mom managed to scrape together enough cash to rent a simple lake cottage in Southern Michigan where her six kids and a couple of the neighbors' somehow squeezed in. So I went for it—perhaps to recapture those cherished weeks from my childhood on Berry Road.

Red Cottage was small, rustic, and renter-equipped with indestructible furniture and primitive cooking utensils. It had a tiny downstairs bedroom, one micro-bathroom with a dwarf clawfoot tub, a fair-sized living room featuring a foldout couch, a large screened-in front porch, old squeaky wood floors, and lots of knotty pine. It was one block from the beach on a secluded side street; big deck, privacy fence, hummingbird feeders, blooming gladioli, an old garage full of tools and junk, and a little garden space. But above all, there was a master bedroom in a converted attic with a dormer view of the Pacific. From that bedroom I could hear the soothing sound of the surf.

The owners, Vicky and Al Paladini, rented Red Cottage by the week, but found this a difficult task from their home in Roseburg. They resembled Michael J. Fox's TV parents in *Family Ties*. They loved Volvos, and liked us. They asked few questions and let me book the place—keeping the utilities in their name—for a monthly rate through

August. By May first, we were Manzanitans.

Until June, our base camp was a ghost town. Arnie rejoiced in the joys of another regional golf tour. Kim and I became preferred customers at a local garden shop, made the nearby Otisville Cafe our Sunday breakfast stop, caught delicious Dungeness crabs from the sea, and discovered a prolific crayfish hole in the upper Nehalem River—all while continuing to explore the coast. We made pilgrimages to Portland and San Francisco, too. And, of course, maintained contact with the other fuges.

Gradually, sleepy Manzanita came alive with summer people. On weekends—Pacific breezes permitting—cars and vans lined the narrow beach road to watch windsurfers swarm our tranquil shores in skin-tight wet suits with their neon-bright sails unfurled. The weekend visitors built driftwood bonfires in the sand, illuminating the coast all the way to Cape Falcon. Many nights between the lapping of waves I listened to their laughter and beach music, and watched strolling lovers' faces flicker then fade into fine sea mist from a sheltered dune beneath a shared blanket with my wife, remembering simpler days on freshwater, Midwestern shores.

There was a charity Bach Festival held in the Otisville Fire Department's garage that Kim and I attended in our Sunday-go-to-meetin' clothes, but local nightlife consisted of pinball, pool, or shuffleboard at the neighboring watering hole, the *Sand Dune*—a rustic beer and wine place not two minutes walk from Red Cottage. Everything was a two-minute walk away. Everything being the beach and a tiny Italian restaurant, from which we ordered many pizzas.

We were just like some all-American family on summer vacation, reading, gardening, fishing, golfing, and swimming. On those misty June mornings, Kim read fashion magazines—plotting her next raid on Nordstrom's in Portland—and numerous cookbooks whose recipes would be tested on us. I read my sacred *Fishing Oregon* book (often venturing out at low tide to seek the elusive surfperch), studied London stocks, and researched methods for procuring identification overseas. Arnie read newspapers, novels and golf magazines. Our harebrained kitty, Ms. Whitey, chased butterflies and hummingbirds, while old Ben chewed slimy rawhide bones on the front lawn. We certainly *looked* like a normal family.

Arnie—who had left a true but forbidden love with a friend's wife in South Bend—was understandably lonely and showing signs of 'third-wheel syndrome', if not full-blown depression. Missing his large Labrador retriever, Toke, also left behind, he began borrowing old Benjamin for daily walks on the beach. And there he befriended a fellow dog lover—a divorcée from Portland whose grandma's Manzanita cottage had become her weekend refuge. The brunette-on-the-rebound was ripe for romance. Ultimately, we came to see more and more of her.

One day we returned early from a trip into Portland to find our "Cousin Johnny" and his squeeze scantily clad, smoking pot and lounging in the living room. I flashed back to the summer before our marriage in Tahoe, when Kim's undercover daddy paid us a visit and lived up to his macho image in a similar scene.

This scene with Arnie stirred mixed emotions in me. For all my craftiness, I could not imagine a one-sided fugitive-romantic relationship, finding it tough enough lying to landlords and casual contacts like the Greek down in San Francisco. I felt good for my old friend when he stared at me with those glazed eyes and that *got me some* smile. But this stranger in our sanctuary—she worried me. What post-carnal questions did she pose while they were stoned, afterglowing and giddy? "So, where did you grow up, ya big hunk? Please, pretty-pretty-pretty please, tell me about your past, Johnny!"

It gave me the jitters.

We spoke candidly about it the following night. "I don't want any tension between us," I said, shaking my head. "Shit! I used to hate hearing my step dad say, 'As long as you live under my roof,' but ours are special circumstances. For almost a year now, it's been just the three of us." I cleared my throat. "I don't want to have to be on guard in my own living room."

Arnie nodded and reassured me he'd keep his summer fling at arm's length.

"Lighten up," Kim said later, as I stared out our dormer window like a nervous father, watching the lovers in our midst walk toward the ocean and wondering what they were talking about.

Birds of a feather flocked together and female fugitives craved the company of their kin. As we approached the anniversary of our first year on the run, I discovered how hard it was to live in isolation. I longed for the company of our colorful friends. Resigned to the fact that Manzanita was nothing but a summer fling, and of no mind to venture far from home, I invited all the others up for the Fourth of July. Recent phone conversations with Bill led me to believe we could fairly settle our financial differences, and so the Fishers flew in to Portland from their new residence in Boulder, Colorado. As we drove them to the coast, then helped them settle in to the vacation rental I'd arranged—once again—the presence of Leigh and little Shannon made us feel good, but bad vibes still lingered between Bill and me.

A huge motor home tooled into Manzanita the next morning and lurched to a halt in front of our Red Cottage. It was the Ohioans' new toy and marijuana transport vehicle, which would also serve as a mobile bunkhouse until July fifth when the second vacation rental I'd reserved became available. Right behind them came Sonny, with longtime ladylove, Missy. They'd driven the Jew Canoe—fueled by premium gas and high grade cocaine—non-stop from Southern Cal, and were about to kill each other. We'd never met Missy, and I watched with great curiosity as she emerged from the Jew Canoe brushing lint from her black, ribbed Lycra leggings. She was terribly overdressed, wearing spiked-heels that helped her perky buns protrude properly—until they sank in pea-gravel beside our privacy fence. Missy, who resembled Lizza Minelli, opened a black, velvet-lined jeweler's case on the hood of the Canoe, sized up an overcast sky, and selected one of her many "healing crystals" which, before she left, all the wives would be wearing.

I recalled what Lizzy had said about Missy on the phone the week before: "She's a little quirky. You know, typical L.A. Jewish Princess, into La-La-Land mentality, holistic medicine, the whole nine yards." I had detected competitive female cattiness in Lizzy's Connecticut Yankee tone. "Missy's not a fugitive *yet,*" Lizzy had predicted, "but she's been with Sonny for years. I think she'll come around."

"Hi! You must be Timmy," Missy said with a hug and a kiss.

"Tim," I said, studying her warm, genuine smile. "And this is Diane."

The guests piled out of their machines and reassembled behind our privacy fence where warm greetings were exchanged. They toured Red Cottage's tiny grounds, marveling at our normalcy. "Pets, fresh garden produce, crab traps, fishing poles, flowers, a barbecue grill...amazing,"

Missy said. "Not exactly what I expected a fugitives' hideaway to look like."

"We've had a good season," Lizzy interrupted with a frown. "The boys have been on the road for months, and—"

"Sold all the Mexican weed we could get," Smiley said proudly. "Need a break from the rat race. Say, what gives with these gray skies? Thought you said it was nice here."

"Gray skies, cool seas and misty rains nine months out of the year are what preserves Manzanita's pristine coastline," I explained, "as well as most of the Pacific Northwest. Don't worry, be happy. It'll burn off by noon."

"It's beautiful, I'll give you that," Smiley said. "We stopped at some sea lion caves down the coast yesterday."

Lizzy—batting her finely plucked eyebrows—draped one arm over my shoulder. "I'm just dying to know our activities schedule, Tour Director Timmy!"

"You said you wanted to unwind, right?" I asked. They nodded. "I've reserved a fishing charter boat, day after tomorrow, at the Port of Garibaldi. The salmon are in and..."

Missy's face turned white. "*Fishing?*" She stroked the shining crystal dangling between her breasts. "But I've never been—"

"You'll love it!" Sonny exclaimed, slapping her ass. "After all, you are pushing forty. Don't you think it's time you learned a few new tricks?" Missy's brow furrowed. She plucked some hairs from just below Sonny's knee. "Ouch!" he cried.

Smiley Jim laughed, too, until Lizzy jammed an elbow in his ribcage.

Kim pinched my side. It was like a live performance of the female Three Stooges. "See, honey," she said. "Not everyone likes the same things you do. Don't be so controlling. They just got here. Maybe us girls will get our legs waxed tomorrow."

The three wives exchanged high-fives. Instant bonding occurred. Our better halves were in their glory. And we men knew right then they'd be a force to be reckoned with in the coming days, just as we knew how badly they needed each other's company, and this reunion.

Sonny saw the hurt expression on my face. "Everyone knows what a good host we have," he said. "Tim's a master fisherman. We'll all have fun on a boat."

"I promise we'll never lose sight of shore," I said.

"Count us in," said Sonny. "Hey! I brought the latest hi-tech bird kites from La-La-Land. Can't wait to fly them on the beach." He was smiling like a kid. We all were.

"What else have you got planned, Timmy?" whistled Lizzy.

I sighed. "Thought we'd hike the Coastal Trail at Ecola State Park." Missy stared at me like some overbearing drill instructor. "It's six miles of…" Even Sonny's jaw dropped. Missy mouthed, S-I-X. I saw pain in her pampered L.A. eyes. "Easy scenic trail," I went on, thoroughly enjoying their reactions. "We'll have a picnic halfway, and watch for whales and sea lions. I'll pack in our lunch. Well, what do you say?"

The Ohioans, always game, gave thumbs up. The other troops nodded approvingly.

"That's the spirit!" I declared. "This is gonna be like *The Big Chill*. We'll do it all. Hawaiian luau on the Fourth? Fuge volleyball in the sand?"

Their heads bobbed briskly. I was excited, and pleased to know I had not lost my touch as a motivator. "They're blocking off Main Street for a small parade the morning of the Fourth, to be followed by an old fashioned pancake dinner."

"Yummers!" shouted Smiley. "Hope it's all you can eat."

Lizzy patted his beer gut and shook her head. "Hope not."

At the table of the motor home they called *The Enterprise*, my guests pulled the curtains, emptied seat cushions, pockets, and purses, and formed an impressive pile consisting of various IDs, hundred dollar bills, and excessive, but personal, drug stashes. "Hate to have some scumbag break into our rigs and ruin this vacation," Smiley said, giving me the eye.

"I've got just the place for this crap," I said. "With mine in the crawlspace of our cottage."

"I knew ya would, Timmy." Smiley slapped my back. "God bless ya, guy! Now, where's Leigh and the baby?"

He had met her and Bill at one of my gala early '80s, Summit Club dinners back in South Bend. In those days, I kept a close eye on such players so they wouldn't cut me out and do business together on the sly. Now that I was a retired dealer, this fear had evaporated. So we strolled to the Fisher's rental house where I made the necessary introductions.

Everyone shook hands. Leigh—always a gracious hostess—served snacks, her brown eyes glowing at the sight of company. Bill put his best foot forward and fired up a pre-rolled joint. Little Shannon was elated. "Unca' Timmy! Auntie Diane!" she squealed. Suddenly she also had *Aunties* Missy and Lizzy, and *Uncas* Johnny, Sonny, and Smiley.

That night Red Cottage's tiny kitchen was hopping with happy, giddy wives, sipping the grape and sharing their mothers' recipes. Lovable Shannon Fisher floated room-to-room like a whirling dervish, dancing with delighted adults and having her fill of genuine affection. Inevitably, we separated into gender groups for the official cocktail hour.

On the front porch, male discussions ranged from marijuana markets to stock markets, currencies to gold coins, and new sources for identification. Sonny had circumvented the California driver's license problem. California required a thumbprint, not something a fugitive wanted on record.

"I've been screwing this little blond license bureau employee," he announced, then lowered his voice so Missy wouldn't hear from the kitchen. "See," he whispered, displaying his Los Angeles license, while keeping one finger over the name. "For five hundred bucks, I can get all of them I want. Want one?"

"Not me," I said. "What did you tell her you wanted it for? Don't forget, hell hath no fury like a jealous DMV woman." I paused to drink. Smiley chuckled. "Especially for a fugitive from justice."

"Oh, she doesn't know squat," Sonny blurted. "Thinks I'm some crazy musician escapee from MTV! Speaking of craziness..." He produced a pill bottle and spilled its contents on the table. "Ta-ta! Presenting two of La-La-Land's hottest new designer drugs, Ms. Ecstasy and Mr. Halcyon. Ladies love 'X', 'cause it's the *love* drug."

"Got no problem there," I said.

"Good old Dr. Bliss! God bless ya, guy," Smiley shouted, rubbing his palm and reaching out. "Just wait till you've been married a while, Timmy."

"Bush is hooked on these." Sonny displayed a tab.

"Come on," I said.

"Serious as a heart attack, Tim! The Vice President and Mr. Halcyon are best friends. Word is, this little gem helps George forget things like Ollie North's drugs-for-arms missions, pizza-faced Noriega's Panamanian money laundering, Iran-Contra, and some shady S & L deals by his sons."

"Nothing's taboo for a chosen few," I remarked as Dr. Bliss filled Smiley's outstretched hand. When he tipped the container my way, I waved him off. "I'm afraid anything more than good old pot might take me out of the fugitive mindset and make me paranoid. Wouldn't want that, would we, guys?"

They exchanged glances. "Gonna get nerved-out like you did at Christmas if we cut loose in Manzanita?" Smiley asked.

"Hell, no! Place is too darn small for you fuges to get in trouble. Your pagers are out of range. You promised no business calls. You can stagger these streets until dawn and not get lost. If we travel far, *I'll drive* or hire someone. So, eat, snort, drink and be merry! You'll find me a mellow host." They toasted that. "Now, what other juicy gossip have you overheard from your Jewish celebrity friends down in Beverly Hills?"

Sonny took a deep breath. "Ant head Nancy Reagan runs the White House by the stars. Dame's got the Gipper staring at the Big Dipper! A doctor friend of mine can remove these." He pointed to his fingerprints. "With laser surgery. The effect lasts about six months. The doc does faces, too. Want an introduction?"

I sang a couple bars of *I've Got To Be Me.* "Too weird," I said. "Anyway, I'm no Robert Vesco and this fuge thing ain't forever."

"Says who?" Smiley retorted. "I've got one for ya. I talked with our Hawaiian Island friend a few weeks ago. According to him, American justice *is* still for sale if you can get enough cheese to the right rats. That is if Ed Meese III and all the president's men don't resign or get indicted. We're gonna know soon enough because..." He paused, hesitant to mention Maui Bert's name in front of Bill McCarthy.

I wondered if Bert really had found a way to bribe his way out of a major prison term, or if he was considering testifying against the rest of us in our absence. And what became of Bert's right hand man, Maui Ray? "I thought he was going to disappear," I said.

"Evidently not. If whatever he's up to works, and we make enough dough, maybe we can all follow his lead." Smiley winked one freckle-framed eye. "Speaking of making money. What-cha think, Timmy? Come to Tucson for the fall crop. Turn us on to Tony. The wives can spend our money shopping and hang out at the pool. And—strictly under the guise of business—I know some firm young cuties who can do nasty things with the bearded clam." He ran his tongue across his lips. "Yummers!"

"You're crazy! Working and fugin' don't mix. Let alone whoring around on your old lady."

"Fuck that noise! We're outlaws, face it. What-cha gonna do, Timmy, go fishin' and play in the garden all year?"

"Maybe."

"How 'bout loaning us some venture capital then? No involvement, big monthly interest."

I shrugged my shoulders, but McCarthy's blue eyes bulged.

"How 'bout you, Bill?" Smiley asked. "You're awfully quiet."

"Tim here's the clown. I'm one of those quiet, serious types." Bill tilted his curly head to one side and flashed me a cocky smile.

"Excuse me," I said, smelling the birth of another conspiracy. "But it's time for me to go play host."

In the center of Red Cottage, sitting on the sofa next to Benjamin, I gently peeled off the worn lead seals on four bottles of 1952 Lafitte Rothschild, which I'd brought out of storage for this reunion. Without losing a cork, I opened them. Then, while the wine of '52 breathed the air of '87, I petted my Irish setter and tuned in to some interesting discussions.

"Oh, he's just adorable!" Missy declared from the noisy kitchen. "But does he buy you things?"

"Sure," Kim said excitedly. "Wait till you see the designer coat I got him to spring for at North Beach Leather in San Francisco. And look at the new stone in my ring."

"Yeah, yeah, they're nice," Missy replied. "But a knockout like you needs *things!* Rubies, cars, crystals, pearls—"

"Evening, girls," I announced, entering the kitchen. "How's it going?"

"Great!" Kim sighed, pinching my thigh. They all giggled. "Nothing against you, honey, but it sure is nice to have some girl talk."

"Good," I said. Suddenly I pictured Kim as Elly May Clampett, her nonmaterial pureness being siphoned away by the Beverly Hills sun beside the cement pond. "Ready for some sunset wine?" I asked them.

Minutes later, with four foxy ladies following close behind me, I approached the porch in time to hear the tail end of another sensitive conversation.

"What-cha think, Arnie?" Smiley said, rubbing his temples. "We sure could use another driver. Lord knows you're experienced! And Sonny's old workhorse, Sarge, needs rest between trips."

Arnie didn't answer.

"You'd pay me how much a month on 200 grand?" a surprisingly animated McCarthy asked, drooling in his drink.

"Ten percent. On *whatever* amount you want to loan us. But only during the pot season."

That's when I noticed Todd's divorcée friend, her face inches from the porch screen door, her knuckles frozen in the knocking position. I coughed loudly. An eerie silence set in. "Hi, Diana," I said, opening the door. "Come on in." I could smell whiskey on her breath.

"Didn't mean to disturb you," she slurred.

Arnie's face turned red.

Above a flickering candle in the corner, I tended to my wine with a towel draped over one arm, carefully tilting bottle to glass with Kim's assistance, and sorting ancient sediment from sweet nectar in the neck.

"You know, that's another thing I've noticed about you, Tim," Arnie's Diana said, eyeing my presentation. "You're quite the connoisseur."

I nodded and continued without spilling a drop. *What else have you noticed? And how much did you overhear?*

"Want to introduce me to your interesting friends, John?" Arnie's lady asked. "Or should I call you...*Arnie?*"

Arnie froze. All eyes focused on me. I took control. "We're into nicknames, dear," I explained. "Everyone calls Johnny, Arnie, for his exceptional golfing talent." I handed her a glass of wine, then cleared my throat. "These are the Fishers from Florida and their darling daughter, Shannon. This is Smiley and Lizzy."

They exchanged greetings. My friends loosened up, but Sonny kept giving me the eye.

"And these crazies are Missy and...*Moon.* Moon's in the music biz. They're from L.A.," I added, nodding. Sonny had been his nickname for his entire adult life until his pointed stare told me it was time for a change. And from that moment on Sonny was Moon.

"At least it's still celestial," Missy whispered in my ear, nervously stroking her crystal.

Our group of ten, my red dog Ben, and Arnie's lady friend, walked to the sea for the sunset ritual we Manzanitans had grown accustomed to. Shoeless, we dug our toes into the refreshing beach and raised our glasses high.

"To sweet freedom," I said.

And as the ocean swallowed another sun, friends—new and old—echoed the refrain. The sand, washed wet by a retreating tide, reflected kaleidoscope watercolors around our sinking feet. A sliver moon hovered above the same Pacific salmon fleet we'd watched in Mendocino when embarking upon this odyssey. One year had passed, and none of us were suffering in prison. I stood drinking and thinking, my negative thoughts flowing outward with the undulating sea, truly feeling free.

In this moment of peace and brotherhood I decided to lower my expectations when settling with Bill McCarthy. Maybe my instincts were wrong? Maybe he did lose our rental properties to the feds. Sure, he should have liquidated like I did in Truckee, but what was he guilty of—negligence? I vowed to discuss things with an open mind as twilight's spell set in.

"Oh, my! That was lovely," shuddered Arnie's Diana. "I'm sure you all have lots of catching up to do, and Grandma is expecting me for dinner. Drop by later, *Arnie...*" she said with an enticing wink. "If you're feeling up to it." Then she handed me her glass. "Thanks, Tim. That was nice."

And as I watched her disappear—Birkenstock sandals swinging from her slight shoulders—the summer vacationer's driftwood fires flared along Manzanita's pristine shores, mirroring the shadowy Pacific salmon fleet.

Shortly after dinner I invited Bill to the patio to talk. He took my open-minded approach for weakness, pressed his luck, and said, "Anything I had coming for our joint interests that did sell was offset by repairs." I owed him, he declared.

"Impossible," I retorted. Bye-bye peace and brotherhood. We had words. He tried to blame me for his predicament, his wife's depression, and his baby's bad dreams.

The McCarthy/Fishers retired early. When the others asked why, I finally told them the story. Smiley and Moon were pretty wasted, and very concerned.

"You saying we can't trust him?" Smiley asked.

I could have really stung Bill. I was mad enough, but it wasn't my style. "He's out here with us, isn't he?" I said. "Anyway, I don't see how you can lose if you're going to be the borrower."

Moon frowned, realizing I'd overheard their conversation on my porch. Smiley furrowed his freckled brow. "We were just talking. Anyway, you're retired, right?"

I nodded. "That's right."

"And as for this rift with Bill," Smiley said, "hey, we've all lost real estate, guy. We can relate. I mean, it's not like you can't afford it." I cringed at his last remark.

"Yeah!" Lizzy said. "It's only money. Come on, Timmy. Their baby is so cute."

"Yeah, Tim," Missy said, rubbing my back. My wife rubbed a more sensitive spot. "We're having so much fun! Don't get bummed out."

"Come on, come on," they said.

Yeah, right, listen to them. Their advice was the equivalent of the U.N. asking Iraq and Iran to kiss and make-up. *Forget fifty grand I'd counted on?* People killed for a fraction of that! I studied Lizzy as she licked her candied lips—the die-hard businesswoman who calculated each diner's share to the penny when I wasn't paying the tab. If she and Smiley Jim had been in the same jam, they would have blown their tops.

"Open the cognac, honey," I told Kim. "Roll a monster joint, Arnie. Tomorrow, I'll settle it tomorrow, one way or another."

Later that night after the motor home *Enterprise* became a psychedelic Trivial Pursuit palace, I retired with Kim to our attic bedroom sanctuary. I stayed up half the night, pacing, stewing, staring out the dormer window at salmon fleet lights flickering on the far horizon, thinking of McCarthy. *I should have never gotten him IDs! Never invited him to this reunion!* Leigh and Shannon would be better off in Indiana, but because of my decision, they were out here, too. Instinct told me Bill was lying about the money, and probably more. I pondered one of my own fundamental rules, and how I used to chide childhood friends for not following it. "A friend screws you by betrayal or theft, and you still call them friend? Allow them in your house? Not me, stupid! What are you so afraid of? Stuck in a small town, a small circle with too many fond schoolday memories? Can't make new friends—especially at your age? What a weak, small-town mentality. Let a thief make a fool out of you again and again and again, and still call him friend? Not me."

For hours I watched my wife curled in fetal repose with those glorious curves bathed in a pale moonglow that filtered through our dormer window. I listened to the soothing surf until the anger left my head, then joined her in bed. Like it or not, I decided, my new life *was* a small circle. A very small circle indeed.

The next day after two heated sets of volleyball and several cold beers, I called time out. Bill and I walked and talked. Everyone watched. I felt the wives' eyes pushing me toward compromise. "Well?" I asked him. "Sticking to that bullshit story of yours?"

He kicked the sand, hid his smirk, and nodded. "Man, you were gone two fucking years! Every one of those rentals needed a new roof. Niggers trashed out two places when I tried to evict them for not paying rent. You were *Mr. Contractor.* You know what roofs cost, and—"

"And I know how long they last, too. They were all replaced in '83."

"What a crock of shit! You're getting too much garden sun, *Timmy.* I think this fugitive stress is making you senile or something."

"Asshole!" I snarled. "You owe me. *I* ain't paying you shit!"

He smiled like a Cheshire Cat, then extended one paw like a corrupt campaigning politician. "We'll just call it even then, agreed?"

One minute passed, then two, with his hand hovering there. I compared putting his pettiness behind me to blocking out yearnings to see my family. Finally I fought off a ferocious invisible gravity, locked grips, and squeezed firmly. "Agreed," I said. "But I'm only doing this for the girls, and the peace of mind of everyone affected by your fucked-up attitude."

"Let's play!" shouted the wives. "You're holding up the game."

They were right. But the main game was over, and Billy Boy had won.

The rest of the holiday reunion was smooth sailing. We took the fishing charter out of Garibaldi the following morning. The captain issued Dramamine seasickness pills and kept his boat within sight of shore. Morning fog dissipated, sun burned through, and his fugitive crew had a field day. We trolled for salmon, jigged for lingcod, grouper, and sea bass around green kelp beds, and caught our limit. Not only did

L.A. Missy overcome her fear of fishing, but Moon's lady outperformed all anglers, earning the nickname *Killer.* The full-day charter ended early, due to a hold full of fish. And as we headed back to port with four happy wives spread eagled across the bow catching ocean spray, I led renditions of popular '60s tunes, and generous Bill McCarthy announced *he* was paying the tab.

"Thanks," said the others.

Kim elbowed my kidney. I spat overboard. "Gee, thanks," I said, then added, audible only to my wife: "Big deal! He could pay for a hundred fishing charters, and still be way ahead. Guilt money, honey. Guilt money."

On the morning of the Fourth, we stood on Main Street with a few hundred tourists and one elated Shannon Fisher—who waved a tiny American flag—to watch the parade. Afterwards, we ate pancakes on picnic tables beside members of Manzanita's Volunteer Fire and Sheriff's Departments. "Yummers!" Smiley declared into the syrup stained face of a beer-gutted lawman. "God bless America!"

All of us marijuana fugitives echoed his cry, and meant it.

In the days that remained we dined at Cannon Beach's Bistro, and the Central Coast's Salishan Lodge. We hiked the Ecola State Park trail, and toured the countryside in the motor home *Enterprise*, stopping to taste Northwest wines and Tillamook cheese. We played shuffleboard, fed the vintage jukebox and danced at the Sand Dune. We had our version of the *Big Chill,* and most of us grew closer because of it.

Bill McCarthy had gotten everything he'd come for, and more. His wife was content and secure in knowing that contact with other fuge's wives and reunions were a reality in her future. His daughter received a healthy dose of love and affection. And not only did Mr. Bill put one over on his old partner, but he planted the seeds for a very lucrative business venture with Smiley and Moon. These were my thoughts as I waved goodbye to Anna Lee and Shannon Fisher at Portland's international airport.

The others stayed on until their vacation rental expired, then surprised me with my thirty-first birthday present. The plan was to take the *Enterprise* to Glacier National Park and backpack into the high country for a week. It was one of my favorite places. I'd been there last with my brother Bill back in '83, and had fond memories and nothing but praise for the park. Todd even offered to watch the home front. I decided to do it.

We made what was supposed to be an overnight pit stop in Portland, but ended up staying three days so everyone could get outfitted. While I was set with the right equipment, everyone else needed packs and hiking boots. We also bought special water filter pumps and dried foods. During our second dining extravaganza evening, at *Jake's Famous Crawfish,* I felt annoyed by the delay, mentioned this and sensed some strange reactions. Later, back at the hotel, after finding The Ohioans' adjoining door ajar, Kim and I pushed inside to suggest an early morning departure.

"What is this?" I asked, seeing all their IDs spread out on the bed, along with the Yellow Pages open to Alternative Mailing Services. Suddenly, all the Ohioans' mysterious side trips—like yesterday's, when Kim and Missy went shopping on Northwest 23rd, and Moon and I walked along the Willamette River—made perfect sense. The Ohioans were secretly working on Oregon IDs! Lizzy, caught red-handed, stood with her hubby at their bathroom door, smacking her lips, whistling conspicuously through that gap in her front teeth. Smiley glared at her.

"Why didn't you just tell me?" I asked.

Lizzy straightened the folds in her fancy dinner dress, then closed the phonebook in a huff.

"We planned on telling you tomorrow," Smiley said. "I didn't think you'd mind, Timmy."

"Told you, honey!" Lizzy smacked.

"Jesus fuckin' Christ, Timmy! Ya don't own the goddamn state." Smiley produced a plate from beneath a *Playboy* magazine and passed it to me.

Mindful that nosey neighbors might hear us, I turned on the TV and cranked up the volume. "Don't you ever run out of that shit?" I said. "I'll tell you one thing. I sure as hell ain't riding all the way to Montana just to snort coke and play Trivial Pursuit in the *Enterprise*!"

"Chill out! It's the last of our stash," Smiley assured me.

"Yeah, right. Listen, I don't own this state, but Tim Barnes is an established Portland resident, for whom I have big plans. Let's just say I'm concerned, shall we? Why Portland? You know I asked Arnie to get his license in Eugene, just to keep some distance between *our* paperwork."

"Look, we just got these institutionalized patients' paperwork." Smiley blinked excitedly. He fanned the air with one of the rare birth certificates. "I'm gonna be Mr. Bentley," he said, trying to sound retarded.

"And I'm Hailey now," Lizzy whistled demurely with hands clasped at her waist and feet rocking in silver heels.

"What a pretty name," said my wife as she accepted the toot plate.

"Guess I'm the only one who sees danger in the concept of shared cities," I sighed. "Did you get a mail drop yet?"

"Right downtown," Hailey replied.

"What about insurance?"

"She's going to Triple A in the morning," Smiley said. "Listen, guy. Don't get uptight. We'll do the passports in another state. All right?"

I nodded, knowing they were set on things. Just so it's not New Orleans, I thought.

Suddenly there was a knock on the door. *Hailey* peered through the peephole, nervously. "Hide the coke! Put away the IDs!"

"Honey, who is it?" asked Smiley.

"Hotel manager," announced a deep voice. Again came a knock.

Kim and I slipped through the adjoining door to our room, from which I entered the hall nonchalantly. The hotel manager was actually Moon, wearing the Tom Snyder wig from his handy-dandy fugitive-disguise kit, with his eyes glued to the Ohioans' door, trying to keep a straight face. When I brought the prankster around through our room *Hailey* nearly beat him to death.

That night, I did the best thing I could, helped them with their Portland paper trip and steered them away from the places Kim and I had used for our paper trips.

The next morning we called for late checkouts and arranged to meet downstairs for lunch. The Ohioans were supposed to join us by one o'clock, but never showed. Afterwards, we congregated in our room and talked. Missy, her confidence bolstered by Manzanita outdoor experiences, made one last plea for Moon to take the Montana trip with us. "Come on, honey! We can do it."

"They don't allow heels on hiking trails in Montana, *Killer*," he kidded, which drew a strong pinch. "Anyway, they're expecting me in Vancouver in two days."

"They, who?" I asked. "Who's expecting you up there?"

Moon took a deep breath, walked to the window evasively, and peered through the drapes suspiciously. "Just some old friends." His voice trailed off. His fingers drummed erratically on the windowsill.

Everyone had a secret agenda.

The Ohioans were now two hours late from *Hailey's* driver's license mission, and a rising tide of incoming conventioneers forced us to evacuate the hotel. Moon and I filled the motor home with baggage and relocated it a short distance away so we could watch for cops. And there on the table of *The Enterprise*, Missy, Kim, Moon and I played gin rummy, straining not to say what we were thinking. What if they went down? Did they have Moon's pager number on them? Tim Barnes' Barbur Boulevard address, or D.K. Moore's? The map I'd drawn to Manzanita's Red Cottage? A hotel room key? For all their talk, would they hold up under pressure? Stomachs grew tense. Several trips were taken to the tiny toilet seat at the rear of the good ship *Enterprise*.

"They snort too much coke," I said, pounding the table. "Smiley and Lizzy are smooth operators, but there's no way they can keep doing that shit and still maintain their edge. Mark my words, one day it's going to catch up with them."

Silence set in. Missy bit her nails. Kim nodded.

Moon nodded, too. "I told Irene the same thing," he said, tugging at his hair. "I'm getting too old for the shit. It's no damn good. Got to give it up, live long and prosper, and get healthy, like you two." He put an arm around his L.A. princess and looked at me like some forlorn schoolboy. "Think you could teach me to play tennis the next time we get together?"

Missy massaged his back first, then her crystal.

An hour later, an ominous scene unfolded across the street from us. Our jaws dropped open, and our eyes grew wide as silver dollars when an obvious unmarked detective car pulled in front of the hotel, then cruised toward First Street.

"They're canvassing the joint," Moon said, rubbing his temples raw. "Shit! I shouldn't have let them take their road test in the Jew Canoe. It's registered to Sarge." He shook his head and kicked the table leg. "He's babysitting all my cash."

I broke out in a sweat and swallowed hard. We tossed in our cards.

Kim sank her claws into my thigh. I rushed to the cushy captain's chair and sat there with my fingers on the ignition key. Missy tugged at her skintight Lycra leggings, closed her eyes, and caressed yet another magic crystal, chanting: "Please. Oh please, honey, please!"

Ahead of us, the heat on wheels screeched to a halt at the corner, then backed up.

I turned the key and the *Enterprise's* engine roared to life. "We go!" I said.

The others held their breath.

A girl dressed like a hooker appeared from the dark depths of the hotel's parking garage where an open car door beckoned. The streetwalker got in, and girl and dirty Dick disappeared arm-in-arm!

The crew of the *Enterprise* laughed hysterically.

A moment later, Moon's Caddy cruised into view and drove past the hotel twice, looking for us. Missy immediately credited her crystals. And then—by unanimous vote—we made *them* sweat for ten minutes before honking the horn to signal our new location.

"Beam us up, Captain Timmy!" Smiley ordered at the motor home's door. Hailey entered first, triumphantly waving her new license like a high school diploma. Smiley noticed our cold, stern faces, and was alarmed by our silence. "Had to wait two hours to take the damn driver's test!" he said. "You weren't worried, were ya?"

The smell of vodka permeated the air. Wanting to strangle them, we continued to stare.

Hailey batted her finely-plucked brows and curtsied comically. "Had to celebrate with one cocktail, didn't we?" she whistled.

She sure looked cute in her white knee socks and that Catholic school student's uniform. All I could do was laugh.

Seventeen days later: I watched Western scenery through the window of our Amtrak sleeper cabin, lost in the largeness of moon-painted landscapes gliding past me and the grand Montana memories in my head, listening to clicking rails, feeling rocking-swaying railroad cars' rhythm and Kim's heart beating where she lay fast asleep in my lap. I fought the demons these fugitive nights were increasingly bringing me. Was this running ruining Arnie's, Kim's, and my own life? In a moment of weakness I doubted that I had the strength to master this game. I missed my family, and blocked their images from appearing in my mind's eye.

On the floor beside an empty bottle of Cabernet, smoked chicken bones, Ritz crackers box and Brie cheese wrapper, sat Kim's new chewed tennis shoes—recently dined upon by a midnight prowler porcupine. In a plastic bag were her treasures from this trip: dozens of quills pulled from our dome tent, smooth colored glass from a fast-running glacial stream, several small reddish-brown pieces of petrified wood reminiscent of lava found on the Big Island of Hawaii.

I stared at Polaroid snapshots of me carrying a full pack and my ebony, elephant-head walking stick from Kenya; of a snow white mamma and baby mountain goat arrogantly blocking our path beside an ice-cold blue waterfall; of Kim tying big bear bells to the laces of her earthtone Danner hiking boots as sweat rolled down her sunburned cheeks from beneath a green bandana; of a meadow where pink sticky geranium, lupine, bear grass, fox glove and bluebells hid a sow and cub located a comfortable distance away from the cameraman. One photo showed me and Smiley casting Rooster Tails at 8,000 feet with water up to our waists—while the Eastern brook trout we angled for nibbled at our naked parts. Another captured Lizzy squatting by a tree where we had hung our packs and clothes for the night to keep grizzlies away from our campsite.

I remembered making love by moonlight in our little tent—she on top, making noises like a grizzly—when a herd of deer trampled through our campgrounds, pursued by something! We switched positions. I grabbed my walking stick and vowed to protect her. She laughed at me.

The next night I broke out four tins of smoked oysters I'd been saving. Smiley, not to be outdone and after five days on the wagon, whipped out a flask of whiskey, and we dozed off under a million stars, serenaded by a crackling fire. And finally, there was the photo I took of us emerging from backcountry wilderness on blistered feet wrapped in moleskin bandages—Victorious Trekkies!—minutes before I flagged down a fire-engine red, open-aired, many-seated vehicle driven by youthful park employees, whom I paid handsomely to ferry our cheery but weary party back to the *Enterprise.* The following day we parted ways with the Ohioans after their *happen-chance* discovery inside the hollow walls of their ship of yet another encore coke stash.

Presently, I exhaled after seeing my reflection in Amtrak glass, and recalled standing at the train depot in West Glacier staring at this long-haired kid in tattered jeans with his thumb extended roadside, wondering where the years had gone, and were going, feeling fear and asking: Whatever happened to the promising free-bird Kid from Berry Road—future poet/writer? What good was money without peace of mind and family? Who am I? What am I? Answer: a married man whose love-lust for a certain gypsy and flight from prosecution had severed me from any previous fantasies—valuable or otherwise—I'd once craved.

"What were you thinking, honey?" Kim had asked when our train pulled into the platform at West Glacier, sounding its whistle.

"About what a pleasant trip this is going to be," I said, before hauling our stuff aboard.

Sunrise came, and I still couldn't sleep. Like a vintage Van Gogh brushed in dawn's early light, Eastern Washington's golden wheat fields rolled by. The sun climbed high above the cliffs that frame the famed Columbia Gorge, and glimmered in its mighty namesake rock-carving river below. America the beautiful still lived! I knew. For we had met the challenge of her mountains and reaped great rewards. But other challenges awaited me in this chess game I had committed us to. And beyond comfortable survival, the long-term rewards were becoming increasingly unclear to me.

My mind was like an electric motor—always running, planning, conceiving. This could be a blessing or a curse. Presently, it was the latter, and I recalled a phone conversation with Arnie before leaving West Glacier; *disturbing*, to say the least. He had been certain that at a minimum the US Post Office or his mail drop had lost his passport. I agreed—seven weeks was way too long to wait—and we assumed the worst. Then there was that *Diana* woman who'd been coming around daily and asking troubling questions. He had tried to distance himself from her, only to find she was showing all the signs of a fatal attraction. I'd warned him though, and now she would have to be dealt with, too. But even more worrisome, Benjamin was sick, and a cancerous-looking lump protruded from my fourteen-year old setter's jaw.

Kim jerked sporadically across the length of my lap. Perhaps she was dreaming. I wondered what the hell she thought about sometimes. Since going underground, we rarely talked *with words.* Did she think? Often? Of us? She never said, and so I thought for both of us. If *this*, if *we*, were *forever,* I knew it was time to establish a more permanent home once again in isolation; then conduct some serious "shuttle diplomacy". I was concerned that my fuge-friends' conduct, combined with their knowledge of my location, would eventually cost me my freedom. I had money, love, and a logical mind that told me to run farther, to run from America.

My relationship with a Greek in San Francisco had to be nurtured, and now I knew *exactly* what I wanted from him: an identity with a history before I tried to seek residency in another country. An entirely different world with an entirely different cast of characters waited overseas, and *overseas* was no longer limited to the overcrowded European continent. Tucson Tony—wed to an Australian wife—had offered great insight on clearing my path Down Under, where accountants, bankers, lawyers, and ID connections (all tested by him) were at my disposal. My old friend had also mentioned a partnership in an Aussie land development venture. Yes, Tucson and Tony had been part of the big picture since those vagabond days of my youth. And now I knew that Tucson was indeed in my future—just as travel was in my blood.

Finally! I was tired and fading from the troublesome, conscious world. The Amtrak viewing window blurred like a cheap TV screen going off the air, growing fuzzier.

Snap!

My image materialized on some Indiana Crime Stoppers show, "Wanted, wanted, wanted! REWARD!"

My body twitched. A freight train blew by, rocking our sleeper car and waking my wife.

She stretched and made that funny fish face at me—the one she used to get little Miss Shannon Fisher to laugh. My wife's brown raccoon eyes twinkled like stars in heaven.

Tired of worrying, I smiled.

We locked fingers and kissed.

"Morning, honey," she said, yawning, blinking and reaching for her bag of life's simple treasures. "Did you get a good night's rest?"

I nodded slowly and pecked her cheek.

She pricked my ass with a porcupine quill.

True love.

As long as I had true love, I believed anything was possible.

An hour later we pulled into Portland's stately Union Station, and I strained to place my mind back in tune with this crazy fugitive game I was playing.

Arnie, pacing nervously, greeted us in the parking lot.

"Don't worry old pal," I said dramatically. "I've got the perfect solution to your woman problem."

9

Running From America

Early October, 1987: I reclined in the coach section of a British Air 747 while soothing classical music played. The plane penetrated a thick cloud formation, and banked sharply. Sleeping passengers stirred. The Emerald Island of Ireland appeared and disappeared below. I recalled the research I'd read that claimed Irish passports were the easiest in Europe to acquire, then thought about IRA terrorism and dismissed the option again. During our descent to England, I shredded financial notes, secured the elastic money holder beneath my slacks, organized documents, and reviewed the previous seven days. What a week it had been.

After visiting The Vault for a substantial cash withdrawal, Kim and I packed a U-Haul with the contents of our Reno self-storage unit for relocation near our new home in Oregon's Columbia Gorge. On the way to San Francisco—where part two of my mission unfolded—I exited Interstate 80 and cruised down Truckee's historic Commercial Row past the former Lion's Share. Sadness overwhelmed me when I saw that my dead dream had been reincarnated as a booming Mexican restaurant. I envisioned its drunken patrons spilling strawberry margaritas made with cheap tequila on our refurbished oak floors, pulled my hat down over my forehead, and drove on toward the Greek's place.

His son and partner had married and moved east. The seventy-year old Greek got lonely and married a thirty-year old Mexican Holy Roller. Sister Paula, he called her. They made an odd couple. And either our host was a damn good actor, or he actually saw me as a potential surrogate son. Sensing the time was right, I had made a decision, and a one-night stopover in San Francisco lasted three days.

Thinking my scheme was crazy, and being driven mad in the first twenty-four hours by Sister Paula's hard sell of Holy Ghost religion, Kim begged me to leave immediately. "Before I go off and slap her!" But the perceptive and wily Greek charmed my lovely Lady Di with a gift—a British sovereign on a dainty gold neck chain—and her impatience was easily quelled.

The Greek and I spent our days at his shop reviewing and grading coins. At night, the four of us went out for dinner and a movie. The last evening—highlighted by a home-cooked Greek meal—was memorable.

Sister Paula jumped up in the middle of dinner to answer a knock at the door. "It's my friends from church!" she predicted with the glazed doughnut look of a lady who barely made it alive out of the '70s West Coast drug scene. Moments later, a dozen Pentecostals marched into the Greek's humble living room, formed a circle, and began to shout, howl and wail testimony at the top of their lungs.

"Oh, Jesus! Yessss, Jesus! Holy Ghost! Holy Ghost! Holy Ghost!"

My wife shook her head, forced a smile, and excused herself from the table. "Goodnight, honey," she said through clenched teeth. "I've got a headache. I'm going to bed."

The Greek smiled cryptically, and told me some of the church's ministers were regular customers at the depository. After they left we remained seated long into the night, studying coins, sipping retsina wine, and continuing our sensitive negotiations.

"So, you wanna work," the Greek said with a firm, slightly gravelly voice void of condescension. He grabbed a chunk of feta cheese and chewed it. I nodded, then bit into one of the dolmas. "But you obviously don't need money—do you, Tim?" While pointing out a scratch mark on an 1800s era quarter, he added, "Amazing how one little flaw can devalue something."

Seeing where he was headed, I wiped my chin and looked him in the eye.

"You're no shoe clerk, Tim. I know a winner when I see one. You're sharp, kid." He reached for a Plexiglas coin holder called a slab. "You're polite, well read, rare—like this 1922 plain penny." His timing was perfect, his delivery impeccable. "I have a temporary dilemma." He passed me the slab. "You see, I've tied up all my cash."

"Go on," I said, starting to grin.

"I could use some fresh investment capital. Selling off my silver holdings is one option, but silver prices are down. And you, it seems, wanna be on someone's payroll."

"Not someone's—*yours*. So I can live off of my cash inheritance and slowly break into the system, build up credit, pay some taxes."

"I know, I know," he said.

"What else do you need to know?" Perilously close to pulling the plug on my plan, I held my breath waiting on his response.

"Nothing, *morea*. Not a thing, my friend," he whispered, handing me the magnifying glass and another coin specimen. "I like you, *morea*. Like you a lot. But can you at least come down once a month and show your face? Do some coin shows with me, help with inventory, send me some customers. Understand? I don't want my accountant getting uptight."

I pictured all those monitor cameras and some of the clientele I'd encountered at the coin shop. Exposure was not something I needed, but Tim Barnes, possible European immigration candidate, had to have a more in-depth identity/history. I weighed the plusses and minuses of our mutually beneficial proposition, then slowly nodded. We gripped hands firmly.

"Good, *morea*!" He said, laughing like Saint Nick. "We're gonna be friends a long time, you and I. Now, tell me...what's wrong with this 1865 Shield Nickel?"

My landing at London's Heathrow International Airport meant that a successful post-flight return to Europe was nearly complete. I stood in the lengthy passport clearance line for non-U.K. citizens, avoiding eye contact with uniformed Customs officers and airport security people, and acting casual. The line shortened. I took a deep breath and thought about the call I'd made from JFK during my New York layover to John Hopkins University in Baltimore, where my sister Judy, the family saint, worked.

From inside a phone booth she had described as "a confessional," Sis told me my dad had been diagnosed with prostrate cancer and was bucking chemotherapy. She said this cool and doctor-like, as she was accustomed to doing, then artfully changed the subject. "Dad got your post card from France. He said, 'don't worry about dear old Daddy-O! And don't try to call or visit—they're watching.'"

"Damn vultures!" I'd hissed.

"Don't cuss," said Sis.

"How does he know?"

"Dad's noticed the same white Ford parked across the street lately with two men inside wearing suits and pretending to read the paper. Sometimes he wakes up early and catches them sleeping with their heads on the dash beside a bunch of Styrofoam coffee cups. He says it's his new game...the only game in town."

I swallowed some imaginary item the size and shape of a chicken bone, shaken by the probability that my Dad would either die while I was on the run or in prison. I grew angry. "I can't believe this! A guy robs your house and no one comes out for a statement. But for a pot dealer, they spend a fortune." *Dad was right, this wasn't going to just blow over.* I pictured my father housebound in Elkhart, Indiana spending his final years playing solitary and listening to his ham radio. The lump in my throat passed. "How long does he have?" I asked.

"Hard to say," Sis replied. "He's stubborn, like you. He refuses to go to Hopkins for the best care."

Block Dad out, block Dad out. "Give him my love," I said. "What else?"

"Mom misses you. She got the flowers you sent from that beautician."

"Great." I watched a tall man in a dark suit and dark glasses grab the phone two places down from mine.

"We all miss you," Judy said. We reminisced about a dusty camel auction we had attended on the banks of Africa's Niger River, near mythical Timbuktu, back when she was a Peace Corp nurse in the '70s. She had received the code system I sent from Montana, and read off seven-figure sets of letters—each representing a payphone earmarked on the sprawling John Hopkins campus for future contacts. "What about coming in?" she asked.

"When crime and punishment match," I blurted too loudly. "Next question," I whispered, suspiciously watching the crowd at JFK.

"Is that couple from the wedding out there with you? How's Kim?"

"Yes, they are. Kim's fine."

The tall man in the suit was making sweeping hand gestures in my general direction. I envisioned FBI agents running toward me.

"Gotta cut it short Sis," I said.

"When can we see you, maybe meet somewhere?"

"Soon," I told her, meaning it, hoping it, but wondering when, where, and how.

The tall man was no where in sight. A crowd of suited men surged toward me. I hung up the phone, slipped into a rest room entrance where I removed my hat and glasses, then instantly exited and headed for my boarding gate. Fortunately, the suits had been a false alarm.

The passport clearance line at Heathrow moved forward. My wire-rimmed reading glasses started to bother me. I hoped I had bought the right deodorant. In front of me a small child wearing a miniature Armani suit stamped his feet, grabbed his weary mother's arm, and fell to the floor on the verge of a full-blown tantrum.

Unnecessary attention.

The crowd's eyes focused our way. The mother—whose outfit and looks resembled Ivana Trump—was beside herself. In the process of straightening up the boy, she dropped her purse. I handed it to her, crossed my hands behind my back and concentrated on my own strange reality.

If something goes wrong, I'll be wearing zebra stripes instead of trendy sports coats! I thought of Kim waiting for my call half a world away on the banks of the Columbia River, which would give the green light to board *her* plane to London. I pictured that nasty growth on the jaw of my aging Irish setter, Benjamin, how gray he was getting, the way he was slowing down and always limping.

The line disappeared and I shuffled up to the glass booth. Inside, I was all butterflies, but outside, where it counted, I was cool, calm and collected. *Why not?* I had been here before, but as myself. Yet these weren't Social Security clerks or Department of Motor Vehicle employees. This was the big test. These people were computer-equipped professionals trained to smell sweating amateurs, and ferret out lies.

I slid Tim Barnes' passport through the slot with a steady hand and a pleasant smile, while simultaneously reviewing his vital statistics—age, date and place of birth, mother's maiden name. Inevitably, the threat Kim's dad had made to my mom crept into my head. *I have friends at Interpol! I'll get that boy of yours.*

"Morning, Mr. Barnes," said the uniformed officer. He punched in codes and paged through a large record book, *The Book,* the one I definitely did not want to be in.

I forced a yawn. "Morning, sir."

"Purpose of your visit?"

"Tourist."

"Length of stay?"

"Two weeks."

The official tugged at his reddish-brown moustache, glanced at me, then my passport picture. "And what is your occupation, Mr. Barnes?"

"I work in a coin shop," I replied with the face of an honest young man.

"Lovely," he said, reaching for something. "I'm a collector myself. First time in London, Mr. Barnes?"

I nodded as he rubber-stamped my book.

"Very well, then. Enjoy your stay. Next, please!"

Piece of cake. I could have packed a million bucks! No one even checked my baggage. I emerged from Customs triumphantly, scanned the multinational crowd, and found a female courier carrying a placard marked Barnes—just as Blake had promised. I tipped the girl, tucked the envelope she gave me containing an address and key in my sports coat, and made my way to the familiar curbside. The cab line was long. A red double-decker bus's open door beckoned. I breathed a sigh of relief and opted for the long, scenic bus ride into London, craving the feel of the city's heartbeat.

The following afternoon I was back at Heathrow International, standing in a crowd that was waiting for loved ones arriving on a nonstop flight from Seattle—second-guessing myself. It had been my bright idea that we travel alone and I go first; thinking if I went down on an untested passport, Kim could make all the necessary calls and return home to Indiana.

An hour passed after her plane arrived and not a sign of her...too long. I started to worry and watch for security people. The river of passengers being greeted by family and friends slowed to a trickle.

What to do?

Suddenly she appeared, her telltale neck-rash flashing like a traffic light. I handed her a dozen roses. "Welcome to London, Meekla." She whinnied like a Kentucky Derby winner. But when I wrapped my arms around her thoroughbred body, I could feel it trembling.

"They searched my bags," she whispered nervously in my ear.

"Did they play with your panties?" I asked, straight faced.

She nodded, hyperventilating now.

"Uh, huh. That's standard procedure for women of your caliber."

"Ornery shit," she blurted before delivering a wet kiss.

I carried her bags to the curb, and flagged a taxi. I loved those classic London cabs. They reminded me of some black and white movie. I had the driver take us by Buckingham Palace. My wife's tired brown eyes were as big as half-dollars. We were like a modern day *Bonnie and Clyde* touring London Town and necking in that leather backseat.

"What's yer final destination, sir?" asked the cockney cabby.

"Kings Road and Sidney," I replied.

Time for the big surprise.

Blake kept a residence in London for his own clandestine banking missions, affairs, and preferred clients' lodging. It was located in the chic Chelsea district with gorgeous views of the Thames River and world-famous Harrods department store. The flat provided us with all the comforts of home; privacy and easy access to the city's sights. With the help of fresh flowers, bottles of wine, bubble baths, body oils, familiar music on the stereo, and marital passion between silk sheets, my wife's initial fears about our European adventure soon faded. Mine did too.

Mornings we fed ducks in nearby Hyde Park, then I'd row us around its Serpentine Pond while pale Brits in candy-striped folding chairs watched us from the green. We took in the sights each afternoon, and after dark did the theatre district, clubs, and Piccadilly Circus. In our wanderings, we discovered a great jazz joint called Ronnie Scott's. We played dress up in clothes that had been mothballed for months—more than making up for our Pacific Northwest isolation. The world was big again, and I was small potatoes, a minnow swimming in an international sea. My confidence level rose significantly. I felt good. *We* felt good, romantic, and rejuvenated. We were co-stars in my movie, head over heels in love. My dream was alive, and peaceful days passed at #11 Daska House.

Autumn rains were falling. I was in the passenger seat of self-proclaimed financial guru Keith Jones' banged-up Mercedes, fingers gripping the dashboard, recalling that day on Maui in 1983 when Bert had said, "Forget the Caymans, or Switzerland. The Channel Islands are the best place in the world to bank. They've been doing it a long time with lots of old money and a quiet, conservative, profile. Take it from me." But of course, neither of us wanted to share the same money manager. So I had turned to Northern England's Jimmy Collins (my antique furniture shipping connection), for an "in" to the Isle of Guernsey's secretive tax haven's elite. Jimmy's directed me to shady Keith Jones, who gave me a letter of introduction to Fort Group, and Blake.

Jones and I had spent the day talking stocks and touring London investment properties, and now he drove across the city like a madman, straining to see past slapping, worn wiper blades while chomping on a slimy Havana whose hot droppings burned more holes in an old tweed jacket that smelled like my Grandma Daisy. Jones was a big bear of a man, over six feet-two, with an expansive belly and a very expressive face. When he got excited, his eyebrows—the size and color of gray squirrel's tails—jumped and hopped high above his wrinkly forehead. Inch-long nose hairs twitched in the smoke-filled air as he shouted obscenities at shabby taxi drivers and rain-drenched, "lower-class" pedestrians.

"Can I tell you?" he said in his thick, well-to-do British tone. "The bloody Empire should have closed the door on these undesirable immigrants years ago! Yes, well, I get my revenge by selling them secondhand automobiles with doctored odometers. That, and a little aggressive loan sharking," he added with a laugh.

The laugh turned into a violent cough, which catapulted his Havana to the floor. He stomped it out with his feet, tapping the break pedal repeatedly. Finally, he parked the Benz atop the sidewalk in front of Daska House where Blake's flat was located.

I extracted my fingernails from his dashboard and pondered the logic of investing with him. Since our first meeting, Jones had been more of a curiosity than someone I would choose to be in cahoots with. He liked to drop names and remind me that he'd had dealings with the *Royals*—Lady Di's mother's sister, to be exact. The mysterious Mr. Jones also claimed to be connected with the British version of the Mob. I was unimpressed, but the old Englishman was knowledgeable and knew most of my story, or at least enough of it to make me nervous. I had to trust people. Then too, I needed to divide my nest egg and begin my quest toward becoming an expatriate. *Remember the lesson of Bill McCarthy,* whispered a little voice called instinct. *Business and intrigue make strange bedfellows,* said another one, named Greed.

"I take it you are pleased with your situation in Guernsey," Jones said, brushing cigar ashes off his lap. "Having secret money is so bloody wonderful! Blake is good at what he does, and those offshore people pay the best interest in the world. Lloyds works with all of them you know. So does the government. No one cares where the money comes from when they're making a few extra points on million pound deals, do they?"

"I suppose not," I said.

"Yes. Well, I must say you're making all the right moves, Master Tim. It is, Tim, now, isn't it?" He tugged at the poorly-shaven wattles of skin around his throat.

I nodded, wishing I could read the limey's mind and know if he saw me as a future associate, or an easy mark. In many ways, Jones reminded me of the Greek. Accordingly, I reminded myself to be cautious during my education with the limey.

"Right, then. But remember, my young Yank friend, keep all of your financial conversations with our Mr. Blake face-to-face."

"Why?"

"Because my friends in the know tell me that Interpol has listening posts in places like Cyprus that are tuned in to international money centers like Guernsey." He laughed. "Of course they ignore all the well-connected big fish they occasionally discover. Now, someone like you is an entirely different story, my boy."

A chill ran down my spine as I digested his babble. I could believe that Interpol would listen to some of the more obvious offshore centers near the Caribbean for drug money...but Guernsey, too?

"I'll keep that in mind," I said.

"Well, then. No sense in your staying on for this miserable spell of weather is there? When did you say Blake was expected back from France?"

"He called the flat five days ago." I paused to remember the definition of the proper English term he'd used. "He said a fortnight."

"Nine more days in this rain! Can I tell you? Take my advice. Start your search for expatriatism on the Spanish Isle of Majorca. Call Blake's office. Have them book your flights and lodging, and arrange a hire car. Go on! You Yanks have Florida and Hawaii, but we Europeans play in the Mediterranean. Go on! Enjoy the weather and the sea. Do some bird watching," he suggested, with both squirrel-tail eyebrows almost jumping off his face. "Have a look 'round the place—especially Cabo de Formentor. It just might be the bloody safe-haven you're looking for," he exclaimed, slapping my knee. "You certainly can't continue living in America with a *tax problem*, can you? And you wouldn't get on well here in the City, or up north Wigan-way, with that bent crowd of Jimmy's."

I punched the seat and studied Keith Jones. Here was a guy in his '60s—a white-haired former World War II bomber pilot and big shot in the insurance racket, a financial advisor still connected to the Lloyds of London Syndicate who kept his wrinkled puss glued to a stock market monitor screen eight hours a day—calling the kettle black. Our antique dealing friend Jimmy Collins was admittedly risqué, but on the other hand, self-righteous Jones rarely spoke of his dear, aging, sickly wife. Rather, he'd spent much of this day—between discussing real estate and stock picks—describing his charades with his latest and extremely young *darky mistress* from Trinidad. "Can I tell you?" He'd said more than once earlier, like an excited teenager. "Can I tell you, Tim, how much fun it is to dress up and play Plantation Master with my Miss Vicky?"

I rolled down the window of the Benz and gazed through a driving rain to the sixth floor of Daska House, where I saw *my* Lady Di peering through the sheers in #11—cocktail glass in hand. Realizing I was an hour late, I waved to her and turned my attention back to Jones.

"Why in the hell is every Englishman with a pot to piss in so damn sexually deviant?" I asked.

His squirrel-tails flicked. "Can I tell you? It's the bloody National Sport, Master Timothy! That, and our dreadful weather." He was laughing now.

I laughed, too, lost in a flashback of premarital-era orgies.

"I see your eyes scouting all the young skirts," he said. "Give it time, lad. Give it time, and you'll have a young tart, too! After all, you are a man of means." He paused, then grew pensive. "But I must say, your bird, Diane, certainly is smart. Yes, very smart indeed."

I watched the old fart drooling at the thought of her, and snickered as I reached for the door handle. My wife would give him a heart attack in a New York minute, most assuredly. We shook hands. "Thanks for your tips," I said. "All of them."

"Right then," he said, shifting the Benz into drive. "See you in Wigan for the opening of Jimmy's new club. Right?"

I nodded, and made a mad dash for the foyer of Daska House.

In the dusky landscapes of the Almond Isle, Majorca, we found European summer still clinging to life. In Palma, the capital, we admired the ancient cathedral that sits on the chin of the harbor, and shopped the Gothic market, La Lonia, whose doorway was guarded by a radiant Renaissance angel. Turned off by city crowds, we explored the quiet countryside on narrow roads lined with stone walls and windmills. We ate at intimate family-owned cafes and watched skilled artisans carve animated carousel animals like the many we had sold at the Lion's Share.

One day, a Spanish motorcycle cop with an eye for rental cars pulled us over for no apparent reason. "Americans?" he asked, sounding both surprised and elated.

Evidently, we were few and far between. In fact I never saw another Yank during our entire stay. I nodded, showed him my Oregon license, United States Passport, handed over some Spanish pesetas, and we were on our way again.

Our last five days were spent at the Hotel Formentor—whose impeccable grounds, elegant decor and wonderful tennis gardens were still rife with the nineteen-thirties' chic established by the Duke of Windsor set. Each night, German, French, and British pensioners glided harmoniously across a marble ballroom floor as if they'd never fought against one another in the war. I loved watching them enjoy their golden years, and wondered if my mom was enjoying hers. One night it took all my discipline—and Kim's hollow threat to "cut me off"—to keep me from singing Sinatra's version of *San Francisco* at their piano bar.

Our second afternoon at Formentor, we were befriended by a young English couple who ran the stables. Humored by my outfit—a Far Side, Shark Nerds, T-shirt—and thrilled by the prospect of having playmates their own age, they showed us secret places and told us about vacant villas that were available for long term rental. We found one perched high above a rugged coastline with a secret patio dominated by an olive tree. With temptation sparkling in our eyes, Lady Di and I fantasized about the move, but then reality set in. It was a big step for a Midwestern-bred couple who were married-with-pets and on the lam from the law.

During our last night's dinner party at the couple's villa the leggy, lady horse-lover said, "You say you want to be a writer, Tim. A very famous English novelist, Robert Graves, lived and wrote here."

Deep inside me, an old dream stirred. "Interesting," I said. *If only my life wasn't such a lie.*

"But, doesn't it get boring?" asked Lady Di.

"Heavens no," the brunette responded instantly. "Not at all. Unlike most of our fellow expats, we manage to put in a full day's work with the animals. It's close-knit here. You can do all your business in the streets of Puerto de Pollensa. You meet the carpenter who didn't show up yesterday, someone who owes you a few pesetas. The village is very compact."

Precisely why I felt we could not survive as fugitives in Majorca.

"Think about it, man! We'd love to have you over." Her lanky husband poured more thick, green liqueur into our empty shot glasses from an extremely long-necked bottle. "Cheers!"

The next day our puddle jumper circled the Isle of Guernsey off the northwest coast of France. Kim put a death grip on my knee. Her fresh-tanned face turned pale. "I'm afraid of small airplanes," she admitted. And then, there were all her unspoken anxieties—about meeting the Blakes, clearing another Customs check, how her hair looked, and her lips—all of which were again loudly announced by that telltale neck-rash.

"I was uptight my first time, too," I said, squeezing her hand tightly and directing her attention to the window.

We saw rows and rows of pre-war greenhouses where tomatoes were raised year-round for London markets. We saw the offshore islands of Sark, Herm, Alderney and Jethou, and bomb-scarred pillbox beach defenses.

"This was the only British possession occupied by the Germans during World War II," I said, playing tour guide.

My pretty young wife pursed her hot red lips before a miniature make-up mirror—unimpressed.

We saw shadowy submerged reefs in frothy seas that had snared hapless sailors for hundreds of years. We saw rolling lush pastures rising from secluded rocky coves, dotted by dozens of grazing brown and white Guernsey cows.

"Shipwrecks, secret currency transactions, tomatoes and cows—that's the Bailiwick of Guernsey's claim to fame," I whispered.

She furrowed her brow. "Where's the shops? Where's the banks? Where's the money?"

I laughed softly. "It's a conservative, quaint little island, honey. All that stuff's neatly hidden on the cobblestone streets of downtown Saint Peterport. But the cash is actually in Zurich, or London. They just manage it from here."

Our wholesome, cream-skinned, plaid-skirted stewardess stumbled down the aisle, adjusting her beret while hurriedly collecting cocktail cups from mostly balding males wearing colorless business suits, who had been scribbling figures on martini-soaked napkins the entire flight. Wheels met tarmac, toupees were straightened, briefcases clutched, dark shades donned to conceal "dollar-sign-syndrome" eyes, and international tax dodgers queued up, drooling to do battle with the Bailiwick's army of accountants.

Politicians? Policemen? Terrorists? Arms dealers? Spies? I briefly pondered who they were and where their secret money came from as they surged past us, then straightened my tie and stepped in line.

Donald Sutherland descended the stairs one step ahead of us, wearing a hat and trench coat reminiscent of one of his spy movie roles. Kim tugged on the sleeve of my sports coat.

"Yeah, honey. I saw him boarding," I said nonchalantly. I smiled, knowing his presence only confirmed I had hidden my money in the right place.

We passed smoothly through Channel Islands Customs, probably because our passports had been broken in with both British and Spanish clearance stamps. But if only I had known about Bill McCarthy's 1986 letter to Tim Meers (advising him to tell the feds I had an offshore account "somewhere in the Channel Islands") I would have never made this journey.

After purchasing flowers near our gate, we emerged in rare-for-Guernsey bright sunshine to find the Blakes waiting to greet us.

"Hello, Tim," he said, extending a hand. "So nice to see you again. How did you find our flat?"

"I gave a bloody London cabby the address, and 'ee drove me there!" I replied in a cockney accent.

Kim blushed. The Blakes laughed and shook their heads. They had informed me on our second meeting that they found my age and manner extremely refreshing, thus eliminating the need for facades.

"Really, the flat was a treat," I said, handing Judy my floral bouquet. "We appreciated it immensely. Thanks." Kim nodded sheepishly in agreement, then—to avoid further confusion for Blake's wife—I introduced her as my Lady Di.

Perhaps it was because Judy—a forty-something Australian blond—strongly resembled Kim's mother, but for some reason, they hit it off right from that first handshake.

"So this is the ravishing young beauty who cornered our confirmed bachelor," Judy said with a distinct Down Under accent that had survived twenty years of English pompousness. "He's quite a character! How do you put up with him, Diane?"

My blushing wife shrugged.

Half-a-block away Donald Sutherland stealthily got into a black Rolls Royce with tinted windows. We tossed our bags in Blake's Range Rover beside a fresh bale of hay and hopped inside.

"Did you make us a hotel reservation?" I asked.

"Hotel? Rubbish!" Judy announced, sounding genuinely excited about having us for guests. "You'll be staying at The Coppice with us. My Tim's never had a client quite like you."

How true. "But we don't want to impose."

"Nonsense! I insist," ordered Blake.

We motored along curvy, crowded cobblestone streets and soon arrived in the upcountry region of Saint Savior where wide-open spaces prevailed. Upon reaching the familiar, crumbling, former German officers' bunker—which bore a brass plaque reading, The Coppice and marked the entrance to their estate—Blake turned off the main road, uttering an audible sigh of relief.

Lady Di leaned toward the window glass, her brown eyes twinkling like Cinderella's. And I—onetime high school history buff—envisioned 1940 Guernsey, when real German soldiers, not the toy ones I had played with on Berry Road, controlled this land and its people.

The narrow dirt and gravel lane was lined by overgrown shrubs and small trees which gave way, revealing a fine green meadow where Blake's prized horses pranced and grazed. A pond came into sight where geese, guinea, swans and other lucky fowl preened at the muddy water's edge. Peacocks pounced on split rail fencing, screeched loudly, and showed their colors. We unloaded the Range Rover beside the stately manor, breathed air like that of a petting zoo's, and instinctively relaxed until Merlin, a charcoal gray Irish wolfhound, charged wildly, intent upon greeting us.

"He's big as a horse!" I exclaimed, petting his huge head.

Kim hugged the gentle beast like the tattered old Teddy Bear she kept by our bed.

"Yes, I suppose he has grown quite a bit since your last visit," Blake noted calmly.

"Nearly nine stone, that Merlin! And here's our new one." Judy picked up a scraggly, mud-caked mutt by its scruff.

Most of Blake's stuffy clients would have found The Coppice's animals too much, but to Di and me it was a slice of heaven in a strange and distant land, the kind of place we both dreamed of owning someday.

And there was so much more I had in common with Blake. Like knowing money wasn't everything.

"It feeds the animals," Blake once said of his secretive business.

To be sure, I could have searched a lifetime and never found a more likable money manager. Unlike Jones and the Greek, I never felt on guard around Tim Blake. Tall, lean, laid-back equestrian, open-minded, competitive tennis player in the late '50s—beneath the horseman's hat, behind that stately expressionless face, dwelt a complex man locked in to a contradictory lifestyle, not so distant from my own. With all his knowledge of international money matters, Squire Blake was also a member in good standing with the London Buddhist Society.

They set us up in the bottom half of their big stone home where their two boys—now in boarding school—normally slept.

"Right, then!" Blake said, semi-animated and rocking on his heels. "I must tend to the horses, and Judy has to fetch food for the animals. You two freshen up a bit. We've dinner reservations for nine tonight at the Cask, and following a set of tennis tomorrow, you and I can pop into the office and review your finances."

I nodded, but Kim just stood there frozen with her mouth open, admiring the country decor of our bedroom and graciousness of our hosts as if she was living in a fairytale. Inside, I felt the same.

Blake clapped his hands. "Very well, then. Make yourselves at home. We'll see you upstairs for cocktails, half-past seven."

"Bye-bye," added Judy cheerfully. "See you in a bit."

They wore stable workers' clothes, had six horses, countless birds, three dogs, a large Persian cat called Blackberry that resembled one owned by Kim's Grandma Wheezy, and they lived on a farm. I watched as my wife's neck color returned to normal, and her raccoon eyes took on those specs of gold she also developed during afterglow. I knew how she felt, and her joy warmed my soul. We were sharing the world together, as I had promised. We were thousands of miles from home in the company of friends.

In silent awe, she unpacked each neatly folded article of our clothing.

"Told you they were down-to-earth," I said.

Friday, October 16, 1987: At 39/40 High Street, Saint Peterport, Guernsey, the offices of Fort Group, I gazed out the second floor picture window past Castle Cornet's clock tower, over a forest of sailboat masts, past ancient ramparts at the harbor's outer reaches, beyond huge freighters seeking refuge from hungry reefs, beyond black foreboding storm clouds gathering in the tiring arms of the Isle of Sark, reflecting on the first time I sat in Blake's leather wing-backed client's chair pondering such perplexing mysteries as retiring from the marijuana trade and managing my secret money. For me, that trip seemed like a lifetime ago.

Blake hung up the phone.

"Sorry about that," he said. "Now then, where were we?"

Where I *was*, was feeling strong and cocky like some international player about to risk all his offshore money in the market. Suddenly, I got a little nervous about rolling such heavy dice. I took a deep breath, produced a notebook, and confidently announced my stock picks with running commentary: British Petroleum, because they were expanding into the American retail market; British Tar and Rubber, presently paying good dividends; Innoco, heavily investing into stable London properties; Hanson Trust—Lord Hanson was into everything, and cash rich. And lastly, Pearl, the insurance group.

These were my selections based on Guru Keith Jones' tips from the *London Financial Time's* 100 Market. And just for good measure, I added three of my own choices from the New York Stock Exchange: Sunshine Mining, in the hope that undervalued silver prices would soon soar; Asarco, because I'd read they were modernizing copper and silver mining techniques—especially in Montana. And Unical, because oil prices were rising. I also bought silver bullion as an inflationary hedge to be physically held in a London bank.

I directed 30,000 British pounds (approximately $45,000 US) to Keith Jones' English corporation, earmarked for London real estate leveraging. "Jones will fax you a document guaranteeing payments at twelve percent interest rates until I withdraw from the partnership," I explained. "He's betting his big behind on South Africa's imminent collapse sending Apartheid's frightened white upper class to flood London's real estate market with a fresh influx of capital."

"I disagree," Blake said in his strictly-business monotone. "Because many of my clients are extremely wealthy Afrikaners, and believe me—they've no intention whatsoever of leaving."

I paused to question my confidence in Guru Jones's wisdom, and wished that Blake would go against his policy and give me some direction.

"Tell me how you made Leo Investments disappear without a trail?" I asked.

"A simple task," Blake replied. "Speaking strictly hypothetically," he said with a cryptic grin. "Friendly governments, say for example, Panama, accept a transfer of funds—for a fee, of course. Then those 'Leo' monies are physically withdrawn by a trusted party, redeposited, and wired to Dublin, again for a fee. Eventually, they end up right back on Guernsey, in my care. Whereupon, they are reassembled under the Aldershot Trust. As I explained on your first visit, we pay farmers in places like Sark and Jethou to act as the board members of our clients' secret trusts. If someone comes asking about Leo Investments in the future, we can honestly say we are holding no such funds."

"It's all Greek to me," I said, thoroughly impressed by his gambit.

We talked at length about Lloyds of London which Jones had described as "the ultimate scam, a syndicate paying enormous dividends to all its *Names* for merely promising to guarantee action with their personal assets—action which has been running along nicely on auto-pilot for years."

I told Blake I was skeptical and did not fully comprehend the concept.

Blake said there was a lot of paperwork involved with becoming a Lloyds of London Name—even if Jones was willing to stand up for me and approve my proxy corporation Aldershot.

My independent spirit told me the Syndicate was not for me.

Blake concurred.

Years later, Lloyds of London's "ultimate scam" would come crashing down around its fat-cat Names like Keith Jones. A series of catastrophic events from hurricanes to Persian Gulf ship-sinkings during Iran's war with Iraq would drain Lloyds' deep pockets and demand compensation for its insured clients from the Names' personal assets. Jones himself would become an embezzler in order to maintain his lifestyle and his *darky mistress* during his final days in London.

At the conclusion of our discussion, Blake promised me the corporate American Express card I'd requested. "We will show your Mr. Barnes as a consultant to Fort Group," he explained. Blake restated his belief that a rising British pound in tandem with rising interest rates would soon become both an attractive, as well as a conservative long-term investment for clients with large accounts.

In a show of gratitude, I guaranteed him my account would grow in strength, as our mutual trust and friendship had, knowing that he did not need my account.

At the time, I felt great about my investment in the rising stock market. Compared to other marijuana dealers I knew I'd always been fairly conservative with my legit investments. But because of my experience risking every dollar in the pot trade, I was also keenly aware one had to risk big money to reap big gains. But then, I could not tell Blake this.

"What do you think about my investment strategy?" I asked.

"I must say, you've certainly done your homework," he said in that dry English drawl. Then, at length, he underscored his distaste for making his clients' financial decisions. "Tim, I've lived a long, rich life from which the one lesson I have learned above all others is this." He rose and walked to the window. "No one is an expert."

Freed from the details of business, he breathed a sigh of relief. "I'm afraid we're in for some nasty weather," he predicted, gazing toward the Isle of Sark.

He produced two long-stemmed crystal glasses, filled them with a French Bordeaux, and stared lovingly at the large oil painting of his prized stallion, Cariolo III.

We shared a toast. "To a long friendship—*Tim*."

On Saturday afternoon the low, steel-gray sky and wisps of sea mist created a permanent twilight around Blake's estate. When Sunday arrived, the rains were so heavy that it was hard to see the horse barn from the kitchen window. Opening a door became a major operation. Our hosts informed us it was the strongest storm in a hundred years. At two in the morning, Kim and I awoke to the sound of howling winds ripping away roof slates and hurling them helter-skelter. Incredibly, the storm continued to get worse—assaulting not only the Channel islands but half of England—felling trees, downing power and phone lines, shattering greenhouse glass, and shaking the centuries-old Coppice to its stone foundation. My wife and I held each other tightly for the remainder of the night, listening to the black beast cry like a banshee as tree branches crashed about, and the Blakes pace the creaky hardwood floors above us. And while we semi-slept, half a world away Wall Street was crashing, too!

Black Monday, October 19, 1987: Gray dawn came late to Guernsey. A driving rain continued. In the Coppice, we lit candles, boiled coffee water on the fireplace hearth, and waited for the deluge to subside. When it did, we all donned rain gear, rounded up the animals, and inspected the estate. Damage was extensive. Some rare birds did not survive, and Lady Di and I expressed our sympathy for the Blakes' losses. We worked all day chopping trees and clearing debris.

The news did not reach us until dinnertime. We were cleaning mud off our shoes in the drive when the cellular phone in Blake's red Lamborghini rang. My money manager's expressionless face gave no clue to the content of his conversation. "I see," Blake said after five minutes. "How bad is it?" he asked after fifteen.

When he finished talking, Blake led me to the stable and gave me the news. "Sit down, Tim," he said. "The New York Stock exchange dropped 508 points, there's a bloody panic in the world markets."

"What about London?" I asked, already feeling weak in the knees.

"Monkey see, monkey do," he replied matter-of-factly. "There's a wave of selling underway. I'm afraid London's FT 100 is considerably down, too. Sorry, Tim, but there's nothing I can do."

I could have vomited. I had just lost half my fortune in the big crapshoot and there wasn't a damn thing I could do about it! Island communications were a mess, and only the big boys were capable of maneuvering quick enough to get out of the market. We would've had to have been in London with insiders for a snowball's chance in hell of selling in time. Even my backup silver bullion, which shot up dramatically for one day, could not be unloaded. I was totally demoralized and felt like a fool. The best therapy for a hyper guy like me was to continue helping my host clear the lane to the Coppice until well after dark.

Blake understood.

Before bed, I called Todd in Oregon on the cell phone to tell him we'd survived the storm.

"The pets are fine," Arnie said. "Take your time. Enjoy yourselves."

Right, enjoy myself. In London and the Big Apple, people were jumping out skyscraper windows.

Tuesday was to be our last day on Guernsey. In a light rain, I jogged to the sea that morning, doing five or six miles until my legs ached as much as my wallet. That afternoon the sun broke through, and Blake and I walked together in a distant windswept pasture. It was he who broke the initial silence by speaking of his boyhood in England.

"I was lying on my back in a field much like this one during the Battle of Britain, watching a blue sky turn black with man's birds of war, quite certain the world was about to end. It did not," he noted with a fatherly smile.

His metaphor did not escape me. Blake knew I was deeply troubled—by much more than the money. He asked about my dog Ben, then my marriage. He spoke candidly about the lack of passion in his own relationship with Judy.

"Whatever became of the French girl you brought to that dinner in London?" he asked.

I shrugged, stuck a blade of grass between my teeth and gazed across a white-capped sea towards France. "I suppose she's with her family in Toulouse," I said, picturing the blue-eyed, alabaster-skinned Catherine and myself as clear as day, dickering for art deco pieces in busy Parisian markets. Kim had been on her great western magical mystery tour at the time, and I was not yet under her spell.

"I love my wife," I said. "I made the right choice, and I am committed, even under my present circums—" I stopped mid-sentence, and Blake did not pursue the details of my *circumstances.*

We spoke of my impressions of Spain and Majorca, then discussed the possibilities for residency on Guernsey as well. In 1987, Channel Islands residency was achieved by owning real estate—which started out at 400,000 pounds sterling ($650,000) for a bungalow. Many international tax evaders bought their residency, Blake explained. But it was too salty for my blood, especially after the stock market crash. Guernsey was also too tiny and too expensive to disappear into. And Bill McCarthy knew my money was here.

Blake furrowed his brow. "Where will you live then, with this tax problem of yours? The States?"

I nodded.

"Will you be safe?"

Silence.

"Why can't we simply negotiate a settlement fee with the Americans so you and Diane can live a bloody normal life?" He patted my shoulder. "I've grown rather fond of you, Tim."

Why indeed? If it were only money, I'd have gladly given the lion's share of mine to take away the emptiness we often felt inside. Blake was one of the many on my journey I wish I had known under different circumstances. How could I tell him I was wanted for marijuana dealing, even though to me it was more a matter of taxes than morality? I could not.

"Frankly," I said. "I don't know whose palm to grease, or I'd do it tomorrow. I don't believe I'm that important to the authorities. However, I am not thrilled about the prospect of prison time either," I added, biting a nail. "But thanks for everything. I'll just have to be extra careful and play it by ear." I shook his hand.

Blake dropped the subject, and never mentioned it again.

Back in London, the stiff upper lip I had kept on Guernsey began sagging. I started dragging my tail, beating myself up mentally for being a financial fool, and bringing Kim down, too. We wanted to go home, but I'd promised to attend the grand opening of Jimmy's club in Wigan—still several days away.

I journeyed back to Keith Jones' office to assess the market.

"Can I tell you?" he blurted. "You must hang on to your shares until they rise in value, Tim. Remember, nothing's lost unless you sell. It's dreadful though, isn't it? It is the perfect time to buy low now from all these pitiful sore losers, and..."

His financial babble, formerly a source of excitement, seemed to fade into the city street noise many floors below us. He offered me a drink, told me I was part owner in a lovely flat near Harrods that had just dropped forty percent in value, then when I felt like walking, insisted on driving me back to Blake's flat. Our first of many stops was to pick up his young mistress, Miss Vicky, who promptly led us on a lengthy scavenger hunt collecting fashion packages from Piccadilly to Knightsbridge.

After lengthy protests, I was returned to Daska House, very late for the surprise candlelight dinner Kim had prepared. She had watched us pull up from #11's window, and before I could knock on the door, it flew open.

There stood Lady Di, furious, seething, and drunk on vodka. "Where the hell have you been? Huh? Fucking one of Jones' little slut—" Her brown eyed stare wondered beyond me to the jovial Jones and the wild Miss Vicky, who was waving a colorful feather boa. Kim bit her lip. Her Hungarian blood was boiling.

They had planned to have cocktails with us, but the perceptive Jones felt the chill, and not wanting to waste one of his two "weekly performances" with his young aspiring actress, he skillfully excused himself. "Can I tell you? I've completely forgotten my appointment with—"

"Foolish you, love!" said quick Miss Vicky as she laughingly led her sugar daddy to the elevator.

But it didn't end there. Lady Di was beside herself.

"Whoremaster! Playboy!" she screamed. "Can you say *lonely*, huh? Can you, mister drug czar?"

"I didn't do anything, honey. I tried to—"

"Liar!" she shouted, stomping her feet, kicking off those red come-take-me heels, and throwing a strong left hook which caught me in the chest. "You care more about your fucking money than me, don't you?"

"Would you please keep your voice down," I said through clenched teeth. "The neighbors will—"

"Fuck the neighbors!" she declared, flailing the air and diving at me.

I bobbed, weaved, wrapped my arms around her and pinned her to the couch where it took all of my strength to keep her in my grasp until the tension left her body.

"I just want to go home," she sobbed.

Already under plenty of stress—and innocent as charged—I lost all patience. "Honey," I said, shaking my head. "As usual, I'm going to give you what you want. Pack your things tonight. I'm putting you on the next plane to Seattle." When she reached for me, I backed away. "But I need some time alone."

As a child witnessing minor domestic violence on Berry Road, I swore never to strike a lady—and I never have. But the closest I ever came to doing so was that evening in London in 1987 at #11 Daska House.

The next day, I jogged around Hyde Park and rowed for hours on its Serpentine Pond—alone. Pretty women waved from shore, but I was lost in another world reassessing my own insane situation, and paid them no mind. Around dinnertime, I phoned Oregon to check that Kim had arrived safely.

"When are you coming home?" she asked standoffishly.

"Don't know, honey," I replied. I paused, wanting to hear remorse for her actions and accusations. I heard none.

That night—at a trendy London artists club where I dropped Jones' name—I answered a calling, a soft internal roar from my poetic vagabond youth, a domesticated adult lion's sudden longing to be free. All around me I saw writers and painters paw promising students on balcony stairs and rails—playing the *National Sport* while pondering world ailments, history, philosophy, philanthropy, philandering. Salt and pepper jazz musicians jammed beside billiard tables where black cats in berets speaking the Queen's English gambled beneath sweet clouds of hashish laced cigarette smoke. The scene was cool. I sat on a corner stool—*me, the outsider*—observing them, fascinated by them, delighted to be among them, wanting to be one of them. Me, *the old me*, wanting badly to be something more than a faceless fugitive.

Frustrated, craving sidewalks and fresh air, I buttoned the collar of my black lamb's-leather bomber jacket, wrapped a white silk scarf around my neck, and cruised the foggy night. Sensing fear and loathing in the post-crash Financial District, I wandered into the "Werewolf-of-London/Soho" area where I was drawn to a club where familiar music and young people played. And there I stayed for hours drinking, thinking, until the booze eventually allowed me to forget about everything: being a fuge, losing a fortune, my discipline, my marriage, my name...my names.

Around two A.M., I marched up to the stage and asked the bandleader if I could sing. He looked me over. We decided on a tune. "We've a Yank from California, wants to croon for you now," he announced. "Please lend an ear to Leo."

And to a healthy crowd's delight, Leo sang with heart and soul and was asked to stay on until the break. I smoked a hashish cigarette with the band—inhaling—and thoroughly enjoyed myself.

Evidently, Sandra enjoyed me, too. I had noticed her earlier, seated one table away, that dark hair spilling over a full lacey blouse, those sad molasses eyes occasionally drifting my way, but mostly looking down. When I got up, she was with three girlfriends—all of whom had dates. Now she was alone with two glasses in front of her, sitting in the chair next to mine.

"Thought I'd save yer place," she explained with a distinct cockney accent. She handed me a drink. "Don't mind, do ya, Leo?"

Her smile was warm and welcome. I shook my head.

"Love yer voice. Could ya sing another song—fer me?"

Her eyes seemed very large, and her lips were wet. When I leaned toward her to speak, she closed them. "You are remarkably beautiful," I said quietly. When I kissed her mouth, her lips parted immediately, and she returned the kiss with great force. For some reason, in that moment, I tried to remember how many women I had made love to since the late '60s free-love era. I could not recall them all, only the pleasure we had shared. Had my worth as a lover stagnated in marriage, as I often feared about my creativity? Longing to know the answer, I sat down beside Sandra.

"Sing," she said, clutching my knee beneath the table.

"I've had my fifteen minutes of fame." I gestured toward the stage. "Really. It's their show, not mine. I'm not one to wear out my welcome."

"Please," she said softly, her painted nails almost penetrating my corduroy pants.

The wife had already convicted me, I thought. Might as well be guilty of something. So I sang for sweet Sandra right then and there. "All of me... Why not take all of me..." Whispering wet impromptu words between the lines into her ear. "Can't you see that I'm no good without you?"

I sang for her the entire taxi ride back to Blake's flat. I sang in the foyer of Daska House. I sang in the elevator where she removed my shirt.

Werewolf of London.

On Blake's plush floor, just inside the door, I peeled off that lacey blouse, she lost the pleated skirt, and I proceeded to carry her to the other room where, on Blake's bed with a pillow strategically placed beneath her arched back, I alternated between finesse and power until the headboard tapped a telltale rhythm on the wall.

"Wh-wha-what-about-the-neighbors?" she exclaimed.

Werewolf of London.

"Fuck the neighbors," I said, exploding inside her.

From a bubble bath, sipping tea, we saw sunrise over the Thames River.

"You're a wonderful lover, Tim," sweet Sandra sighed.

Her compliment was music to my ears. It seemed our affair was therapeutic for both of us. Sandra, a surgical intensive care nurse who'd been seeing an older doctor, was having some serious romance problems. She needed to talk.

"Tell me," I said.

"Eeza' bloody married man! And—"

"Shhhh," I said, pressing a finger against her lips. "So am I."

She bit me gently, nodding. "Guess I 'ave a genuine problem with married men then—aye, love?" she sighed. "What do you suggest?"

"This too shall pass," I prophesized. When she smiled, I saw curiosity in those big brown eyes. "So, tell me about your work," I said, beating her to the question.

"Me? I suck bloody hematomas and try and be careful not to drop nursing manuals on the chests of my double-bypass patients," she blurted, blowing bubbles and laughing. "Heavens! Look what time it is." She stared at the wall clock. "If I don't get to hospital by half-past seven, I won't 'ave a bloody job to complain about."

"Here." I jumped from the tub and tossed her a towel. "Hurry and dress, Ms. Nightingale. I'll call you a cab."

Feeling guilty did not occur to me as she reached, hesitantly, for the door handle. But the thought of marrying a foreigner and being able to acquire an English passport for Tim Barnes certainly did.

"Sorry to be in such a rush," she said, biting her lip.

The cabby honked his horn again from the middle of Sidney Street.

I kissed her flushed cheek. "It's not over yet," I said. After she left, I unplugged the phone, swallowed some Advil and fell asleep.

That night, she came again. I took her to dinner, then we went for a carriage ride. We shared romance. She was so bubbly, so upbeat, so *appreciative*. No longer that sad-eyed kid from the club in Soho, she was a kind lady trying to make her way in the world. But even though I was still mad at Kim, my anger was fading and being replaced by confusion. I began to feel guilty of premeditated adultery, and finally realized that any arranged marriage for citizenship would only draw me deeper into the dark side of my fugitive illusion. My real marriage was the only pure light in my life, which is why I decided to venture north to Jimmy's bash a day early, to avoid further temptation.

I felt an eerie sense of déjà vu when I kissed Sandra goodbye at Victoria Station then watched her sultry image disappear from the window of my northbound train. The moment recalled the spring of 1984 when I sent Catherine to the coast to catch the Channel Ferry to Calais for the last time, and committed myself to Kim and the Lion's Share.

Jimmy Collins was waiting for me at Wigan Station, standing tall beside his vintage olive green Rolls Royce, stroking his neatly trimmed moustache, rosy cheeks glowing, silver hair blowing in the wind. He greeted me warmly, head bobbing vigorously like Katharine Hepburn's. Soon we were sitting in the third floor living room of his Victorian house—or what remained of it. It was actually a mansion with very lofty ceilings and large, well proportioned rooms. Since the last time I paid a visit, the main floor had been transformed into a hotel lobby and dining area. There was a third floor ballroom—just down the hall from us—and adjacent to it, an enormous bathroom with a ten-person Jacuzzi strategically placed beneath a nymph-adorned dome skylight. Upon this bathroom's walls were painted life-sized, nude Adonis-like males flexing muscles of all kinds. And it was here, in this "romper room" according to Jimmy, that the real Twentieth Century history of his castle had occurred, a rich, risque history which would be retold again, and again, and again by the locals, long after he was gone.

Mr. Collins's house—soon to be Mab's Cross Hotel and Night Club—was one of Wigan's oldest historical landmarks still in private hands. Together with its walled garden and former carriage house in the rear, it occupied an entire city block. Mab's Cross was named after the legend of a medieval maiden who—upon being deemed unfaithful to her Crusading Scottish Lord—was made to carry a heavy wooden cross in disgrace for many miles, to the present site of Jimmy's place. The hotel was grandly furnished with the owner's prized remnants from his lengthy reign as Lancashire County's antiques exporting king. Nowadays, apparently Lord Collins' kingdom had been reduced to the third floor, where he resided with his brash Boy George-look-alike lover, Paul.

Jimmy reclined on the russet settee, I sat in an ornately-carved Queen Anne chair, and he ordered one of his boys to fetch glasses of port. My gracious host lit a long menthol cigarette and gave me an update on the people in his life: Paul, his longtime lover; Max, his alcoholic, embezzling partner and would-be bartender at Mab's; and so forth.

"I've built young Paul a nice salon in the old caretaker's cottage out back," Jimmy said, his slow drawl still smooth as velvet. "The lad's settled down. Spends most of his time styling hair now. Keeps him out of trouble in town." Collins took a two-second drag on his menthol fag, snuffed it in a silver ashtray, and drew another, sword-like, from the pack.

His hands shook. I could hear carpenters' hammers pounding finishing nails three floors below. Sensing trouble in the kingdom, I began to wonder why—beside obvious economic reasons—he was changing professions so late in life. I understood why the early 1980s antiques export boom had faded. The British pound—once as low as 1.35 in 1983—now stood at 1.77, creating a thirty-percent increase for American buyers. Also, unemployment in the industrial north of England had dropped considerably, meaning the local populace was no longer driven to sell their family heirlooms to Jimmy Collins and his pickers for pittances to pay for their meager needs. Maybe Jimmy, obviously moving slower since last I saw him, had merely devised this costly scheme to bring the nightlife he craved a little closer to home.

Our port arrived—a '48 Warres—and Jimmy resumed his oration. "Max still has problems with the drink," he drawled, tipping back his own medication. "June's got herself a bloody poultry stand at Wigan Mall. I'm afraid the same anti-gay crowd that closed down her place, Clowns Pub, is raising a fuss about us. But the brewery is behind me one hundred percent." He paused. "By the way, I really appreciated the money you loaned me. We needed badly to get these damn carpenters and the paddies to push the pace for the opening." He raised his glass. "You're a true friend, Mr. Lion. Cheers."

I raised mine. "Cheers," I echoed.

"Not to worry though," he proclaimed, with some of that old fire smoldering in his tired eyes. "I've called in all my favors for tomorrow. MP's, mayors—past and present—bobbies, our champion Wigan rugby lads, and of course, the best of Lancashire's beauty queen lasses will all be in attendance."

"And they'll all come willingly?" I asked. "Or did that little photo album you keep convince some of these celebrities to attend?"

"You're such a clever lad." Jimmy jammed yet another menthol in his mouth. "Yeah, well, they all *came* willingly first time 'round, didn't they?" He laughed. "Like they say, history repeats itself. Wait 'til you hear what else I've planned."

I listened intently, panning the room that reminded me of my own little kingdom once upon a time in Truckee, California. There were parties planned for every persuasion. A re-enactment of the carrying of Mab's Cross was scheduled for British history buffs. Athletes were to sign autographs. A Miss Mab's Cross pageant was on tap, for which I was to be one of the six judges.

I had to hand it to him. Collins was one helluva host.

Regardless of his lifestyle, the man was a great diplomat—kind of a bisexual Henry Kissinger without the German accent. In between unimaginable wildness, Jimmy's nearly sixty years of living had also been filled with charity work, generosity and kindness. He was a classy, genuine gentleman, but seemed to have surrounded himself with a cast of leeches. This was an opinion I kept to myself, not needing any vengeful enemies.

"Enough about me and my boring, petty life," he said. "Let's hear about you. How's this fugitive act affecting you? You all right?"

I nodded. We talked a little about married life, and why Kim hadn't accompanied me to Wigan. We reminisced about 1985's master plan to make me one of the top wholesalers of English antiques in California. "Other than losing a small fortune in the stock crash, I guess I'm faring well," I sighed.

"I got your package," he said, referring to underground press publications I'd sent which described methods for securing British ID. In a follow-up letter, I had asked him to confirm, denounce, elaborate on, and/or update their claims. He opened a drawer in an oak sideboard and reached inside. "British identity documents," he said, blowing dust from a file folder. "Go on, have a look."

I fingered through them diligently. Collins fell silent for a moment.

"The birth certificate and driver's license can easily be obtained," he told me. "The passport's an entirely different animal."

I frowned. "If I remember correctly, the big requirement for a British passport is a referral by someone of standing who will swear to having known you for years."

"Right you are." He bobbed his head rhythmically and sent a thin stream of menthol cigarette smoke ceiling-ward. "Easy enough though, love. We simply find a drunkard clergyman or physician who's fond of a few extra quid." He coughed, then smiled cryptically. "And you can figure out the rest. I suppose you'll have to do a bit of acting, but then you're such a clever lad."

Clever, yes, but not vain or insane enough to feel secure about testing the English system—even with inside help. When I expressed this thought, Jimmy hit me with the obvious answer—marriage. *Not again.*

"I could easily arrange one for Mr. Barnes," he said. "Then you could stay nearby and help me develop the club."

Nice idea. I was admittedly adventuresome. But his thing was not my thing. And even though the thought of tackling a legitimate project was enticing, our antique business had left a clear paper trail to Wigan, should the feds want to make such a lengthy trip. Not a likely occurrence, but I would always worry about some warped-minded customer snitching on me for a pint of ale... *"Scotland Yard? That Yank yer lookin' fer, 'eez workin' up at Mab's Cross in Wigan!"*

"No, the American Pacific Northwest is where I belong," I said.

"You're crazy to stay there. Come live in Edinburgh, then. There's a large American artists' community up that way. You'd fit in well."

It was appealing, I thought, but Kim would never go for cool windswept Scotland. She was already complaining about Oregon's rainy weather.

"I just don't want to see you get caught! Why live in the States with such insane laws?"

"I'm an American. It's my country. I can get in my pickup truck and drive for days. I speak-a-da language. I'm going to pay some taxes on this new identity, and keep my options open. If and when Tim Barnes immigrates, at least he'll have a few years' history under his belt."

The phone rang. Collins answered it. "Yeah, right. I'm on my way," he said. To me he added, "I have to go play host. The guests are arriving. I'll have Max show you to your room."

The next morning, Mab's Cross Hotel was an energetic beehive of activity. Guests swarmed in from the far corners of the Empire, liquor lorries unloaded their stock, carpenters scrambled to trim out the bar, landscapers arranged potted palm trees around the parquet dance floor beside flaming-pink neon flamingos. Two balding men wearing matching white safari outfits moved in next door. One winked when I left my room and went down to the lobby in pajamas. "Friend of Jimmy's?" he asked when I returned with coffee and a newspaper.

"Yes. Good morning," I said politely. *Not that kind of friend.*

With rain in the forecast, I decided to take a hike. I spent the afternoon retracing the trail of the medieval maiden made to bear the guilt-weight of Mab's Cross from all those centuries gone by. And in the solitude of Lancashire County's woods, I debated the merits of calling my Lady Di, who, like Oregon—half-a-world-away—I was sorely missing. Not yet, I decided.

Opening night festivities began with a black tie dinner party. For local Wiganites, it was the party of the year, and they watched me with not-so-subtle curiosity, wondering who this American fellow, Leo, was, and why I was seated at the host's table, next to the Collins family. I observed them, too, with the inquisitiveness of a 170-pound cat and a writer's eye. Transvestite bobbies, made-up Members of Parliament, boys-in-waiting, bored wives, brash Paul's punk crowd fidgeting nervously in formal attire...everyone maintained their best behavior throughout the seven-course gourmet evening, until the last speech was delivered and the final glass of champagne was consumed. At that time, the crowd roared down the hall to the adjoining nightclub, where the real action began.

After helping the undermanned staff tend bar, I leaned in a corner and surveyed the scene. Soon, a sassy lass in a lion print dress pressed against me, tugged at my wedding ring and asked, "Where's the missus?"

"Back home, in California," I replied.

"Pity," she said, sensually slurping a Bombay martini. "I'm married to an MP...for bloody show," she slurred, swishing a perky booty. "But he prefers bent boys!"

"Pity," I said, estimating the suction power of her high cheekbones. "Such a waste," I added instinctively. I loosened my black bow tie, suddenly feeling a little tempted again.

"Friend of Jimmy's, are you?" she asked, swallowing an olive.

"Yes, only I like women."

"Staying at the hotel?"

Her hair was perfect. I nodded.

Someone put *Werewolf of London* on the stereo system.

She popped two black onyx studs on my French shirt, and ran one ice-cube-holding-finger down to just below my belt. "How 'bout we slip up to your room after midnight, love? Would you like that?"

The music grew louder. One of her girlfriends grabbed her arm. I nodded to the beat.

She blew me a kiss.

Liquor and lust knocked at my brain.

Werewolf of London.

"Max! Hit me again," I called out to Jimmy's embezzling bartender. I could smell the lingering scent of the lioness. "Make it a double, Max!" I watched her mingle through the masses dancing with old men, but glancing, always glancing my way. "One more vodka. Skip the tonic, Max," I said.

By midnight, all pretense of British dignity had disappeared from the dance floor. The silver sphere showering reflected light on the madding crowd reminded me of the '80s disco days—not a favorite era of mine. The sex monster within me wanted another vodka and tonic. Fortunately, my conscience ordered soda water.

In the solitude of my room, I undressed. And there on the bed in darkness, I opened an old leather case containing a slender silver flute with mother of pearl keys. At my request, Jimmy had gotten it for me. It was to be a coming home gift for Kim—the instrument she'd spoken fondly of playing in high school. I took it out, fingered it, pictured her puckered lips in my rain-splattered windowpane, longed for her, and slept.

Sometime later, I was tossing and turning, dreaming she had left me, when a wind-driven shutter slapped, and someone rapped on my door. My heart pounded. Rain resounded off window glass. And then I heard the slurred voice of the lady in the lion print dress: "Leo. Leo? Leo! Are you in there, love?"

I was and I wasn't. Once in London was enough.

The knock came again. But all I could hear was the rain.

I awoke clear-headed on a cloudy day. The party was over, and so was my first fuge European exploration. Mab's Cross Hotel was silent, with the exception of snoring hangover victims. So I ventured into Wigan town, entered one of those old-fashioned red British phone booths, and dialed the number in Oregon. A light rain trickled down the glass. It rang once, twice, three, four...too many times.

My pulse quickened.

"Honey!" my wife answered. "It's three in the morning here. What's wrong?"

"Nothing," I sighed, relieved. "I love you. I miss you. I'm coming home."

When he awoke that afternoon, Jimmy Collins found the note I'd slipped under his door. At the time, he was both surprised and disappointed that I'd ran home "pussy whipped," forsaking my duty to help judge the Miss Mab's Cross pageant. But weeks later when I called, his disturbing news confirmed my instinctive feelings about not moving to England or Scotland, and underscored the magnitude of my dilemma.

"Yes, Leo," Jimmy said. "I've been hoping you'd give a ring. We had a visit from the authorities the other day. Scotland Yard sent two men by to inquire of the whereabouts of a former American client of mine." He proceeded to give me the play by play. "Of course, I denied having any knowledge of this individual's current status. I believe they considered me hostile and uncooperative," the king of Mab's Cross concluded, his not-so-velvet voice wavering between sips of port and drags on menthol smokes. "And so—just in case they come again, armed with search warrants—I've gone and shredded all written communications after July, 1986." He paused to puff. "Oh, one more thing. I received an interesting call from an old friend of yours—*Maui Ray*. He's left a number where he can be reached in Rome. Do you have a pen handy?"

Interesting indeed. Bert's right hand man, Maui Ray, was rumored to be on a grand-jury-avoiding world tour, but was he? My palms got sweaty. My paranoid mind whirled. The last time I'd seen Ray was in Wigan in 1985, when I introduced him to Jimmy Collins—so he could play the antiques game, as I had. But how could I trust anyone after so many deals had been made with the government since my departure? The answer was easy. I could not.

"Keep it, Jimmy," I said. "If he phones you again, don't mention this call. I'm going to lay low for awhile."

The news of the authorities expanding their search for me to England added a whole new dimension of fear to my predicament. My ideas were not bearing fruit, trying to be a happy fugitive was expensive, and I had lost a fortune in the world of international finance. I needed to regroup.

My brother Bill, in tiny Bethel, Alaska, had gotten an official visit, too. While the feds apparently had elected to operate covertly in their surveillance of my other relatives, they decided to play hardball with Brother Bill. Perhaps it was because their training manual taught them to hunt wild beasts like me in the most remote regions of the country. Perhaps it was because their snitches told them Bill was my favorite brother. Or maybe, just maybe—because Bill was a fellow government employee—they figured they could get him to turn on me, like convicted Unabomber Ted Kaczynski's sibling eventually did.

Bill, a younger, clean-living carbon copy of me with nothing to hide, described his encounter in our brief, clandestine 1987 pre-holiday pay phone conversation.

"What's new in the great white north?" I asked him.

"Plenty. You okay?" he answered, sounding nervous.

"I was. I guess so. Why?"

"That babble letter you sent from Europe? It came special delivery, dissected like a frog, and hermetically sealed in a plastic bag from some government lab in Seattle."

"So. No surprise. They put something on you called a *mail cover* order. I just hope they believed everything they read about us moving to Brazil, the baby and—"

My brother chuckled. "There's more. They came to pressure me for information."

"Who came?" I asked. "When? Where? Give me all the details."

"It was the last week of September. Simon, a black man—rare for bush Alaska, and not well liked in Bethel because of a cocky attitude and bad reputation for womanizing—steps into my office with his chest stuck out beneath a too-tight State Troopers uniform. Jim, a thirty-five-ish white boy with a greaser hairdo and a hot dog city slicker suit, struts in behind Simon and identifies himself as a Federal Narcotics Agent. The three Public Health Service staff members I am supervising freak out. None of them know about your situation, Tom."

"Simon says, 'William Virgil Hickey, I'd like to talk to you about your brother.'"

"You know me, Tom. I'm thinking, shit, what a joke! I never enjoyed playing *Simon Says* when we were growing up. I wanted to say, let's play *Environmental Scientist Bill Says*, but I could tell they didn't have much of a sense of humor. I took them to my office where we could talk in private. The fed closed the door, and Simon asked if he could record our session. It really felt weird, Tom. I mean, I don't know the law that well, but you know what I think about the pot laws. And you're my blood."

"Bill, please," I whispered, as a cold wind roared down Mount Shasta, shaking the phone booth I'd selected off California Interstate 5 for this risky payphone contact. "Just give me the details, dude. I'm running low on quarters, here."

"Okay. So, Simon asks if I'd seen, heard from, or knew the whereabouts of my fugitive brother. He said you were armed and dangerous. He said in a deep voice, 'You know, Mr. Hickey, you can go down, too, if you know anything about your brother and don't tell me. It's called aiding and abetting, bro!' That's when I got pissed off. Why no, Simon, I said. I have no idea where Tom is. All I know is that he's my best friend, a kind and honest man, and probably wise to stay away from glory seekers like you who get a hard-on by ruining people's lives over—"

"Bill! Get real," I interrupted, feeling a rush of emotion, and realizing that for everyone else but the fugitives being hunted, these hunts were merely a sporting game. "How did it end?"

"I told them I hadn't seen you since the wedding in Tahoe. I said there were worse demons than marijuana dealers to spend tax dollars hunting. Then I cut it short by saying I had two contaminated water systems to investigate, and an Eskimo village with hazardous waste in their schoolyard."

"Then what?" I asked.

"They assured me I'd be seeing them again—real soon. I walked them to the exit and waved goodbye—the way we used to when Ma made us be polite to the dentist after getting three fillings and a mouth full of spinach-flavored fluoride treatment. I haven't seen the fed since, but Simon is a common sight at the local disco where he comes—in his Troopers uniform—trying to pick-up young native girls. Guess this means we won't go salmon fishing this spring, eh?"

"Guess not," I muttered, thinking about my brother. Like me, he saw the world the way it really was—*gray*—and knew that uniforms, guns and badges, and government mandates did not always guarantee the difference between good and bad.

"Tom," my brother said, sounding serious. "Ma wants to see you, just to know you're all right. I know it's going to be tricky. But she worries a lot. What should I tell her at Christmas time?"

A fresh snowfall blanketed the hood of Tim Barnes' black Ford. I had been on the phone too long and knew it.

"Tell her I'm fine," I sighed, envisioning Mom's face. "Tell her I love her. Tell her to wait for a sign and don't tell anyone, but one way or another—we'll do it."

Alaska State Trooper interview with William Hickey, Thomas Hickey's younger brother, August 1987.

STATE OF ALASKA

DEPARTMENT OF PUBLIC SAFETY

DIVISION OF STATE TROOPERS

STEVE COWPER, GOVERNOR

Arthur English, Commissioner

P.O. Box 268
Bethel, Ak 99559
(907) 543-2294

September 28, 1987

Inspector [redacted]
United States Marshal Office
701 "C" Street, Box 28
Anchorage, AK 99513

RE: FEDERAL FUGITIVE, THOMAS P. HICKEY

Inspector [redacted]

This is in reference to your written request on 08-25-87 on the above subject, Thomas Hickey. I interviewed his brother [redacted]

It is my personal opinion that [redacted] knows where his brother is, or at least how to contact him. He tried to give the appearance of cooperating with the Troopers, but being sure not to give too much information.

I informed both [redacted] they could be charged with Federal crimes for keeping information about Thomas's whereabouts from the U.S. Marshal. They were told it was illegal to keep that information or to interfer with an official investigation, by lying about the above information, or allowing Thomas to stay with them or hiding him in their residence, to avoid his arrest.

If I can be of any further assistance to you or your office, please feel free to contact me, and I will attempt to assist your office in anyway I can.

Attached is a written copy of interviews conducted by officer [redacted] Alaska State Police on subjects [redacted] and [redacted] The interviews were conducted as per requests from USMS-N/IND. and USMS-AK. The statements made during the interviews did not reveal the whereabouts of fugitive THOMAS HICKEY. Officer [redacted] advised both subjects on 8-25-87 of the harboring statute and that in his opinion [redacted] is in contact with fugitive Thomas Hickey. [redacted] further advised that he will continue to encourage [redacted] to reveal those whereabouts..... Investigation still continues at this time...

[redacted]
Alaska State Trooper
D Detachment / Bethel Post
(907) 543-2294

cc: [redacted]
D Detachment Commander

10

Tucson Tony Rides Again

Early December 1987: I had promised to help the Greek do a coin show in California, and Kim had not seen her mother, Donna, in fifteen months. Having read that the families of fugitives are most likely to be watched around Thanksgiving and Christmas, we decided the gap between holidays was the perfect time to do both of these tasks. I put her on a redeye in San Francisco and she flew directly into Buffalo, New York.

The next morning, Donna slipped her key into the door lock to open her lamp shade shop for business. Between the swirling snow-snakes on the sidewalks, Donna noticed a hauntingly familiar woman in a stylish European hat, suitcase-in-hand, head down into the wind, walking toward her fast. Donna shook off intuitive feelings and opened the door to her shop.

The strange woman dashed in behind her.

"Excuse me, Miss, but we're not open for business."

"Motho! It's me," announced her daughter, my wife. She tossed her hat, exposing her short perm. "Missed ya. Like my new look?"

They hugged and kissed, quickly drew the blinds and hung the CLOSED sign on the display window. Minutes later Donna sneaked her daughter out the back door.

By the next afternoon they were in Toronto for several days of fantasy Christmas shopping and worry-free quality time.

A week later on our drive back to Oregon, Kim gave me the family, and fugitive updates. "First the good news," she said. "My sister Kelly was at *The Hacienda* when your picture was shown on that Crime Stoppers show."

"The Mexican restaurant in Mishawaka known for bottomless pitchers of margaritas and rowdy patrons? What's so good about that?" I asked, shifting into third to scale a mountainous stretch of Interstate 5.

"A couple of drunks at the bar said: 'Hell! They'll never catch Tom. He beat 'em, and they're pissed because they look like assholes. Haven't you heard? They're living in Brazil and Kim had a baby! The dude's a fuckin' legend.'"

The Ford sputtered toward the summit of Grants Pass. My wife watched me break into a sweat and laughed. *A legend?* Perhaps my plan had backfired. Talk like that would only taunt the government into intensifying their manhunt for me. *A legend?* All I ever wanted was to be left alone. I fidgeted in my seat, hands wet on the wheel, wondering who was spreading my misinformation. Kim's dad, I suspected, was disclosing information being leaked to him by his contacts at the FBI.

"So, what's the bad news?" I asked.

"Motho got a visit from the feds," my wife mumbled, rubbing a red splotch on her slender neck. "My dad's former partner on the force, an FBI agent named Hanis, is in charge of the hunt for you. Hanis is good at what he does." She paused, and took a deep breath. "This agent and my dad are pretty close. They've been through a lot of things together."

"And?" Former partners shared secrets which indebted them to each other for eternity. I wondered how much pull her dad—now released from the force on a disability pension—had with this agent Hanis.

"And they told Motho my life will be in danger if they raid our house and there is gunfire."

"Scare tactics," I blurted, turning down the volume on the radio. "What did she tell them?"

"Nothing! She laughed and said you were nonviolent. She told them not to forget she was once married to one of their kind and knew all their dirty little tricks."

"Did they get pissed?"

My wife lowered, then shook her head. "Nope. They just grinned and said they were going put you on *Unsolved Mysteries*."

"I can't believe this." I ground the Ford into fourth for a downhill stretch. "Great. Fucking great. They're full of shit." I felt convinced it was a bluff. "They'd never waste that kind of money looking for a pot dealer. What do you think, honey?"

"You're the thinker."

It was a quiet ride home.

§

The week before Christmas we drove Kim's new 1985 beige Volvo in a blinding snowstorm to Boulder, Colorado, for a brief visit with Leigh, Shannon and Bill. We spent the Christmas of '87 in Durango at the Blackwells' hilltop home, nestled in the shadows of majestic Silver Mountain—and strategically located in the Four Corners area for easy access to the Southwest's marijuana-smuggling border towns. All the same players from Manzanita attended, Moon, Missy and more. Thanks to McCarthy's sizable hunk of investment capital, the southwestern chapter of Fuges Anonymous was in the midst of a very profitable season.

Spirits were high. So were our hosts. They told me little had changed in Tucson except the potency of the product, and the prices. Weed wholesaling for six to seven hundred dollars a pound in Tucson was bringing over a grand in hundred lots at the other end of the pipeline. It was a far cry from the hundred dollars a pound, twenty-five dollars an ounce days of the early '70s. Apparently, America's appetite for marijuana—contrary to government statistics—had not diminished, but the Drug War marched on anyway, driving up marijuana prices and making cheaper, harder drugs more affordable than pot to the nation's youth.

Of course, this was great news for folks like Smiley and Moon, for upon arrival in Eastern markets—which were short on supply and high on demand—each load was quickly cashed out to their happy customers, who always clamored for more. It was every salesman's dream. And gadget master Moon had developed a State Trooper-proof fleet of cross-country contraband transport vehicles, too.

"Our main problem is getting the money back here quick enough," Moon said. "Our connections can't warehouse what little inventory they acquire and risk being busted. It's first come, first served. We've been Fed-Exing our chips to Phoenix so we can slap a down payment on the next load."

"Sounds crazy," I said.

"It is," admitted Moon. "And we want to expand our market. Which is why I want to ask you for a loan, to help with our cash flow. How do you feel about us using Arnie as a money driver so our pot crew can rest between missions, then fly down to Tucson fresh for the road?"

"Arnie's his own man," I said. "He'd probably like the money. Talk to him." I thought about the last of my cash reserves, sitting in a box in

Reno. "I might consider loaning you a hundred grand, especially after losing my left nut in the stock market."

"God bless those dirty Customs officers, each and every one of 'em!" Smiley offered the toast, alternating between snorts of Christmas cocaine and gulps of his beloved *Crowny*. "One or two more seasons, and the wifey and I can retire to Mexico with a couple of million. Right honey?" He pinched her ass. "Speaking of money. I'd like to learn about your banking arrangements, Timmy."

A blushing Lizzy nodded, blinked and fondled her new diamond bracelet. "Actually," she said, smacking her lips, "we're thinking of renting a workhouse in Tucson or Phoenix for next season. Something with a pool. You and Kimmy will simply *have* to visit, for the weather, of course."

We skied, dined and played marathon games of Trivial Pursuit together. I was shocked because they had lived in Durango less than a year, yet everywhere we went they knew someone: the ski instructors, lift shack operators, restaurant workers, and an interesting couple who told stories of international travels and were actually invited to party with a nest of fuges on New Year's Eve. I figured they were either sexual swinger-playmates or Smiley's customers, but something about them didn't feel right.

Being drawn into the holiday drug scene again was bad enough, but consuming coke with strangers was ignorant. Kim and I checked out of Smiley's guestroom, and into Durango's historic Strater Hotel, where we spent our final Colorado nights—and our second wedding anniversary—recovering from the relapse.

That last day in Durango while skiing together, I watched from a cornice ridge as Smiley disappeared in a puff of white snow-mist down a black diamond run at the Purgatory resort. I shook my head and listened to his war whoops echo off the canyon walls. Smiley skied like he lived—too fast. I wondered how long they would last, and if this resort would live up to its name for them, before they could retire to Mexico with their millions.

I had not been to Tucson since 1982, and after my flight from prosecution, wild horses could not have dragged me there. But here I was, where it had all begun in earnest—the easy money, my early mastering of entrepreneurial business skills from negotiating to marketing, and the all-important earning and giving of trust—driving into the boonies of northwest Tucson. I clutched the Volvo's steering wheel with my stomach churning, about to share another chunk of my colorful past with the woman beside me.

"Was that a roadrunner?" Kim asked like a kid at the zoo. "Just look at all those giant cactus standing out like telephone poles against that flaming sunset sky! It's beautiful here."

"Yes, beautiful," I mumbled, mesmerized by an approaching flatbed truck driven by two Mexicans. The rig was carrying a full load of hay, and when I pulled onto the shoulder to let them pass I read their sweaty poker faces and envisioned marijuana bales concealed below their cargo! Maybe it was the gold Rolex on the wrist of the driver when he waved at me and mouthed *stupid gringo.*

Tucson Tony's latest ranch was isolated, like all the others in this barren dealers region. Fortunately, there was no need to knock on the door of his humble adobe home and hope I had followed his directions correctly. The minute the Volvo's engine came within earshot, *El Gato* was waiting at the gate with his trusty golden retriever, Rusty, wagging his tail beside him. Tony's suitable nickname meant the *Cat.*

"Thought you'd never make it, T," he said, shaking my hand through the open driver's side window. "It's been a long time. Too long. You know you're always welcome on the ranch."

"Thanks, Gato. You look good."

The scent of mesquite charcoal wafted from his barbecue-chef's apron. I studied the Italian-American native of the Big Apple who'd come West after Woodstock, and never returned to New York, except to peddle his goods, or collect money. He had not changed much, this olive-skinned, curly-headed, soft-spoken man known to play a mean guitar.

"What the hell is that?" I asked, pointing to a shiny black BMW parked beside the same primer colored '54 Chevy pickup he had driven since I first met him. "Thought you always went low profile?"

"Bought it for the wife," Tony mumbled. "What about this yuppie-mobile of yours, huh?"

We laughed as a crescent moon appeared on the horizon.

I introduced him to Lady Di. "She wanted a silver Jaguar," I explained. "But I convinced her something conservative was in order. Her looks get enough attention. I wouldn't want my neighbors always wondering where the foxy blond in the silver Jag got her money, would I? Anyway, it's highly rated in crash tests and has an extremely efficient heating system."

"Like me, honey?" My blushing wife winked and extended a hand. "It's a pleasure to finally meet you, Tony."

"Pleasure's all mine," the Cat purred.

We sat down to dinner with his Australian wife, Aggy, and his hired hand, Eugene—an eighty-two year-old leather-skinned pensioner, lifetime pal, and part-time pot driver. Aggy regaled us with stories of the wonders Down Under and its many opportunities for young people seeking a fresh start. Raven hair, high glossy cheekbones, pleasant demeanor and an enchanting accent—Aggy was pretty, and pregnant. The mere fact that my fellow conservative marijuana millionaire had committed himself to her enabled me to drop my defenses, assume she had an equally impressive brain behind those brown eyes, and listen attentively.

What I gathered was that Aggy, like most careful dealer's wives, was lonely—part of the great compromise for living the good life on an outlaw's salary. BMWs and diamond necklaces may have secretly been this seemingly down-to-earth Aussie's best friends, but she was obviously starved for female companionship—fugitive or not—with whom she could talk honestly and openly.

"Tony speaks highly of you," Aggy said at one point. "Now I see why. You're such a charming couple. If we weren't flying to Sydney day after tomorrow, we could all go on holiday at Tony's friend's resort in Monterey."

I believe I could have listened to her sultry Aussie accent, which ended each sentence trailing off like a question, for a few more days, but they were flying to Sydney, packing boxes were everywhere. Tony proceeded to describe his Mexican buddy's Monterey resort, and how Mexican government officials protected such investments for a fee.

When Eugene went to bed and the Australian cabernet ran out, the conversation shifted to "twenty-questions" on our life as fugitives. Activities that had become mundane to us fascinated them. Then Kim became fixated on the topic of Aggy's pregnancy. When Tony and I rose from the table and started for the door my Lady Di looked at me with maternal eyes and blurted, *"Baby."* Her brown eyes saddened. Her classic smile became a pouty frown. I felt a powerful tugging at my heart strings, and in that instant—for the first time—I realized the fabled feminine biological clock in my no-longer-a-kid wife's thoroughbred body was ticking like a time bomb. I had felt ready for a tow-headed lion cub back in Truckee, but how could I do this to a child? Maybe the answer was Down Under.

Beneath a starry desert sky, El Gato and I smoked after-dinner cigars and stared at Mount Lemon. "Remember the time I snuck you into the university Student Union lounge to drink and enjoy the air conditioning," he said, "and we wound up watching Dustin Hoffman in *The Graduate*?"

"Sure as hell do. How could I forget?" Proudly I puffed on my stogie. *"Plastics..."* I whispered. "I was seventeen, we were tripping on magic mushrooms, and a thirty-one-year-old lab tech who believed I was from London took me home. My first Mrs. Robinson," I sighed. "Seems like only yesterday."

"Yeah, it do, don't it? You know, herb has been good to me, but the times they are-a-changin', T." Gato stared at me with far away eyes and shook his head sympathetically. "Look at you. You were so conservative, so cautious. What happened to your happy ending?"

"Conspiracy," I hissed like a snake to mask the hurt inside that speaking the word produced. "Good God, Gato! Don't feel sorry for me. There's probably several million people who'd cream their jeans to be in my shoes. How about you? How you feeling these days?"

"Good, T, real good. I'm finally happy." His round face glowed in the desert moonlight. "I'm going to be a father. I should be—"

"You should count your blessings and quit while you're ahead," I said, gripping his shoulder.

"I know. I know." He nodded. "Shit T, you sound just like the wife. But I've got to tell ya, I have one more season left in me."

"Why?"

"Because. I've got to sell this house and these vehicles. And with a little more money I can get my boat restoration company idea off the ground, and do some serious land development projects." His gray-muzzled golden retriever limped over to his side, and the Cat scratched the dog behind an ear. "Rusty's getting old, and Eugene's no spring chicken. There's nothing left for me here, T, and I'll be an Australian resident next year. It's time to move on. Come and join us. It'll be like old times. I can arrange everything. You can invest through your offshore corporation. We can be partners. Give me until next Christmas, and I'll have all the paperwork ready for you. What do you say, T?"

It sounded good. I was tempted. A fresh start with another like-minded-couple who knew my past? "I'm willing to give it a try."

"Great." He handed me an envelope. "I'm checking on a contact to buy passports out of Hong Kong. Meanwhile, here's the pictures and the info for my US ID set. When will your people get it done?"

"Give me a month or so. What's with these passports? You in some kind of jam? Is there something I should know about?"

"Nope. A man can't have too many identities. Can he?"

I shook my head. A coyote howled. Rusty barked and limped off into the mesquite thickets.

Gato said, "I'm coming back—alone—in March for the last few spring smuggles until fall. Then I'll return in November and ride that final season hard. How about bringing my paperwork down and helping me move some weight? You still have people?"

I choked on cigar smoke. "I'm out, Gato. Haven't handled one ounce of weed since '84. I don't need money—only peace of mind." I pawed at the desert floor, realizing what an oxymoron my statement was. "I just don't feel like that old magic I once had is still protecting me. And anyway, all my people are either informants, or fugitives. Now, I'm sure my fellow fuges would love to hook up with you for your last hurrah. Matter of fact, they've already offered to pay me for an introduction to the infamous desert Cat."

"How much?"

"Twenty grand."

"Shit! Is that all I'm worth after all these years in the biz?"

"No comment. I could ask for fifty, but I figured you—"

"You figured right. I'm too close to retirement to meet new faces. Why couldn't you intermediate? You wouldn't have to touch anything, just be their eyes. What kind of stash vehicle do they have? The road between here and Phoenix is hotter than hell these days."

"They're running two dual-wheeled Silverado pickups. Each one's hauling a heavy steel construction site generator that's hollow inside. They were custom welded by some Hell's Angels friends of theirs. They can hold a thousand pounds, concealed. And every time they load it, they glue on a new gasket and seal it by drilling in dozens of metal screws. I have never seen a better transport rig."

"Impressive," said the Cat.

"Definitely. And every rig is registered to a jive transport corporation that leads to a mail drop. They're pretty crafty, but I don't want to deal again. I've already done three years cold turkey."

"But you wouldn't be dealing, per se," Gato argued, scratching the whiskers on his chin. "It would be simple. My beaners drop the bales off here, Eugene picks up your people's rig with half the cash stashed inside and brings it here. You do what you're good at—quality control—and Eugene loads it, then drives it to the shopping mall parking lot off Ina Road. You and I watch from inside the wife's BMW, and when everyone is in place, you walk over to your guys' car, hand them the Silverado's keys and get a suitcase with the rest of the cash. You're a trustable guy. They trust you. I trust you. And in the process, you pick up a few extra g's mad-money to buy your wife some baubles. By the way, I know a great jeweler in town. Think about it. You're an outlaw already, right? It'll be my last season. Who's been your buddy since those days of yesteryear? Who's yer pal?"

Tucson Tony had my number, and was playing a familiar tune. I was like a recovering addict looking relapse in the eye. I felt an old familiar churning—akin to a drunken gerbil on a treadmill—in my stomach. Elation and fear flowed through my veins. I thought about how vulnerable I would be making a sizable marijuana transaction in a public parking lot—as opposed to the Aardvark Construction pole barn arrangement I'd used in the '80s. I thought about all the money I had just lost in Europe, and felt a rush of adrenaline.

"We leave tomorrow," I said. "Send a note to my Portland mail drop before you come back in March. Put a time and a payphone number on it. Use our MEXICANFLY code. Don't mention this around my old lady. I made her a promise."

"Mum's the word, mate," purred the Cat.

"Now, where's this underground stash you've been bragging about?" I asked.

"You're standing next to it." El Gato pointed to a stack of mesquite.

Fifteen minutes later we had relocated the woodpile, dug a foot deep into the desert sand, and were descending into an air-conditioned custom-concrete pot smuggler's bunker. The pungent smell of Mexico's finest *sensimilla* filled my senses.

Suddenly the sound of a low-flying plane penetrated the desert silence. Gato grabbed the match I had lit to see my way along some steel stairs and snuffed it. He quickly slid the metal plate above our heads to its former position. We dropped to the dirt floor below, held our breath...and waited for the eye in the sky to pass.

Nineteen Eighty-eight was an unusually cold, gloomy winter in Oregon's Columbia Gorge. It spawned at least three confirmed cases of cabin fever. This ailment—combined with the mysterious loss of his *Johnny P. Morgan* passport application, and a strong desire to completely disappear from his potential fatal attraction, Manzanita-fling—influenced Arnie to expedite his assumption of identity number two, *Patrick O'Hara*, and accept seasonal employment as Moon's money driver.

Arnie's decision to hit the road brought much needed privacy to our latest refuge on the banks of the Columbia River near mighty Bonneville Dam. In my haste to disappear from Manzanita after our fuge-reunion exposure, I had considered the small, three bedroom ranch on rare waterfront acreage to be quite a find. The practically immobile octogenarian landlords—Carl and Marie Obermier of Canby, Oregon—were sweet folks who asked few questions and accepted not only my well-honed story, but our animals as well. There were no neighbors per se, only two vacant places barely visible through the thick hedges on either side of us that were primarily summer homes. But there were surprises, which required some adjustments for Kim and me.

Perhaps it was the *Unsolved Mysteries* warning from her mother, or the trains that rumbled along the too-near tracks that vibrated our bed some nights; or maybe it was those enormous river barges cruising down the Columbia at three in the morning, tossing tidal waves ashore, sounding their horns, and beaming a barrage of strobe lighting like alien aircraft through our windows. Regardless of the cause, sleep became a rarity and Kim developed a nervous condition of grinding her teeth—which our kindly Portland dentist promptly cured by prescribing a bite guard. My wife joked that the unappealing device was for my protection from her vampire tendencies, but we both knew damn well it was another troubling sign of the times.

After her mother's warning we became reluctant, regular viewers of *Unsolved Mysteries*—even though the idea of wasting national media exposure on a marijuana fugitive seemed ludicrous to me. Each Wednesday evening Kim made popcorn, we flopped on the couch clutching stiff drinks, and listened to the voice of host Robert Stack. Inevitably, after each no-show showing, the wife and I breathed a sigh of relief. Then I scanned the airwaves with my satellite dish for old black and white reruns of Mr. Stack's early days as Elliot Ness in *The Untouchables*, a show that chronicled America's *other* lengthy prohibition war.

Our last cat, Miss Whitey, whose natural winter camouflage evidently failed her, disappeared forever one day after I spotted a cougar on the ridge behind the house. With her bio-clock silently clamoring for motherhood, Kim felt an urge to be surrounded by pets. She saved a calico kitty at a nearby farm from a Humane Society death sentence; filled two aquariums with tropical fish—naming each one; and brought home two hand-fed parakeets from a Gresham petshop. When Arnie agreed to adopt our animals if we moved to Australia, I retrieved a gray and white striped Manx from an Eagle Creek Park ranger's unwanted litter, hoping the cats—Smokey Bear and Punkin'—would give my fading Irish setter a boost. To my great delight, Benjamin immediately took the two feline brats under his wing, and they became the best of friends. By February of '88, our isolated sanctuary was alive and bustling with active, happy, surrogate children.

In early March of 1988, I got a letter from the Englishman, Jones, asking me to host him for a fortnight holiday in the states. Kim was not keen on him coming, but realized that my partnership with Jones in London property required that I maintain a relationship with him. He brought his nephew, Jeremy Springs—a scrappy young, prematurely balding, unkempt cricket player—to our tranquil river home, explaining that Master Jeremy, his heir apparent, was someone I should know just in case the older Jones passed away. Within days, both Londoners grew tired of my laid-back routine of mountain hiking, playing with pets, putting in a terraced garden, fishing in my backyard trailed by hungry cats, and gorging myself on Lady Di's increasingly gourmet-quality cooking. To satisfy their craving for skirt-gazing action, I took them into Portland for St. Patrick's Day, where the Brits had good fun until a kilted Irish bagpipe corps came busting through the louvered doors of Schmicks and McCormick's bar blowing *Danny Boy*.

"Can I tell you? This establishment has developed a foul odor," Jones scowled, his turned-down squirrel tails revealing a deeply furrowed brow. "If and when America experiences the kind of terrorist carnage which we have from these bloodthirsty Irish paddies, then displays such as this one will leave a bitter taste in your mouth, too. If I were not sworn to secrecy, I would tell you some of the unfortunate encounters these paddies have had at my associates' and my own expense. Even the liberal *Royals* despise these creatures! Now, please be a good chap, and take us back to your home."

I had never seen him so humorless.

The next day, Jones suggested we spend their final week in America somewhere warm and dry...Arizona. I paged Moon and Smiley, who returned my call from Tucson.

"God bless 'em!" declared Smiley, after I explained my intentions. "You wouldn't come down for your fuge friends," he taunted, "but for your new foreigner crew... Sure. Bring on your damn limeys. We'll entertain 'em. And while we do that, you can pay your man, Tony, a little visit. Whatta' ya say? Huh, Timmy? We're having some serious problems filling our orders down here."

"I'll see what I can do," I mumbled.

"Great!" shouted Smiley. "Oh, by the way, Timmy, the wifeys didn't make this trip, and there's some wild titty bars in town."

"See you day after tomorrow," I said.

With the guilt of London still fresh on my conscience, I asked Kim to come along, but she insisted on staying with the pets.

As the plane circled Tucson, I could clearly see how much the city had grown, gobbling up desert in all directions on either side of Interstate 10 to accommodate its approximately half-a-million residents. Most of Golf Links Road, all of Oracle, even Ina Road was developed.

Beneath us Jones spotted the government's massive graveyard for retired military aircraft and Davis Mountain Air Force Base, then after landing, babbled on about his WW II bombing runs until his sixth sunset cocktail ran dry on the balcony of the Brits' Ramada Inn suite.

"Can I tell you?" he then said, stopping to chew the butt of his Havana and hassle the nightly gathering of mockingbirds in fragrant lemon trees below. "Can I tell you? Those dirty buggers will drive me mad!"

"I'll switch rooms with you," I said, grabbing his wrist before he could dump the ice from his glass over the balcony rail. "Those birds are music to my ears."

"Mm, yes, I see. Well then, what about these friends of yours and their ladies of ill-repute—preferably firm, young darkies?"

"Patience, my dear Jones," I said. "Patience."

March in Tucson marked the end of another marijuana season. I reclined in my lawn chair pretending to read an Ann Rice novel, peering through reflective Vuarnet lenses, watching New York scammers scattered around the pool sipping piña coladas with mistresses half their age while they waited for shipments and dirty Customs Agents' shifts to change on the Mexican border. There were undoubtedly deep cover DEA agents in those lounge chairs, too—wearing confiscated Rolexes, packing seized handguns with their Hawaiian Tropic lotion, rubbing well-tanned elbows with the underworld while soaking up desert sunshine and taking plenty of notes for both personal and governmental purposes.

Same old Tucson.

Smiley and Moon showed up at the Ramada around noon.

"Some associates of mine are having an Arizona Wildcats tournament party tonight out at their place," Smiley said, after I introduced him to the Englishmen. "How would you and your friends like to come?"

"Can I tell you?" replied Jones with both squirrel tail eyebrows wagging excitedly.

"Please do," said Moon sarcastically.

"Can I tell you, Mr. Smiley? It sounds like a smashingly brilliant idea!"

"Great! It's a date, then. We'll pick you up around nine."

After my fellow fuges departed, I explained to Jones that the Arizona Wildcats were the local college team, and one of the favorites to win the NCAA basketball crown. "March madness, we call it," I added.

"Can I tell you?" said a dejected Jones. "I find your American sports to be dreadfully boring, and—"

"Trust me," I said. "This party will be anything but boring. And, there'll be plenty of tanned brown *poontang* there, too."

Light beamed from his brown eyes. The bristles on his brows stood erect. "Lovely. Well done, Master Timothy! Now then, *can you tell me* what to wear to this gala affair?"

On the way to Shorty Bob's place, Moon drove the Jew Canoe in circles around the foothills near Sabino Canyon until he was satisfied that not even a local—let alone two drunken Englishmen—could remember the secret location in the black-of-night desert landscape. Shorty Bob's sprawling red tile roofed ranch house was rocking! Svelte coeds skinny dipped in a dimly-lit pool. Smugglers, middlemen and drivers snorted coke off silver trays during TV time-outs from the big game. Every one had an alias, and no one asked prying questions.

The Brits arrived half-crocked on Bombay gin, then smoked joints with people like *Shorty Bob, No-Show-Steve, Fuzzy, Weed*, and *The Glove*. When the game ended, the giddy Jones told entertaining stories detailing his WWII radar-evasion tactics behind German lines to bemused young smuggler pilots, and was the hit of the party. He even hinted of some flights across the Mexican border back in the '60s, when he was a legal alien working the insurance racket.

"Can I tell you?" I overheard Jones say suggestively to a glassy-eyed Wildcat who could have been his granddaughter. "Battle-tested pilots are the very best...at whatever they do."

At one point, Smiley, Moon, and I disappeared to a small outbuilding where I was shown several cellophane-wrapped twenty pound bales of Mexican pot of varying quality which had been kept in a freezer for freshness.

"Here's what's been on the market this season," Smiley lectured, slicing the packages with a Buck knife for my inspection. "Be sure the Cat's product is this grade or better."

"Tony's in Mexico until tomorrow," I said, studying the fine red hairs on a giant bud of *skunkweed* beneath bright fluorescent lighting.

"Fine. How 'bout we take your friends with us to *Nogey* tomorrow so you can do your thing in peace?" Moon asked.

"Sure." I swallowed hard and rubbed pungent resins from my sweating palms.

Moments later, back at the party—perhaps because of the two lines of whiff I had consumed—I started feeling paranoid, caught a ride back to the Ramada Inn, and called my wife from the phone booth across the street. "Yes, honey, I'm being a good boy. Uh-huh, the Englishmen are both asleep. Love ya. Miss ya. Be home soon." I hoped she could not hear the cocaine rattling round my brain.

The next morning—at the crack of noon—Smiley and Moon drove the Brits south of the border to Nogales' red light district for their dirty deeds. Tony wasn't due back from Sonora until that evening though, so I drove my sporty rental car—a new benefit provided by Blake's credit card—to Sabino Canyon, where I hiked the Bear Creek Trail and meditated.

The heat was intense. My gaze drifted from tall cottonwoods, which shivered lima bean green beside a shimmering snowmelt stream, to jagged bluffs capped with saguaro cactus and occasional juniper, to the summit of Mount Lemon. I lay down to rest on a large flat rock above a reflecting pool, and recalled the first time El Gato had brought me to this special place.

The desert Cat played his twelve-string guitar that spring day in 1974, I sang Simon and Garfunkel songs, and our young dogs, Rusty and Benjamin, howled harmonically. College kids on recess from their "higher education paper-trips" dove naked from the cliffs. I considered coming to the U. of A. campus to live and further my education in the fields of writing and art. Everyone passed reefers around blanket-to-blanket saying, "*Sit and sing a song. Take a puff. Peace, love.*" It was mellow. The local cops didn't care about kids getting stoned in the canyon. Tony was going to be a rock star, and I was going to be a writer. But like well-meaning politicians and desperado gamblers, we decided to make a little easy money first.

The heat was intense. A small plane circled overhead, and somewhere along memory lane I fell fast asleep like a modern day Rip Van Winkle, only to awake hours later in 1988—a wanted man.

"They're right, you know, Mr. Lion," a little voice told me as I high-tailed it back to my rental car ahead of the setting southwestern sun. "Like it or not—you are an outlaw."

May 1988: The frisky senior citizen flew to Baltimore for a weeklong visit with her forty-two year old doctor daughter. The two single women dined, talked and went to bed. The younger woman never slept. Instead, she paced the floor, occasionally peered through a gap in her curtains, and watched the clock. At exactly 2:45 A.M. she walked to a corner payphone and called a cab. At 3:00 she gently shook her mom, our mom's, shoulders. "Wake up!" Judy, the family saint, whispered. Grab your things, Mom. We're taking a trip."

"When?" asked Mom, rubbing sleep from her eyes.

"Now. *Right now*. Our taxi is waiting."

"Where? Where are we—"

"Can't say," Judy said, biting her lip.

"I'm your mother, young lady. Now tell me what you're up to. Is this about Tommy?"

Judy nodded, Georgette dressed in record time, and both lady spies scrambled out the door to an idling Yellow Cab. It was a short ride to the subway, which they took to the train station. The trip to New York was quick and quiet. The next train carried them to Quebec where they caught a bus to Montreal and checked in to a low-profile bed and breakfast.

From across the street, a man in a dark suit pulled up the collar on his Irish wool overcoat, rubbed his cold palms together, tightened his white silk scarf and waited, his bated breath breaking skyward in short, sharp bursts.

When the lights went out in his subjects' second floor room window, he checked the time on his gold 1910 Policemen's Ball pocket watch, and walked away.

At precisely 11:00 A.M. the following morning, the women came to the appointed place, Dominion Square, a noted tourist center. And there, the cloak-and-dagger dames, engrossed in their spy games, patronized some shops; then sat on a predetermined park bench where—with sweaty palms, palpitating hearts, and wandering eyes—they fed pigeons and waited for a sign.

The man in the suit watched his nervous subjects from the shadow of his hired carriage until he was completely satisfied. On the fourth approach to their position, he gestured at his driver. The quick rhythmic clicking of horseshoes on cobblestone slowed, and the familiar faces came into focus. For over two years now, he had envisioned this moment and the manner in which it would come about. His disciplined heart—hardened by his profession—grew soft. He swallowed hard. The carriage lurched to a sudden halt, and the man lunged forward and reached out for them.

"Excuse me," *I said,* tipping my hat. "Would you two ladies like a ride?"

I gazed into my mother's misty green eyes, took her trembling hand and helped her up first, then my sister. They started to speak, but I shook my head, pecked their cheeks and spread a blanket over our laps. With hands clasped so tight our knuckles turned white, we toured Mount Royal Park in silence for nearly an hour, unwinding.

Much later—when the initial shock had worn off—we walked the streets of Old Montreal where they brought me up to date on family matters; then bombarded me with questions about life on the lam. *How was Kim? What about Todd? Do you sleep well? Are you always looking over your shoulder?*

"It's not like that, Jude," I said. "Really."

"What's your house like? Where is it?"

"Nice, Ma. It's simple, like it was in Mishawaka—only out in the wilderness. You'd like it." I wished I could take them there like a normal human and let them see for themselves. "We spend ninety percent of our time at home. I planted a vegetable garden, and Kim put flowers everywhere. We have cats, birds, and fish. Kim's a great friend and wife."

"Any neighbors?" Judy asked.

I nodded, then thought about how chummy Adolph and Chevon Trogg—who had been spending weekends at their summer home next to ours since the weather broke—were becoming. "They ask us over for dinner, take us fishing in their boat, mushroom hunting, and—"

"Aren't you afraid they'll find out?"

"No, Ma. All they know is what they see and what we tell them… nothing. They think we are the all-American couple next door. Us, and our cousin Todd, too. Remember all those school plays I was in? Well, every day is just another performance now."

We passed two longhaired French kids puffing on an ivory hashish pipe, and I nodded to them. "The only thing I worry about," I said, "is getting too close to some of the good people I meet."

"You're not doing anything illegal anymore, are you, son?" Mom stared hard into my eyes.

"No, Ma. Not even jaywalking," I muttered, looking away and picturing all those passports, Social Security cards, birth certificates, driver's licenses, and Tucson Tony's underground stash. I did not like lying to Mom, even if it was for her own good.

"Guess what?" I asked, artfully changing the topic. "Kim's becoming a gourmet cook! Ain't nothing in *Fanny Farmer* that girl can't bake! And, we still make love everyday—at least once."

I grinned.

"Lucky you," the ladies sighed in concert.

"I'm dating a sixty-nine year-old German whose idea of romance is cross-country skiing and watching wildlife mate." My sixty-two year old mother chuckled forlornly.

"That's nothing," Judy blurted uncharacteristically. "I'm seeing a former Buddhist monk whom I've known since my Peace Corps days."

"A monk?" I asked curiously. "Still suffering through your midlife celibacy era?"

"Very funny," Sis snapped. "I said *former* monk. Anyway, Loc has moved to Australia to open a Vietnamese restaurant and be with his extended family. I'm going to visit him 'Down Yonder' this winter." My sister blushed and bit her lip. "Might just surprise everyone, and stay. Say, maybe you and Kim could show up there mysteriously?"

"Never know, it's a small world," I said. "By the way, it's Down Under, Doc."

"Is this your fugitive look?" Judy asked. "You look so much younger, little brother. Oooo, I like him without his moustache," she cooed playfully while rolling back one of my shirtsleeves.

"See, Tommy," said Mom. "I told you having a baby face would come in handy someday."

"And he's so healthy, too," Judy added, coaxing me to flex my forearm. "Doesn't your boy look healthy, Mom?"

Instinctively, I took my sister's cue and participated in her reassurance game while our mother—hiding behind her *humor armor*—listened intently.

"Fugitive life ain't so bad, Ma. I play tennis with Todd, hike, make love and garden with Kim...and I row whenever I can, just like we used to."

She squeezed my hand. A tear formed in one faded green eye, and trickled down her cheek. "I miss you rowing me around Diamond Lake with old Ben's nose pointing into the wind and his soft funny ears flapping like Dumbo the elephant's. I miss hearing you sing *Rump-a-pum pum* at Christmas time, and Frank Sinatra songs at dinner. I mi-miss you," she stammered, shaking her head. "I miss you, son. Do think we'll ever—"

"Shhhh-sure," I hissed, pressing a finger to her lips and fighting raw emotion.

"How is Benjamin?" Judy asked, rummaging through a gigantic African handbag.

My mind raced back to an April afternoon spent sitting in a Portland veterinarian's waiting room reading a poem on his wall about *knowing when to do the right thing for your best canine friend when his time comes.*

"Ben is dying," I mumbled. Like another part of my identity, I thought.

"From what?" quizzed sister Judy, cool and doctor-like.

"Salivary sarcoidosis," I replied, surprising her with the correct pronunciation of Ben's disease. The term had been forever ingrained in my brain the moment it left the vet's lips. "He has this huge, gross lump hanging off his jaw. The vet quit in the middle of the operation, and...and..." I swallowed a lump of my own. "Ben's too old. The vet said he couldn't remove it. Said it would either kill him, or leave him brain dead." I choked up, knowing I would eventually have to play the part of Dr. Jack Kevorkian, and put my old pal down.

"That's so sad," Sis said. "Everyone loved Ben. He's such a good dog."

"He's had a great life, Jude. Story book. Big Red. How many Irish setters slid across the marble ballroom floor of the Boston Marriott on prom night, traveled coast-to-coast, barked out their orders for cheeseburgers at McDonalds drive-through windows all over America and lived to be fifteen?"

"Not many, I suppose." My sister produced a 35-millimeter Nikon from her purse. "Smile! You're on Candid Camera!"

"Sorry," I said, covering her lens with the palm of my hand. "No pictures."

"You're kidding, right?"

"Wish I was, Jude. But I'm not," I sighed. "Listen, let's just have four stress-free memorable days—like old times. Okay? And to guarantee they are stress-free, I've got a few simple fugitive rules for you to follow."

Because I had met an intriguing French Quebecois girl in 1979 at Olympic Stadium's Sugar Ray Leonard vs. Roberto Duran boxing match and toured Montreal in her inspirational company on subsequent visits, I qualified as tour guide for our clandestine holiday. Deciding not to bring relatives to my room at Rue Sherbrooke's, Delta Park Hotel, we met each morning at different predetermined subway stations, and said our good-byes at others. We toured museums, art galleries, Chinatown, and Isle St. Helens' famed botanical gardens. We shopped and ate in the Underground City. For their last day, I got a car and drove them north to the Laurentians, where we lunched at a lakeside French chalet and discussed renting a cottage or villa for future Montreal rendezvous.

"Here, Australia, Europe, it doesn't matter," my mother assured me as I rowed her and Judy in a weathered wooden rental boat before we returned to the city. "We'll travel anywhere to see you, as long as it's safe and you're free."

Our family reunion ended with me escorting them to their bed and breakfast after a late dinner at a French cafe. For four wonderful days I had again experienced the priceless magic of family. And when they left me with nothing except the fresh scent of their lipstick on my cheeks, I was The Kid from Berry Road again, staring at their twin silhouettes in that second floor window, awkwardly walking backwards and waving, reliving a lifetime of memories, wiping away tears until I could not see anymore, mouthing the words *love ya*, stumbling over a steaming steel sewer grate, shoving my trembling hands deep into the pockets of my gray Irish wool overcoat—then disappearing around the corner into my own private *Twilight Zone* world.

"Ou sont les jours d' an-tan?" I muttered. Where are the days of yesteryear?

The next morning when they were on a homebound train to Baltimore I met Moon for brunch at Winnies, on Rue Crescent.

"How's mom?" he asked.

"Good," I said, studying Moon's new look: a Don Johnson/*Miami Vice* five-o'clock shadow, Steven Segal slicked-back hair tied in a pony tail, and a designer leather jacket from which a cell phone hung like a purse.

"I know you're probably wondering why I asked you to meet me here," he said spreading cream cheese on his bagel. "Let's just say it has something to do with an olive boat from Afghanistan that's on its way to Vancouver."

"Yeah, go on," I said. "So, what gives with these olives? You getting into the commodities markets, or—"

"Oy vay! Please. Fuck olives, already," Moon bellowed, flicking the green one from his martini to the bustling sidewalk below. "My ship's come in, T," he whispered. "There's twenty tons of primo Afghani hash hidden in those olive cartons!"

"Jews and Muslims doin' biz," I mumbled. "If that don't take the cake."

"Yeah, yeah. Happens every day. Listen, we're talking some serious shekels here for ol' Sonny Boy." He tapped his chest. "So, my employer—soon to be proud owner of this olive shipment—has been asked to put up some extra, last-minute collateral for his consignment south of the Canadian border, Southern Cal, to be exact. That's where you come in. How would you like to dump a couple hundred grand in gold at fair market value, and be paid up here—with interest—in Canadian dollars? Your buddy McCarthy is doing it. But before you decide, let me tell you how much easier it is to send money from here to your offshore account. My people have a connection at Citibank—any amount, anywhere, two percent. Think of it, T. No more fooling around with those funky certified checks! Just trust me with your gold, then take a trip up here in a few months, and binga-banga-bong!" He snapped his fingers. "A mutually beneficial transaction, Mr. Barnes."

I sipped a Bloody Mary and measured my response, simultaneously thinking of strengthening my marriage while watching a garden grow, and the river flow, and as many sunsets over Mt. Saint Helens with my faithful Irish setter as fate would allow. After Ben's final season, we would follow Tucson Tony to the Land Down Under and permanently disappear.

Seeing Moon's fervent desire for the ultimate *Royal Scam* scared me to death. It was another wake-up call, and made me all the more determined to leave the country. I had to go. I had to be one of the few who retired and made it.

"Well?" Moon asked.

"Meet me in Reno at the Peppermill Casino next week," I said. "I'm emotionally drained, Moon. I've got a life to live, and this is going to be the last trip I take for a while."

The FBI was closing in on Bill McCarthy.

3-10-82

FEDERAL BUREAU OF INVESTIGATION

Date of transcription 10/28/88

On October 21, 1988, GORDON DELANEY, date of birth July 22, 1928, Comptroller at MARK LAPRADES AUTO IMPORTS, 3493 Tyrone Boulevard, St. Petersburg, Florida, telephone number (813) 345-9999, was advised of the identity of the interviewing Agent and the purpose of the interview. He then provided the following information:

DELANEY provided a copy of the sales contract of ANNA LEE FISHER. A review of this contract showed that ANNA LEE FISHER, 4401 Birkshire Manor, Apartment 924, Tampa, Florida, telephone number (813) 864-1663, purchased a 1983 Saab from them in December 1986. It could not be determined from the sales contract if FISHER paid for the vehicle with cash or credit. No further information could be obtained from the sales contract that was provided by DELANEY.

Disconnected or no longer in service

245F 159-550

Investigation on 10/21/88 at St. Petersburg, Florida File # ~~Tampa 245F-269~~

by SA MICHAEL J. BRADLEY:sle* Date dictated 10/21/88

This document contains neither recommendations nor conclusions of the FBI. It is the property of the FBI and is loaned to your agency; it and its contents are not to be distributed outside your agency.

11

Dog Days

We spent that fugitive summer of 1988 sheltered beneath the pro tective cliffs of Oregon's Columbia River Gorge, fishing, gardening and getting mentally prepared to make the permanent move to Australia. It was not an easy decision, for we were torn between two worlds—one we had created with our animals and gardens, and another offering new challenges with my good friend Tucson Tony, far from the reach of America's fugitive-hunting TV programs and its law.

Many dog day afternoons were spent on the sandy beach at nearby Rooster Rock State Park pondering the pros and cons of becoming expatriates. I decided we could not trust anyone except Arnie with the knowledge of our move. I also wanted at least two years of employment history in San Francisco for my Tim Barnes identity before applying for Australian residency. But I was afraid that if we stayed in Oregon too long finalizing our plan, we could find ourselves featured on *Unsolved Mysteries* one night, and be turned in by our neighbors. Accordingly, we kept to ourselves, avoided socializing with the neighbors, and planned an exploratory Australian trip for the spring of 1989. Meanwhile, the others—from Canada to Arizona and parts unknown—carried on with their risky business.

It was after returning from a visit to our Portland mail drops one afternoon that Kim and I walked into a nearly fatal situation. We were in the garden when I noticed smoke plumes rising from the riverbank through the neighbor's trees. A cheery young Christian couple had purchased the dilapidated bungalow on the next lot, and I remembered seeing them sweating that morning as they worked, tirelessly raking and piling brush at the rocky shoreline. We had passed them on the highway on our way back home from Portland, and waved.

The Columbia Gorge's winds kicked up, and from the tall, dry grass between the neighbor's trees, smoke soared high into the sky. I ran into the garage and grabbed two five-gallon buckets.

"Honey," I shouted. "Get all our garden hoses! The neighbors have set the woods on fire!"

I ran into the swift and slippery Columbia River with my buckets in hand, and repeatedly charged the blaze. Within minutes Kim had managed to stretch our garden hoses far enough to reach the flames with a steady spray of water.

"Careful, honey!" she screamed as the winds shifted, sending flames dangerously close to me.

Benjamin barked feebly behind her. Our cats cowered beneath the satellite dish, their fur standing on end. For nearly thirty minutes we maintained a Mexican standoff, preventing the blaze from breaking through the trees to the Smith's dry wooden structure. The pressure on our water pump was waning when to our great relief, the neighbors returned from their trip to the grocery store and joined in the great battle. Nearly two hours later, a tired, soot-stained foursome sat on tattered cloth lawn chairs surveying the charred aftermath.

"I just praise God that we have you for neighbors," said Angela Smith as she poured lemonade in our glasses.

"Amen," whispered her husband, Mike.

From that day on, each time the Smiths drove out from their Portland apartment to tackle yet another renovation dilemma in that dilapidated dream country bungalow of theirs, we were invited to dinner, church, or a movie. "We've told all our friends about you two," Mike assured us on one such occasion.

"That's nice," I replied pensively.

And so it was that we became known to all of the dozen or less inhabitants along the isolated Interstate 84 frontage lane called Star Route B in Cascade Locks, Oregon. No longer could we slip away to the freeway like wandering tourists in Tim Barnes' Ford pickup or Lady Di's Volvo unnoticed. No longer could we take our morning walks to Horsetail Falls and be incognito. Within a week of the fire we began receiving curious waves, winks and nods from not only the sturgeon hatchery and bait shop owners at the end of Star Route B, but also from the hard drinking Native American family three lots down who often loaded semis full of salmon in the dark of night destined for God only knew where. Their suspicious operation often triggered flashbacks to the days of Maui

Bert's first marijuana shipments. But each time we came upon one of these midnight maneuvers on the lane, we merely smiled and waved.

Fugitive life dragged on during that summer of 1988. My wife often complained of being bored and isolated. I bought *Writers Digest* magazines, and half-heartedly contemplated attending workshops or conferences. We both scanned the Sunday papers, dreaming of working together again in a business like our Lion's Share shop. I got nervous every time I tried to envision our future, and was certain that the exposure owning a business or writing could create would be best attempted in Australia.

In my third summer on the lam I was discovering that retirement drove me crazy. Life was good, but lacked self-fulfilling goals. Playing the identity game was taking away my identity, and some days only the natural beauty of our surroundings preserved my sanity. Of course I never admitted this to Kim or Arnie. Instead I became addicted to the Financial News Network—tuning in for hours, hoping to see my European stocks rebound—and reluctantly continued laying the groundwork for leaving the country. Tim Barnes filed his taxes as an employee of the Greek's place in San Francisco, and even received state and federal tax return checks at his California mail drop residence. With Mr. Barnes' identity/history growing stronger all the time, a 1989 Australian adventure loomed ever larger in our future. But the continued threat of our exposure on television's *Unsolved Mysteries* also lurked on the shadowy horizon, as Kim learned from another call to a payphone in Buffalo, New York.

"Oh my God, Kimberly!" her mother reported as I stood by timing the call and watching for suspicious cars entering the Interstate 5 rest stop. "They stopped by again last week. They still say they're going to put Tom on *Unsolved Mysteries*."

"We've watched that show until I can't stand it anymore," said Lady Di sarcastically. "Anyway, it's summer reruns season now, Motho. So, what other rumors have you heard?"

"None. Can you believe they still actually expect me to turn you in? They keep saying that if you get caught up in a raid, someone could get killed."

"Right, Motho," my wife replied, squeezing my hand tightly. "Everyone knows what a cold-blooded killer Tom is."

The day after her mother's latest *Unsolved Mysteries* warning, I crossed the river into Vancouver, Washington, and did something I had been putting off—acquired an Evergreen State driver's license for my backup identity, Paul James Kelly. Mr. Kelly's US Passport and Social Security card had long since been forwarded from a New Orleans mail drop to another one in San Francisco—where I had picked them up; then cancelled the box to eliminate the paper trail. Instinct told me not to neglect my other alter ego, and now Kelly's ID set was complete.

After consulting with Arnie, I decided not to mention the TV show warnings to the others when I invited them to what I felt would be our final Northwest reunion. Moon—basking in financial afterglow from his Afghani olive boat windfall—settled into our spare bedroom with L.A. Missy. Arnie—road weary, but richer and ready for another golf tour—likewise stayed with us. The Blackwells of Durango, Colorado and the Fisher family from Boulder set up quarters in my neighbor Adolf Trogg's summer home. After word of the Smiths' wildfire incident reached him, my fellow fisherman, Adolph, insisted that "my friends in the music business" stay at his place when I mentioned the reunion. Kindly Mr. Trogg's offer was for free, but I told him they were well off and would insist on paying a rental fee.

This gathering went surprisingly well. Mornings we drank Arnie's fresh-squeezed health concoctions, took walks along the lane and picked berries with which the ladies baked tasty pies reminiscent of our mothers' recipes. Afternoons, bare-chested fuge females smelling of cocoa butter chatted side by side in half-submerged lawn chairs behind Adolph Trogg's riverfront home. We men, upon returning from golfing or fishing, initiated games of badminton and croquet, or found shady places to lie down. We spent two nights camping at Lost Lake on the slopes of Mount Hood. There was an excursion to the Port of Astoria, a tour of Bonneville Dam, and massages for everyone at historic Carson Hot Springs. The Blackwells slipped away one day to "see a movie in town." I suspected they were completing their Oregon paper trip, but believed we would soon make the move to Australia, let go of my Northwest protectionism policy and merely bit my tongue. Perhaps it was the calming familiarity of his wife Leigh, or the precious innocence of Bill's rapidly growing daughter Shannon, but regardless and to my great surprise, I began to second-guess both my instinctive suspicions of Bill

McCarthy and my earlier decision to excommunicate him from our fuge chapter.

Moon seemed increasingly disturbed by L.A. Missy's reluctance to go underground, especially in light of the fact that he was again on the verge of becoming a very rich man.

"I have family, honey," I overheard Missy say one morning. "And I have nothing to run from."

"Well, I do," Moon snorted. "What about running to something? What about being together?"

"It would be nice. But what about my peace of mind, honey? You can't run forever." Missy sighed. "I've got to tell you, Kim and Leigh don't sound like the happiest wives in the world."

"Oy vay! Peace of mind. Define peace of mind in the real world for me, please. Is it any better than this? Would it buy you that jewelry case full of magic crystals, or pay for all those visits to holistic healers every time you have a pain? Hell, no," Moon snapped. "Peace of mind, like beauty, is in the eye of the beholder."

Outside their open bedroom window, where I knelt in moist garden soil petting Smokey the cat, I wondered how often Missy's questions arose during those private sunbathing sessions at the ladies' makeshift nude beach. Did Kim's true feelings come out when she was with the girls? My stomach knotted as I recalled my young wife—all of twenty-six—recently asking me if she looked old. "Mature, Meekla, not old," I'd replied, pecking her cheek. And just last night the once-rebellious and cool Lady Di had admitted how much missing her sister Carrie's high school graduation bothered her.

Then my wife had announced with furrowed brow, "Leigh says Shannon's nightmares are getting worse. She told Bill she was considering going home with her daughter."

"What did Bill say?" I asked.

"He laughed and told her if she went back, it would be alone."

After Kim inserted the bite guard that protected her teeth from their nervous grinding, I turned off the light and whispered, "Love ya, Meekla. And you know you are always free to leave."

"I know, honey," she mumbled. "I know."

We were changing, I thought in the darkness that followed. We were all getting older. Our priorities were changing, too. I pictured Leigh:

her once fresh face now creased by encroaching lines of age, her raven hair suddenly harboring streaks of gray, the way she spoke so openly and often about religion for the first time in years, reminiscent of her family upbringing. Arnie the natural athlete was going bald and putting on a paunch. He often lamented the pain he caused his aging parents. Moon was a millionaire again, but was constantly on edge, his health failing, and only seemed happy when he was spending money. Smiley and Lizzy mystified me. Perhaps it was because they were constantly medicated and engrossed in the trade, but they never seemed afraid or stressed. To them, life was one big party.

Something was also happening to my marriage. Although Kim never said it, I could tell she was tiring of waiting for some miracle solution. She was physically content, but spiritually unfulfilled. She wanted a baby and a normal life to raise the child in. She was a good, loyal wife, and I loved her deeply.

What had happened to my promise to her to become a writer and have kids? What had happened to the highly anticipated era of spiritual and mental growth that my retirement, marriage, and move West had been all about? Partying and wandering from place to place in a life without meaning was becoming less palatable every day. I was not happy. I was not some Butch Cassidy desperado, or a Drug War martyr, either. There were no heroes among us. As long as we stayed in America with the same old crowd, my idealistic hopes were nil. I was a restless man with too much drive to accept an early retirement along an Oregon riverbank. I was a dreamer without a dream to pursue, and for all I possessed, I would never be happy without this. Even for my gypsy wife, the fool's gold glamour of fugitive life was fading fast.

Each night while the barbecue grill got hot and fugitives bantered between the hedges with cocktail glasses in hand, I would sneak away with my wobbly-legged red dog to the grassy knoll behind our satellite dish. And there my canine friend and I stared west across the great river in reverent silence to where the jagged rim of Mt. St. Helens swallowed a sunset sky. Often times, as pastel plumes exploded upon the horizon and I petted the thinning hair on old Ben's weary head until his leg twitched the way it did, I recalled the tale a drunken sturgeon fisherman had told me that spring.

"Before the blast in May of 1980 she stood nearly 10,000 feet," slurred the leather-skinned gent clutching a pint of Jack Daniel's and pointing toward Mt. Saint Helens. "Yessir, she lost over 1600 feet and tons of mass in a matter of seconds."

"Plenty of people and trees perished that day too, didn't they?" I asked the smelly old timer.

"Trees? To hell with trees, boy! A legend died that day. By the way, I was a logger half my life, ya know. Say, you ain't one of them tree huggers, are ya, son?"

Three years as a Pacific Northwest fugitive had taught me not to engage in debates on politics, the environment, or religion. I shook my head.

"No, sir," he said before pausing to take a belt. "The biggest loss that day was the life of one Mr. Harry Truman, owner of Spirit Lake Lodge. When all them fancy scientists saw that big bulge of lava building they tried to make Harry abandon the place. 'Course ol' Harry told 'em to go to hell every time, right on up till that last ride down the mountain. The next day...*kaboom*! She blew," he shouted, crashing his empty bottle on the rocky shore. "And Harry was buried alive right there at the lodge. Give 'em hell, Harry," the old man muttered.

After what seemed an appropriate period of silence I asked, "Why did he stay?"

"For one thing, Harry's wife had died there." He twisted the cap off a stinking jar of slimy sturgeon bait. "Then too, things was just too damn familiar on that mountain for him to pull up stakes and run. Understand, son?"

I certainly did.

At sunset during that last fuge summer reunion, I often compared my plight to that of Mt. St. Helens' most famous hermit resident, Mr. Harry Truman. I was falling in love with the Pacific Northwest, and not at all at peace with the idea of leaving my country for some new frontier. However, ignoring the rumblings all around me could well result in a similar, explosive fate.

"Decisions," I sighed, hearing the muffled laughter of my fugitive comrades rise to an audible crescendo in the distance. I rubbed the baseball-sized tumor on my Irish setter's neck, and he forced a crooked smile. A tear ran down my cheek. And while last light of day faded away, I recalled our long, colorful past, sadly realizing that nothing lasted forever.

"Honey! The grill's ready,"' my wife called out when this nightly ritual was done.

"Coming, Lady Di," I replied in mock Brit-talk, while raising my red dog to his unsure feet and willing him to once more walk with me away from the setting sun.

On the second to the last day of our reunion three of us rested on slick, dark, moss covered rocks, panting from the quick pace of our five-mile hike. Golden sun shafts filtered through an evergreen canopy like soft stage lighting to capture our flushed faces. Cool mist born of Mt. Hood's glacial peaks wafted from cascading falls, which fed the picturesque pools before us near the headwaters of Eagle Creek. I passed the quart of carrot juice I had ferried in my daypack to the Blackwells, who proceeded to cure their parched throats.

"Thanks for bringing us along to your special place," Lizzy whistled through her gapped front teeth.

"Yeah, guy," Smiley bellowed. "God bless ya for sharing! This is as nice as some of those spots it took us days to reach in Montana last summer."

The Blackwells paused unnaturally as the echo of their voices faded in the canyon walls. When nature's silence returned, I watched them fidget, then exchange cryptic glances. Say what's really on your mind, I thought. You sure as hell didn't drag yourselves out of a hangover bed just to see the scenery.

"Bill says Kimmy's going to Boulder to house sit and watch Shannon while they take their little trip," said Lizzy.

I skipped a stone across the mirror-surface of the water and nodded. "I know. Bill told me about it yesterday."

We spent the next thirty minutes talking about international banking. Smiley confessed to pressing my drunken English associate, Jones, for information about the Channel Islands during their Arizona jaunt to Mexico. The conversation switched to Bill's plan to carry several hundred thousand dollars to Zurich where he would open a second secret account. He'd eliminated the trail from his over $800,000 Cayman Islands account by wiring those funds to a sympathetic Swiss bank and physically carrying them down the shadowy cobblestone street to the open arms of another money manager. Now Bill intended to build up a backup account with his remaining cash reserves—recently retrieved during a clandestine trip back East. His strategy of having two distinctly separate accounts was a sound one, which I also felt a need to employ. If arrested, one account could be "fully disclosed" to the feds in exchange for leniency, and the other one would be waiting when you got paroled. Then too, there was always the possibility to consider of being ripped off by your money manager.

"We've shared a lot of dinners with them since they moved to Boulder," Lizzy announced. "Leigh is wonderful—as you know," she said suggestively. "And Shannon is precious! Granted, Bill is not as charming as you, my dear, but he's no dummy."

"Yeah, guy," Smiley said. "Ol' Mister Fisher seems all right to me. He's a little stiff until he gets a few drinks under his belt, but he's certainly not the enemy just because he lost your rental properties. Right?"

"Yeah," I sighed. "He told me about your business deals and the money he loaned Moon. Said he didn't want to sneak behind my back. I can't believe Moon's paying him ten percent a month on that much money." I bent down and splashed water on my face. "But like I told him, I don't give a damn what any of you do together. God knows I'm not looking for any handouts." I laughed. "You know, he even asked if I'd go down to Tucson to make sure your last run was successful. Said he'd feel better about his investment capital if I was involved."

"I don't suppose you told him you already were?" Smiley grinned. "Speaking of Tucson. I've got a proposition. We found a great rental in Phoenix, right off Camelback Road, only minutes from the airport."

"It has a pool and a fireplace," whistled Lizzy. "It's in a quiet neighborhood on a cul-de-sac. The perfect workhouse."

"You're kidding, right?" I asked. "Don't take this personally, but with your party habits, you two will stick out like sore thumbs."

"We will not," Smiley interrupted with a frown. "Just listen. Bill wants to sell us his cars. Ten grand for both Saabs! Can't beat that. I'm going to register them to an imaginary landscape company I set up and keep them parked in Phoenix so none of us will have to deal with rental cars."

"Why?" I asked.

"Because we don't have a credit card like you yet," Lizzy replied. "I've found a bank that promises a Visa card—no questions asked—if you deposit two grand or more."

"Gee! I'll bet no federal agencies investigate their clients," I snickered.

"Listen Timmy," Smiley snapped. "Here's the bottom line. I know you. After three years of doing nothing, you've got to be bored to death. I'm offering you a limited partnership. Invest your spare cash with us, split the cost on this Phoenix house and Bill's cars. You live here and play Doctor Doolittle with your animals. We'll live on the ranch in Durango. And when small connoisseur shipments come across with my connections, or a big load is available with your friend, we zip down to 'Zona for some fun 'n games."

"Wait a minute. You said, if I connected you in Tucson and helped you get your money to the right place, you'd retire. Right?" I watched the gambler's curse beam from his blue eyes. "Believe me. I'm not interested in any other partnership besides my marriage for the rest of my life. And as for these cars of Bill's, are you that tight, crazy, or what? You of all people should realize how important clean, dependable equipment is in the business."

"What do you mean by that?"

"My God, Smiley! Mixing paperwork between two fugitives has got to be one of the most ignorant moves I can think of."

As he recoiled with a bruised ego, I flashed back to one of my monthly payphone calls with Bill when they were still living in Florida. He'd received something in the mail from his insurance company, about them canceling his policy without a reason. I remembered how he laughed and cursed the insurance company like he cursed the rest of the inferior world in which he lived. Then there was that nerve-racking call when I actually heard him shaken after running into some people at a restaurant in Tampa. Then there was his emergency evacuation to Boulder.

"By the way," I asked Mr. Blackwell. "Why is Bill selling you both his cars anyway?"

Somewhere in the distance a tree branch snapped. Smiley looked over his shoulder, then back at me. "Because. He's already applied for their tourist visas through some private passport company in L.A. His plan is to get extensions over there at the embassy, and eventually apply for residency. He says his research shows they can get citizenship by having another baby over there. Hell, they'll be gone for good by Thanksgiving."

"Gone where? Where are they going?" I asked.

The Blackwells eyed one another nervously. "Gee, Timmy," Lizzy whistled. "Didn't he tell you?"

"Tell me what?" Other distant voices began echoing in our canyon.

"Bill says America sucks," Smiley said. "According to him, the only way a federal fugitive can make it is to become an expatriate. So he's taking his family to Australia."

My jaw dropped. My mind reeled. Apparently, one of the biggest decisions of my life had already been made by Billy Boy. In the microsecond that followed I both cursed and thanked him. For months now I had been preparing for yet another trip my heart was not into. Was it such a small world? Did we really think so much alike, or had Smiley mentioned my friend Tony's Australian connection during one of their cocaine dinners? If he had, it was my own fault for slipping. I stared into the reflective pool, picturing quaint koala bears and bouncing kangaroos as they faded from my future. Perhaps if the Fishers succeeded we could still go Down Under? No. Damn it! No, if he went down, we would be sitting ducks trying to get out of the country. I watched my face contort in the mirror-like waters.

Suddenly the blue surface exploded. I whirled around to see a group of hikers emerge in the clearing above us, and heard a young mother scold her son for tossing a stone. What else was Bill running from? And what would I say to Tucson Tony? It did not matter. For Lady Di and me, the Aussie move was out of the question. Once again, my ex-partner's decisions had effected my fate.

"Loose lips sink ships," I muttered as we headed home on the trail.

By October, Ben grew so weak he could not walk to our sunset spot on his own. The cancerous growth had spread to his jaw and he could barely eat. His elegant, shiny coat—once nurtured with special vitamin E oil and egg white potions—was no longer plush but patchy. His leathery elbows were so cracked that I had to apply Bag Balm to prevent them from becoming open wounds. Often when I called his name, Ben would stare off into the distance with those glassy eyes as his disease stole another part of him from me. I felt powerless. I became melancholy. I questioned my reasons for postponing the inevitable as—like the bare trees along the riverbank and the broken summit of Mt. St. Helens—my once proud bird dog regressed to little more than a skeletal image of his former self.

bird dog regressed to little more than a skeletal image of his former self. Lady Di, Arnie, even the neighbors watched as I carried that animal around for weeks whispering into his floppy ears and always, always hoping to hear Big Red tell me himself that it was time. Until that last day I think everyone knew, except me.

One morning when I left the driveway for a jog down Star Route B, Ben leaped up off his blanket to follow and fell sideways in agony. His shrill howl sent shivers down my spine. We spent the next few hours sharing a blanket and watching bald eagles pluck spawning fish from the swift and unforgiving currents of the Columbia. Fifteen years, fifteen years of uncommon friendship were about to end. Becoming a fuge was an easier decision for me.

And so on a crisp fall day, feeling much like the Kid From Berry Road again, I wrapped my best friend in his favorite flying-duck flannel sleeping bag and gently placed him in the front seat of Tim Barnes' black Ford. For our final ride together, I took the Scenic Loop Road. I cracked the vent window and cradled his heavy head so he could feel the mist from Horsetail Falls, hear the birds take flight as we approached them, and smell the salmon breeze which sent bright red leaves flying across our windshield.

The vet was waiting for us. "Your wife called," he said when I walked in with Big Red in my arms.

I paused one more time to read that poem on his wall.

I swallowed hard, and tears welled up in my eyes.

When the deed was done the kindly vet inquired, "You all right, Mr. Barnes?"

"Yeah, fine," I lied. But I was not all right. I jumped into that truck and drove like a madman to Rooster Rock—visually, mentally, spiritually impaired. And there I walked for hours crying, mumbling, mourning, kicking stones and wondering where the hell my life was headed.

When darkness fell cold and lonely on the autumn shores of the Columbia River, I regained my composure, drove to the rear of the Sea Gull Cafe, and crammed that flannel duck sleeping bag, his leash, half-chewed rawhide bones and everything *Ben* into their rusty trash dumpster. And then I went home to my worried wife, where I didn't speak a word until the following day.

§

For weeks after Ben's demise, the vodka bottle we kept in the freezer became a frequent companion of mine as I, Mr. Health & Exercise, extended the nightly cocktail hour. I realized that losing Ben meant losing another piece of my true identity, of the real me. I also knew our continued association with the others would only lead me into backsliding down to Tucson. Kim was growing increasingly unhappy with our geographic isolation—often making the forty-five minute drive to Portland where pet shops, jewelry stores and fashion comprised her second passion. The dog days of summer were giving way to another long fugitive winter. The garden died, fish quit biting, skies turned gray, and November winds howled up and down the Columbia Gorge.

Feeling the need for a serious change, we relocated to our sixth home in three years—a condo in the heart of Mt. Hood's ski country at Rippling River Resort. The move gave our marriage a lift. Morning walks on the mountain were rejuvenating, and our cats and birds helped fill the void Ben's passing had left in me. Besides the geographic change, the decision to get a small condo encouraged Arnie to find his own place. My friend was finally financially and emotionally ready to live on his own. This meant that Kim and I would have privacy for the first time in three years.

Arnie was also very close to his parents, and on many depressed days he mentioned turning himself in while they were still healthy. His role in our Midwest based conspiracy was not as serious as mine, and we both felt he could admit his guilt and get a survivable sentence. If and when Arnie chose this path, the FBI would inevitably investigate his last place of residence and interview neighbors and such for any leads to me. Accordingly, Arnie finally took flight from the nest, renting a place in Sandy, Oregon, about twenty miles away. He started living his own life by signing up for classes at a community college. After a clandestine meeting with his sister Molly in Las Vegas, he returned to report a sad but touching story about his dad.

By employing various mail-forwarding services, Arnie managed to send his parents a letter which was delivered by some neighbors. Noticing that the final postmark and address was from Canada, Arnie's father drove north, driven by a desire to see his son—only to find a Toronto mail drop whose owner kept his promise of preserving a client's privacy.

"I've made arrangements to talk to them next month," Arnie told me. "Oh, I almost forgot. Molly said we're still a regular feature on South Bend's weekly *Crime Stoppers*. The only good news is that the photos they're showing are ancient."

Meanwhile, my disposable J.P. Simms answering service kept us abreast of the other fugitives' activities. The Fisher family had made it safely past Australian Immigration Officials and left the number of their Queensland condo for us to call. The Blackwells—to whom I had finally given our home phone number—secured that Phoenix workhouse and were moving small loads of connoisseur Mexican herb back East with Moon.

Tucson Tony sent a postcard to Tim Barnes' Barbur Boulevard address as well, saying: See you in December, mate. Remember to remind your friends that all the pretty girls get asked to the dance very early during the holiday season.

I decided to keep his coded message about pending high-grade marijuana shipments a secret from my wife, fearing her reaction at any sign of a return to Tucson.

One November evening during dinner with Kim at Mt. Hood's historic Timberline Lodge, I made an impulsive decision. I had been reading Catherine Ann Brown's book, *Famous French Chateaux and Inns*. France had always intrigued me, and the tiny principality of Monaco was another tax haven I'd researched extensively. In light of the loss of the Australian option, Europe deserved another look. I also needed to speak to Blake in person about dividing my assets, or getting a lawyer to serve as a buffer between us in case I got busted. Then too, there was that favor the Blackwells kept pushing for. *Busted*, I thought, then shook off the dark images the word conjured up and tried to act wild and crazy.

"Lady Di," I said seductively between wet kisses on her slender neck. "I've been thinking."

"You drool too much when you drink," she said, gently biting my finger. "Just what are you thinking about, my green-eyed gremlin?"

"Taking my beautiful wife to the land of fashion, perfume factories, and gourmet dining." I paused to watch the air she breathed expand those amazing breasts. "Going swimming in the Mediterranean Sea. Making passionate love in the boudoir of a castle."

"France?" she whispered, leaning closer yet.

"Oui, ma fille sucrée," I replied, straining to show some resemblance

of the old me she'd fallen in love with—the me I feared was dying more each day. "We shall tour 'ze shops, sun on 'ze beach, and play roulette together at Monaco's casino whilst staring at the paintings of naked nymphs on the ceiling above." Our eyes met with the intensity of that moment when we'd exchanged vows in Heavenly Valley's cable car. I blew out the candle. "*Voulez vous couchez avec moi ce soir*?" I inquired in the universal language of love.

"Who are you tonight?" she asked through those trembling red lips.

"Fantasize," I said, reaching beneath the table for her thigh.

Our stay on Guernsey was brief. We met the Blackwells, travelling under the name of Bentley, at Dove Cottage, a quaint little bed and breakfast I'd reserved for them. We shared a dinner. I gave them the name of a firm recommended by Blake and some tips on how to go about their business. The next day while I met with Blake they set up their first offshore account, then flew home to do another dope deal.

Unable to bring myself to trust another money manager with a separate account, I decided to ask Blake if he could control a second trust for me in a country other than England, Switzerland, the Caymans or Channel Islands.

"One of the trendiest new places to set up trusts is Dublin," he informed me. "And," he inquired with the expressionless curiosity of a British banker, "what will the purpose of this second account be?"

"I want to buy some real estate and employ a friend of mine, Mr. Paul James Kelly, as an investment consultant."

The day before he and Judy departed for a "Save the Elephants" photo safari in Africa, Blake and I strolled the meadows of The Coppice once again and spoke of our personal lives. I explained why I hadn't wanted the Bentleys to open their account with him. "Speaking for myself, you will never have to worry about me using you or anyone you've introduced me to save my skin, should the United States IRS ever have me in their grasp. As for mixing money business with my other, unusual friends," I added, "trust me. You don't need it."

In our five-year association, Blake had brought me, like some novelty, to dinners attended by some of his wealthiest and stealthiest clients. In an ever-changing world that was steadily losing the concept of loyalty, I wanted him to know where I stood. When I asked why he seemed so melancholy this trip, he surprised me by saying that he and Judy were considering divorce.

"We're growing apart," Blake sighed. "I'm seeing a younger woman in London. Judy is disgusted by the amount of time I spend with my financial duties. The children are grown. I've purchased a boutique in Saint Peter Port for her to manage. How is your Diane holding up?"

I thought about the sarcastic remarks my wife made on the mornings I became mesmerized by television's Financial News Network. I considered the irony between her growing desire for jewelry and her jealousy of my energy spent managing the money that provided the good life for us. "I guess I see her changing too," I admitted to my friend, and myself.

"That's life," Blake said, slapping me on the back. "Even in the most normal of marriages, one must work at keeping romance alive."

I wondered if I had enough energy to keep my fantasy romance alive, and remain a free man.

Blake winked at me. "I, however, haven't a doubt in my mind that you are a master of romance. I am also quite certain you'll have a wonderful holiday with Diane in France."

We landed in Nice the day after a terrorist act in Paris. It was a nightmare. We were taken out of the immigration line to a special Interpol interrogation room. All non-French citizens had to go through the same procedure. Kim was visibly shaken, and it took all my energy to stay calm. I made slang French remarks about my wife's breasts to the huge policeman with the handlebar moustache as he scanned our fugitive passports. The entire time I thought about the threat her dad had made: "I have friends at Interpol. I'll get even with that boy."

We made it through, but Kim was so shaken that we never recovered enough to fully enjoy the romantic aspect of our adventure. In the beginning of this fugitive game, close calls with the authorities and ID scams energized us. Now they were a major drain.

Monaco did not hold the magic we were looking for. Instead, it seemed a shallow, plastic playground for the type of jet setters that appeared on the covers of grocery store tabloids. We got drunk one night and wandered around the marina babbling about buying a boat and living on it, but we knew we'd never fit in.

We made the best of it though, strolling Nice's cobblestone boulevards, sipping cappuccino at sidewalk cafes and slipping into colorful, narrow boutiques. We visited Roman ruins at Triomphe des Alpes and ventured north past Grasse where perfume factories piled flower-petal mountains along the winding road which ended in Saint Andre. We found beauty in the gardens of the village monastery at Eze, where author Sidney Sheldon set his novel *Sands of Time*. We were entertained by minstrels at the Chateau Eze, and made love on one of their ancient stone balconies with the blue Mediterranean Sea for a backdrop. But there was no Oz for us to discover in France. Once again, whatever it was we were seeking remained elusive.

Within days of our return from Europe I received a call from Tucson Tony. "Ho-ho-ho," he said. "'Tis the season, *amigo*! Got a pen handy?"

"Go," I said. He read a series of letters from our MEXICANFLY code—CEEFLYF—and asked me to repeat them. I scribbled 522-8908 on a note pad.

"Nine o'clock tomorrow morning," he said. "If it's busy or there's no answer after two rings, try again at noon. Remember where you're calling, T. There's tons of heat in town, and I can't be hanging around the phones."

"Got ya, Gato," I said.

The next morning, payphone to payphone, Gato told me the goods were positioned for an impending border crossing. "If your friends want to play," he said, "you'll have to get a place in line before the game begins. The price is right and the quality is right on. Lime green, red hairs, no BB's. I saw a sample on the other side. This is your calling, T. You're a pot man. Are you coming?"

The excitement in the Cat's voice stimulated that dormant James Bond side of me. I pictured the early days of my pot career, counting money at Tony's ranch, then later at the construction company landing spot for Maui Bert's semis. I thought about the conversation I'd had with Smiley earlier in the week. The timing was perfect. Even as we spoke, Moon was en route to Phoenix with a suitcase full of cash that would be given to the man who could fill their holiday orders.

"Count them in," I said. "I'll be there tomorrow night."

"Great. Bring your wife."

"Nope," I snapped. "Don't want her near it."

"Aggy will be disappointed," he said. "She wanted to show Di the baby, but I understand. Have a safe flight, T."

As I packed my luggage, Kim appealed to me one last time.

"Please, honey. You don't need this. What about the risk? What about your promise?" she pleaded. "I'm afraid."

I was afraid, too. Actually, my feelings were somewhere between fear and elation at the prospect of becoming a player again. I didn't really know why I had to go. But I did. Did I want to get caught because I didn't have the guts to turn myself in?

"Don't be afraid," I said, wrapping my arms around her slender waist. "It's their last run." But as I stroked her hair and stared at my reflection in the dressing mirror, I realized she was right. No matter how I excused it, I was breaking my promise to her and myself to stay away from the business. Regardless of what I thought about the legal or moral issues of selling pot, I was just another vampire bitten by the gambler's curse.

"Don't worry, Meekla," I assured her. "I'll be home in a couple of days, then we'll spend Christmas in Hawaii."

That was how it was supposed to go—a couple of days, in, out, and gone. But as any experienced pot scammer knew, it rarely worked that way in Tucson—or anywhere. Ninety percent of the time, the big score turned into a waiting game; wait for the underpaid Customs man to get on duty, grab the dirty dollars and do his thing; or wait for the Mexicans and Indians to mule the harvest from underground pit to underground pit across the desert chessboard until another crew could liberate it from the reservation in a truckload of fruit or vegetables. Now there was a new twist. Gato's Mexicans—who back in the '60s and '70s pre-paraquat heyday simply crushed their low-quality crop into one kilo "mini-bricks" for easy transport—had not only learned the importance of growing with care, but also understood that manicuring and putting a light press on their precious product meant gringo connoisseurs would better appreciate their goods, and pay more per pound.

And so I waited while wetback laborers worked like Santa's elves at a stash house south of Tucson clipping, pruning and compressing tons of weed into twenty-pound, cellophane-wrapped gift packages destined for happy holiday puffers. Actors, artists, athletes, computer wizards, insurance agents, musicians, politicians, policemen, prosecutors, school teachers, stock brokers, writers, AIDS and glaucoma and cancer and chemotherapy patients and their doctors, virtually millions of Americans waited, waited on the marijuana men to deliver a seedless bud to their Christmas stockings.

As I waited, I felt the old rush of excitement which had eluded me since the early '80s.

I spent most of my slack time between the Embassy Suites Hotel on Oracle Road and nearby La Canada health resort where the desk clerk had conveniently arranged afternoon tennis matches. I talked to Smiley and Gato once a day, and called my wife every night. I never considered how lonely and frightened Kim must have felt, and she never once complained. I just figured I was keeping her out of harm's way while I chased my rush, or death wish, or whatever it was that had brought me back to Tucson.

For the first few days I felt like a normal businessman visiting a familiar town on his sales route. I'd exercise each morning in my room, then gather with the other guests—mostly retired snowbirds—for the complimentary continental breakfast. On the fourth morning a hush fell over the hotel breakfast crowd. As a local newscaster made an announcement, a leather-skinned gentleman adorned with turquoise jewelry lunged forward and turned up the volume on the TV.

"Drug Task Force agents arrested two illegal aliens after a brief chase today and seized approximately 5,000 pounds of marijuana valued at more than five million dollars. This latest bust," concluded the newsman, "brings the total amount of pot seized this season to nearly 20,000 pounds."

Suddenly feeling self-conscious, I panned the room to see if anyone was giving me strange looks; then relaxed, confident that my short haircut, tennis outfit, and athletic appearance cancelled out any suspicion. As I watched the old man by the television shake his head like he'd just lost a family member, a blue-haired grandmother gumming a jellyroll addressed me.

"This Drug War is terrible, isn't it?" she asked.

"Yeah, terrible," I replied, wondering which of these retired Good Sam Club members were really hired pot drivers—similar to Moon's or Tucson Tony's—waiting for their Winnabagos to be loaded with contraband for the long drive back East.

"Ah, hell," said the little old lady. "It's only pot."

One day after Moon arrived with the money, he and Smiley got bored with babysitting it in their hotel room. Unlike me, their therapeutic response to the waiting game was to party. They flew in Moon's seventy-year old driver, Sarge, to sit on the cash, and invited me for a night on the town. Following a lively dinner, Smiley drove to a stripper bar where he knew all the girls. Many mixed drinks and too much casual cocaine snorting later, Smiley announced we were going to another party after closing.

"With these coke whores?" I asked, feeling paranoid as hell, and thinking about all the movies I'd seen where cops squeezed hookers for information.

"Why, Timmy?" Smiley chided me. "You pussy whipped? Even fuges need to live a little."

"What do they think you do for a living?" I asked. When he didn't answer I pictured the romantic card Kim had hidden in my luggage, signed: *Remember I love you, Lion—Always.* "Take me to my hotel," I said.

Two days later at high noon, the desert Cat and I emerged from the underground pit at the back forty of his ranch after counting stacks of cash and removing our cut from the deal. We slid the steel cover over the entry, shoveled sand over it and tossed mesquite firewood around the area.

"This place has been a good friend to me," Gato said as we walked backwards, sweeping our tracks until we reached a dry, rocky wash leading back to the house. "Good friends are rare," he added with regret. "You sure I can't change your mind about coming Down Under this spring?"

"We'll have to play it by ear," I replied. "If my friends survive, maybe next fall. Say, you gonna leave that stash pit when you sell the ranch? I mean, down here it could be a big selling point. Don't you think?" A second of silence followed, then my laughter broke the ice.

"Yeah, right. After the holidays I'm covering it with a bulldozer—before the realtor brings out any potential buyers. It's over for me now, T. I don't care who buys the ranch, long as they have legal money. But if they're scammers, let 'em dig their own damn hole."

We shared lunch. I showered off the reefer dust, dressed in my businessman flight outfit and left two brightly-wrapped Christmas gifts in their guest bedroom: a bottle of Perrier Joet for the proud parents, and two baby ensembles thoughtfully selected by my wife. Moments later I stood at the door of my rental car saying goodbye. Gato gave me directions to his jeweler friend in town where I intended to spend my profits on pearls and diamonds for Kim. Aggy handed me a tin of homemade Christmas cookies and let me hold their infant son in my arms.

"He's beautiful, isn't he?" Gato said.

"Yeah, beautiful," I whispered, returning him to his mother. "Kid's lucky, too." My friend and I shook hands firmly. "He'll never hunger for money like we did growing up."

I tightened my grip, then broke away and slid in behind the wheel of my rental car. "A kid that cute deserves a full-time, legitimate daddy," I hinted, hoping with all my heart that Kim and I would survive this twilight zone to start a family of our own.

Tucson Tony flashed that big Italian grin and hugged his wife and child. "The next time you see me, T? I will be officially retired."

"When will we be seeing you again, Thomas?" asked Aggy.

I shrugged my shoulders, slipped on my shades and turned the key. "One never knows. Do one?" I gave him a wink. "But happy trails till then. And take care of those guys, lady."

Then I tapped the side of the car and headed for the highway with the strangest feeling in my gut—like I'd never see them again.

12

The Phoenix Affair

December 31, 1988: On the Big Island of Hawaii, five minutes remained in our third year as fugitives, and even though I believed the FBI was well aware of my love for these islands, I had returned here once more. This was Moon's first trip to Hawaii, and this setting was his choice for New Year's celebrations. Living "the lifestyle," that's what it was all about for Moon now. Maybe once that's what it was all about for me, too. This night, I would have been content having a moonlit dinner at our simple vacation rental by the sea, but I was happy to be anywhere in Hawaii—one of the few places in the world that had always given me energy, as opposed to taking it away.

Liza Minelli sang *Auld Lang Syne* on stage with an orchestra. Moon and L.A. Missy, and Lady Di and I slow danced on the parquet ballroom floor of the latest garish resort to encroach upon the sacred shores of Paradise. Outside on the moonlit grounds, international high rollers rode the tram or were poled in gondolas around the manmade lagoon that incarcerated pet dolphins whose job was to entertain. All around us inebriated couples glided across the floor in white tuxes and satin dinner gowns. Men ogled my wife whose red and black party dress hugged her hourglass figure like a glove, whose double strand of Christmas pearls and anniversary diamond earrings turned as many heads as her natural beauty. L.A. Missy, in a sequined designer dress with an egg-sized pearl cameo resting snugly in the inviting nest between her exposed breasts, drew her share of attention, too. I wished I were wearing my aloha shirt, instead of the sports coat my wife had dressed me in.

Lady Di sighed and lay her head upon my shoulder. I felt her heart beat. I smelled the sweet scent of the gardenia flower in her hair. And as we danced I stared into the spinning silver sphere above me, and saw the year in review. The neighbor's fire; the relocation moves; the Montreal rendezvous; Ben's death; Tucson; Monaco, our close call in Nice the day after a terrorist act required all American travelers entering France to have visas.

One minute until midnight. We continued to dance and I recalled the various fugitives' New Year's resolutions. Arnie vowed to travel Europe and golf the historic course at St. Andrews; Moon—unfortunately for Missy—pledged to cut all past ties by summer and purchase residency in one of several countries with passports for sale. The Fishers had fallen in love with the Land Down Under and planned on having a second child there to secure residency. The Blackwells firmly believed their Shangri-La lay south of the border in Mexico, and had gone all out to move their money to their new offshore account in Europe. My wife wanted a home of our own again by summer. And I—the meticulous planner—continued to struggle with the frustrations of living the rest of my life as a lie within the restraints of this fugitive game.

The Greek invited us to tour Greece with him, hinting that he had relatives in high places who might be able to help me. Help me with what? I wondered what he thought about me. Perhaps his country deserved some consideration, but I worried about my exposure with the cunning coin dealer. I also considered trusting my instincts, telling him part of my story, and enlisting his help in relocating overseas.

I sensed that the stress of this life was tearing away the delicate fabric of my fairytale marriage, and a version of Maui Bert's gambit came to mind. If the others all left the country, Kim and I could stay in the West, buy some land in the mountains with my new Dublin corporation, Peacehaven, and build a dream home together. I believed having no more landlords to contend with and sharing a goal comprised a great formula for continued marital bliss. Regardless, if my two identities continued paying taxes and building their histories, I would be prepared for any decision the future brought. I thought about the leather-bound writer's journals Kim gave me for Christmas, and doubted that I could ever relax and focus enough to revive my childhood dream.

Massive fish netting above released hundreds of balloons all around us. I tried to block out negative thoughts and think good ones. My wife and I kissed. Glitzy baubles were not on my list of favorite things, but she looked happy with her holiday jewelry, and that brought me joy. I was glad we had put some distance between ourselves and Smiley and Lizzy's cocaine habit this holiday season. I wondered what my family members were doing tonight, and if they offered a toast to me, as I did to them. A rose-cheeked Arnie joined us on the crowded floor where New Year's revelers stomped colorful balloons. Like Moon and Missy, he looked happy, too. They all seemed so very happy just enjoying this day, and every day of freedom. I wondered if I was the only one who stayed awake at night ulcerating about the future. At last all the cast members of our fuge troupe were flying high, financially strong and feeling confident and comfy with their new identities, but I sensed a cloud of pending separation hanging over us.

Liza Minelli sang *Life is a Cabaret.*

"Life is a cabaret, ol' chum," I muttered, "so come to the cabaret!"

"What's the matter, honey?" my wife asked, fondling her Christmas pearls.

"Nothing, Meekla," I replied, entranced by the silver sphere suspended from the ceiling. "Nothing at all."

"Happy New Year!" all present pronounced. And all in all it was. Within hours my beloved Fighting Irish football team would even win the national championship. But like the elusive surfers' wave, it was not to last, for a tsunami of change was rolling toward each and every one of us.

New Year's had always been my time to reflect back and look forward with hope and vision, but I had made some bad decisions in 1988 that left my created illusion of happiness deeply shaken. I believed in karma, and my trip to Tucson had given me bad vibes about mine for 1989.

Easter Sunday, 1989, Phoenix, Arizona: The after-dinner atmosphere at 3611 East Mariposa Street was graced by gaiety and celebration. It had been a glorious sunny day spent poolside enjoying Arizona's springtime within the friendly confines of the Blackwells' privacy fence. Diamond Liz pulled out all the stops to be "hostess with the mostest" and now served dessert for seven on china she had shipped from Harrods of London especially for the occasion.

When the silver cocaine tray came our way Lady Di gave me the eye.

"Honey?" she said with a nervous grin. "We've been too good lately. How 'bout a little reward?"

Drunk, among friends, eager to please her, and admittedly feeling the urge, I made the same old peer pressure mistake and nodded approvingly.

Next, on a whim, our hostess produced a camera.

"No pictures," said Moon rising from the table.

"Oh, come on, Sonny!" Lizzy pleaded. "Don't be a party pooper. You act like the feds are going to have copies sent to them."

I agreed with Moon.

Numerous lines later, Lizzy clicked off several shots of Kim and I. Smiley gave her a dirty look. The rest of us complained halfheartedly again, but we were hopelessly mesmerized by the "Peace/Love" stage of our high. Within minutes, Lizzy had her medicated models posing, and before we knew it she was out of film and our impromptu photo session was over.

"Listen everybody!" Lizzy announced, pausing to curtsy and lick her lips. "We received a letter from the Matthews in Australia."

"Matthews," I muttered. I knew she was talking about Bill and Leigh, but I'd never heard them called the Matthews. Obviously, they had assumed new identities before travelling to Australia. Mysterious, I thought, like selling his cars and leaving the country so quickly.

Lizzy pulled some pages from an envelope. "Please allow me to read it to you. *Greetings. Hope this letter finds you both well. We are fine, thank you.*"

As Lizzy read wordy descriptions of the free and easy life in Australia, feelings of envy filled my heart. Bill was touring the wine regions and beaches Down Under while I was here with the same old crowd doing things I didn't really want to do. I fidgeted in my seat. Our hostess smirked while she read, and I sensed she was enjoying my reaction.

"Here's an interesting part," Lizzy said. *"Down to two months on our visas. Next month after I receive Sonny's check (to make my bank account balance better) I'm going in to try and renew our visas. I hope it is truly no problem as my lawyer has stated. If there is a problem, we'll probably go to New Zealand for a week or so. The Australian government did me a favor and devalued their currency to where I get an extra $800 to $1200 a month now. Interest rates are still high. I'm now getting 14.2% on my checking account, 16% on any time deposits. I think after my visa interview I may lock in at a higher rate. Until I buy a house or business my only problem will be fighting boredom. Since I've now had almost three years of practice with that, it should be easy going for awhile...*"

When Lizzy finished reading Bill's six-page correspondence, she handed me a glass of Cognac and said, "That was some letter. Huh, Timmy?"

I watched her snort another line of cocaine from the mirror Smiley was holding under her nose. "Yeah, some letter," I said. As the party continued I wondered why my old partner had sent such a detailed letter to Smiley's Phoenix work-house, and signed it with their newly assumed names.

It was 3:15 A.M. Everything seemed normal. Kim and I feigned fatigue to avoid hearing, for the thousandth time, Lizzy's cocaine conversation about her wasted education. Moon and Missy followed suit and gathered their things to go to their room at the Biltmore. Arnie sipped a pre-sleep beer on the sofa. Smiley stubbed out another joint in the glass ashtray perched precariously on the end table, glanced over at Moon with nervous blue eyes and shook his head. Lizzy hugged Missy, pecked Lady Di on the cheek, then stormed off to bed alone.

As my wife and I retired for the night, many recent observations gnawed at my stomach lining. For a man who had recouped his losses, Smiley Jim Hagar had been tense, quiet and jumpy since we'd arrived—not at all like him. Once, driving home from the market in one of the Saabs he bought from Bill, Smiley circled around the block with one eye glued to the rearview mirror and returned to the store claiming he forgot something. I saw him answer the phone and hang up—like it was a prank caller. He mentioned changing their phone number after only having it for a few months. He and Moon had many private discussions. I was concerned they may have some heat they were not telling me about. I wondered if Smiley had screwed somebody's wife, drawn the attention of rip offs, or made an enemy in business. There were strange vibes between him and Lizzy. They used to always travel together. Now Smiley was spending more time on the road. Perhaps the passion had gone out of their relationship, but I still thought they were so compatible.

"I hate coke," I muttered loud enough for Kim to hear.

"Then why do you do it every time we have a party?" she asked.

"Good question. Guess I'm just stupid."

At 4:30 A.M. my wife and I were in the guest bedroom, naked beneath a down comforter, unwinding from the high. Moon and Missy had left for the Biltmore Hotel over an hour ago. Arnie was crashed on the couch. Smiley finally gave up channel surfing, slipped his empty Crown Royal bottle back into its purple bag, turned off the TV and headed for bed. Suddenly the house was so quiet that I could hear Lizzy sobbing between chopping and snorting coke across the hall. When Smiley entered their bedroom he was assaulted with a torrent of words.

"Well, we fooled them all," Lizzy declared. "Didn't we? They actually think we're happy."

"Honey, please don't—"

"Don't honey me, you bastard," Lizzy slurred. "Don't you wish I was at the house in Durango so you and Sonny could bring some more young coke-whores here? Huh? Maybe even catch another batch of the clap?"

"Shhhhhh!" Smiley snapped.

Kim's body grew tense beside me. We heard the sniffing of more nose candy.

"Give me that!" Smiley demanded.

"No! Don't pretend you care. You may not love me," Lizzy sobbed in a soft little girl's voice that belied the hardened middle-aged businesswoman she had become, "but I have a daughter who does. And a sister who's—"

"Married to a snitch!" Smiley said.

"So! Who's to say you wouldn't have done the same thing if you were in his shoes? Gary did what he had to do. At least their hell has an end in sight." After a moment of silence, Lizzy spoke rapidly and breathlessly. "I have my mother! My God, my poor dear mother."

Clearly she was strung out to a fine thread. And after calling her husband every name in the book, she threatened to go back to Ohio and turn herself in.

"Over my dead body!" Smiley declared, apparently having had enough. "It's not that simple you know, honey. You're in this up to your precious ass. Or did you forget the feds indicted you, too? Don't kid yourself, those prison dikes won't give a damn about your college degrees."

"I hate you," Lizzy cried. "I'll take my half of the money and move to—"

"Like hell you will."

We could hear what sounded like a struggle. A glass shattered on the floor. I threw back the covers, my heart racing out of control.

"I, I'm sorry, honey," Smiley apologized.

"Yes, you are," Lizzy said. "We are. Something's got to change, Jim. I'm serious. We can't go on the way we are."

Kim became almost unhinged with frustration and fear. "No wonder Lizzy's such a nervous wreck," my wife whispered while retreating to the far corner of the bed. She pulled her knees to her breasts, pressed her back against the wall and glared at me. Moisture welled up in her raccoon eyes. She swallowed hard between irregular breaths. "Tell me the truth, Tom. Have you been screwing around on your business trips, too?"

"No. I, I swear," I stammered, reaching for her with the trembling hands of a worried husband who had no chance in hell of displaying believable reassurance, confidence, or honesty when he was wired on coke. When I touched her she recoiled, and my guilty conscience conjured up the image of my brief affair at Blake's flat in London. The sight of Kim's tears hurt far more than her words.

From the living room we heard the television come back on. Over in the Blackwell's bedroom, someone turned on the radio and cranked up the volume. It was a sleepless night in Phoenix.

Our flight home to Portland was on Wednesday. The day before, Arnie and Moon went east on money-collection missions; Missy returned to L.A., and Kim and I spent our last day with the Blackwells—one on one—attempting to assist them with their most serious marital situation.

In a small wooden boat in the middle of Arizona's Lake Pleasant, I watched Smiley Jim Hagar attempt to relax.

"Now I know why you spend so much time fishing," he said. Then he furrowed his brow and asked me a question that came as no surprise. "Timmy, do you ever think about how much easier it would be to just disappear alone, without a wife?"

I paused to recall how many times I had done just that since going underground with a cop's daughter. Then I blocked out the thought and passed on my final remark before rowing my fishing buddy and I back to shore. "Just think of how screwed up being a fugitive would be without a woman you loved who knew your situation."

Smiley emptied our red worm container overboard and an armada of carp exploded on the glassy surface. "I know," he said, nodding. "God bless ya, guy. I know you're right. And part of me agrees with you. After all, I am finally a millionaire again." He sighed and extended a hand for me to shake. "So what? So, maybe I should retire and go live south of the border like the old lady wants. But shit, Timmy! I'm not some decrepit old fart. I'm good at what I do. I provide a necessary, honorable service to the pot smokers of America. And I'm damn sure not ready for the rocking chair."

"I hear you," I said. "Hell, I'm only thirty-two. Believe me, I know how you feel. Don't forget about your offshore bank account, though. With it, the possibilities are endless. You're smart. I'm sure someday you'll find a way out of this maze." I took a deep breath, then broached a subject not discussed since the beginning of our adventure. "Given any thought lately to all of us negotiating to go in voluntarily? Maybe give up half the money and—"

"And what, get screwed?" Smiley demanded. "I ain't giving up a goddamn dime! God bless ya, guy. If I knew who to bribe to get us all a skip bit I'd have invited them to Easter dinner. But if you can't get the money into the right hands, you'd have to rat out a dozen people to get a decent sentence. It's not that easy anymore. Too many judges, prosecutors and agents have got caught with their hands in the cookie jar. These tough new laws have created a nation of snitches, so they're jumpy, just like us. Oh sure, for every twenty people some hard-ass judge hammers, one still gets mysteriously slapped on the wrist." Smiley snorted with a twisted grin.

"Like Maui Bert?" I mumbled.

"Exactly," Smiley replied, frowning. "By the way, word is Bert got off with a five year tax charge. God bless him," Smiley sighed.

"Five years?" I echoed, wondering how the guy who sold boatloads of Colombian pot and put away millions ever managed that sentence without selling any souls to hell. I pictured myself in a prison cell, spending twenty-four months with my writing in peace while my secret bank account collected interest and my loyal wife waited. "That means he'll get paroled in two years. What I wouldn't give to get that."

"Yeah, dream on," Smiley remarked. "That was then. This is now. Only snitches get off light these days. If someone gets a short sentence, someone else is doing time because of them. You and I will do some serious time."

My heart sank as the elusive door to a survivable legal solution, briefly ajar, slammed shut again.

"Listen, here's my decision. A friend of mine has a little villa down in Guaymas, Mexico. Me and the wifey are going there to relax. There's good rum, great marlin fishing, a nice marina, and no phones. After a few weeks in the Gulf of California sunshine, either the old lady and I will reconcile, or we'll get ourselves a Mexican divorce. Why don't you and Di come with us?"

I locked my hands on the oars and dipped their paddle ends into Lake Pleasant. At this point in time, the worst thing in the world for my marriage would have been to go watch them snort coke and argue. Unlike me, Smiley surrounded himself with a cast of shady characters, many of whom were probably closer to him than I. He didn't need my company, and I didn't need to meet any new faces. Then there was my natural distrust of Mexico where—as Gato warned me—men on the street sold information for a fistful of pesos.

"Well? Whatta ya say, guy?" Smiley asked.

I shook my head and pulled on the oars. "Sorry, pal, you're on your own," I said as the boat surged forward toward shore. "But don't take it personal. It's not your company, it's the water," I muttered.

"Laugh now, Mr. Honeymooner. But mark my words, one day you and Di will be dealing with this shit, too."

Not if I can help it, I thought, suddenly feeling queasy.

April 13, 1989, Phoenix, Arizona: Two plain sedans turned off Camelback Road, and cruised through the selected neighborhood in synchronized slow motion. The men-in-black scouted the alleys and cul-de-sacs with trained eyes. Then, in the rapidly dimming light, the raiders spotted the yellow block home and the two Saabs they were looking for.

"Bill McCarthy's cars," one man declared.

They unzipped their windbreakers and checked the loads in their weapons. One drew a hunting knife from its sheath.

"Time for this punk to pay his dues," mumbled another.

"Let's hit 'em," said the man in charge.

Three days later the Arizona sunset sky was alive with color. It had been a long road trip and Arnie was looking forward to relaxing on the links with his new set of golf clubs. He cut his engine, coasted into the cul-de-sac and zipped right under the Blackwell's carport behind the two black Saabs. As he lifted the red patio brick that concealed the spare house key, he noticed the newer of McCarthy's former cars was drastically leaning to one side.

"Bad shocks," he muttered to himself, making a mental note to tell Smiley.

Arnie breathed the cooling, mesquite-scented night air appreciatively and gazed at an emerging crescent moon. But when he pushed open the house door and flicked the light switch, he felt sick inside. Fifteen minutes later, Arnie placed a call to Rippling River Resort, Oregon.

Kim and I had shared a wonderful, romantic day on the mountain. We'd walked for miles in a lush rain forest, come back, made love, and ate a steelhead trout I'd caught just outside our patio door. The cats were well fed and wrestling on the back deck. The birds were freed from their cages and squawking merrily on the TV dinner tray I had turned into a tinker toy playground. She was contentedly arranging flowers in a vase. I was reading the real estate section of *The Oregonian*, and pondering buying a cabin in the mountains and laying low. Only three people knew our number—and none were expected to call—so it was a great surprise when the phone rang.

"Tim, it's Arnie," said the voice on the other end of the phone. He paused to clear his throat. "I've run into a problem down here, Bud."

The tone of my normally calm, cool and collected best friend's voice was ominous. "Where you calling from?" I asked.

"Phoenix. I'm at a mall on Camelback road. Listen close. I just left Smiley's place. It's a mess. Ceiling panels torn down, pillows slashed, the freezer's contents tossed onto the kitchen floor. Even the firewood box has been rifled. When I saw the slider ajar I ran out and drove here to call you. My golf clubs are still inside. What should I do?"

My mind reeled with possible scenarios. The Blackwells, incommunicado in Mexico, had been expected back any day. Had they been ripped off? Abducted? "It sounds like they've been ripped off by professionals," I said, watching my wife's face turn white at the sound of my words. "Did you notice anything else? You sound pretty shook."

"Yeah," Arnie sighed. "I saw three lawn chairs hidden in the shrubs along the fence. There were Kentucky Fried Chicken boxes and empty bottles beside them. And the cars..."

"Yeah, what about them?" I asked.

"All the tires had been punctured. What do you think?"

"If you're up to it, go back and get your clubs. Whoever did this is long gone. Take a look around. Make sure there's no dope left out where the cops can see it. Secure the place, turn on a light and wipe your prints off the door when you leave. I'll page Moon and see if Smiley can be reached in Mexico. Maybe you should head home."

"Will do, Bud. I'll call you from the road tomorrow."

"Ten four. Be careful, big guy." Within seconds I dialed Moon's Sky Pager number and punched in #44, my code for home.

Two hours passed and Moon had not returned my page. Suddenly I was struck with a vision of the Blackwells bound, gagged and being tortured by a gang of thieves demanding to know the location of their drug money. My wife sat silent on the couch, her thoughts known only to herself. I wondered who Smiley had mentioned us to, what kind of records and addresses he kept in Phoenix, and if we were in any danger.

The phone rang and I lunged for the receiver.

"Hey, Bud, it's me again," Arnie announced, his deep voice wavering and shaky. "I did what you said. Got my clubs, put a metal bar in the slider track, gave the place a thorough going over and wiped my prints. On my way out I noticed something hanging on the refrigerator." He swallowed hard between words. "I'm afraid the shit just got deeper."

"Why?" I asked, expecting him to say he'd found a ransom note.

"Because. Their house was hit, all right. But not by rip offs, by feds! I've got the search warrant and seizure list they left behind right here in my hands. When I realized what went down, I got the hell out of there," he blurted. "I'm in Flagstaff now."

"Who were they searching for?"

"It's a three-page document. Issued from the US District Court, District of Arizona. Page two is called, Exhibit A, and it looks like a history of the feds tracking of Bill McCarthy's 'Fisher' ID beginning in 1987. There's another name, Scott J. Harris, on this page. It also describes the two cars Smiley bought from Bill; then lists what they were searching for."

"And what's that?"

"Books, records, receipts, notes, controlled substances, weapons, safety deposit box keys, cashiers checks and other items evidencing the obtaining, secreting, transfer, and/or concealment of assets and the obtaining, secreting,

transfer, concealment and/or expenditure of money. They found twenty-two lines of shit."

"Read it to me," I said.

"Various identification—top right dresser drawer; scrambler device and various papers—top left dresser drawer; pager, business cards etc.—floor of master bedroom; photographs; various tickets; controlled substances; letter dated 2/27 with money order and photos of William McCarthy; briefcase; deposit box key…"

While he read, I wrote each item down along with its location, with every stroke of my pen speculating as to what damage might result. I pictured us mugging for party photos at Easter and felt like an ass. I recalled Lizzy reading Bill's letter to us.

"Arnie, what's the date on that list?"

"April thirteenth. Why?"

"That letter they found is probably the one from Australia." I paused briefly, deep in thought. "The feds know where they are, and you can bet that Interpol has been contacted by now. I'm afraid the clock is ticking for them, pal. Maybe for us all."

In the ensuing silence Kim moved closer and we locked hands.

"What are you going to do?" my best friend asked, aware more than anyone of the hard feelings between McCarthy and me which had began during the Aardvark Construction Company years.

My wife rubbed my temples. Seconds ticked away on our Session's clock. "The right thing," I replied. "Assume the worst. Warn everyone. Are you stopping over anywhere for the night?"

"Are you kidding? I couldn't sleep if I had Moon's Valium stash!"

"Yeah, I hear you. Think you can swing through Vegas and get a couple hundred in quarters from a casino? I got a feeling I'll be donating heavily to the payphone gods in the next twenty-four hours."

"Sure. Good luck, Mr. Barnes," Arnie sighed.

I was tempted to utter my typical response, *fuck luck,* but this time prayed that luck would be on our side.

Ten minutes later Moon called during a layover at an East Coast airport. Our conversation was brief. He had a plane to catch and I was concerned about his flight name and pager number having been compromised by the Phoenix raid. I told him what I knew. He listened intensely. After cursing intermittently and slapping the phone enclosure he informed me that Smiley's Sky Pager was out of range in Guaymas where he believed the Blackwells remained on vacation.

"But," Moon added, "that idiot called someplace in Guaymas from his home phone one night when we were trashed out. By now the feds have checked the phone records. If the Blackwells are still free, there will be DEA agents swarming Guaymas by tomorrow looking for two fugitive gringos. Oy vay," Moon mumbled. "I've got serious shekels to collect, other fuges to warn, and I'm out of Maalox and Rolaids. We need to get word to Guaymas ASAP."

His final boarding call blasted over loudspeakers in the background.

"Gotta run, T. Page me in two hours and I'll have a plan," Moon said.

"Will do," I replied. "It'll be a Portland number. So don't freak out when you can't find an area code on your pager. You understand?"

"Sure-sure. Just sign it #44."

Our Session's clock chimed eleven times. I decoded the number to the Fishers' Queensland condominium in my address book and tucked it in my shirt pocket. It had been a long day and promised to be a nerve-racking night spent chasing change at convenience stores, paging Moon, and waiting at out-of-the-way phone booths chosen to keep potential heat away from the location of our Mount Hood home. Before Arnie's second call Kim and I had been drinking liqueur. Feeling drained, I explain the situation to her, my voice flat with fatigue.

Lady Di took my hand and led me to the kitchen table. She uncovered our stoneware sugar bowl exposing a small amount of white powder. "A gift from Lizzy to me," she said coyly, obviously concerned about my love/hate relationship with cocaine.

I was aware she had brought back a stash, but thought it had run out already. Okay, fine. For her this little dessert was all right. In moderation, it only seemed to make her more talkative, and horny. I, however, after our sleepless night in Phoenix, had sworn off toot for good; declaring we would never keep it around us so I'd never again be tempted to consume any and regret it. But here I was with the lady I loved staring down into the magic sugar bowl, smelling its ether-based contents. My stomach churned, my pulse raced, my palms began to sweat. My wife dipped one long fingernail into the pile and stuck it under my nose.

"Not for me," I said, before breaking away for the door.

The digital clock on the dash read 4:06 A.M. I was driving back up the mountain in a steady rain, hands wet on the wheel, eyes glued to the centerline on Highway 26, evaluating the latest rash of conversations.

Moon informed me he had reached a fuge in Tucson—the Glove—who could get word to a fishing boat captain in Guaymas who would warn the Blackwells they were in danger.

"Smiley's going to want to know what was on that DEA list Arnie read to you," Moon said. He recited a series of numbers, which I wrote down. "I've told The Glove you'll be calling this public phone in Guaymas at three A.M. If he's there, Smiley will answer. If he does, tell him I'm en route to Sky Harbor. Tell him they'll be looking for them to enter the country together by car, or at the airport. Tell him to wear tourist clothes, carry souvenirs, put about thirty minutes between him and Lizzy and walk across the Nogales border with the lunch hour traffic. The Glove will meet them on the other side."

"Got it," I said. "But what about you? Don't you think it's insane to fly into Phoenix after everything that's happened?"

"Oy vay," Moon responded with strained coolness. "Piece of cake, T. I'll be wearing my Tom Snider wig and a polyester leisure suit."

The loud drum of rain drops beat upon the black Ford's roof, drowning out melancholy cowboy music that was fading in and out on the radio. The road blurred like a wet watercolor as I entered a cloudbank that engulfed Mount Hood. I cracked the window, slipped a Doors cassette into the player, leaned forward and flicked on my low-beam headlights. Morrison sang *Riders on the Storm.* The truck kept climbing, and I recalled my second conversation—with my former business partner Down Under.

For a man in his precarious position, Bill McCarthy's overall lethargic response to my warning surprised even me. He spent the first few minutes belittling Smiley and the government. He complained that Moon's latest twenty-thousand dollar a month interest payment had not yet arrived to his Queensland bank account—which he boasted was bearing seventeen percent on the Australian dollar. He mumbled about having to wait for some important letter mailed to his condo from a European money manager. "If I get away clean, but they get my account information, I might as well surrender," Bill said.

Like me, it was important to my old nemesis to hold lots of money against tomorrow's uncertainties. But short on quarters for this costly, international payphone call, I became short on patience as well, and quite vocal about the seriousness of the situation.

Once convinced that the feds' windfall acquisition in Phoenix would indeed lead Interpol to his doorstep, Bill pulled out of his version of shock and started thinking out loud.

"The feds aren't as sharp as you think," he said laconically and slowly. "It will take days for them to figure out who and where we are. In the meantime, I'll lay down one helluva trail for those dumb fucks to follow. We'll fly to Hong Kong on roundtrip tickets. I'll take care of some banking business there, then buy tickets to Vancouver—roundtrip, of course. When we arrive in Canada, Moon can bring us our backup set of ID. Yeah. I'll rent a place at a ski resort and lay low. Fuck the feds."

Although I considered his timetable a bit presumptuous, it was at least a practical plan. And William Charles McCarthy, if anything, was a most practical man.

Between the swish-swish-swishing of the windshield wipers I saw a big buck jump out ahead of me and rear up helter-skelter. I hit the Ford's breaks and swerved. My heart throbbed, and for an instant I felt wired from the adrenaline rush. Which reminded me of my last conversation—just over an hour ago—with Smiley Jim Hagar.

He was high as a kite and talking crazy, with Lizzy by his side. When I asked if my address or phone number were contained in the stuff the feds found, he took a long time to answer, then sounded more insulted than reassuring. I repeated the items on the seizure list several times and passed on Moon's instructions.

"My jewelry!" I heard Lizzy cry. "Ask him if they got my diamond necklace."

Smiley could not silence his wife, and they actively debated organizing a rescue mission to retrieve the contents of their ransacked home. They cursed Bill McCarthy and his cars.

"You were right," Lizzy sobbed. "We should have never mixed paperwork with them!"

I held the phone away from my ear, watched a swaggering truck driver and a two-bit hooker head for a cheap motel room across Portland's infamous 82nd Street, and wondered how much attention two wired gringos were drawing at 3:00 A.M. down in tiny Guaymas, Mexico. The debate at the other end of the line grew louder, with Lizzy suggesting that Jim's womanizing was the cause of their dilemma.

"Listen to yourselves," I said. "That's crazy talk! You're free, man. You have money. You're retired. Write this loss off. Let me get you a vacation rental somewhere so you can lay low and regroup."

"God bless ya, Tim, Timmy," Smiley stammered. "I might just take you up on your offer. But even if we can't rescue the wifey's jewels, I still have to return to Phoenix."

"Why?" I asked. "What in the world could be that important?'

"Money. I have cash stashed in a storage unit. And, more importantly, one of Moon's custom-designed rigs is sitting in Sky Harbor's long term parking lot. If the feds find it, then my fail safe method for delivering loads will be ruined."

I had to pause after Smiley's remarks. I had to pause to shake my head, stare at my reflection in the phone booth glass and come to grips with one of my own fundamental beliefs: no one can save the world. Maybe a small portion of it, perhaps only that portion we love.

"Are you sure we're not in any danger?" I asked him one last time.

In the eerie silence which followed I heard snorting sounds between the whispers.

"Do I have to move and change my name?"

"Nope," Smiley said.

"Are you certain?"

"Positive," Smiley finally replied with cocaine confidence. "Ya worry too much, Timmy. Tell Moon to page The Glove at one o'clock. Tell him we have a mission. Talk to ya tomorrow night, guy. Bye."

"Yeah, tomorrow," I muttered. "Be careful."

It blew my mind. The feds were on to them, yet these material things and doing more coke were all they seemed concerned about. They were out of touch with reality. Hell, maybe I was, too.

Bright lights materialized in the gray soup outside my windshield. I heard a siren wail, then the whir of a trooper's tires as he blew past me headed downhill on Highway 26. The digital dash clock read 4:38 A.M. Suddenly I realized I'd been gone over five hours and had neglected to call home.

"Stupid!" I said to myself, slapping the steering wheel. "She'll be worried sick. No, she's always calm, cool and collected. She's trained—a cop's daughter. Remember?"

How could I ever forget? And now detective daddy-in-law—eager to get my face on national television—had fresh, revealing photographs from Phoenix to show his FBI friend.

The road leveled off. I entered the village of Welches, and the rain changed to fine white snow. Bent tree branches formed a welcoming tunnel when I made my final turn. The scene was serene and relaxing, like the one I expected to return to momentarily.

I opened the door to our Rippling River condo and found my wife on the living room floor surrounded by photographs. She had a pair of scissors in one hand and a drink in the other.

"Hi, honey," she said in a clenched-teeth tone of voice I recognized as toot-induced. "What did you find out?"

As I brought her up to date she snipped Jim and Irene's heads off one of our Tahoe wedding photos and tossed it in a pile.

"What are you doing, Meekla?" I asked softly as she proceeded to surgically remove Arnie from a Polaroid taken at the Lion's Share.

"They're your friends," she said, frantically searching for another victim.

Snip.

"What if they get busted at the border?"

Snip.

"What if someone breaks down our door in the morning?"

Snip.

Her face turned as red as her favorite pair of heels.

"Oooo," she squealed. "Why can't I just be barefoot and pregnant?"

A rash crept up her long neck.

Snip.

"I hate this life," she hissed, pulling her hair into little bunches.

Snip.

She started to hyperventilate.

"Tom, I can't take it anymore."

I wanted to tell her that what she was doing made absolutely no sense. I wanted to say the obvious: honey, if the feds are ever looking at our photo album, then I'll already be history. I wanted to grab her and shake her to her senses, but it was simply not my style. Maybe I should've congratulated her for being human enough, being feminine enough, to finally release the very same feelings that I as a man kept hidden inside. Regardless, for a woman who seldom showed emotion, this was a major cry for help.

"Maybe you should just run away by yourself!" she shouted, flailing the air with her scissors. "You'd stand a better chance alone than with me."

"Shhhhh!" I said, having heard the school teacher couple in the condo above us stirring. "Remember what I promised you in Mendocino?" I asked, kissing her on the lips. "This Lion's not going anywhere without his raccoon."

Our big gray Manx, Smokey Bear, pounced on the newspaper beside my wife. The paper slid along with the cat, revealing the Ziplock baggie that was concealed beneath it.

Without a word, without hesitation, I seized the quarter ounce of cocaine and walked briskly into the bathroom.

"What are you doing?" Kim asked, two steps behind me.

"Something I should have done a week ago," I said, lifting the toilet seat.

While unsealing the Ziplock, I saw her face in the medicine cabinet mirror.

"You're nuts," she said, staring at me as if I'd just taken leave of my senses. "You've lost it, Tom!"

"Not yet," I replied. "But if we have another binge of this crap, I might."

"Give me that!" she demanded.

I shook my head, blocked her hand, and extended the precious stash beyond her considerable reach.

"You know I know what you're feeling, Meekla," I said, facing the wall. "You're craving that famous one more, that endless last line. Aren't you? You know how I know? Cause if I hadn't heard what I heard tonight we might both be snorting, babbling, douching our noses, biting our nails and looking through the louvers on our window blinds for the boogie man."

I tilted the baggie and let some powder spill out.

"Because of this shit, Jim and Irene's marriage, if not their freedom, is in jeopardy. Each time we do this shit together I feel we lose another part of the magic that brought us together."

"I know. I know, honey," my wife whispered, wrapping her arm around me from behind and breaking down in tears. "Go on, flush it."

"Take a good look," I said as the cocaine hit the toilet water. "Because it's the last time."

"Hold me, Tom. I'm scared," Kim sobbed.

And as I did I thought, *me too.*

I did not ever want to wake up and pull away from the warmth of my wife's body, and so it was noon when I finally raised the window blinds and fed the pets. Outside, last night's snows melted and mountain sunshine danced in the shimmering ripples of the Sandy River. In our bed, my wife lay fast asleep in her normal, innocent fetal position with our calico kitty Punkin curled beside her. I brewed some coffee, crossed my fingers in support of my fellow fuges, and hoped an "all clear bulletin" would soon be received from Arizona.

At 12:30, Arnie called from a gas station on the Warm Springs Indian Reservation. "Everything all right?" he asked.

"Should be. Might be," I said quietly, trying not to wake Kim. "But no matter what, we need to talk. Why don't you drive straight here with that list."

At 1:30 Moon phoned from Phoenix. "It's me with your afternoon fuge update, T," he announced. "They made it."

I smiled at my wife and gave thumbs-up.

"Now talk some sense into them," I suggested to Moon.

"I intend to. Right after we complete our mission."

At 3:30 Arnie arrived, and we three Hoosiers spent the balance of the afternoon discussing things. In the beginning we tried to downplay the significance of the Phoenix affair and convince ourselves that it would not affect our presently comfortable lives. But logic prevailed, and we decided to grill Lizzy and Smiley in person when the time seemed appropriate, to determine how much damage had been done to our security.

We were having dinner with Arnie that night when the phone rang again.

"Man, I can't believe this," Moon wheezed, sounding very, very tired and quite possibly in shock. "They're gone."

"Turn down the stereo, honey," I said, covering the receiver. "What'd you say Moon? Is there a television on in the background? I can barely hear you."

"Shit!" he screeched. "It's already on the local news. I have to go. My driver is waiting."

"What happened?"

Moon's normally energetic voice dropped another notch as he made the official announcement. "We lost 'em," he said like a doctor. "They...they got them, T," he sobbed.

"Where? How?" My stomach turned at the thought.

"What does it matter? They're history."

"What's wrong?" my wife cried, clutching my arm.

I shook my head and envisioned Jim and Irene face down on the hot Arizona pavement surrounded by government agents with guns drawn. In a microsecond I remembered the day they appeared in disguise at the Lion's Share and enlightened us with the fugitive way out of my pending predicament. I pictured them at our South Lake Tahoe wedding; teaching us about IDs; touring Lake Powell together, Mendocino, Bend, Sunriver, Manzanita, Montana, Durango, the Columbia Gorge, Guernsey.

"They're gone," I mumbled.

Kim grabbed my shoulder and shook it hard. "Honey, what's wrong?" she asked again, her face drawn with tension.

Arnie rose from the dinner table, his mouth agape. "Busted?" he blurted.

"Good night Irene. They got 'em," I whispered with shaking hands.

Suddenly my thoughts switched to self-preservation, and I wondered about our fallen comrades' strength of will under pressure.

"Tim! Tim, you there?" Moon shouted. "I've got to go. I'll call you tomorrow when I can."

I cleared my throat. "There may not be anyone here to answer after tomorrow," I muttered ominously.

"What do you mean by that?" Moon asked. "They're our friends! How can you assume Jim or Irene will snitch us out?"

A car horn honked outside Moon's hotel room.

"Don't assume anything," I said. "Cover your own ass until the smoke clears. Our friends are facing a shit load of prison time."

The horn honked again.

"Don't lose touch," Moon pleaded nervously.

"I won't," I promised. "I'll page you tomorrow night."

"We love you, Moon!" shouted Arnie and Lady Di. "Be careful."

"Be careful out there, Mr. Barnes," Moon said.

"Tim Barnes is dead," I replied. "Goodbye."

When I got off the phone I marched into our bedroom closet and started pulling clothes from their hangers. Exactly what happened in Tucson, Arizona on that April day would be the subject of conjecture for years to come, but certain things were obvious to me as I packed my suit bag. Jim Hagar, two-time loser, had his priorities pretty damn screwed up in the months preceding his arrest. He had put his coke habit, his sexual desire, then his money ahead of marriage, friendship and life.

I remembered what Diamond Liz said to him about her snitch brother-in-law that night in their Phoenix bedroom: "Who's to say you wouldn't have done the same in his shoes?" I also remembered the silence that ensued.

I tossed my leather bomber jacket on the bed, burdened by the doubt I had about the depth of our fuge clan's courage once the shit really hit the fan. Indiana had taught me this lesson in mistrust. The code of honor I once thought was written in stone had been erased by harsher drug sentences, and a pacifist like me was no threat to any snitch wanting to cut his time.

Lady Di came in to the bedroom. "Where are you going?" she asked.

"To the coast," I said, leaning over to consider the cold realities of our circumstances and glaring at my wife. "Pack up the house. I'm putting you in a hotel tomorrow. I'm going to get us a vacation rental. And when I return we'll have to move the storage unit by Vancouver Mall, too."

"Why?"

"We called the storage once from this phone. There's a paper trail. Don't worry, Meekla. We have plenty of money and each other. We can do anything. There's no sense taking chances."

She bit her lip, and nodded in agreement. Tears formed in her eyes.

I grabbed hold of her, seeking strength in our embrace before doing what I had to do to survive in the coming months.

"Feel any different?" I asked, after forcefully kissing her on the lips.

"Why? Should I?" she asked.

"Uh huh," I replied. "You just divorced Tim Barnes and became Mrs. Paul James Kelly."

Arnie stuck his head around the corner. "Excuse me," he said shyly. "But did you say you are moving?"

"Yeah, we're moving. They had your phone number, too, didn't they?"

His face turned ghostly white.

I gestured to my best friend.

A spontaneous group hug ensued.

"We're all moving then, I guess," I said reassuringly. "Back to the coast where we know our way around, just in case."

Arnie bent over and picked up Smokey the cat. "Jim and Irene busted," he mumbled as he flopped into our couch. "Shit! I can't believe it."

"Believe it," I said as a deafening silence set in.

Friends were a rare commodity in the fugitive world, and two of ours were gone. I had worked for three years at legitimizing Timothy Alan Barnes, now all of it was down the drain. And we were moving again—for the sixth time.

"Damn them," I muttered while hugging my wife. "Why couldn't they listen?"

She dried her eyes with a tissue, then started rubbing my temples and acting strong again. "Let's get to work," Kim said. "It'll be all right, Tom. It'll be all right, as long as we're together."

I closed my eyes and blocked out the voice of reason, which was telling me that staying with my wife was my biggest liability. For the first time, I seriously doubted that my waning energy could continue to support this marriage and my own sanity, but I could not relax my guard and give up.

In Smiley's case, the feds' plan of patiently waiting for the fugitive to fuck up had paid off. Smiley and Lizzy had made their fortune selling drugs, and ruined their fugitive run by doing them to excess. The people who had introduced us to the underground were history, and all that the rest of us could do about it, was run like a bunch of scared rabbits.

Federal Search Warrant for Arizona "work-house."

AO 93 (Rev. 5/85) Search Warrant

130

United States District Court

DISTRICT OF ARIZONA

In the Matter of the Search of

(Name, address or brief description of person or property to be searched)

3611 East Mariposa Street,
Phoenix, Arizona

SEARCH WARRANT

CASE NUMBER: 89-0103MB

TO: SUSAN SCHILLIE and any Authorized Officer of the United States

Affidavit(s) having been made before me by SUSAN SCHILLIE (Affiant) who has reason to believe that ☐ on the person of or ☒ on the premises known as (name, description and/or location)

3611 East Mariposa Street, Phoenix, Arizona, described as a yellow colored block house with white roof located on a cul de sac with the numbers 3611 on the front of the house next to the front door

in the ________ District of Arizona there is now concealed a certain person or property, namely (describe the person or property)

See attached Exhibit "A"

I am satisfied that the affidavit(s) and any recorded testimony establish probable cause to believe that the person or property so described is now concealed on the person or premises above-described and establish grounds for the issuance of this warrant.

YOU ARE HEREBY COMMANDED to search on or before 4/23/89 (Date)

(not to exceed 10 days) the person or place named above for the person or property specified, serving this warrant and making the search (in the daytime — 6:00 A.M. to 10:00 P.M.) ~~(at any time in the day or night as I find reasonable cause has been established)~~ and if the person or property be found there to seize same, leaving a copy of this warrant and receipt for the person or property taken, and prepare a written inventory of the person or property seized and promptly return this warrant to Michael Mirzolla, Jr. (U.S. Judge or Magistrate) as required by law.

4-13-89 @ 2:45 PM at Phoenix, Arizona

Date and Time Issued — City and State

MICHAEL [illegible]
United States [illegible]

Name and Title of Judicial Officer

[signature]

Signature of Judicial Officer

PP HQ IP HON OTT (Priority, HeadQuarters, InterPol to HONg Kong & OTTawa)
DE CAN #0157 1600050
ZNR UUUUU (Unclassified)
P 090300Z JUN 89 (Priority, 3:00 AM GMT June 9, 1989)
FM LEGAT CANBERRA (245F-IP-159) (RUC)
TO DIRECTOR FBI/PRIORITY/
FBI INDIANAPOLIS (245-IP-159)/PRIORITY/
LEGAT HONG KONG/PRIORITY/
LEGAT OTTAWA/PRIORITY/
BT
UNCLAS
CITE: //5800//
PASS: (1) HQ-OLIA, FOREIGN LIAISON UNIT, SSA R. D. DUNKLE;
(2) HQ-DRUG SECTION.
SUBJECT: WILLIAM CHARLES MC CARTHY, AKA-FUGITIVE(B); ET AL, OCDETF, OO: IP.
RECANTEL 70 HQ, IP, HON, OTT, 6/2/89.
RETEL CONFIRMED CAPTIONED SUBJECT, WIFE AND DAUGHTER, USING ALIASES MARK DAVID MATTHEWS, LAURA LEE MATTHEWS, SHANNON MARIE MATTHEWS DEPARTED AUSTRALIA 4/23/89, EN ROUTE HONG KONG VIA QANTAS 27. HONG KONG VERIFIED SUBJECT, ET AL ARRIVED HONG KONG AND DEPARTED 5/1/89 VIA CANADIAN PACIFIC CP8 EN ROUTE VANCOUVER.
CLOSE, BUT NO CIGAR□
INQUIRY AT THE DIPLOMATIC TELEPHONE ANSWERING SERVICE, BRISBANE, REVEALS ON 4/21/S9, MC CARTHY DEPOSITED $130 AS SERVICE FEE TO FORWARD URGENT LETTER EXPECTED FROM SWITZERLAND. THE LETTER NEVER ARRIVED AND MC CARTHY LATER CALLED TO CANCEL THE SERVICE. HE NEVER PROVIDED A FORWARDING ADDRESS FOR HIMSELF FOR THE LETTER.
OTHER FORWARDING SERVICES IN THE AREA WERE CHECKED WITH
NEGATIVE RESULTS.

The FBI was convinced by this encounter that Thomas Hickey was in Colorado, when in fact, he was five states away.

FD-302 (REV. 3-10-82) FEDERAL BUREAU OF INVESTIGATION 117

Date of transcription 8/2/89

ANN M. GORDON, date of birth August 29, 1962, 1285 Vivian Street, Golden, Colorado 80401, telephone number (303) 238-5469, after being advised of Agent's identity and nature of interview related the following:

GORDON is currently a teller at the FIRST NATIONAL BANK OF LAKEWOOD, located 143 Union Street, Lakewood, Colorado, telephone number 989-8888, and can recall making out a cashiers check in the amount of $7,000 to STAR LITE PHOTOGRAPHERS which was purchased on October 28, 1988, cashiers check number 42657.

GORDON recalls the transaction and stated that it stood out in her mind due to the fact that the individual who purchased the cashiers check paid in cash. She stated that to her recollection the majority of the bills were hundreds or twenties. During a brief conversation with the individual who purchased the cashier's check, the individual stated that he was going to buy a Toyota Truck at STEVINSON CHEVROLET. She advised that the individual was wearing longer hair and a mustache but was very nice and pleasant in nature. His actions and way of speech did not arouse GORDON's suspicion. She felt that the subject was being up-front with her. She stated that the subject did wear light brown sunglasses, but did take them off while doing the transaction. The individual told GORDON to make the check payable to STEVINSON CHEVROLET and to put it as being purchased by STAR LITE PHOTOGRAPHERS. She stated she vaguely remembers the name ROBERT being spoken but could not recall the last name of WILSON.

After reviewing photographs of subject's involved in this case on file with the Denver Division, GORDON stated that the individual who purchased the cashiers check for $7,000, on October 28, 1988, was THOMAS PAUL HICKEY.

245F-159-731

Investigation on 5/4/89 at Lakewood, Colorado File # DN-245F-253

by JOHN W. PIATANESI/llm Date dictated 5/4/89

SEARCHED ___ INDEXED ___ SERIALIZED ___ FILED ___ AUG 1 ? 1989

No stone was left unturned.

FEDERAL BUREAU OF INVESTIGATION 92

8/2/89

Date of transcription

- 1 -

CHRISTEN CARLSON, Manager, THE MAIL BOX, 2888 Bluff Street, Boulder, Colorado, stated that she bought the business, which was once called MAIL CALL, located 2111 30th Street, Boulder, Colorado, from the Owner/Manager KAY KENDALL, approximately one year ago.

According to CARLSON, her records indicate that JAMES N. FISHER and ANNA FISHER were receiving mail at THE MAIL BOX using box number 519. She stated that on March 22, 1989, a caller identifying himself as JAMES N. FISHER requested to belong to their answering service. The caller stated that calls may be coming into her place of business, either by the name of JAMES N. FISHER or MILE HIGH INVESTMENTS. CARLSON related that, to her knowledge, no calls were ever taken for either name. The post office box 519, which is in the name of JAMES N. FISHER and MILE HIGH INVESTMENTS has been prepaid in advance and is good until October of 1989.

CARLSON related that her instructions on the P. O. box 519 was to send all mail received to 2303 North 44th Street, Suite 277, Phoenix, Arizona 85008. CARLSON said that, as of this date, there has been very little mailings to that address as it appears all activity on mail box 519 has ceased.

She did have an application for delivery of mail through Agent in the name of JAMES N. FISHER, which she provided investigating Agent with a photographic copy of. She stated she never met FISHER personally, but believes she did talk to him or someone identifying themselves as JAMES N. FISHER. JAMES N. FISHER had post office box 1059 when mail was being delivered at the MAIL CALL located 2111 30th Street, Suite M, Boulder, Colorado.

CARLSON located a contact number for FISHER which was left by the caller identifying himself as FISHER. The telephone number was 258-7994.

245C-159-732

Investigation on 5/5/89 at Boulder, Colorado File # DN 245F-253

SEARCHED ___ INDEXED ___ SERIALIZED ___ FILED ___ AUG 4 1989 FBI—INDIANAPOLIS

by SA JOHN W. PIATANESI/blm Date dictated 5/5/89

This document contains neither recommendations nor conclusions of the FBI. It is the property of the FBI and is loaned to your agency; it and its contents are not to be distributed outside your agency.

13

Last Chance

The Phoenix affair really got to me. I began having graphic dreams about our house being raided, federal agents firing guns, and one of us being killed. I never told Kim or Arnie about this or showed any sign of losing my nerve. I simply did the same thing I'd been doing since I left Tahoe and reality behind me; run and survive. We ran back to the familiar Oregon coast where I assumed the identity of Paul James Kelly and rented a cottage. My wife and Arnie kept their same names, and we rarely ventured far from Devil's Lake. Isolated and paranoid, for us the beautiful setting became in essence a prison without walls.

The Arizona raid provided the government with a wealth of leads which they immediately began to pursue. Smiley's address book gave FBI agents scores of names and phone numbers to decode, and Lizzy's Easter photo collection killed any illusion I had created to convince the feds we were living overseas. The letter and photos Bill had sent to the house on Mariposa Street quickly led the FBI and Interpol on a manhunt to Australia. Accordingly, Bill and Leigh flew to Hong Kong, then barely missed being busted at Vancouver International airport. Fearful of crossing the Canadian border under the names Mark and Laura Matthews, they rented a ski condo in British Columbia and lay low, waiting on new IDs from Moon.

Moon moved to Montreal and hung out with the crew he had assembled to help move the Afghani freighter's cargo of olives and hashish across the country. With help from his Hell's Angels friends, Moon somehow managed to keep abreast of Smiley and Lizzy's fate.

One of my worst fears of facing the music of American justice for my marijuana crime was magnified when Moon phoned to tell us the latest news about Smiley. According to Moon's sources, Smiley had been hanging tough and planning on going to trial. Then, in a county jail cell, he had an argument with two gang kids who wanted his carton of milk. After failing to verbally intimidate Smiley, the gang members stuffed a pair of socks with soap cakes and used this makeshift weapon to beat Smiley's head while he slept. Word was, Smiley was in a coma for some time. When he woke, he had amnesia, and could barely speak.

Arnie and I had been discussing a voluntary surrender since Smiley's arrest, hoping to build the strength to make some exploratory moves in that direction through my attorney. Smiley's beating killed those thoughts. The possibility of our smiling friend being disfigured for life sent shivers down my spine. We may have been lawbreakers, but we were nonviolent ones. More than ever, a long prison stretch sounded like a death sentence to us.

August 1989, Devil's Lake, Oregon: Sitting on the quiet pier at Devil's Lake, Arnie and I reflected on the four months since the raid in Phoenix. We had decided to separate in case the feds were showing our pictures around the Northwest. Arnie had rented a small retreat in Hood River, and I found a home on an island in Puget Sound. Our vehicles were packed, and Kim was getting the pets together in preparation for yet another journey.

"What happened?" I asked. "We used to have such carefree spirits."

Arnie nodded in silent agreement.

"So many of us made it, put the money into something productive and went on without this witch hunt. My God, why did it have to come to this?"

"We sold a product as recreational as beer," Arnie said, "but illegal. We took the risk and reaped the rewards. But at what cost?"

"I'm tired. Tired of running, tired of hiding. This damn paranoia is wrecking my nerves," I admitted.

"I know, Bud. I know. Mine too."

I skipped a stone across the water. "Doesn't this place remind you of all those summer luaus we had back in Michigan? Remember the look on our parent's faces when we ran around with grass skirts on and yams stuck in our Speedo swim suits?" My stomach knotted as I thought of how much I missed my family and friends.

Arnie let out a long sigh. "You think turning ourselves in is still an option, Bud?"

"No. Look at what happened to Jim. It's safer hiding from the government than being locked up with a bunch of mutants."

I raised my beer in a toast to Jim and Irene, our fallen comrades. What did the future hold for them? What did the future hold for us? We needed normalcy in our lives. Despite the risk, I had decided to relocate Kim and me and our menagerie of pets to Bainbridge Island, where we could try to mend our frazzled nerves.

Arnie wanted to take some classes at an Oregon community college. "I need to be around normal people," he explained.

"Me, too," I said. "Some days this is like being on a bad trip with no hope of ever coming down. My brain's turning into mush. Bainbridge has a tennis club, and Seattle's cultural treasures are only a ferryboat ride away. Kim wants to take tennis lessons."

"She told me," Arnie said. "She sounds excited."

We shook hands.

"Friends to the end, Bud," Arnie vowed.

"Forever," I said. "There's only a three-hour drive between us. When Notre Dame takes the field this season, we'll make a day of it. Tennis and TV. What do you say?"

"Sure, Bud," Arnie said. "Tennis, ND football, and beer."

I headed toward my Ford truck, which contained all I was allowed to love in my fugitive world, my wife and my animals.

"Are you all right, honey?" Kim asked as I climbed in.

Putting aside my melancholy state, I tweaked her on the cheek and smiled. "On the road again," I began to sing in my Willie Nelson impression. And I drove away from Devil's Lake, hoping to somehow enjoy life again with my beautiful wife on an island in Puget Sound.

Summer 1990, Bainbridge Island: A full year had passed. On the surface, life was very sweet. We had a rustic place in the woods with a huge, therapeutic garden where we worked side by side. We decorated the house with many comforting antiques from the old store in Truckee. We fed wild birds and raccoons. We had our pets. We took fishing trips in nearby wilderness areas and sought oysters, clams, and crabs on the Olympic Peninsula. We took the ferry to Seattle for romantic dinners, football games and garden shows. We were befriended by our landlords, Steve and Cathy Wallace. We became members of the Bainbridge Island Racket Club. We stayed physically healthy, and our recreational drug use died with Smiley and Lizzy's demise.

I had managed to create a stable world that revolved around my marriage, without the external stress of jobs, family conflicts, or fugitive reunions. We never spoke about the deep-seated fears we still harbored. For a while, we were able to kill our dark past and bury it beneath the green cedar forest on tranquil Bainbridge Island.

The tennis club let us feel like we were part of a community again, and I enjoyed the older crowd. Slowly but surely it became the center of our social universe. We developed genuine friendships with several of the club's members, and soon were being invited to dinner and cocktail parties. At first I declined these invitations, suspecting there were questions in the minds of our tennis friends about my California cover story and my real estate consultant job. Part of me saw the club as a soap opera setting where the affaire du jour with the tennis pro and island gossip were not the kind of things we needed to be around. Another side of me saw the club as an emotional rescue for my wife and me that allowed us to feel we belonged somewhere and were still normal people.

Our paranoia about blending into the social scene eventually faded, and a false sense of security set in. Kim took lessons and was befriended by several ladies at the club. We became good friends with our neighbors, the Brewer family. Our first Christmas Eve on the island was spent with fellow tennis player and local greeting card artist Fred Schafer, singing carols at the Bloedell Mansion. Arnie arrived on Christmas Day and spent a week.

Life was stable for him, too. He was taking classes at a community college near Hood River, and had made friends with a New Age couple in his neighborhood. He immersed himself in reading books and watching movies. Although he thought about becoming a pro at a local golf course, like me he feared that any job exposure in the real world could lead to questions and an arrest. Arnie decided to be a professional student and live off the money he'd made driving for Smiley and Moon. He joined a tennis club at The Dalles, and we alternated tennis and football weekends between Hood River and Bainbridge.

Throughout this post-Phoenix period, I had kept my Tim Barnes alias alive. There were millions of Barnes listed in America's phone books. Tim was still working in California, where the Greek was constantly asking us to go to Greece with him. Because Smiley had sworn to me during our last conversation that my Barnes identity was not in danger, I saw no harm in keeping Barnes alive two states away from where we were living. I trusted the Greek, and believed that if the government got a trace on Barnes' Social Security number, he would be the first to know and I would be the second. On one trip to San Francisco, I nearly told him my entire story.

"I don't know what you're running from, kid," the old man interrupted, staring at me with fatherly eyes. "And I don't want to know. But I like you. Believe me, *Morea*. Trust me," he whispered. "I have relatives who are connected in Greece. Maybe you can have a business and a family there. Maybe I can help. Maybe I should sell off this business and move there, too," he sighed. "Sometimes I get an urge to return to my roots."

"Thanks," I replied, touched by his apparent sincerity. Since embarking on this odyssey, I'd met dozens of people who saw me as a good man and wanted to befriend me. Such encounters always bolstered my sagging self-esteem. But I could never forget that the government saw me in a different light, the standard image of the dangerous drug dealer. "I'll talk to the wife about making the trip to Greece with you."

As Paul J. Kelly, investment consultant for Peacehaven, the offshore corporation Blake created for me, I looked at many parcels of land in Washington. Sometimes Kim accompanied me. But because of the pets I often went alone, camping, fishing and communing with nature while calling home every night. In eastern Washington near Wenatchee, I fell in love with Lake Chelan and bought some acreage there through Peacehaven. The Chelan Valley was magical. Part of me longed for a place of our own like the chalet I'd built on Grandma Daisy's land a decade earlier. I began having a crazy vision of building a mountain home with Kim while Paul Kelly's employment history with Peacehaven developed. Another part of me knew the government was pissed off because we were still somewhere living free, and they were hell-bent on putting me away. Staying in the Northwest was an illogical move.

One day Moon informed us that Smiley had pleaded guilty in a federal court in Ohio and was sentenced to twelve years. Lizzy, he was told, received six months. Moon was concerned that the math meant Lizzy had supplied the government with information. He'd also heard from one of their customers that Smiley had bragged to a cellmate that he was faking his amnesia. The cellmate passed this information to the prosecutor, who promptly confronted Smiley with it. A plea agreement soon followed. After this news, Moon ceased his efforts to monitor the situation.

Our world on Bainbridge was a blessing, but there were normal, human feelings inside us that Kim and I could not block out forever. Out of fear, we had not called our family members since the Phoenix arrest. Kim's mom, Donna, had gone to a certain payphone once every four months and returned home without hearing from her daughter. Finally, we decided to re-establish the connection.

On the appointed day we drove Kim's Volvo to Neah Bay, the northern most point of Washington's Olympic Peninsula. We decided to make a day of it, packing the cooler with fresh fruit, cheese, and a bottle of wine. Pulling off the road, I discovered the perfect spot for a "pre-call" picnic, an isolated beach just out of view from the highway.

Our mood was light. Kim chatted like an excited schoolgirl, talking about her last visit with her Mom, and wondering what kind of mischief her siblings were getting into. It was the most she'd talked in ages, and I sat back listening to her for a change, enjoying the moment, happy that she could reconnect with her mother. We had both agreed to stop talking about our families long ago, but I knew that the separation of a mother and daughter was difficult.

Sipping the wine, we lay in each other's arms, gazing out to the Pacific Ocean. I spotted a pod of killer whales breaching in the distance. Watching the magnificent creatures play in the natural beauty of the Northwest was a spiritual experience. I squeezed Kim in my arms. As we shared the special moment, the whales frolicked in their freedom. I felt free with them.

"Honey," I said reluctantly, not wanting to interrupt the mood. "It's time to make your call."

She looked up at me and gave me a gentle kiss, ending our afternoon lunch with the promise of further passion.

After driving further up the point, we came upon our destination, an isolated telephone booth. I grabbed my pouch of quarters, and we squeezed in together holding hands. She dialed the long distance number, and then I fed coins into the slot. Far away in a New York shopping mall, a payphone began to ring. It rang once, no answer, twice, no answer. Kim's head drooped.

We had a rule about these prearranged calls. If no one answered after three rings we hung up, fearing FBI heat.

"Hello?" Kim said. She started nodding excitedly. Her face lit up, and she began her conversation with her mother.

My job was to keep feeding the coin slot so the call would not be prematurely disconnected.

"Really?" my wife asked. "No way!" she blurted.

Kim's animated responses to her mother's gossip and news gave me a warm feeling inside. I smiled as I watched my wife soak up information about friends and family from home. Home. How I longed to talk with my own family at that moment.

"Oh Motho, really! Here, say hi to Tom." Kim handed me the phone with a hug.

Hearing this woman's warm voice filled a void within me. I assured her I loved her daughter very much, then handed the receiver back to a bouncy Kim.

When I gave her the signal to wind it up she gave me a pout. I put a few more dollars in the slot and left the booth, allowing them a few moments alone to say good-bye.

I leaned on the Volvo's hood and watched Kim closely. Suddenly the joyous expression on her face changed to one of pain.

Dark clouds covered the sun and rain threatened. Kim hung up the phone and marched toward the car. Tears streamed down her cheeks.

"What's wrong?" I asked, afraid of the answer.

There was none as she silently climbed into the passenger seat and slammed the door. I sat beside her and reached for her hand. She swatted it away, then covered her face with her hands.

"Is your Mom okay?" I asked softly. "Your sister?"

She pulled her hair into little bunches. She drew her knees to her chest and shook her head. Drizzle began coating the windshield.

"Honey, what's wrong?" I asked again.

"Just drive us home, Tom!" she screamed.

Tom? She hadn't called me that in ages.

Silent minutes became uneasy hours. The drizzle turned into a downpour, and she didn't say a word during the long drive back to Bainbridge. When I pulled into our driveway, it was night. "Now tell me what happened," I asked, after killing the engine. She glared at me a moment, then punched the dash and looked away. "Please tell me," I whispered.

She raised her feet to the windshield and pressed her tennis shoes against it with all her might. "My Grandma Wheezy died, and I wasn't there when she asked for me. Okay, Tom?" She kicked the windshield with both feet. "Are you fucking satisfied?"

"I'm so sorry, honey," I said, remembering the kind old lady with the Persian cat she'd introduced me to back in Indiana.

When I tried to hug her, she went crazy and began kicking the windshield repeatedly and cursing. "Sorry just doesn't cut it, Tom!"

I tried to grab her legs, but she blocked my arms and went into a frenzy—clawing and kicking the Volvo's windshield until it bowed and shattered. I jumped out, ran to the passenger side and pulled her from the car. I held her tight and said, "That won't bring her back, honey."

She grew limp, lay her head upon my chest and sobbed, "You're so right. Right as always, Tom. Nothing we're missing, not one damn thing I'm giving up for this can ever be brought back."

I felt sick inside. She was right. I wondered how I'd feel if my mom died while I was on the run. I tried to picture going back and turning myself in, but all I could see was a dark prison and Smiley being beaten in his sleep with socks stuffed with soap cakes.

Her lip was bleeding. She lifted one foot gingerly and I led her to the door. "Make me a drink," she hissed. "Make us both a good strong drink."

After the news of her grandma's death, Kim went into a depression. When Moon called to invite us for a visit to Canada, she opted to stay home with the animals, her African Violet collection, and her tennis friends. She made it clear that with the exception of Arnie, whom she considered family, she wanted nothing to do with our fugitive circle. It had been months since I'd seen Moon, and I felt a meeting was necessary. I appreciated his friendship, and he had offered to buy all my gold and help transfer the money overseas to my account through his banking connections in Montreal. The business side of me believed it was time to put all but a fraction of my remaining assets overseas where they would earn interest, as opposed to collecting mold.

I still called Bill and Leigh on a monthly basis. They had moved to

Vancouver Island and rented a home there as Scott, Laura, and Shannon Daley. Shannon was attending a day school. Bill was working on an elaborate scheme to acquire solid Canadian ID in Alberta, and had found a banking connection in Vancouver he could trust. Bill was involved with Moon in his ID scam and still investing in the hashish trips, although he denied the latter. Like me, he was convinced he could start a business and somehow blend in and hold his family together. Like us, they had joined a racket club for health and friendship. When Moon mentioned meeting in Canada, I decided to visit the Daley family, too.

The ferry left from Port Angeles, Washington. I went alone. Moon met me at Victoria on Vancouver Island, and took me to his hotel in Oak Bay. Other people staying there had come to meet him for business discussions. Moon had talked about his "crew" before, but I'd never met them. That night, I agreed to have dinner with his workers, one of who would drive to San Francisco and pick up the gold coins I was cashing in.

It was an interesting dinner table.

Moon introduced an enormous gentleman with no visible neck as Cowboy. He wore a ten-gallon hat, western clothing, and spoke in a soft, cultured manner. "Please to meet you, Kelly," Cowboy said with a distinct Texas accent as he crushed my hand in his.

"Cowboy's my right hand man up here," Moon said. "He's a former Green Beret, and a present chapter head of the Hell's Angels. This is Mad Max." Moon gestured at a dapper-looking gent whose single gold earring looked out of place with his conservative business suit. "Max is my money man. He's going on a mission for me next week that will give me the same set up you've got offshore, different place of course."

"Pleased to meet you," said Max with a hint of French in his tone. "Any friend of...*Moon's* is a friend of mine."

"Last but not least," Moon said. "This large but lovely lady is on my driving team."

The big brunette with a model's face and a weightlifter's build extended her hand. When I kissed it, she blushed coyly. A second later she shook my hand with more force than Cowboy had.

"We call her The Wrestler," Moon snickered. "Because before she met Cowboy here, that's what she did for a living."

The next day, Bill and Leigh came to the hotel. He had hired a fishing boat for a luncheon and a half-day salmon-fishing trip in the bay. It was a revealing afternoon for me.

Bill was relaxed. He spoke candidly and in great detail of his plan to acquire Canadian ID. He was convinced that even if he were arrested in the years to come, Canada would not extradite him to face America's harsh sentencing laws for pot dealers. After a few beers, Bill casually mentioned marrying a Vancouver hooker if he had to, to achieve residence status.

I had to laugh, even though his remark underscored the hidden desperation in both of us. The one thing I knew for certain about Bill was that he loved Leigh and Shannon. That afternoon, I sensed a mellowing between us. After all that had happened, for all our differences, we still had a lot in common. We wanted to keep our wives, our money, and our freedom. Deep inside we wanted to get off this mad train ride as bad as our better halves. But we couldn't, and wouldn't face the music voluntarily. We were strong Leo men, but not that strong.

Moon and I went canoeing and fishing. I hit tennis balls with Bill and Leigh and spent one night at their home. On what became my last evening, we went to a restaurant with Moon and his crew. It was just a social gathering, and that's all we did, socialize. Minus the cocaine from the Smiley era, we had a great time that ended at a local nightclub. I was drunk and feeling like one of the gang. After dancing with Leigh and flirting with the cocktail waitress, around eleven I decided to call Kim on Bainbridge.

While I fed the payphone quarters to complete the connection, I flirted with the talkative lady operator. When my call went through, Kim was beside herself. She had overheard my discussion with the operator and blew up like she had in London. I hadn't done anything wrong, but I knew she was still hurting from the call to her mother. It was time for me to head home.

Before I left, Moon told me what had been obvious: he was gearing up for one big last run. He also made it clear that he was laying the groundwork to make the permanent move overseas. He didn't say where and I didn't ask.

"I'm seeing a little Jewish number back east," Moon said. "What if we can get together around the holidays and celebrate your fifth wedding anniversary with some skiing? Maybe you and Kim would like to meet her." He cleared his throat. "We're thinking of living together in another country."

I was surprised to hear him even hint of being lonely enough to consider cohabitation. "Maybe," I replied. I drew a deep breath and wondered how I'd managed to keep my marriage together for nearly five years. "Sonny," I said. "I like you, man. You're generous and caring. We're friends. You've got your millions now, right? You believe in karma, right?"

Moon frowned. "What's your point?"

"Why do you need the proverbial last run?"

He shook his head. "Why? Oy vay," he sighed as he put an arm around my shoulder. "A man can get tired of marriage. A man can get tired of running, too. But a man can never get tired of making money. The big money is mine now, man. Shit. They could legalize pot in Canada next year and all the profit would be gone. All I can say is that when there's a damn Drug War going on, you don't surrender, Chief. You keep on trucking."

That September the Greek bought his tickets and offered me one last chance to meet his mysterious Uncle Nikos. Kim was terrified about flying under her paper trip passport again, and it took weeks for me to talk her into going. "I need to see Blake and Jones, and want to give Greece a look," I said. "Arnie says he'll come and stay with the animals. I don't want to leave without you," I pleaded.

Taking that last trip together out of the country was one more mistake in a long line of mistakes. We didn't need to go, and we weren't mentally up to the task. Kim was still shaken by the death of her grandmother, and the Phoenix raid and Smiley's beating were always in the back of my mind. Although we encountered no trouble at any passport checks, I perceived a frightening change in my own demeanor. I was definitely losing my nerve.

In London, Keith Jones managed to avoid me during our five-day stay at Blake's flat. Lloyds of London was in the beginning stages of a long, hard fall from grace that began with Iran sinking oil tankers in the Persian Gulf, and was accelerated by a series of worldwide storms and disasters. Lloyds' primary business was insuring people, places and things. It was time for the "Names" like Jones who'd been living on easy street for years to start paying their dues. It wasn't just me. Keith Jones the financial player was avoiding all his creditors.

We stayed a weekend in Guernsey with the Blakes, whose marriage was once again healthy. Blake and I discussed my pending trip to Greece and the possibilities of buying land there. "Be very careful about investing in Greece," Tim advised me. "It's easy to move funds into Greece, but quite difficult to extract them."

Athens was a mess. Greece had just lost their Olympic bid to Atlanta, and I perceived some heavy anti-American sentiment. The airline, the trash collectors, the utilities, the whole country was on strike. We met the Greek and his wife at a hotel in Athens and were introduced to several of his relatives during the following week. One night at a restaurant in the city we met the mysterious Uncle Nikos.

Talk about cold. Nikos was a stout bowling ball of a man with black eyes that beamed barbarously at mine from across the dinner table. As he carved his lamb, Nikos conjured up images of a military dictator who took expatriate Americans like me to his torture chamber. I envisioned myself hanging upside down in a dungeon with electric wires connected to my tender mercies. I envisioned Nikos nodding to the man with his finger on the electric power button, then saying in his gravelly voice, "This can all end at any time, Mr. Kelly. Kindly call your banker and have the money transferred to my Swiss account. Oh yes, *Morea*, did I forget to tell you that your wife Diana has the body of a goddess?"

After dinner I took the Greek to the bathroom for a heart-to-heart. I told him I had changed my mind about having a frank talk with Nikos concerning my questions about protection and permanent residency in Greece.

"The guy is packing a gun under his jacket," I told the Greek.

"*Morea*, he's a high level member of the secret police."

"He gives me the creeps," I said. "I don't feel relaxed in Athens, and my wife's scared to death."

"I understand," replied the Greek. "Maybe you are better off staying in America. After all, in ancient Greece, the harshest punishment was exile."

The Nikos encounter made us want to go running back to Bainbridge, but I had rented a romantic villa in Lindos on the Isle of Rhodes. Our flights were booked and the villa was paid for. Even as a kid in Indiana on Berry Road, I had always dreamed of vacationing on a small Greek Island with a beautiful woman at my side.

The Greek came to Rhodes for one week. He and his wife stayed with us in the villa. We took a few trips to the old markets looking for coins, and we talked about my strange situation and the two names he knew me as, Kelly and Barnes. Before the Greek headed off to Thessaloniki where he had relatives and ancient gold coins to see, I told him I was selling off my collection. I admitted that friends of mine had gotten in trouble with the law, and said I didn't want him getting involved. Someone would come to get the contents of my box, and soon I would also end my employment with him.

The Greek nodded slowly. "You're a good man, *Morea*," he said. "I hope you don't have to run forever. Keep in touch."

Alone in Lindos, and for the first time in our fugitive run, my wife and I reflected at length and from the heart about the life we were living. She told me I was losing my sensitivity and the zest for life that had first attracted her. Living on the edge was killing her, and she asked how we could ever really enjoy life again without some peace of mind about the future. Hearing her finally air her thoughts fueled a growing self-doubt in me.

One night we got drunk at a restaurant in Lindos and wound up sitting beneath the stars with the owner and his mistress. The owner looked like Cuba's Castro, and we spoke for hours about politics, love and excessive government control over its citizens' daily lives and decisions. Long after the restaurant closed, Kim and I wandered the narrow paths of Lindos, talking about our marriage.

"You fit in anywhere," she told me. "I don't. I don't like politics, and I don't care about government interference. Sometimes lately, I don't care about anything. I think I'd rather be barefoot and pregnant in Indiana."

"Do you still love me?" I asked, fearing the answer.

"I love you," she said sadly. "But I don't love this life anymore. I don't like meeting people like Nikos and that man at the restaurant tonight with his slutty mistress. I don't like the way you're always thinking about managing your money, either."

The writer in me had always enjoyed the freedom to seek out interesting people and talk openly with them. I did not regret remaining open to such meetings, but the money remark made me think. Was I really too absorbed in taking care of it?

"Blake will be managing my funds from here on out," I said. "By next year all my assets will be making money for us. We won't have to worry about whether a storage building or a safety deposit box has been broken into."

"I don't worry about the money," she said. "I worry about us. What are we going to do about us?"

My mind drifted. On that night in Lindos I knew beyond a doubt that she wanted to leave the madness as bad as I did, but lacked the strength. The concept of leaving my wife and living alone somewhere like Greece while my account made hundreds of thousands a year was as impossible for me as surrendering to my Drug War pursuers and voluntarily going to prison. I was committed.

"Try and stay together," was all that I could say.

Rhodes was a peaceful place, but we were not at peace. Kim acted cold and distant after our discussions. We argued and drank more than we ever had right up until the last few days, when we decided to do what we'd been doing for most of our five years on the run, enjoy the moment and drink life's poetry.

We sat on the roof of our villa and watched the moon and stars at night. She modeled for my camera in the villa's courtyard, and we rented an open-aired jeep and drove to the valley of the butterflies. We combed the beaches for bits of smooth aged glass, seashells and brightly colored stones. From the shores of Rhodes, we could see the coast of Turkey on the hazy horizon. Iraq had invaded Kuwait that August, and as we gathered life's simple treasures in Kim's netted bag, I sensed dark clouds of war and turmoil gathering all around me. For nearly five years I'd been trying to keep our love alive and build a dream we could hold onto and share. But just like the warplanes I saw in my mind as I stared off toward Turkey, there were no dreams out there. It was getting harder by the day for me to separate fantasy from reality.

Back on Bainbridge, we fell into a pattern of tennis, home, pets, Seattle weekends, and pretending to be the cunning Kellys, safe in our fantasy island world. Months passed, and when the demons of reality haunted our minds, we slew them with drinking, love making, and

and cuddly sleeps—then stuffed them back in their dark Pandora's box.

A monster storm slammed into the island just before the Christmas of 1990. The wind howled for days and nights and rare snow piled high against the cedars outside our door. Wells froze and power lines fell. People on the island banded together to weather the storm. I rescued tennis club friends with my four-wheel drive truck. Many of us took showers at the racket club, which had hot water and a generator.

Our neighbor Ginny Brewer and her boys came over to share our fire and some company. In a living room lit by candles and warmed by a Ben Franklin's hearth, we listened to NPR report on the pending war in the Gulf. At the end of each night I'd stoke the fire that kept our animals and us warm. In the middle of the night I'd wake to check the stove, and end up having the same foreboding thoughts about our house being raided, shots being fired, and me being arrested. It was strange. I couldn't shut my mind down, or stop the nightmare. I decided that news of war and the many dark days of the storm were stirring my anxiety.

When the skies cleared over Bainbridge, we walked to Battle Point Park and saw six ducks frozen to death in the pond, where their sleeping limbs had been shackled in thin ice when the great storm came. The scene conjured up visions of my arrest in broad daylight, as if I intuitively knew my run was coming to a close. I felt like I was cracking up, but never said a word about it to Kim. That evening, I wrote my first prose poem in years.

Things change, it began. *We are vain enough to think we can control destiny. One day our world is built on solid ground, then suddenly the earth trembles, tectonic plates collide and the illusion of life is shaken from its fragile foundation.*

I did not remember all the words that filled two entire pages. But I did remember coming home from Seattle after seeing a live performance of *The Nutcracker* with Kim, and having her confront me with the poem. It was two days before our last Christmas together. She called it morbid.

"What does this mean?" she asked me with misty brown eyes.

"I don't know," I answered.

"Are you all right, honey?" she asked. "Are you sure you want to take this ski trip?"

"Sure, Meekla," I said. "We were married in a ski gondola, and this is our fifth wedding anniversary. It might be the last chance we get to see Moon, too. We're going to Sunriver."

On Wednesday January 9, 1991, I was in Sunriver, Oregon on the last full day of a fugitive rendezvous and ski week with Moon and Arnie. My disappearance act was in its fifth year. That night I reappeared on *Unsolved Mysteries*. I never saw the show. Calls came in to the studio from several parts of the country, where people swore I was the fugitive neighbor living next door. The most damning call was rumored to have come from a member of a tennis club on Bainbridge Island.

Without knowing any of this, the next morning Moon, Arnie and I packed our cars and left the keys inside our vacation rental. We said our good-byes. Moon and his jeweler friend climbed inside their silver 1991 Lexus. Arnie crammed his big body inside the cab of his little Nissan truck, and Kim and I boarded our warm Ford full of squawking birds. This three-vehicle convoy motored north on Oregon's scenic Highway 97, until Arnie took the fork in the road towards The Dalles and his Hood River hideaway. Moon and his mistress waved as we passed them at the entrance to a Madras, Oregon gas station.

I have not seen any of them since that day.

It was 11:40 on the morning of January 14, 1991. Three days had passed since Moon called to warn me that one of his crew had thought they saw me on *Unsolved Mysteries*. After five years of living a lie, I didn't have the heart to run any longer. I had just slipped on my lucky gold lion ring, tucked my brown leather valise under my arm and exited the house on Bainbridge Island, locking the door behind me. The sky was blue, the island uncommonly quiet. Two cats relaxed upon the rail, fat and sassy in the noonday sun. I hopped into my Ford and started the engine.

Seconds later, Smokey pounced on the hood and pawed wildly at the windshield. When I stepped out and grabbed him, he rabbit-kicked my gut, hissed and jumped to the ground. The little calico, Punkin, let out an eerie cry, catapulted from the rail and dove beneath the deck, where Smokey promptly joined her. And there, crouched side by side, eyes bulging, whiskers twitching, they screamed a silent warning for me to come and hide.

Then I heard the sounds: engines revving, spinning tires spitting gravel, heavy bodies snapping tree branches! I held my breath. The sounds grew louder.

The thought of running never occurred to me. Forget the movies. Forget dreams. This was it. Time for a dose of pure reality. As precious freedom seconds ticked away, my heart raced and I stood my ground straight-faced, knowing this was the only way for it to end.

They came through the woods. They came from behind the red horse barn—fast-moving men wearing matching dark windbreakers with US MARSHAL in yellow lettering. A plain looking sedan slid sideways blocking my truck, and two agents jumped out with guns drawn.

"FBI! FREEZE!"

In late January of 1991, the Bureau of Prison's Con-Air transported me from Oklahoma's El Reno penitentiary to Chicago's Metropolitan Correctional Center. From there a team of US Marshals took me back to South Bend. This journey was the reality I'd been unable to face for five long years. It was like stepping back in time. I stared out the mesh-covered van windows at the flat countryside along the Indiana toll road, then saw Notre Dame's golden dome at the South Bend exit. As we approached downtown I scanned the sidewalks for familiar faces. Flashbacks filled my head, longing for my wife burned in my heart.

That night during a phone call from the county jail, Mom told me that my dad had died a few weeks earlier from cancer. She didn't have any way of telling me when I was in solitary confinement in El Reno, and she'd decided I didn't need any more bad news. After all the years of post-divorce bitterness, I was happy when Mom said they'd been friends again in his final months. I went to bed staring at the bars, regretting how my running had prevented me from seeing my father during the last five years of his life.

The last thing I thought of before I slept was the intense "out-of-body" dream I had in an El Reno prison cell. Part of that vision had depicted my dad dying, the other hinted my wife would leave me.

With my Houston attorney present, I plead not guilty to all counts in a federal courtroom. Mom and Kim's heads sank when the government declared I was facing 240 years in prison for my part in a marijuana conspiracy. I held my head held high during the hearing, but it dropped when I was whisked away to the marshals' holding cell where I had a depressing talk with my Houston lawyer.

Jerry Patchen told me he had concluded that because of the Northern District of Indiana's attempt to indict him on obstruction of justice charges during my run, he felt it was best for me to hire another attorney. I needed someone from the area who could detoxify the negative image that had been developed during my fugitive years. Patchen was also against having any involvement with my offshore bank account.

"Bill McCarthy has hired an attorney named Rick Kammen," Jerry said. "Bill is fighting his extradition hard in Canada and stands a fair chance of succeeding. His lawyer is rumored to despise clients who take plea bargains. Looks like you and Bill will both be going to trial, if he does in fact return."

It happened so quickly. I didn't fully comprehend why Jerry was distancing himself from me. All I could do was listen and nod as he concluded by telling me to interview a list of attorneys and promising to work closely from Houston with whomever I selected. As we shook hands and said goodbye, I sensed I was losing my best chance at winning my battle in the Drug War before it ever began.

Chicago's Metropolitan Correctional Center, a federal holding facility, was a high-rise purgatory, a hotbed of smoldering tempers, a depression pit designed to make criminal defendants crack under pressure, or so its more astute occupants claimed. They were made up of organized crime figures, porno kings, rapists, robbers, abortion clinic bombers, and a few murderers, but most of them were accused of dealing hard drugs like cocaine and heroin. Men with bitterness and hate beaming from their eyes hung around phones in a haze of cigarette smoke, waiting to talk to their wives, lovers, family, friends and lawyers. Everyone was on edge. People shuffled around the dining floor babbling mindlessly with food dangling from their faces, medicated with psychotropic drugs like thorazine because they couldn't handle the pressure. The place reminded me of the nut ward in *One Flew Over the Coo-coo's Nest.* There were bloody fights every night. Someone got convicted or sentenced every day. Someone secretly agreed to testify against their homeboy, their mother, or their brother every week, then were quickly relocated to the "snitch floor" for protection. It was primarily a male-dominated institution, but one level was filled with women. The black brothers called it "the bitch floor."

Three types of men were housed in the MCC-Chicago: predators, prey, and people like me who wanted to keep to themselves. Keeping to yourself was an impossible dream. I was sent to one area designated for pretrial defendants, floor fifteen. On fifteen I was assigned to one of the scores of two-man cells. My cellmate was a huge white man in his late twenties. Brian was the first institutionalized person I ever met. He had just finished a five-year "bit" in Manard state prison for armed robbery, and was waiting for the feds to dismiss a detainer on him. Brian called our cell "the house." He had an arrest record dating back to puberty and a rap sheet longer than a Michener novel. Like many prisoners, Brian could not read or write. In an effort to get along, I read the letters his mom sent him, and wrote a response. He quickly befriended me.

Brian was a psycho and a racist. He could talk about his ex-wife lovingly one minute, then scream; "I'll kill the cunt when I get out!" He ranted and raved about how the black El Rucan gang ran the MCC. "They control the laundry, the drugs, and even the fucking food! Most of the damn guards are niggers from the same hood as the El Rucans. Just 'cause Jesse Jackson's half-brother is one of their leaders they get to run things. I can't even get a joint in this place."

Brian scared me. The last thing in the world I needed was to be stoned in a six by eight cell with a psycho who bragged about beating dope dealers with gun butts until they told him where their money was. The racial tension also got under my skin. Things sure had changed since the '70s when I used to pass joints at concerts to afro-headed blacks who were grooving to the same Jimmy Hendrix tunes as I was.

There were some basic things I needed in prison, like stamps, greeting cards, and shower shoes to protect my feet from the rampant foot diseases. I discovered it would be weeks before I got a few dollars cleared into my MCC commissary account. For more years than I could remember, money had not been a problem. Suddenly I didn't have fifty thousand legal dollars to hire a new lawyer, or even five bucks to acquire a few comforts in prison. All my money was in Europe, and it couldn't buy a can of soda from the MCC vending machine. Valentine's Day was approaching fast. I got a set of colored pencils from the prison chaplain and made cards for Kim and my mom. When the men of floor fifteen saw the beauty I created from the pain in my heart, I was overwhelmed with prepaid requests for my cards and poems.

"Make up one for my old lady, Writer Man," they'd say.

Like my spending account, it would be a while before my visiting list was approved and entered in the system. At least every day I was able to call Kim or Mom collect. I also received greeting cards in the mail. Sometimes I'd be on the phone and a fight would break out a few feet away. I'd try and cover the receiver so they couldn't hear the fists and the cursing, but they heard. "Be careful in there, Tommy," my mom would say.

Most fights were over homosexual involvement, drugs, booze, or gambling, none of which interested me. I'd reassure my mom by telling her that no one in the MCC wanted to fight with an old pot dealer. But the reality was that people got beat up for just looking at someone wrong after they'd had a disturbing phone conversation.

Kim had moved in with her girlfriend's parents in South Bend and was having trouble eating and sleeping. It hurt me inside to hear her telling me she wasn't whole without her cuddly lion sleeping beside her. I hungered for her more than freedom, or family, or money. It drove me crazy every time I had to hang up the phone when my fifteen minutes was over. I'd head to my cell holding back tears and reread the greeting cards she'd sent me.

Thomas, when this is over I'll pick you up like Kirk Douglas or Bert Lancaster in one of those old convict movies. We'll hit the first rest stop and make up for lost time! I promise. Thomas, this time will pass and no one and nothing will ever separate us again! Love forever, Raccoon.

In our seven years together I had never seen Kim write anything. Her words meant a lot to me. I'd read them again and again, then arrange them on my bunk like an altar in hell, and worship our love.

After lockdown, I spent my nights on the top bunk listening to Brian crack his knuckles and grunt between pushups. "Don't let your ass get weak in here, cellie," he'd say. "And don't expect your woman to do this time with you. I know what I'm talking about. I've been where you're going, to gladiator school. Speaking of war, there's a couple of fucks here on fifteen whose necks might need to be snapped if they don't quit glaring at me in the chow line."

I'd spend hours staring though our small window slit at the bustling streets of Chicago below, where hookers and crack dealers sold their stuff beneath the neon lights of a rundown Chinese restaurant. I'd reread Kim's cards, then write long love letters to her. I'd think about my dead dad and recall our house-painting days on Berry Road. Eventually, Brian would burn up his hyper-energy and plop his 240 pounds in the bed below mine, sending a cloud of body odor my way. The nights always ended the same, with him asking me to describe one of the places I'd traveled to, and me talking until he started snoring like a freight train.

I didn't sleep much, but when I did Brian would inevitably wake me with one of his nightmares, screaming and cursing satanic phrases and threats in voices that would curdle the blood of Stephen King. Sometimes he'd shout so loud that the guard would come by and shine his flashlight in on us. I'd lie on the top bunk with my pillow over my face, trying to fight the fear of uncertainty I felt inside as my downward slide accelerated.

Two months later I was working on my fifth cellmate and a stomach ulcer. Brian had been taken to the hole after a bloody battle with a black guy whose tattoo job he'd botched. In my initial months behind bars I saw more violence than I had in my entire life. I hated violence, and seeing it on a daily basis was beginning to get to me. Reading my wife's greeting cards became the most comforting thing in my life. Inside the MCC and Indiana's county jails each day seemed like a week. Outside in the real world, things were moving fast—and always in the wrong direction.

My new lawyer, who I'd selected for his apparent sympathetic views on pot laws as well as the pro bono work he did for death row inmates, had filed many motions on my behalf and reviewed stacks of government documents compiled during my fugitive years. The longer Charles A. Asher studied the facts, the more certain he became that my only chance for survival was to plead guilty and cooperate. The government had found letters in my mail drop that led to our main self-storage unit in Oregon. The money and art in it were seized. The government also claimed to have found a letter detailing my offshore account. I thought it was a bluff. I could not remember having saved such a letter in our storage or anywhere, but Asher swore they had one and were taking steps to freeze the account. I thought about Bill in Canada where our northern neighbors were still refusing to send him back to face America's pot laws. I wondered if his cash and account had escaped the arrest, and if his now-freed wife was able to help him conceal them from the government.

I had counted on my wife to be my partner and keep in touch with my English money manager, but Kim had long since said she was afraid to call Blake again. I could not push her to communicate with him against her will, yet Kim was the only person Blake would talk to openly about my account. Oddly enough, she swore no one was influencing her or questioning her. I assumed her dad was, but every time I mentioned the possibility of him trying to help us, she refused to discuss it and got nervous, then mad. I could only hope Blake was hiding what he could, because at this point, my crisis mentality was putting money down the list and making preserving my marriage a top priority.

Every time my lawyer filed a motion I was chained and transported back to an Indiana county jail to spend a few nights sleeping in a filthy crowded cell on a floor mat next to a toilet. Then I briefly appeared in court before the judge. Kim managed to talk the marshals into letting me wear a suit and tie for these appearances. Putting on the suit made me feel like Superman. Smelling Kim's perfume and feeling my old clothes became a comforting, strengthening ritual for me, just as wearing my old shirts to bed had become one for her. After each appearance I would change back into my prison jumpsuit and battle depression.

In the initial weeks Kim put on a strong face for our visits. She would take the train from South Bend or drive with my mom. We'd all hold hands for hours and feel warm inside. We'd discuss my case, but legal talk was like a foreign language to them. We'd kiss when Mom got up to walk, and the guard would come and warn me of the penalty for kissing my wife more than once at the beginning and once at the end of our visit. The sick thing was that while he was saying this, one of the local gang members would be lifting his lady's skirt by the vending machine and shaking all the candy inside it. I couldn't believe they allowed that to go on, especially with children in the room. My mom wanted to say something when she saw this sex act, but I told her I'd learned at the MCC that it was best to mind your own business. I said according to Jesse Jackson's half-brother, Noah, who was one of the jailhouse lawyers I talked to, the government was providing sex, booze, and drugs to members of the El Rucan gang with the hope of turning key members into snitches.

"I have seen the drugs and booze myself," I said. "How does heroin, cocaine, and fifths of vodka get into a secure place like this?"

"Our government would never do that," Mom said.

"Don't kid yourself," I snapped. "It's a dirty little war on both sides and the only goal is grabbing the money and showing statistics." I lowered my voice and whispered, "Word is they even bug the attorney-client rooms."

Kim and my mom looked at me like I was talking crazy, but the story of government misconduct in the MCC would eventually be reported in the *Atlantic Monthly.*

All we could do was talk about our hope for winning a trial, and my future plans as a free and normal person. Mom wanted to put up the money for my legal fees. She'd also spoken to my new lawyer and wanted me to take a plea. I told her I couldn't and didn't want her or my relatives spending their hard-earned savings on my defense.

I had always been a positive person in a position to give, and taking was not a palatable option to me. Every time they left with pained expressions I smiled and waved while my insides turned to jello. My loved ones were hurting inside because of me, and for the first time in my life I was turning negative, and powerless to help them. My depression got worse after each visit.

Prison paranoia was a dangerous disease. It didn't take long before all the negative energy in the MCC started making me become distrustful of everyone from my lawyer to my wife. All around me people were saying that a drug conspiracy defendant didn't have a chance in hell of winning a trial. "At least your case is under 'old law' sentencing guidelines," the jailhouse lawyers told me. "You're gonna get some time, Thomas. Just be glad your case isn't under these tougher 'new law' guidelines. At least you'll get parole. Even some of the worst judges are bitching about losing their sentencing discretion to harsh mandatory minimum sentences."

My *real* lawyer echoed this cry. And when the government offered its first plea bargain to save the cost of going to trial, Asher advised me to accept it. The plea would have had me doing over twelve years for carrying on "continuing criminal enterprise." I'd studied the "discovery" documents my lawyer gave me listing all the other co-conspirators' sentences. Bill McCarthy's suppliers in Florida who had delivered tens of thousands of pounds did less than two years in prison. Maui Bert's sentence was also light. My main customer, a repeat offender named Dan Morissette, had gotten only eighteen months from the judge in

Indiana. I couldn't understand why I was being advised to take such a plea. Recent conversations with MCC jailhouse lawyers had me imagining my attorney dining with government prosecutors in South Bend and joking about how quickly his former millionaire and *Unsolved Mystery* client was falling apart.

'Continuing criminal enterprise is like some Mafia charge," I said to Charles A. Asher. "Is it the TV show publicity, or what? I'm not some evil sacrifice whose blood will make Americans stop smoking pot. Whether you agree or not, I'm going to trial."

Asher told me he had no fear about going to trial, only the outcome. He reminded me it was the '90s and that my case was in northern Indiana. He also suggested I find a way to pay the fifty thousand dollars he estimated his services would require. He asked me to think about it.

There was nothing to think about. Only a madman would give up his money and friends and agree to go to prison for twelve years. And I wasn't that crazy yet.

I didn't know if it was my paranoia or my intuition, but suddenly I perceived a change in my wife. I didn't want to believe it was happening, but all the signs were there. Some nights she wasn't home for my calls, and the love-cards weren't coming as often. The visits dropped off to once a week and she came alone. Her brown raccoon eyes, normally bright and cheery, seemed sad and evasive. We'd exchange small talk about the pets and the job she took with an old school friend's construction company, but more and more of our visits were spent watching gang members poke their women by the vending machine while we sat in awkward silence. I sensed that she wanted me to confront her about my fear, but it was like turning myself in voluntarily. I couldn't do it.

Instead I tried to rationalize my fear. This was not the young rebel wife and partner who had spent the last seven years of her life with me. Lately she spoke of "being on the edge of a breakdown" and "wanting to see a priest." Like me, she was growing insecure, sleepless, neurotic, and troubled with the task of redefining right and wrong while surviving as best she could in a world that again included family and friends. She was working for the first time in years doing heavy lifting and painting. I should have been happy she had a job to keep her busy and get some cash coming in. Someone had broken into her storage locker and ransacked it looking for drug money. Our cat, Smokey, had been hit by a car. No wonder she was acting strange.

In the MCC I had too much time to worry, and worry was chiseling away at my sanity. Every time I returned from seeing Kim I suffered from migraines and heard voices in my head for hours. Maybe ours was more of a physical marriage. Maybe if I was no longer there to have and to hold she could not survive on emotion alone. Unlike her I had no choice but to hang on to my love and memories, or I'd be doing the thorazine shuffle like all the guys on psychotropic drugs. I needed her love more than anything, but I didn't want to push her away. I could feel the pressure in my head building every day. My June trial date was getting closer. I needed all my energy to keep it together. I dismissed my intuitive visiting room observations and decided it was just prison paranoia.

The fugitive chapter of my life was history, but by the spring of 1991, I had already relived it a thousand times. The underground life I came to hate seemed like heaven after a few months in Chicago's MCC and Indiana's county jails. My marriage was fading, the government froze my money, and my lawyer was advising me to take a plea that would have me doing twelve years in prison. Every day I read legal documents, hoping to find a way out. All I did was discover the depth of my old friends' betrayal. Their words cut like a knife. The two things I wanted to see most, Smiley and Lizzy's FBI debriefing notes and the letter the government claimed to have detailing my account, were never provided. Legalese, love sickness, prison paranoia, and sensory deprivation from being locked in a skyscraper for months were scrambling my brain. Cards and visits from my wife were fewer and far between. Kim's mom wrote to tell me how much her daughter loved me, but I rarely heard it from Kim. More and more of my phone time was spent talking with my family. I felt I was headed for a total breakdown.

One day my lawyer handed me some new documents. One was a letter Bill McCarthy had written while we were on the run, telling the feds about my offshore bank account. Asher told me he had gotten out on bond in Canada. The US government was furious and concerned that Bill would run again. My lawyer looked me in the eye and said the United States Attorney was offering me one last chance to plead guilty. "It's a good offer," he explained. "They want you to plead to five counts and they'll drop the rest."

I focused on the initials CAA that my lawyer had embroidered on his shirt pocket, and asked what the bottom line was.

"They want you to not contest the money and tell your story...all of it. It's called an open plea agreement. If the judge gave you the maximum on all five counts and ran them consecutively, you could get forty-two years."

"Screw that!" I said. "For pot? That's a murderer's sentence! I thought you said you fought for death row inmates for free."

"I do."

"And you want me to plead to that? No way! Get ready for trial, Charley."

"Listen, Tom, hear me out. With a show of faith on your part, some diplomacy by me, and a little luck..."

"Fuck luck," I said. "I like guarantees."

"No guarantees, Tom," he said matter-of-factly. "They won't go for it. But if we can get the judge to run your sentences concurrently, you could possibly get a ten-year term and come out on parole in forty months."

"I want that in writing."

"Damn it, Tom. Will you listen to me? You hired me to get you the shortest sentence possible. I'm going to tell you how. Give up the money first. It's the best chance you have of surviving this thing and preserving your marriage."

"I'm listening," I said, wishing I were privy to his closed-door conversations with the government about me. "And how will I pay you for your services?"

He wanted me to send a letter to my banker requesting a full disclosure of my assets. With such a show of faith, he believed he could convince the government that I was not the gangster I was being portrayed as. He had discussed my cash dilemma with his colleagues as well. None of my family members would have to borrow money for my defense, he assured me. He would be paid from my forfeited account by the government.

"Think about it, Tom," he said. "It's definitely your last chance for a survivable outcome in an Indiana court."

"I will, Charley," I said, feeling the ultimate pressure of being between the proverbial rock and a hard place.

That night on floor fifteen, a huge black man who I'd spoken to several times about art and poetry returned from his last day in court. He had been found guilty of dealing cocaine and carrying firearms. The brother was older than me, and tougher from his many years in the street. He had a gentle spirit, but no one on fifteen messed with him. When he wanted the phone or extra food, he got it. In return for my advice on poetry he had offered me some on surviving prison time, since this was his third offense. After chow he went off the deep end and "bitch-slapped" a guy until he was senseless. He'd slammed another guy's head into the concrete wall and split it open like a melon. Then he stripped off his jumpsuit and proceeded to rinse the blood off his body in the shower. When ten o'clock count time and lockdown came he stayed in the shower singing Gospel music and refused to go to his cell as required. It took five guards from the goon squad to remove that big naked man from that tiny shower in cuffs and chains. As they dragged him to the elevator en route to the hole, every man on fifteen could hear him screaming that he'd rather die than get anotner long bit in prison.

The plan came to me on the roof of the MCC. It was a gray day and I was walking in circles wearing the ratty green parka the guard had draped over my shoulders. The roof was where we went for recreation once a week or so since the weather had broken, and it was the only place that came close to the sky and nature that gave me energy during the fugitive era. I felt like the lost alien in the movie ET. I was dying from the inside out. I held a damaged Walkman radio I'd taped a dozen times, and wished I could use it to contact a spaceship that would beam me off my crazy world. I'd found an "oldies" station and was listening to tunes that reminded me of better days. I had a tough decision to make, and the time had come to make it.

Mom, my siblings and my lawyer wanted me to take this last chance plea bargain. Kim said it was up to me, but she said it in a way which made me think she was embarrassed by the idea of my cooperating. A jailhouse lawyer said, "Go to trial and don't give the government a goddamn dime. Take a bit of advice from an old timer, you'll miss the cash long after the girl has deserted you." I smiled and told him he was talking to an incurably romantic marijuana man.

If I lost a trial in Indiana, I could end up doing more time than my marriage, my mom, or me might be able to survive. But there were other things to consider, like my conscience and the code of the herb business I'd vowed to keep since my first deal at Tucson Tony's ranch.

Moon and Arnie were still fugitives. I could not tell the government that I knew their various aliases or that they were engaged in a hashish smuggling operation. I had recently studied FBI documents that showed my Tim Barnes phone number and address circled in Smiley's address book, but did that prove Smiley had betrayed me? Could the 1989 Phoenix raid coup have enabled the government to intercept a letter from my banker to my Portland mail drop that detailed my account's assets? I did not know beyond a reasonable doubt that Smiley and Lizzy had disclosed their post-flight Arizona dealings to the government as part of their plea. If they hadn't and I did, they could face more charges. I recalled their faces and all the good times we had shared during our adventure. I thought of Tucson Tony with his new wife and baby, safely retired to Australia.

Looking down on the Windy City through the strands of barbed wire on the roof I saw Lake Michigan in a distant haze, and Lincoln Park. I remembered the summer weeks when Mom brought us here to her dad's row house on Belmont Street. Grandpa took me fishing and to football games back in the '60s when the Bears were called the Chicago Cardinals. I imagined the crowd cheering. I heard a marching band and pictured my kind and gentle grandpa carrying me around Riverview Amusement Park on those sweltering summer nights during the closing parade ceremonies saying, "Be a good boy Tommy, always listen to your mom."

Mom wanted her son free as soon as possible.

Big, scattered raindrops started falling on the roof of the MCC. I picked up the pace. I heard James Taylor singing *Up On the Roof* on my Walkman, and suddenly knew what I had to do to try and save my ass and my honor. Some would call my plan telling half-truths, but I'd also heard it called walking between the raindrops. It didn't matter what it was called. As far as I knew, Bill McCarthy was the only one who could dispute my version of our fugitive years. Bill was out on bond in Canada, and I gambled he would run again.

§

In a FBI debriefing room where poster-sized aerial photos of Aardvark Construction's infamous pole barn decorated the walls, I told a less detailed version of my story than the one recorded here. I did as my lawyer advised, and let my natural personality come through. The process lasted days, and it began by chronologically admitting to most of the '70s and '80s dealings that had already been divulged by my co-conspirators. What had not been known or mentioned by others remained unmentioned by me.

Phase two of my debriefing consisted of my fugitive recollections. The government was fascinated by the methods I employed to create my identities and hide money overseas, money that I pointed out Mr. Blake had no idea was made from dealing. I also pointed out the fact that they were getting my pot money back "with interest" that amounted to several hundred thousand more dollars. I made no mention of Smiley and Lizzy's trip with me to the Channel Islands, where I arranged a contact for their offshore account. The ease with which I was able to travel internationally also surprised them. At times some of the agents seemed humored by my story, but my father-in-law's friend, Special Agent Hanis, sat stone-faced and made notes throughout the entire debriefing.

In our final session we dealt with the forfeiture issue. This group consisted of my lawyer, an IRS Criminal Investigation Division agent, a DEA agent, FBI Agent Hanis, and a shapely US Assistant Attorney named Barbara Z. Brook. The government began by showing me scores of photos of antiques and art, and asking me to prove which of them had not been bought with marijuana profits.

"Sure." I surprised them by saying it like some TV game show host. "Let's play the wheel of forfeiture with Barbara Z. Brook! I'll take the reverse painted lampshade for twelve hundred, Barb."

Eventually we addressed the issue of my stocks and currency held overseas. The agents, the lady United States Assistant Attorney, my lawyer, everyone except me was smiling over what had to be one of the biggest government cash coups in Indiana history. I watched with a sense of horror as my up-and-coming young lawyer flirted with Barbara. Here I was putting on a strong face, but dying inside as I surrendered my assets to the government. I rationalized my losses by asking myself, "What was a year in prison worth?" then answering, "All of it."

But as my lawyer ogled the government's representative, it suddenly dawned on me that he might not be working for me alone. After all, the feds had just agreed to pay him $88,500 from my seized funds for a plea bargain. No wonder all the legal eagles were happy. It seemed unreal, like a scene from some TV sitcom.

In the closing minutes of my debriefing I was asked point-blank if I had any knowledge of post-flight activities by Smiley, Arnie, Moon or Bill McCarthy.

Special Agent Hanis glared at me, and I slowly shook my head.

"Like I said, we got together for holidays out of loneliness," I told them. "Kim and I mostly kept to ourselves in the Northwest."

Everyone closed their briefcases. The head prosecutor, Bill Grimmer, who looked like actor Wilfred Brimley, made a cameo appearance to talk to his crew. Everyone seemed satisfied, even me. My "between the raindrops dance" was done. My integrity was preserved. I may have given up the money, but I wouldn't be helping send anyone to prison for selling pot.

During my transfer from South Bend to Chicago the marshals made a rare stopover at Hammond Indiana's US Marshal headquarters to pick up other prisoners. I was sitting on an empty wooden apple crate from Washington State when I saw a normal telephone on a stand. It was six in the morning and I had an uncontrollable urge to call Kim before she went to work. I wanted to let my wife know what was going on. I wanted to tell her we could survive this thing. I wanted to say that I understood what she was going through. I glared at the phone through the bars and asked the marshal if I could call my wife.

"Sure, call her," he said, handing me the phone and walking away. "I'll be right back."

As I punched in her number excitedly, it occurred to me that I had not had access to a direct dial phone since my arrest. I waited anxiously to wish her good morning while the phone rang. When there was no answer, I left a cheery message on her machine and hung up.

I sat there thinking how strange it was for the machine to be on so early. I remembered that Kim had said her mom was in town from Buffalo and staying with her. Suddenly three numbers popped into my head, 4-3-4; the code I had programmed into our answering machine on Bainbridge which we used to retrieve our messages when we were away.

After straining to see if the guard was in sight, I entered the number again and nervously punched 4-3-4 to retrieve her messages. There was only one, but it was a killer. "Hi Motho. I'm spending the night at Kevin's again. See you in the morning."

It was my wife at some other man's house. I could hear dogs barking in the background. She sounded happy.

I hung up the phone, covered my face with my hands, and fell to my knees in the corner of my cell. My eyes started watering. My head started spinning so fast that I thought about banging it on the floor. I had just lied to the feds and given up my assets, all for maintaining a shred of hope for a future with my wife as the "normal couple" we'd craved to be so often during the fugitive run.

For weeks I was like a zombie. Every time we went for rec on the roof, part of me wanted to jump through the barbed wire to the street below, but another part of me just wanted to believe my marriage and my sanity would survive the summer heat.

It was the evening before my sentencing. I lay on my bunk reading dozens of letters people had written to the judge on my behalf, pleading for leniency. There were letters from my landlords and neighbors on Bainbridge Island. There were letters from business owners, school friends and family, all stating that I was a nice, warm-hearted, caring guy who had made some mistakes. I read the defense sentencing memorandum document prepared by my lawyer that recommended a six-year parolable sentence, thinking I could survive the time by writing a novel. So I was a nice guy, and many agreed. But I had made my money selling pot, was being sentenced in Indiana, and hadn't given the government anything but my assets to mitigate my fate. It was all in the judge's hands. All I could do was hope.

When the noise from the TV in the hall started bothering me, I listened to WBBM's old time radio programs on my Walkman. Rebroadcasts from a simpler era with shows like *The Shadow*, *The Bickersons*, and *Abbot and Costello* had become part of a soothing ritual that helped me sleep.

Suddenly a loud shout from out in the hall startled me.

My cell door swung open and a crowd of prisoners popped their faces inside.

"Get your ass up, Thomas!" one man said.

"You got to see this, Writer Man," said another. "*Unsolved Mysteries* says after the commercial they're going to announce the sentence you got."

I thought they were joking. Seconds later I was being dragged down the hall to a front row seat at the almighty TV set. Sure enough, the host came on and gave the updated status of my case. He concluded by saying that I had been sentenced to forty-two years.

The guys grabbed me and shook my shoulders.

"Forty-two fucking years and you never went to court!"

"You're a goddamn magician."

"You one bad ass muthafucka! Talk about getting the hammer!"

I stood there in shock. I couldn't believe they could tell such lies on TV. I went back to my cell wondering how this would affect my case. I couldn't sleep, and the more I thought about it, the angrier, then more paranoid I became. I stayed awake all night freaking out and obsessed about calling my lawyer.

In the morning I asked him how they could prematurely announce my sentencing as the maximum possible amount on national TV.

"Forget about what they said on TV," Charley replied. "Tom, your sentencing has been postponed. Bill struck a deal in Canada and came back. Did you lie? Who did you think you were saving? That couple from Ohio who introduced you to the fugitive world may not be proud of it, Tom, but they plead guilty, too. We have a serious problem."

14

Crime & Punishment

On August fourteenth 1991, I entered the federal courtroom in South Bend escorted by two marshals. I glanced at the government's table where Special Agent Hanis stood expressionless beside federal prosecutor Bill Grimmer. As I moved to join my lawyer at the defense table, I scanned the gallery. The court was filled. In the front row sat my mom, my brothers and sisters, and my wife and some of her family. Seeing my mother and her children together holding hands for the first time in years triggered flashbacks to the days of Berry Road when we had been a poor but happy family. The hope beaming from their faces gave me strength. Behind them sat many of my old friends, some of whom had dabbled in the business before I retired. They were regular people, devoted to their families and involved with the community, but if I'd played my cards differently, they would have also had to face this day of reckoning.

Judge Robert Miller, Jr. entered the courtroom and we all rose. My lawyer made a brief speech that focused on a letter to the court delivered the day before. The letter was from one of my former friends and main customers, Dan. During my absence he'd made many statements about me in his cooperation debriefings. Most were true, but some were greatly exaggerated in order to lighten his sentencing posture for a repeat offender down to below two years. Dan basically said I was not an evil or a dangerous man and asked the court to consider leniency. It was an admirable attempt, but too little too late. My lawyer had already stated our case in his defense sentencing memorandum document, and in light of Bill McCarthy's return and his accusations of my attempted cover-up there was little else to add.

Judge Miller shuffled some papers and asked if I had anything to say.

Of course I did. I was a man of many words, but it was impossible to express everything that weighed on my heart. My emotions and my beliefs about fairness in sentencing brought me to tears. Suddenly all I could speak of was families, remorse, and pain.

Sensing negativity in the air but hoping my guilty plea and letting go of the money would be enough; I gazed up at the bench and envisioned the judge giving a speech. It would be reminiscent of some of my favorite old '60s family-oriented TV shows like *Leave it to Beaver, My Three Sons,* or *Hazel.* He would address me by my real last name. "Yes, Mr. Hickey," he'd say, "you broke the law by selling pot, but a lot of good people have appealed to this court on your behalf. You have no violence in your history. This is your first offense. Accordingly, I've decided to use my considerable discretion in this matter and give you a sentence befitting your crime."

Judge Miller cleared his throat and opened his mouth, and my real sentencing was off and running. "Mr. Hickey, I am not here to sentence you as a man," he said. "I leave that to a higher court."

Something about the tone and nature of his opening remark made it clear this was going to be a very bad day. I wanted to speak again, and quickly, before his words were written in stone. What am I but a man? I thought. But it was too late.

The written version of the judge's words, which I was soon given, led me to believe my sentence had been decided long before this day. Words rattled around my brain and echoed in the silent courtroom, my words, my lawyer's words, the words of my wife and Mom and family and jailhouse lawyers like Jesse Jackson's eloquent half-brother, Noah, from the cells at the MCC.

"Mr. Hickey was the subject of exhaustive governmental efforts to find him over the past five years. His use of false names enabled him to remain free; he placed his assets in a foreign country. The life of a fugitive doubtless is less comfortable than that of a law-abiding citizen, free to come and go, to visit friends and relatives, and to make family decisions without concern of being discovered. The life of a fugitive whose criminal activity has made him a millionaire, though, is doubtless more comfortable than that of one who has been imprisoned."

I closed my eyes and pictured places, people and events that had been part of my five years on the run.

"As for the need to provide the defendant with correctional treatment. Nothing in the record indicates that Mr. Hickey is in need of correctional treatment better provided in prison."

I saw hope in the court's written assessment of my need for correctional treatment.

"The greatest sentence this court has imposed on any other defendant is fifty-four months, a sentence given to one described as Mr. McCarthy's highest-level assistant. Mr. Hickey notes that those persons who delivered much of the marijuana to the pole barn, whom Mr. Hickey describes as more deeply involved than he, each received a year of imprisonment or less. Trying to reconcile those sentences against his role in the offense, and recognizing that his role and conduct warrant imprisonment, Mr. Hickey recommends imposition of a six-year prison term. The court cannot evaluate the sentences meted out to others. Those sentences were imposed in other cases in other courts, and whether those sentences were based on the conduct involved in this case is unknown."

"Mr. Hickey has tendered pleas of guilty to five counts of the indictment pursuant to a written plea agreement. He pleaded guilty to participation in a conspiracy to distribute marijuana. He pleaded guilty to filing false federal income tax returns for the years 1982 and 1983 by failing to report his drug income. He pleaded guilty to one count of causing interstate travel in the aid of marijuana transportation, and to a count of possession with intent to distribute marijuana. Mr. Hickey also agreed to cooperate with prosecuting authorities and to forfeit and assist with the forfeiture of approximately $1.4 million in assets and cash. The government agreed to dismiss the remaining counts of the indictment and not file additional charges."

Standing with my hands clasped tightly behind my back, I prayed for all the words to go away. The whirl of emotions and images inside me churned faster and faster still, like the twin tornadoes in the '60s that took out our great willow tree beside the house on Berry Road. Suddenly I looked at the judge with a solemn expression, and heard the terrible bottom line.

The hammer fell hard.

"The court believes that a sentence of twenty years gives proper deference to the seriousness of the crime, the nature and circumstances of the offense, and the need to deter criminal conduct by others."

The words reverberated in my head. *Twenty years!* I felt weak in the knees. The room started spinning. I heard sobbing and screaming and jeers, but no applause. I tried to focus on my wife and Mom's face, to no avail. I looked at my lawyer with disbelief. "Charley, how can this be? You've got to appeal this."

"This is a good sentence, Tom," he said, gathering up his papers. "Believe me, this is a good sentence. We can live with this."

We? I wondered if he was the same lawyer who once said, "no one should do more than eighteen months for pot," and been paid $88,500 of my seized account by the government.

"This is a good sentence. We can live with this."

We? There was no we. While I sat in solitary confinement my lawyer could be dining with the lady prosecutor tonight, toasting the latest windfall provided by another prisoner of the Drug War.

We? I was the one who'd be living with this for a long, long time.

Two marshals came to whisk me away to the county jail.

"I want to talk to my mom and Kim," I pleaded.

My lawyer whispered something to one of the marshals.

Two minutes later I was seated in a back room behind a wire-mesh divider where convicted clients conversed with their attorneys. *Twenty years, twenty years, twenty years! I might as well have been on death row.* I took several deep breaths and tried to regain my composure while my lawyer ushered Kim and Mom into the tiny area on the other side of the mesh divider.

"Five minutes," said a marshal.

Mom, Kim, and I were alone.

It was as quiet as a tomb.

Kim's face was all broken out in a rash. Mascara was running down her cheeks. She squeezed my mom's hand and looked toward the wall.

Mom looked me in the eye and asked, "What will you do?"

"We'll appeal the sentence," I said, as her faded green eyes grew wet.

"I just want you to come home," she sobbed. The real love of my life's wrinkled hand trembled when she put it against the wire mesh to touch mine. "Go back to your writing, Tommy," she whispered.

"I will, Ma. I'll write a book. It'll be all right."

Her head drooped from the exhaustion of the day, and she started shaking it repeatedly in apparent disbelief. "No!" she exclaimed, pounding one fist on the table.

I looked for my wife to comfort my mother, but Kim was apparently beside herself with a myriad of thoughts and emotions. I watched in shock as my mother cried and cried until her head came to rest on her arms. "You've been gone so long, Tommy," she muttered. "I just want you to come home."

She had raised six kids under tough conditions and never lost her nerve or her smile. It was the only time in my life I ever saw her break down.

"I will, Ma, you'll see. I'll come home a writer, I promise. You'll be proud of me. I love you."

"Sorry ma'am," said a US Marshal. "It's time to go."

I watched her slowly get to her feet, and hung my head in shame.

15

Purgatory

Life Inside

Prison is Purgatory. You never want to go there. With no disrespect intended to the Marines, it is the ultimate test of a good person's mettle. The movies have taken many of you "inside" for a glimpse at the life, but I assure you it's a different experience for each and every one who endures a sentence of any length. Many prisoners come out as bitter, better criminals. During my time there were faces burned with hot oil over ten-dollar gambling debts; fires set in locked, occupied cells; fatal stabbing and beatings; suicides; consenting and forced homosexual acts, and countless fights. It would take a whole book to describe those prison years.

Prior to being assigned to a federal prison in Kentucky, I spent months in limbo at the MCC Chicago battling chronic depression. The loss of my freedom, fortune, and faith in lovers and friends did quite a number on me. I nearly lost my mind, even gave suicide a day of deliberation. That's when I decided to slap myself around to the reality I had to confront. For the first time in my life I truly understood what down and out was, and while staring into the abyss decided to reconnect with the dream once cherished by the Kid from Berry Road. I wanted a purpose, a goal, an identity: *to be a writer.*

It was macho for a man to be able to handle his time, so I suffered quietly, did my morning janitor job and slept most of the day. I stayed up nights looking out the window and listening to "Old Time" and talk radio. Blocking out the warped world around me enabled me to focus on two short-term goals: filing an appeal to make my two ten-year sentences concurrent, and healing the gaping wound in my heart. I started keeping a journal, partly out of a need to capture my fears and feelings, but mainly to practice my powers of observation and prepare me for writing books, as I had promised Mom.

At the request of my lawyer I wrote to my fugitive friend Arnie. The objective was to encourage Todd to come in voluntarily so the government could close the case. I was told that if he did and acknowledged the influence of my letter, it would increase the chances of my appeal being granted. I did not want to testify against anyone for a time cut, but saw no harm in writing the letter. Todd's father met me in the visiting room with no officials present, and after a lengthy discussion, I personally passed on the letter.

In the winter of 1992 I became resident #00071-522 at the Federal Correctional Institution in Ashland, Kentucky. Other convicts said that my new home was the most dangerous FCI there was at the time, next to Petersburg. They preferred to call Ashland "The Butthole of the BOP," but to me it was a big improvement from Indiana's filthy county jails and the sensory deprivation of Chicago's MCC. That first winter day when I walked the circular outdoor track in the prison yard and gazed beyond the razor-wire fence tops to Kentucky's rolling hills, I cried tears of joy.

I was assigned to C Block, Ashland's toughest housing unit, reserved for men with plenty of time on their hands. The two-tiered cellblock was a world of its own, separate from the rest of the prison. When you said you were in C Unit, you immediately got respect on the compound. It was an alley community, Hell's Kitchen, a cross between L.A.'s infamous county jail and the movie *Midnight Express*. Thieves caught practicing their trade in C unit received their justice from a convict court. Bed sheets over bars covered cells which featured stingers (homemade cooking devices) boiling freshly stolen goods from the officers' mess, bottomless moonshine glasses, drugs of choice, pseudo-women prostitutes and high-stakes poker games. Every night the steel doors slammed shut at precisely 11:30, every morning they opened at 5:30 for "work call."

There were white supremacists, West Virginia strike breakers, abortion clinic bombers, murderers, New York Mafiosi, Jamaican Posse, Bloods, Crips, Latin Kings and Cornbread Mafia in C Unit. Rumor was there were even witness protection people hidden within its smoky confines. Belonging to a group seemed to be the norm, but I decided to keep to myself and get along with everyone—just as I had in high school. At first I was terrified and had to learn to control it. Psychos and killers in

C could smell fear.

All new recruits were destined for kitchen duty, but an old convict taught me a trick to get around the system. After irritating the skin near my TB test, I was deemed "positive" by the medical staff and taken off the kitchen roster. I needed work, or a *catch,* some place where I could help people and improve my mind. I despised all the tension between groups and gangs and the head-trips they caused. *Only ignorant people embrace violence,* I thought. I accepted a teaching job in the education department.

I was the new kid on the block and everybody had a story to tell, especially after they learned I wanted to be a writer. Being around books, paper, pencils and a typewriter five days a week was heaven-in-hell. At night in C block I played with words like tinker toys, finding solace and escape in them while penning a manuscript in which I lived my future. Deciding I was going to be a writer was easy, becoming one in prison was an exhausting journey that would take every ounce of patience and energy I could muster.

In spite of everything, the summer of '92 was filled with hope. Arnie voluntarily returned from the fugitive world and said my letter played a part in his choice. Many months had passed since my appeal to the court, and I often dreamed of a sentence reduction that would render me eligible for parole in forty months. Jailhouse lawyers said the disparity between my co-conspirators' sentences and mine was a travesty of justice. Again and again I heard, "You plead guilty, gave up the money and still got two dimes? Who'd you piss off, Writer Man? Maybe they're just playing with your head." The longer the judge delayed answering my appeal, the more I believed he was giving it serious consideration. At mail call on August fourteenth I received a belated thirty-sixth birthday present from the United States District Court in South Bend. My heart pounded like a drum as I tore open the letter, then sank like a stone after I read the decision: DENIED. Smiley was a few months away from being paroled and Bill McCarthy was nearing the halfway mark in his bit, but I couldn't even see the light at the end of the tunnel. My sentence remained *twenty years.*

FCI Ashland never became my world, but I grew comfortable there and soon knew all the interesting activities. People trusted me—guards and convicts—because I had never testified in court to cut my time. It wasn't hard for an experienced fugitive to discern Ashland's underground economy. Like the small, glass-enclosed, pet ant colony Dad made for my sixth birthday, it was easy to see everything going on: how the drugs got in, gamblers made payoffs to staff, real pussy was sold at R & D, and medical treatment could be purchased for thousands in postal money orders. Some low-level officials were busted by inmates wanting time cuts and prosecutors craving brownie points, but just as in the real world, the fallen corrupt were quickly replaced by other eager entrepreneurs.

But they weren't all bad, cons or staff. By the time I left the education department to take the job as chapel clerk, I'd met some good, caring people on both sides of the bars, people doing whatever they could to make Purgatory a better place. I made a conscious choice to become one of them.

When President Clinton was campaigning, I huddled with my fellow convicts and watched him play his sax and joke about smoking pot on MTV. At the inaugural ball, Bill and his entourage of Baby Boomers danced as Fleetwood Mac played, "*Don't stop thinking about tomorrow...*" Those ironic scenes stirred hope for sentence-relief among a prison population that was rapidly expanding with first time nonviolent drug offenders. It was false hope.

On December 21, 1993, I earned the privilege of being appointed MC for the prison's Christmas Party for orphans. For weeks I had helped raise money from hardened cons to buy toys. It was my second Christmas in prison and I was determined to give something again. The old biker we elected to play Santa even trimmed his white beard and showered. Singing *Rudolph the Red Nose Reindeer* with those wide-eyed Kentucky boys and girls was more rewarding than any drunken bar-performance I'd done. It was the best present I could have ever asked for—the giving of Christmas Spirit, returned tenfold.

In my first two years at Ashland I'd sent hundreds of letters, poems, handmade cards, and had many visits and phone calls. Despite this communication, I felt myself slipping out of touch with the outside. As time went on those things that reminded me life was going on without me left more hurt than happiness in their wake. My Italian American friend, Tony, a talented artist in his seventies who had done over nine years and enlightened me on prison life, said he'd learned to stay away from the phones and limit family visits to twice a year. Once Tony said softly, "You're an aspiring artist and romantic like me. In here all we have is our art, nothing else matters. Don't let the negativity around you seep in. Dive into your work and forget about the outside. You'll understand what I'm talking about when you hit the five-year mark." He wrinkled his forehead and raised his voice in anger. "Nothing positive comes from putting men like you away for more than five years." He clenched his fist. "I've only seen one person as determined to make it as you are, Writer Man." I understood what he was saying, and it scared me. Communicating with Kim's mother to maintain a connection with my lost love was one of many things I had to let go. My justification for visits was to allow family to watch me clown around for hours so they could leave relieved and thinking I was holding up under the pressure—even though I fought off tears when they waved goodbye from the exit, and whispered to myself, "Hold on, Thomas. Hold on." I often asked Tony if I was going to make it. "You just might," he'd answer with a twinkle in his tired eyes, "but you'll have to stay strong and fight the natural urge to become bitter."

In three years of captivity I'd lived with dozens of different men in crowded cells—black men, white men, Latinos, Native Americans. It was like taking people from the local mission and living in the bathroom with them for days, weeks, months. The last convict to share a cell with me at Ashland was by far the biggest test of my diplomacy and patience. *Piglet*, an obese white man, was a chronic liar and an obnoxious attention seeker. Piglet hated my writing, and did everything he could to hinder my productivity. He left chicken bones on our floor, played loud music on his headphones, sang off key, and farted continuously from the bunk below mine. Piglet's snoring was so intense that I prayed for popcorn kernels spilled from the sack on his bloated gut to get sucked into the nostrils of his snout. Worst of all, Piglet was a pseudo-jailhouse lawyer who made his vice-money by typing incompetent appeals and motions to the courts. Everyone in the joint soon knew what he was about, so he preyed on the new inmates, literally waiting for them to arrive with long faces at the legal library seeking help. It was sad. In many cases, all a convict got was one shot at an appeal. People like Piglet who sold such false hope were dangerous, and I was living with one of them in a vulnerable cracker box.

At last I earned a single in G, the honor unit. It couldn't have come at a better time, for after five months with Piglet I was nearly driven to poison him with a ptomaine mayonnaise sandwich. The day was January 6, 1994, and occupying the six-by-eight-foot cell felt like moving into a sprawling new home with an ocean view. Finally, I could lower my guard and relax at night. I cleaned and organized until three A.M. I arranged my reference books on a makeshift shelf, then wrote until dawn. I fed big black crows crackers from my tiny window and, even though the heat was not working, felt warm inside.

Tony and I became close friends during that harsh Kentucky winter. We ate meals together, and spent many late night hours walking the halls of the honor unit sharing our memories. I watched him draw in his cell, and he suffered through countless readings of my work. We smuggled bread out of the chow hall in our underwear and fed flocks of starving pigeons and wild birds. One day we found an injured white dove with chocolate-tipped wings in the courtyard outside G Unit. The bird had been attacked by a hawk, and was unable to fly. I suggested sneaking it into the unit and nursing her back to health. Reluctantly, Tony agreed. I named her White Dove, and we taped popsicle sticks to her broken wing and hand-fed her for weeks. We hid her on the window ledge outside Tony's cell during the day, and brought her in at night. Tony procured some hard-to-find ointment, and White Dove grew healthy. When her feathers came back she preened and let us rub her soft breast. Eventually a guard told Tony that envious convicts had complained about his pet. All the staff loved the resident artist, but the bird had to go. I placed White Dove on a branch of the small, bare, tree we'd found her in, and went back to my work. She was able to fly, but stayed around G Unit waiting for us to bring her food and affection.

One day we found a pile of bloody white feathers on the frozen dirty ground. A guard told us the hawk had returned. Tony was beside himself. That evening I peeked though his cell window and saw him crying. "Go away, damn it," he said after I entered without knocking. "I knew better than to get close to anything in here. I knew better than to lo...love," he stammered. I placed a hand on his shoulder. "It's my fault," I said. "I'm the rookie who hasn't been down five years yet." He wiped his eyes with a sleeve of his tattered robe, and picked up his drawing pencil. "Well, I have," he mumbled, "and I should've known better." I stared at the huge scars on his chest, remnants from recent open-heart surgery, and pointed to them. "There's no shame in knowing that old ticker of yours does more than pump blood," I whispered, "or in discovering time hasn't ruined us yet."

I returned to my cold cell to reminisce and write for the remainder of the night, and was warmed by my final words of self-talk. "Some people travel light, secretly afraid of the hurt that inevitable loss can cause them. Okay, that's a plan. But I would rather have the good memories for eternity, even at the cost of short-term pain. Understand? I loved a lady who was my wife. We shared a lifetime of good times in a short time. I'll never forget. I hated like hell to lose her, or my parakeet, or my sixteen-year-old Irish setter, or my Manx cat, or... Get the picture? For one month of a dreary winter at a prison in Kentucky I and my old artist friend fed, petted, coo-cooed and helped a small, injured White Dove with chocolate-tipped wings regain her strength and dignity...and we are better men for having done so."

On April 10, 1994, I signed a contract with a publishing company in Salt Lake City, Utah. I had sent my manuscript *Chelan* to several New York publishers and endured each of their rejections: *Keep writing, and feel free to send us your next work. Sorry, not the kind of material we are looking for this year. Although your writing shows promise, we regret to say...* I was hungry for an experienced editor to take me under his wing, but it seemed no one wanted to edit, market and nurture an incarcerated writer. When Northwest offered to publish *Chelan* I jumped at the opportunity. Tony witnessed my official rebirth as *author.* "But are you good yet?" he asked. "Who knows," I said. "What is good? Who decides? The public? The critics? The marketing department?" He scratched his balding head and answered, "Thomas Lion, you're damn good for in here. And by the way...history decides." When Tony left my cell for midnight count I thought about how much my life had changed, realized I was on the way to fulfilling a lifelong dream, and wished Mom could have been the one to witness me sign the contract.

In November of 1994 my number appeared on a list of inmates to be relocated to the federal prison in Lexington, Kentucky. Shocked and disturbed, I appealed to my boss, the regional chaplain, to pull some strings and keep me in Ashland as his clerk. Several chaplains spoke to numerous staff on my behalf, but the order was written in stone. "I'm sorry, Thomas," said the chaplain. "We certainly don't want to lose our clerk, and we realize how much this move will disturb your routine and your writing, but the BOP moves in mysterious ways." My counselor told me I was needed in Lexington, and it was a privilege to be selected to go there. I didn't get it. I loved my job, got along well with the staff, had a few friends, two completed manuscripts, and was well into the rough draft of *I Was An Unsolved Mystery*. Suddenly, after only nine months of cherished solitude in my single room, I was headed back to square one at a rundown joint a hundred miles down the road. I wondered if the order had come from some official in Indiana, intent on continuing my punishment as a favor to Kim's dad.

As our rickety prison transfer bus climbed the hill to the prison on the outskirts of Lexington, I watched sunrise paint golden glitter on the Kentucky bluegrass. "This joint's in the Guinness Book of Records for having the most single-pane glass panels on any building in the good old US of A," one of Ashland's old jailhouse lawyers said. "They say there's a housing unit called the *Dog Pen* where cons volunteered to be guinea pigs for heroin and LSD endurance tests in exchange for early release." A Latino passenger cleared his throat and bellowed, "Sign my ass up!" Everyone broke into laughter. "They say a lot of famous people checked in here for recovery in the fifties," the jailhouse lawyer continued, "back when you druggies still had a choice between hard time and rehabilitation." I stared at the words *Narc Farm* etched in stone above the gate as we approached it, then thought of the new drug offender program I'd heard about. "There's so many miles of walkways and tunnels," the old man added, "it takes weeks to learn your way around." A small black kid hung his head and muttered, "That means plenty of nooks and crannies to get cornered in and get a shank stuck in your back! All them brothers coming here from joints like Petersburg and Atlanta with tons of time, they don't give a shit about nothing." No one said a word as the gates to our new Purgatory parted and we were swallowed up inside.

In the waning days of 1994 violence at Lexington was a daily occurrence. Opposing gangs and groups from prisons around the country fought for position and power as the pecking order was re-established. Noise levels, confusion and general conditions made working on my memoir impossible. I shared a cell in Cardinal Unit with a former marshal and his son who wanted me to write their life story. Wayne had also done time in Ashland, which is where he'd heard about my writing. He was a pilot who'd flown over domestic marijuana fields with his son and targeted them for eradication. In his many years in law enforcement he'd arrested hundreds of hard-drug pushers and violent people, but never felt right about busting marijuana growers who were trying to save the family farm. In the end he'd protected them, was sold out by an informant and convicted on federal charges. In hundreds of hours of talks, Wayne and other law enforcement officials I met inside confirmed my suspicions about "equal justice" in America and the rampant corruption associated with the Drug War. To a man they said that who you were, who you pissed off and who you paid off played key roles in deciding who went to prison and for how long. I put my memoir on hold and began writing another book called *Both Sides Now.*

Early one rainy March Sunday morning a guard entered our cell and shook me from my sleep. "The chaplain wants to see you," he said with a somber expression. "Now." As a former chapel clerk, I knew convicts got calls like this for only one reason—a death in the family. My mind whirled with possible scenarios and locked on to my worst nightmare, *Mom.* I jumped into my khakis and hurried down the hall. The chaplain, who was on the phone, waved me into his office. "Good morning, Thomas," he said softly. "Someone wants to talk to you." My stomach churned as I reached for the receiver in slow motion. Pictures of my mother raced through my mind. Please, God, no, not her, I thought. The caller was my old boss from Ashland, the caring man in black, Father John Noe. He knew that Tony and I were very close, for he had also befriended the old artist. Shortly after I left Ashland, Tony got out on an early medical release. We kept in touch and I knew he was about to sign a contract to sketch sports figures and market numbered lithographs. In a gentle and wavering voice, Father Noe told me our friend had died of a massive stroke during a business trip to New York. "At least he died a free man," the Father said. "I thought you would like to know." I hung my head and envisioned Tony's amazing works: the charcoal sketch of Mother Teresa that was sent to her and prompted a personal response; the pencil drawing of a huddled, homeless family done for Habitat for Humanity and President Jimmy Carter; and the sketch of the black *Buffalo Soldiers* that Colin Powell and others marveled over. Rest in peace my dear, free, friend, I thought on the long walk back to my cell.

On April 19, 1995, I returned from work and saw an agitated crowd gathering in the TV room. Convicts were cheering and saying things like, "Yeah! Fuckin'-A! Now these assholes will think twice before taking a cushy government job." The Murrah Federal Building in Oklahoma City had just been bombed. Scenes of federal employees crying as their murdered children were retrieved from the rubble drew more jeers from the convicts. I bit my tongue and headed back to the cell with a sick feeling in my heart.

Five days later I was pacing the floor outside the room where parole hearings were held. I had waited four and a half years, believing that only a detailed prison record compiled by people who knew me could neutralize the negative influence I anticipated from my former father-in-law or his pals. "Calm down, Thomas," said Jim, a soft-spoken, gentle giant who'd befriended me. "These people don't care about you. It's my sixth try at an out date, and this hearing examiner is supposed to be a real motherfucker. You should've brought a lawyer with to speak their language." I nodded, then reminded myself that Jim was convicted of a gruesome double murder, not dealing pot. The door opened and another convict walked past me with his head hung low. "Remember," Jim said as I went in, "you got nothing coming." A small black man with receding salt and pepper hair stared at me over the top of tortoise shell framed glasses, introduced himself, and got down to business. The examiner flipped through a thick file and read the government's history of my case. He asked if I accepted responsibility for my actions and what I thought about my sentence. "I was guilty of being a member of a large marijuana conspiracy," I answered, "but have bad feelings about the sentencing disparity in my case." I knew what was at stake, but had to speak my mind. I was nervous but thorough while mentioning the roles, unexplainable amounts of cash forfeitures, and sentences of those co-conspirators known and unknown to me. What I believed the court had failed to consider, the examiner apparently did. "According to your progress report," he continued, "your institutional adjustment has been good. No infractions, an excellent worker, very talented, very trustworthy..." He paused and flipped through my collection of awards and recommendations. He noted that I spent my free time writing and had signed a publishing contract. "I also see you have a job and housing arranged for your parole plan," he said. Although he seemed sympathetic to my circumstances, the examiner explained that he could not release me within the 40-52 months parole guidelines for my offense. Because of my consecutive 4205A adult sentence I could not be paroled in less than 80 months, or one third of twenty years. The news was not new to me, but it still hurt. "The sooner I can get out of this nuthouse the better," I muttered. "People around me applaud kids getting killed on TV, and I just have to sit there on my hands. I've got to go. Five years is enough." The examiner shook his head. "It's unfortunate," he said. Then he closed my file and stood. "All right, Mr. Hickey, I hope once you get out of here this lifestyle is behind you." We shook hands. "Oh, it's behind me," I said. "I have something I always wanted, this writing career. I'm totally absorbed in it." I returned to the unit and called Mom to let her know there was an end in sight. The next week I applied for the new nine-month drug offender program that promised inmates who completed it a year off their sentence.

That autumn Minister Louis Farrakhan called for Monday October 16, 1995 to be, "a Holy Day of Atonement and Reconciliation—a day of fasting and prayer for those who are able." The highlight was to be a Million Man March on Washington DC. The BOP announced that the sixteenth would be a normal workday for the entire prison population. But as the day of the march grew near, rumors of work strikes, sit-downs and rioting among black convicts resulted in a rare decision by worried officials. The rigid BOP blinked, and made Million Man March day an excused absence for blacks wanting to watch the event on TV. Many of the brothers serving lengthy sentences for crack cocaine were convinced their treatment by the Department of Justice was a national conspiracy. Like me, they wanted hope. Sympathetic toward first time nonviolent crack-cocaine offenders of any race, I watched TV as the scene unfolded in an orderly manner on the Federal Mall. Speaker after speaker eloquently asked the Black Community to be with their children, teaching them the value of home, self-esteem, family, and unity; and to passively work with them to realize the mission of the Million Man March: to improve the quality of life for their people. Occasionally a group of white prisoners passed the TV and jeered, but overall the audience inside the brick walls of Lexington was calm and attentive—until the Reverend Jesse Jackson spoke. His voice reminded me of my talks with his half-brother Noah at Chicago's MCC. Part of Jackson's speech addressed the inequality in sentencing for blacks convicted of drug offenses. He described UNICOR—the BOP's profitable convict labor factory—as being run by "Wall Street" corporations like GE and Dupont. I'd read and heard similar accusations before (some of which compared our prison labor force to China's), but many of the brothers had not. Soft mumbling among the men soon became shouting. I could feel rising anger in the TV room. One of my black friends took me aside and said to stay out of common areas for a few days.

Four days later, tension was still high. The grapevine buzzed with reports about other prisons going off like bombs, and the alleged failure of a bill to reduce crack cocaine sentences fueled the explosive situation. All week we'd heard SWAT teams firing automatic weapons on the range beyond the yard, trying to send a message to would-be rioters. Lexington was a powder keg and everyone was on edge—cons and staff. Inmates calling family members in the Motor City were told the *Detroit News* reported massive, nationwide prison rioting, with scores of injuries and millions in damage. Talladega, Florida's joint, had eight staff and thirty inmates injured and many buildings destroyed. In nearby FCI Memphis, it took firefighters all night to put out blazes at three housing units that resulted in fifty guards and inmates being treated for smoke inhalation. In Greenville, Illinois, convicts took over parts of the prison and refused to return to their cells. On Saturday the Department of Justice ordered most of the nation's 88,000 federal prisoners confined to their cells. When the phones were shut off and TV privileges suspended, I listened to my Walkman for news from National Public Radio. On the second floor of Cardinal Unit my cellies and I discussed our options. Even though a part of us understood and empathized with the pro-riot convicts' intent, we decided to keep to ourselves and not to be swept up in the madness. The night of the twenty-first ended with several trash fires being set in Cardinal Unit. The housing unit next door had been torched, and evacuated by guards. Through the window I saw government buses, cars and vans moving into the parking lot until the outside lights were shut down. I went to sleep remembering C Block stories of men being burned alive in their cells and wondering...*was this the big one?*

At first I thought the chanting was part of my nightmare. Then I smelled smoke. The synchronized pounding of men's work boots on concrete echoed like rolling thunder in the corridor. "Burn, baby, burn!" convicts shouted. "Pump it up! Burn the bitch down!" A flash of light lit up the glass panel in our door. Alarms sounded. Arguments erupted. Soon the goon squad was grabbing burning bedding, tossing it from cells, and herding men toward the common area. Minutes later I stood at the end of our range watching thick, black smoke rise to the ceiling and swirl down toward the floor where mattress fires burned. One guard shouted something about making room for a fire crew. Another restrained an old convict who wanted to rescue a letter from his cell. Suddenly I envisioned the only copies of my manuscripts going up in flames. In panic I pushed my way to the front of the crowd. A guard who knew me put a hand on my shoulder. Another guard from the goon squad threatened to throw me in the hole if I took one more step. A trip to the hole would be my only infraction in almost five years. Disobeying a direct order in an emergency could endanger my parole date. I remembered Tony's words in Ashland, *In here all we have is our art, nothing else matters,* then took a deep breath and ran as fast as I could into the smoky corridor.

There were more depressing days. In 1996 Mom was diagnosed with ovarian cancer, my publisher went bankrupt, and the one-year-earlier parole date I'd been promised by the BOP in return for taking a nine-month drug offender course was not approved by my sentencing judge.

Eventually the heavy gates of Purgatory swung open, and I was free again—paroled after doing six years eight months. When I drift back to my prison years, my mind rides an emotional roller coaster of memories. Some are bad, some are good, but over all I get a feeling of pride. I taught grown men to read, and offered survival wisdom to frightened nonviolent kids, as Tony had done for me. I kept my promise to Mom by working days and writing until dawn on hundreds of nights. I completed three manuscripts during my sentence and started two others. My debut novel *Chelan* was released in June of 1997.

Once in a while someone tells me I am amazingly "normal" for having gone through all that I have. I always laugh and ask them to define normal. When asked how I survived prison, I remember writing a poem on April Fools Day 1992 that I called, *Captured Body, Free Mind Poetry.*

Nature
I am without the therapy
of your being.
And because of this,
confusion
lingers longer some days...
these days
than I ever realized
it could.
Clarity
comes in the comfort
of knowing without a doubt
that you at least
are "Out There"
for always.
And even though you struggle
to retain your own health,
I know you wait for my return
with a mother's patience...
And because I know,
I carry on with a smile.

Should I have told the whole truth and nothing but the truth? Should I have never become a fugitive in 1986, or married a cop's daughter? Could I have come in, testified in court against my friends for pot and possibly been allowed to serve a fraction of the time and keep a sizable amount of cash? Would I have ever written this story if I hadn't forfeited my fortune? Should our government spend millions of tax dollars to retroactively seek out and prosecute people like me? Would have, could have, should have. It's all spilled milk, water under the bridge.

I was not a minor player in the marijuana game. Even Jerry Patchen later said that although I had suffered far more than other members of the vast conspiracy I was a part of, my sentence could have been worse in Indiana. I am simply one of the marijuana guys who got caught, did his time, and want to put it all behind me. There are plenty like me who made it and went on to be musicians, marina owners, California vineyard growers and such. But I believe that if you gamble long enough, you eventually lose it all. Casino owners count on this fact. I also believe that things happen for a reason, and that what goes around comes around. One thing's for sure, being an outlaw takes a ton of energy, the kind of energy that if directed elsewhere might allow a person to accomplish almost anything they set their mind to. Maybe it took a twenty-year sentence for me to get my priorities right.

Today I don't have to worry about a federal agent or someone I helped send to prison breaking down my door in the middle of the night and blowing me away with a gun. Today I can spend quality time with Mom, my siblings, and my friends. Today I can make new friends who will know the real me. Today I can sit at this computer and create. Today I am a free man facing the second half of life and chasing a childhood dream of being a successful writer. Today I know that our identity is so much more than the driver's license, the passport, or credit cards we carry—it's who we are, what we do and stand for, where we came from, and ultimately where we are going. Better late than never, I guess.

Epilogue

"It's an emotional issue. It's right up there with gays in the military and abortion. Everybody's got an opinion on it, it touches everybody in America."

—DEA Agent Steve White, 1998 PBS Frontline

America's war on marijuana is a complex issue, especially for us Baby Boomers who came of age in the '60s and '70s. Millions of Americans believe the decision to smoke pot medicinally or recreationally should be a moral rather than a legal one. I myself have not smoked pot in nearly eight years, and would not want a child of mine experimenting with pot or alcohol before the age of eighteen. I do, however, believe that morality is more of a family than a government matter. The Drug War is not my cause, but I feel obliged to raise a voice on behalf of the tens of thousands of nonviolent first-time drug offenders who fill our prisons today. Few outside of their families may care. You also may not care—unless it's your child who's in prison one day.

But it must be said that all marijuana users, growers, or dealers are not threats to society. Many of them became involved during an era of experimentation. Many dealers and growers would probably need no more than having their assets taken and serving two years in today's prison system to decide that they had taken their shot at being financially secure and had had enough. Many nonviolent marijuana offenders I met during my prison term, who had received more time than I for much lesser offenses, may not survive the mandatory minimum sentences they are now serving. The only lesson they are learning is how to become better, bitter professional criminals. I wonder what physical and mental condition they will be in when they emerge from a crowded system wracked with violence, corruption and sexual abuse. I survived the riots of 1995, but will they survive the next ones?

Today we have a booming prison-industrial-complex fueled by Drug War politics. It is a war that has gone on for over thirty years. Who is winning? Can we mandate morality? Is recreational marijuana use a bigger moral issue than drinking? Is pot a "ladder drug," or is every addictive personality destined to find its addiction beneath the kitchen sink, in a model airplane kit's paint or glue, or on the streets of our inner cities? If we removed the profit and illegality factors from soft drugs like pot, would the thrill to kids and the lure to dealers be gone? Commentator Andy Rooney recently said he believed that cancer-causing tobacco is far more damaging to its consumers than pot. "No one ever died from smoking marijuana," Rooney said on *60 Minutes*. The main result of America's war on marijuana has been to drive up the price and make it an even more lucrative, tax-free business in the underground economy.

I often think of Robert McNamara's last book, in which he states his regrets twenty years after his term as Secretary of Defense for sending young men into battle, death and imprisonment in Vietnam. Is America's war on marijuana another war that can never be won? Is the mental, social, and financial "collateral damage" incurred by continuing this war worth the costs? Will some former president one day write a confession similar to McNamara's, long after he's quit worrying about being re-elected?

I studied many examples of sentencing for both violent and nonviolent crimes during my prison years. I met millionaire professional bookies and gamblers, who caused physical and financial suffering to American families with another kind of addiction, get less than a year in prison. I saw rapists and repeat child molesters who bragged about their next offenses get out in less than three years. But for me the most disturbing study during my prison years had to be the sentencing of Sammy "The Bull" Gravano. As mobster John Gotti's right hand man, he admitted to nineteen murders during his lifetime of crime. Mobsters I met in prison said he bragged of the figure being closer to thirty-six. Regardless, Sammy cooperated with the government and was given a five-year sentence, much of it rumored to have been spent in protective custody dining on room service at taxpayers' expense. On the night I heard that one, I looked around at all the nonviolent drug offenders in my cellblock serving double-digit bits and shook my head in disbelief.

In the past decade I've met many people in respectable fields like corrections, police work, the military, social services, Red Cross and even parole officers, who have privately said that our nation's enforcement of pot laws is an enormous waste of tax dollars. Since my release I've run into many ex-dealers, mostly at book signings, who survived unscathed and became respectable entrepreneurs, even considerable success stories in prominent businesses. They and countless present or former recreational smokers continuously cheered me on to write this story. According to the 1995 National Household Survey on Drug Abuse, approximately 65.5 million Americans—about one third of the general population—reported they had tried marijuana at least once in their lifetime. Are you or were you one of them?

What's wrong with this picture? Why does our government bring this juggernaut of law and justice to bear with such force on those who use a plant that has been and will continue to be around for centuries? Conservative columnists, PBS documentaries, retired law enforcement officials, and even outspoken federal judges have posed similar questions about comparative sentencing in America's war on marijuana.

William Charles McCarthy's sentencing was postponed again and again. Eventually, Bill was given fifteen years. This was his second drug conviction, normally an aggravating factor in sentencing, as he had been arrested in 1975 for selling LSD. The record indicated that Bill had been responsible for bringing tens of thousands of pounds of marijuana to Indiana after Thomas Hickey moved to California. Bill's total forfeiture in cash and property was $340,000. There was no mention of the large block of hashish seized from Bill's home at the time of his arrest. In his sentencing memorandum, Judge Miller cited a number of mitigating factors: "No indication in the court record that Bill had been involved in any drug activities while a fugitive; Bill's apparent devotion to his wife and daughter; Bill's admission of wrongdoing and acceptance of responsibility for his actions. He ultimately waived extradition and complied with his bond provisions in Canada. To the extent that rehabilitation remained a goal of sentencing, Mr. McCarthy's remorse, guilty plea, and cooperation were viewed as the first steps toward rehabilitation. The court had no doubt that he had learned a lesson. Mr. McCarthy also pledged cooperation with the government's investigation, and had been truthful and helpful in ferreting out another's lack of candor. Just as the *Sentencing Guidelines* provided illustration of the seriousness of an offense, they also illustrated the importance of this factor. No provision of the *Sentencing Guidelines* allowed as great a downward departure as that for substantial assistance to authorities."

Bill McCarthy was paroled after doing less than five years in federal prison. Leigh McCarthy served no time in prison. They remained married.

Kim was never charged with any crimes. She filed for and was granted a non-contested divorce in the fall of 1991. She has since remarried and started a family of her own.

Arnie spent nearly a year driving around the American west pondering what to do after Thomas Hickey's arrest. During this time he golfed 191 courses. In 1992 Todd surrendered voluntarily. He was sentenced to nine years and paroled after serving one third of that time. He married his long time ladylove, who had visited him during his prison years.

James "Smiley" Hagar served four years of a twelve-year sentence. Irene served less than six months. They forfeited several properties to the government.

Maui Bert served less than three years. His multimillion-dollar offshore account was not forfeited to the government.

Maui Ray served no time.

Tucson Tony remained retired and happily married Down Under.

Mad Max and the Lady Wrestler were never indicted.

Moon is still out there somewhere.

Blake still manages millions in secret offshore accounts. The company has expanded and opened a new Caribbean office. For him and his colleagues, business is booming.

The Vault's clients are still stashing untraceable treasure.

Con men continue to use alternative mailing services to scam Americans.

The Greek is still matching wits with customers.

Lloyds of London "Name" Keith Jones died from a massive stroke that occurred in a London bank while he withdrew a sum of cash.

Jimmy lost his hotel and nightclub to receivership. He exports antiques from his humble abode in Northern England.

Jerry and Charley still practice law.

Special Agent Robert Hanis retired after Bill McCarthy's sentencing.

Unsolved Mysteries continues to feature America's fugitives.

And the war goes on.

Acknowledgments:

This memoir would have been half the book, or a pipe dream without assistance and gentle encouragement from some key people at crucial times. To them I say thanks for helping me put my past on the shelf, and thanks for being there in all phases of this project, from start to finish: Elizabeth Coulter, Rick and Gayle Gilpin, Sandra Harris, Lynne Van Husan, Sandy Koopman, Carol and Brad Lasater, Donna Peifer, Waimea Williams, and last but not least my agent, Roger Jellinek, who coaxed, coddled, pleaded, prodded and provided the editing energy for me to go the extra mile and put out a quality book I am extremely proud of.   We did it Carol!

CHELAN

By Thomas Lion

Come visit the not-so-serene Pacific Northwest in this gripping debut novel.

A struggling writer with a haunting past—not unlike the author's—and a diverse array of locals, learn that international events can indeed affect their way of life. A foreign corporation is buying up resort property and bribing vote-hungry politicians into doing its bidding. Not so fictional, you say? Business as usual? True, until the residents of the Chelan Valley discover too much about their new neighbor's sordid past.

Signed copies of Lion's debut novel are available for $14.00US/ $19.00CAN. The price includes shipping. Checks and money orders are accepted. Please provide name, address, and telephone number with your order for promp delivery.

♌ **The Oregonian:** "Chelan...*a colorful thriller...*" ***Paul Duchene***
♌ The Colombian: *"Suspenseful..." Dave Jewett*

To order:

Leobrand Books Phone: (808) 671-6161
PO Box 893548 Fax: (808) 671-6160
Mililani, HI 96786